THE CHRONICLE OF JAZZ

THE CHRONICLE OF JAZZ

MERVYN COOKE

Abbeville Press • Publishers
New York • London • Paris

For my parents

Acknowledgments

This book would not have been possible without the unstinting support
of the staff at Thames and Hudson. Thanks are also due to my old friend
Roland Robertson, without whose influence I might never have delved
into this extraordinary music in the first place, and to George Double
and Charlie Furniss for teaching me more about jazz than I could ever
hope to teach them.

First published in the United States of America in 1998 by
Abbeville Press, 488 Madison Avenue, New York, N.Y. 10022

First published in Great Britain in 1997 by Thames and Hudson Ltd.,
30 Bloomsbury Street, London WC1B 3QP

The text of this book was set in Rotis
Printed and bound in Singapore

First edition

10 9 8 7 6 5 4 3 2 1

ISBN 0-7892-0399-5

On the jacket: front, l. to r. (with detail on front flap) Max Kaminsky,
Lester Young, "Hot Lips" Page, and Charlie Parker at Birdland, 1949,
Corbis-Bettmann/UPI; *back: top, l. to r.* Sarah Vaughan,
© Redferns/Photo Max Jones Files; Tommy Dorsey, © Redferns/Photo
Max Jones Files; *bottom* Donald Byrd, New York, 1959, © William
Claxton/Special Photographers Library; *spine* Louis Armstrong,
The Frank Driggs Collection.

Frontispiece Saxophonist Courtney Pine, who inspired a creative surge
in British jazz during the 1980s.

Right King Oliver and his Creole Jazz Band at the time of their
pioneering recordings in 1923 (*l. to r.*): Honore Dutrey (trombone),
Baby Dodds (drums), Oliver (cornet), Louis Armstrong (slide trumpet),
Lil Hardin (piano), Bill Johnson (banjo) and Johnny Dodds (clarinet).

CONTENTS

Above A Chicago vaudeville performance in 1915, with scenery suggesting a steamboat.

Left Sonny Greer, who provided Duke Ellington's orchestra with endlessly resourceful drumming for twenty-eight years.

Right The raw emotion of jazz: Billie Holiday singing in the 1940s.

Left Piano virtuoso Oscar Peterson, one of the most prolific recording artists in the history of jazz.

Below The legendary Louis Armstrong: a revolutionary spirit in his youth and, in later years, one of the most popular entertainers of all time.

INTRODUCTION

A Century of Jazz

"Jazz became many things – frenetic, destructive, hysterical, decadent, venal, alcoholic, saccharine, Lombardish, vapid – it has enriched stuffed bellies; it has corrupted the innocent; it has betrayed and it has traduced; but, everywhere and in all its forms, something jazz acquired at the moment of its origin has profoundly touched all its hearers. What was this thing that set folks dancing and smiling from the slums of New Orleans to all the capitals of the earth?"

Alan Lomax (1950)

The extraordinarily varied nature of jazz can only be understood by considering the exhilarating rapidity with which it has established itself at the forefront of the modern musical world. Like cinema, that other major American contribution to twentieth-century culture, jazz is currently celebrating its one-hundredth birthday (the first ragtime compositions were published in the 1890s). Over the course of its first century of existence jazz has adopted and transformed many of the technical innovations of earlier classical music with astonishing speed, compressing four centuries of musical expertise into a dazzling array of styles and structures. The result is an audience appeal that ranges from the mass pop market to an intellectual cliquishness even more exclusive than that of the 1960s avant-garde in art. Along with these achievements, jazz has managed to summarize most of our instinctive feelings about music and reshape the art for the future.

The story of jazz is one of lively interactions and tensions between performers and composers of widely differing temperaments. The chronological diary at the heart of this book vividly illustrates the exciting and often unpredictable nature of these creative encounters, tracing the history of jazz from its largely disreputable beginnings, through the height of its popularity in the Swing Era, to its gradual evolution into a serious art music capable of sustaining intellectual and emotional interest on a par with any other modern art form.

Never far below the story's surface are the racial tensions that sparked off the early development of jazz. Slaves transported from West Africa to the New World took their musical traditions with them, and adapted their tribal work songs and dances to sustain them in their forced labors (● p. 17). Fundamental elements of jazz were born when the dynamic rhythmic language and expressive pitch-bending of African vocal music became fused with structures and harmonies borrowed from the European music favored by white slave-owners. After universal emancipation in 1865, black religious music (which also synthesized techniques of African and European origin) paved the way for the two genres that would directly lead to the early jazz style: RAGTIME and the BLUES, both of which appeared in the 1890s.

Ragtime (● p. 20) – "white music played black," as it has been aptly described – derived from white dance forms such as the polka and march, and superimposed a SYNCOPATED rhythmic style reminiscent of black BANJO music and plantation songs on simple harmonic structures built from western CHORDS. More adventurous ragtime composers (including some white musicians) began to borrow elements from the BLUES, a vocal form characterized by a greater degree of IMPROVISATION and distinctive tonal colorings retained from African music (● p. 27). Ragtime began to disappear around 1920, although it had already influenced classical composers such as Debussy (● p. 24) and Stravinsky (● p. 43). Its style formed the basis for later jazz piano playing and spawned the Harlem STRIDE school of the 1920s and 1930s (● p. 46). The blues, which continued to flourish in its own

Left The banjo, based on traditional West African prototypes, was typical of the homemade musical instruments to which slaves had to resort. It remained popular in jazz until the 1930s, when it was supplanted by the more versatile guitar.

Right A 1920s jazz band in Berlin, where the new music flourished until the Nazi Party attempted to suppress it in the 1930s (● p. 81).

Below Duke Ellington at the keyboard, in a characteristically suave mood. Coming from a middle-class background, Ellington combined social respectability with phenomenal compositional talent and in the process raised the intellectual standing of jazz in the 1930s.

right and led both to the BOOGIE-WOOGIE style of piano playing and ultimately to rock'n'roll in the 1950s, donated to jazz the universally popular TWELVE-BAR harmonic progression, as well as a new emphasis on improvisation.

Ragtime pianists usually eked out a living in brothels and saloons, some of the few employment opportunities open to black musicians after emancipation. Another source of work was provided by the celebrated brass bands that appeared in funeral processions in southern cities such as New Orleans (● p. 28) and flourished due to the availability of cheap second-hand instruments abandoned by Civil War military bands. Band marches borrowed the ragtime idiom, often to "jazz up" classical pieces such as Chopin's Funeral March. When this style merged with rougher blues elements, early ensemble jazz in the DIXIELAND style (● p. 37) was born.

Jazz recordings first appeared in 1917 and began to proliferate after 1923 (● pp. 51–2), by which time the centers of musical activity had moved northward to Chicago (● p. 64) and eastward to New York (● p. 29). The growing popularity of dances such as the Charleston led to the development of a livelier style in which the original march-like mood was abandoned in favor of headier tempos and snappier rhythms. In the 1920s jazz developed further at the hands of many brilliant pioneers, including the innovative composer Jelly Roll Morton (● p. 45) and virtuoso improviser Louis Armstrong (● p. 56).

With the work of Duke Ellington at Harlem's Cotton Club (● p. 62) in 1927–32, jazz at last found a composer worthy to be hailed as equal in intellectual stature to his counterparts in the field of classical music.

9

Ellington produced a stream of tightly organized masterpieces in the three-minute format ideally suited to the technical limitations of 78rpm recordings. He then broke new ground by constructing pieces of considerably greater length.

In spite of its growing intellectual respectability during the 1930s, jazz had still not quite succeeded in shedding its early links with sex and low living. The music continued to be tarnished by an inevitable association with illicit drinking during the Prohibition years (1919–33) and, later, with the addiction to hard drugs that caused the premature and often impecunious deaths of many a talented musician. Jazz seemed more respectable in Europe, which had not endured social problems of such magnitude as those in the US arising from slavery and racial disharmony. From the early 1930s onward many American jazz musicians opted to emigrate to France, where greater social status and appreciative audiences made them welcome.

Left A poster by Charles Lévy, designed in 1879 for the *Folies-Bergère* in Paris, reveals how the stereotyped view of black minstrel shows prevalent in the USA was exported wholesale to Europe.

Left A scene at the *Moulin Rouge* club in Vienna in 1925 vividly illustrates the inextricable link between jazz and the sheer hedonism of its early years.

Right A young couple dance the jitterbug in Harlem in the 1930s, to the accompaniment of Erskine Hawkins' popular swing band.

Right The Band, painted by Edward Burra (1905-76), depicts a group that includes a sousaphone to the left of the drummer. This derivative of the tuba was named after the "March King," John Philip Sousa. Both instruments were retained from New Orleans marching bands and replaced by the doublebass during the 1920s.

In the 1930s the three strands of art music, popular music and jazz came closer together than they had ever been before – or have been since. The growing commercial success of jazz ensured that it became the pop music of the immediate pre-war years, while the distinguished SYMPHONIC JAZZ cultivated by composers such as George Gershwin and Aaron Copland (● p. 55) seemed destined to fuse highbrow and lowbrow into a cogent and enduring synthetic idiom. With Benny Goodman's and John Hammond's concerts at Carnegie Hall in 1938 (● p. 91), jazz at last proved itself to be an art form worthy of appreciation by critics, scholars and audiences in full evening dress.

Predominant in these years was the SWING band, its extended instrumentation exploiting the contrast between massed saxophone and brass sections as a background to exciting improvised passages performed by featured soloists, many of whom became international stars. The most successful swing bands were based in New York; although some originated in Kansas City (● p. 64), where Bennie Moten's work influenced the young Count Basie (● p. 86). Alongside the HOT and inventive style of the black swing bands, white ensembles, such as that led by Paul Whiteman (● p. 55), produced a more restrained but suavely polished dance music. The virtuosity and commercial success of the more enterprising white bands, notably those led by Benny Goodman (● p. 84) and Glenn Miller (● p. 107), were spectacular, and did much to spur on the growth of jazz in Europe.

White commercialization of jazz seemed at its height in the later 1930s, and the attempts of black musicians to regain the artistic initiative ultimately led to the decline of the swing band after World War II. The "be-bop" (or BOP) revolution began around 1941 when rebellious musicians like Charlie Parker (● p. 136), Dizzy Gillespie (● p. 219) and Thelonious Monk (● p. 154) began experimenting with a new style in which outmoded harmonic progressions were replaced by more startling chord sequences, and melodic improvisations became increasingly characterized by distortion, fragmentation and metrical ambiguity. Traditionalists lamented the alarmingly esoteric and abstract nature of bop. It was described by poet and jazz critic Philip Larkin as "bloodless note patterns," and Duke Ellington likened it to "playing scrabble with all the vowels missing." The modernistic forcefulness of this new sound in jazz (later to become the HARD BOP of Art Blakey and countless

11

Opposite, above In one of the most bizarre experiments in jazz, blind saxophonist Roland Kirk (who avoided the word "jazz" in favour of the phrase "black classical music") developed a technique for playing three reed instruments simultaneously.

Opposite, below Wynton Marsalis, a prodigious talent who assured jazz a continuing audience of young enthusiasts during the problematic 1980s.

Above Trumpeter Donald Byrd, photographed by William Claxton in 1959, in a picture that says it all: a solitary black musician communes with his instrument, while the body language of the white onlookers ranges from indifference to grudging curiosity.

imitators) was allied to a political need to reclaim jazz for the black Americans who had invented it in the first place: as with modernism in the other arts, the deliberate inaccessibility of the idiom protected it from a casual audience.

After his early work in bop, Miles Davis (● p. 216) rapidly established himself as the most creative figure in post-war jazz. His achievement in developing not one but several new styles has remained unparalleled, and has largely accounted for the profusion of possibilities available to the contemporary jazz musician. Seeking first to temper the unfortunate aggressiveness of bop, Davis initiated the COOL style in the late 1940s (● p. 120), in which dark instrumentation was coupled with a laid-back mood and sophisticated harmonies. This new restraint proved to be influential on the emerging WEST COAST style (● p. 134), which grew up in Los Angeles in the 1950s and was dominated by white musicians. Next came Davis's experiments with MODAL JAZZ (● p. 146), which abandoned chord progressions altogether and consisted of extended improvisation on unchanging groups of notes. Davis's SIDEMEN in the 1950s included pianist Bill Evans (● p. 156) and tenor saxophonist John Coltrane (● p. 160), both of whom later revolutionized the styles associated with their instruments.

A serious crisis in the mid-1960s was caused by the wholesale defection of a new generation of potential jazz fans to the relatively fresh pop and rock markets. Disaster was partly averted by Davis's canny synthesis of rock and jazz elements into a new hybrid style: FUSION (● p. 170). This became the characteristic (and largely electronic) sound of jazz in the 1970s, and scored exactly the commercial success jazz then so desperately needed to survive. Fusion also rescued jazz from the avant-garde dead-end into which the eccentric talents of performers such as saxophonist Ornette Coleman (● p. 150) seemed in danger of leading it in the 1960s. Radical departures from fundamental concepts in earlier jazz included the rejection of TONALITY, a move not likely to guarantee popularity. The growth of avant-garde jazz paralleled that of avant-garde classical music prominent in the same period, but was potently symbolic in likening its lack of formal constraints to the spiritual and political freedom that African Americans still found it necessary to demand.

By the early 1980s, fusion seemed to have run its course and many musicians who had made their names in the synthetic arena returned to playing a brand of jazz that (sometimes self-consciously) resurrected elements borrowed from earlier styles. Since the 1940s, when the obsolete genres of ragtime and dixieland were systematically revived by both performers and scholars, jazz has had its own "classic" idioms that survive in a healthy state today. Sometimes these early genres are pursued authentically in liberal doses of musical nostalgia, and in other cases they are modified from a modern perspective in a kind of jazz "neo-classicism." The young virtuoso trumpeter Wynton Marsalis (● p. 196) has been an outspoken advocate of this return to wholesome musical values, lamenting the commercialism behind the entire jazz-rock fusion movement.

But jazz has always had a concern for popularity at its very heart, and attempts to place it on an élitist pedestal have always been doomed to failure. Ever since the 1930s, when Louis Armstrong was criticized for "selling out" to commercial interests, the feud between the élitists and the populists in jazz has been as vitriolic as that between black and white. And Marsalis's own commercial success has, ironically enough, been partly secured by the untiring promotional efforts of CBS (now Sony) – the same company that pushed Miles Davis in the direction of fusion nearly three decades ago.

The plurality of jazz styles with which the often perplexed listener is surrounded today is almost as diverse as that in classical music: in just one hundred years, jazz has caught up with its illustrious musical forebears, both in quality and quantity. As they have in the past, jazz musicians today move in and out of each other's spheres of influence, the only difference now being the international flavor these migrations have acquired. Styles continue to be transmitted and transformed through an exciting process of musical osmosis that, in essence, is comparable to that which spawned the beginnings of jazz not so very long ago.

1895–1916
Origins

West African musical traditions, kept alive by slaves on US plantations in the nineteenth century, gradually coalesced with the tonality and structures of European classical music to create an exciting new American art form.

The only surviving photograph of the legendary cornetist Buddy Bolden (back row, third from left), a famous image often printed back-to-front in an attempt to correct the left-handed positions of the string players.

1895-1905

The Ragtime Era Begins

Black composers and their white imitators popularize a new style of light music based on catchy rhythms and appealing melodies. This "ragtime" is refined by the capable hands of Scott Joplin, who hopes to turn it into an art form. As it begins to merge with the rougher blues style, the beginnings of jazz are heard.

1895

February The Czech composer Dvořák, director of the National Conservatory in New York, publishes an article in *Harper's New Monthly Magazine* entitled "Music in America." He causes considerable controversy by advising American composers to build their future music on the basis of negro folk melodies.

● Ben Harney composes his RAGTIME song "You've Been a Good Old Wagon," and has it published in Louisville, Kentucky. He later styles himself "Inventor of Ragtime."
● Scott Joplin (● p. 21) publishes two songs in Syracuse, New York.

1896

3 August Ernest Hogan copyrights his ragtime song "All Coons Look Alike to Me," published by Witmark and Sons in New York. The title sets the racist tone of the genre, which rapidly grows in popularity.

5 August Ben Harney copyrights "You've Been a Good Old Wagon" and issues a revised version under the Witmark imprint.

● Scott Joplin publishes his first instrumental pieces in Temple, Texas. They are both marches, one (*The Great Crush Collision*) inspired by a railway accident.

1897

January William H. Krell, a white composer, publishes his *Mississippi Rag* in Chicago. It is the first RAG for solo piano to appear in print.

December Tom Turpin publishes his *Harlem Rag* in St. Louis, the first piano rag by a black composer to appear in print. At least twenty more rags by other composers are published in this year.

● Ben Harney issues his *Rag Time Instructor*. ● The first recordings of ragtime are made for the newly introduced disc-playing gramophone, in versions for solo BANJO and orchestrations for band.

Right A landmark publication in the early development of ragtime: Ben Harney's song "You've Been a Good Old Wagon."

"Ragtime is a certain type of syncopation and only certain tunes can be played in that idea. But jazz is a style that can be applied to any type of tune. I started using the word in 1902 to show people the difference between jazz and ragtime."

Jelly Roll Morton

Plantation Roots

Above William Aiken Walker's painting *Plantation Economy in the Old South* (c. 1876) presents a typical scene on a cotton plantation, and seems to suggest that, even after the Civil War, life in America's Deep South carried on much as before. Walker was born in Charleston, South Carolina, which later gave its name to the most famous jazz composition of the 1920s (● p. 58).

Hundreds of thousands of African slaves were relocated to North America between the sixteenth and mid-nineteenth centuries, torn away from their tribal homes by European traders. Although the importation of slaves to America became illegal in 1808, domestic slavery continued to flourish in the southern states until Abraham Lincoln became President. He forced the issue, and the bloody four-year Civil War between the industrialized northern states and the secessionist southern confederacy began in 1861. Slavery was finally abolished by the Thirteenth Amendment to the US Constitution in 1865. If freed slaves rejoiced at the news, their elation would prove short-lived: severe problems rooted in violent racism and strict segregation continued to blight black Americans for more than a century afterward.

In the popular imagination, jazz was born directly out of the hardships and repression of slavery and emancipation. Slaves had from the earliest years been systematically deprived of their cultural heritage, including their rich African musical traditions. On the cotton and rice plantations of the Deep South, slaves were forbidden to touch any musical instruments that might be used for secret communication, including drums or loud wind instruments. However, resourceful musicians produced home-made instruments such as the BANJO, which was based on a type of West African lyre. Although slaves from the same tribe were split up and dispersed to weaken their morale, African workers from disparate backgrounds soon forged a common musical language through work songs and FIELD HOLLERS.

Unaccountably anxious to please their masters, many slaves began to learn European musical styles and became proficient on Western instruments, such as the violin, in order to perform popular white dance music. When white entertainers began imitating what they saw as quaint black music-making (their faces duly blackened with burnt cork or boot polish), the MINSTREL SHOW was born. After emancipation, many black musicians – including early jazz practitioners – started their careers in minstrelsy. Other genres that arose from black music-making and proved influential on the development of early jazz included religious music based on European hymns (SPIRITUALS, later supplanted by GOSPEL) and the secular BLUES (● p. 27).

"Jazz came to America three hundred years ago in chains."

Paul Whiteman (1926)

> "A wave of vulgar, filthy
> and suggestive music has inundated the land.
> Nothing but ragtime prevails, and the cakewalk
> with its obscene posturings, its lewd gestures."
>
> *Musical Courier* (1899)

WORLD EVENTS

1894
- Accession of Czar Nicholas II, Russia

1895
- Birth of cinema ● Discovery of X-rays
- Creation of Rhodesia

1896
- Racial segregation upheld by US Supreme Court
- Gold rush in Alaska ● Revival of Olympic Games in Greece
- Marconi demonstrates radio technology

1897
- Queen Victoria's Diamond Jubilee ● Discovery of electrons

1898
- War between Spain and USA ● Discovery of radium
- Opening of Paris Métro

1899
- Boer War commences

1900
- Chinese Boxer rebellion
- Oscar Wilde dies

1901
- Death of Queen Victoria and accession of Edward VII
- Picasso's first exhibition, Paris
- Assassination of President McKinley, US
- Nobel Prizes instituted ● Giuseppe Verdi dies

1902
- Emile Zola dies ● Boer War ends

1903
- Wright brothers' first flight, US ● Paul Gauguin dies

1904
- Antonín Dvořák dies ● Anton Chekhov dies
- Completion of Trans-Siberian Railway

1905
- Civil unrest in Russia ● Einstein's theory of relativity
- Norway gains independence from Sweden
- End of Russo-Japanese war

● New prostitution legislation regulates the red-light district in STORYVILLE, New Orleans, where brothels have been conducting their business legally since 1857. Storyville soon becomes an important center for early jazz musicians (● p. 23).

1898

● Will Marion Cook and Paul Lawrence Dunbar stage their revue *Clorindy, or The Origin of the Cakewalk* on Broadway, and subsequently take it on tour to London.

1899

Summer The publisher John Stark visits the Maple Leaf Club at Sedalia, Missouri, and hears its resident pianist, Scott Joplin, perform his *Maple Leaf Rag*. Stark signs a contract with Joplin on **10 August**, pays him an advance of $50 for the piece and immediately publishes it. It sells over one hundred thousand copies within a year of publication.

● Joplin publishes his *Original Rags* in Kansas City. The title page describes it as "picked by Scott Joplin," a reference to the figurations borrowed from BANJO music that characterize the RAGTIME style. ● Irving Jones publishes his song "I Don't Understand Ragtime" in New York. ● Baltimore pianist Eubie Blake composes his rag *Sounds of Africa*.

Left Tom Anderson's "Arlington Annex," a leading establishment located at the junction of Basin Street and Iberville Street in Storyville, New Orleans. In the background is Lulu White's Mahogany Hall.

Below Tom Turpin's *Harlem Rag*

1900

23 January A CUTTING CONTEST between ragtime pianists is held at New York's Tammany Hall. The winner, Mike Bernard, receives the title "Champion Ragtime Pianist of the World."

May Banjo player Vess Ossman performs *A Bunch of Rags* in London, where he attends a recording session. This year he also participates in two New York recording sessions.

● John Stark moves his business from Sedalia to St. Louis, and Joplin follows. ● Tom Turpin opens his Rosebud Café in St. Louis, which becomes a meeting place for jobbing pianists. ● John Philip Sousa takes his famous band on a European tour, performing ragtime arrangements at the Paris Exposition.

Traces of Africa

While several characteristics of jazz reveal affinities with techniques common in West African music, these have frequently been over-emphasized by commentators keen to promote the image of jazz as an exclusively black phenomenon: jazz could not have developed in the way it did without the wholesale borrowing of European HARMONY (a concept alien to African music) undertaken by black musicians under strong white influences. Although the harmonic dimension of jazz is thoroughly Western, its harmonies are distinctively colored by BLUE NOTES which probably originated in the African technique of "bending" pitches for expressive effect. Blue notes flatten the third, fifth and seventh degrees of the Western major scale, and this undoubtedly dictated the choice of harmonies underlying the TWELVE-BAR BLUES, which later became the most important harmonic sequence in jazz (● p. 27).

In terms of structure, jazz reflects African influences in its widespread adoption of CALL-AND-RESPONSE patterns. In slave work songs, passages for a solo lead voice were answered by a choral response from the workers. The solo passages, however, might be elaborated by a process of melodic IMPROVISATION, the characteristic that most obviously differentiates jazz from classical music. The "dirty" vocal tone of plantation singing was directly carried over into jazz where, in contrast to the pure sounds favored in classical music, a singer's or player's idiosyncracies are prized for their unique expressive effect.

But it is in the sphere of RHYTHM that jazz's debt to African music is most clearly detected. Observers of slave music in the nineteenth century noted the unorthodox use of SYNCOPATION in their melodies. Deprived of drums, slaves habitually used the regular pulsation of hand-claps or axe-blows to set up a solid rhythmic foundation above which they could sing in catchy CROSS-RHYTHMS. This technique, ultimately a simplification of the complex POLYRHYTHMS in African music, soon became the basis for the exciting rhythms so characteristic of jazz.

Ragtime

The popularity of SYNCOPATION in black music of the 1890s is apparent in ragtime, which derives its name from the image of "ragged" rhythmic patterns. Unlike the BLUES (and unlike later jazz), ragtime was PRE-COMPOSED and circulated in printed form. The genre reflected the higher musical aspirations of the new generation of black musicians seeking to broaden their horizons after emancipation: along with their widespread commercial success, composers of ragtime such as Scott Joplin ultimately hoped that they would create a new black American classical music.

The ragtime style first appeared in songs with banjo (later piano) accompaniment, but became famous when adapted for solo piano. Its pianistic origins lie in nineteenth-century salon music, especially in the work of Louis Moreau Gottschalk, who based some of his pieces on slave melodies; its sectionalized, repetitive structures were borrowed from the march idiom popularized by John Philip Sousa, composer of *The Stars and Stripes Forever*. A typical ragtime texture consists of regular "oom-pah" patterns set up by the pianist's left hand (sometimes termed "boom-chick" after the alternating bass-drum and cymbal strokes in march rhythm), over which the right hand plays a highly syncopated melodic line. The HARMONY of ragtime may seem tame when compared with classical music of the same era, but the importation of BLUE NOTES from the blues (● p. 27) marked the next important step toward the early jazz style.

Ragtime disappeared in the early 1920s when it was rapidly supplanted in popularity by New Orleans jazz, but it enjoyed revivals in the 1940s (● p. 116) and 1970s (● p. 180). It also directly spawned the most important of early jazz piano styles – the Harlem STRIDE school (● p. 46) of the 1920s

1901

January A ragtime CUTTING CONTEST is held at the Tomlinson Hall, Indianapolis, Indiana.

7 June The Sousa Band records an orchestrated version of Gottschalk's piano piece *Pasquinade*. Originally composed around 1860, the work was a clear stylistic precursor of RAGTIME.

● Charles Booth records J. Bodewalt Lange's *Creole Belles* for the newly formed Victor recording label. This is the first ACOUSTIC RECORDING of a piano rag to be commercially issued. ● The American Federation of Musicians votes to suppress ragtime.

1902

16 June The Sousa Band records the NOVELTY ragtime number *Trombone Sneeze* under the direction of its composer, Arthur Pryor.

July Lincoln Park opens in New Orleans and becomes a center for performances by ragtime and early jazz ensembles.

● Scott Joplin publishes *The Entertainer: a Ragtime Two-Step* (● p. 180), and composes his ballet *The Ragtime Dance*. ● The eccentric American composer Charles Ives, an insurance salesman who also happens to be a musical genius, begins a set of four *Ragtime Dances* for piano or small orchestra. He is the first American classical composer to respond positively to the ragtime craze. ● Tony Jackson, a famous "Professor" (i.e., piano player who can read music) in STORYVILLE, composes his ragtime *Naked Dance*. ● The revue *Joyeux Nègres* is staged at the Nouveau Cirque, Paris. ● Decades later, Jelly Roll Morton claimed to have invented jazz single-handedly in this year – even though he was only twelve years old in 1902!

1903

18 February Scott Joplin registers the copyright of his unpublished (and now lost) ragtime opera *A Guest of Honor*, and takes it on tour.

● Eubie Blake publishes his first piano rags. ● *Maple Leaf Rag* is issued by Stark as a song, with lyrics by Sydney Brown. ● The Sousa Band performs at the British Royal court, and tours Prussia and Russia.

Below The title page of Scott Joplin's *Maple Leaf Rag* (1899).

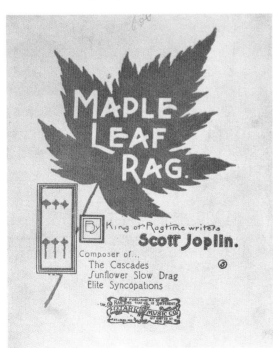

1904

22 February Louis Chauvin wins the annual CUTTING CONTEST organized by Tom Turpin at his Rosebud Café in St. Louis.

● Scott Joplin composes his rag *The Cascades* for the St. Louis World's Fair.
● Cornetist Buddy Bolden (● p. 25) is becoming established in New Orleans as the leading exponent of a musical style that fuses elements from ragtime and the BLUES: in a word, "jazz."

1905

● Joplin's *Bethena: a Concert Waltz* transforms the ragtime style into triple METER.
● Joseph Lamb publishes his first compositions, not yet in the rag idiom. ● Stark moves his company to New York, which is becoming established as the major music publishing center. ● Jerome H. Remick founds his publishing house in Detroit and New York, going on to publish over three hundred ragtime pieces. ● A black newspaper in Indianapolis strikes out against the racism of coon songs, and declares: "Composers should not set music to a set of words that are a direct insult to the colored race." ● Jelly Roll Morton (● p. 45) claimed to have composed his *Jelly Roll Blues* in this year.

Scott Joplin: The Entertainer

The most famous composer of piano rags was born in 1868, the second son of an ex-slave who worked the railroads and his banjo-playing wife. Scott Joplin learned classical music from an immigrant German teacher and began to forge a career for himself as a pianist, appearing at the Chicago World's Fair in 1893. He soon settled in Sedalia, Missouri, where he was employed as house pianist at the Maple Leaf Club. It was here that he was discovered in 1899 by the white publisher John Stark, whose edition of Joplin's *Maple Leaf Rag* met with such commercial success that the two men moved to neighboring St. Louis and prospered. Stark's publishing house also promoted the work of Joseph Lamb (1887–1962) and James Scott (1886–1918) who, together with Joplin, became established as the so-called Missouri School of "classic" ragtime composers. They did their best to keep ragtime restrained and refined, but were ultimately swept into obscurity by the jazz craze. Stark's company went out of business in 1922, but not before he published many of the finest hits of the ragtime era.

Joplin's rags include the famous *Pineapple Rag* and *The Entertainer*, both of which show his mastery of an essentially limited genre. Later in his career, he attempted to branch out into more ambitious compositional projects, such as ragtime ballet and opera. After moving in 1907 to New York, which was rapidly becoming the center of the popular-music industry, Joplin channeled his energies into the creation of what was to be his final stage work, an opera with an all-black cast entitled *Treemonisha*. Published at his own expense and performed privately in Harlem in 1915, the work flopped badly and the composer's resulting nervous breakdown and deep-seated bitterness precipitated his early death in 1917. It was 1972 before *Treemonisha* was rescued from obscurity and given a public staging (● p. 179); shortly afterward, Joplin's complete works were published and the composer was awarded a posthumous Pulitzer Prize.

Above A pensive study of Scott Joplin, who aimed to transform ragtime into a kind of black classical music.

Right A photograph from the first professional production of Joplin's opera *Treemonisha,* performed in Atlanta in 1972.

1906-9

New Orleans: the Musical Melting Pot

As the ragtime craze peaks and begins to influence composers of classical music, New Orleans establishes itself as the cradle of the emerging jazz style.

1906

26 March Buddy Bolden attacks his mother-in-law and is placed under medical supervision.

● James Scott meets Scott Joplin in St. Louis. John Stark publishes Scott's *Frog Legs Rag*, and Joplin prepares an orchestral version. ● Stark publishes Joplin's ballet *The Ragtime Dance* in a truncated version for solo piano. ● Jelly Roll Morton composes his *King Porter Stomp* which, more than two decades later, becomes a smash hit in the Swing Era (● p. 82). ● New Orleans trumpeters Freddie Keppard and Bunk Johnson begin to make names for themselves.

1907

13 March Buddy Bolden is arrested and, three months later, committed to an asylum for the insane. His promising career is cut short, and the first jazz legend passes into obscurity without having entered the recording studio.

● Joseph Lamb meets Joplin and Stark; the latter publishes Lamb's *Sensation Rag*. ● As part of a growing migration northward and eastward, pianist Tony Jackson heads for Chicago and Scott Joplin moves to New York. ● Jelly Roll Morton later claimed to have invented SCAT singing in this year.

Below Canal Street, New Orleans, in c. 1905.

"He was the blowingest man ever lived since Gabriel. They claim he went crazy because he really blew his brains out through the trumpet."

Jelly Roll Morton on Buddy Bolden

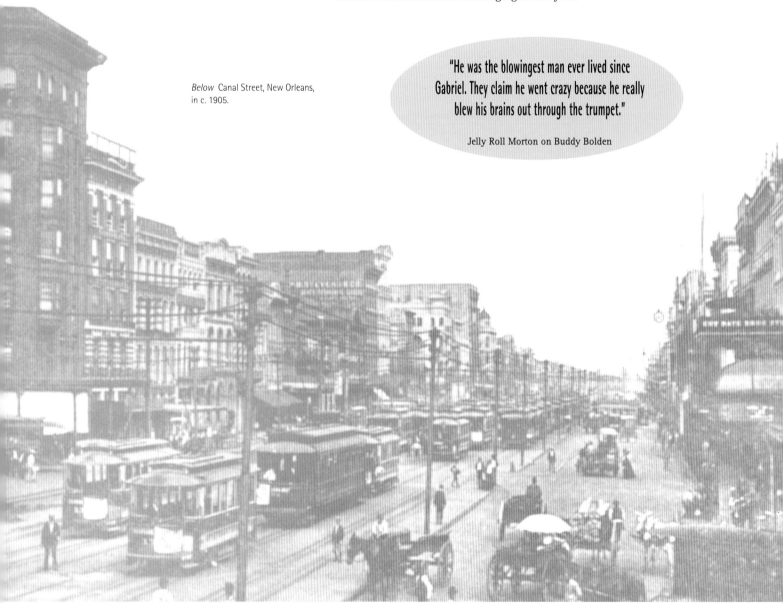

Funky Butt Hall: New Orleans and Storyville

Above Basin Street, New Orleans, showing the adjacent railroad and (at far left) part of Tom Anderson's Annex.

Below, right Music and sex are the prime commodities on offer in this 1906 advertisement for Anderson's establishment.

Those who today associate the word "funky" with musical earthiness may not care to learn that its original meaning was obscene, referring to vaginal odor. The aptly named Funky Butt Hall was one of numerous houses of pleasure in New Orleans that provided employment for RAGTIME and early jazz musicians. It was located on the outskirts of the red-light district known as Storyville, bordered by Canal Street and the railroad, which offered various services to visiting sailors and doubtless many others.

"The District," as it was universally known, was named after Alderman Story who boldly initiated legislation in 1897 regulating prostitution in the city. The region comprised thirty-eight blocks, and was sufficiently well organized to issue its own consumers' guide, known as *The Blue Book* (published by Tom Anderson). Over two thousand women plied their trade in the "Tenderloin," as it was also known, and Creole musicians could find plenty of work in ragtime bands, as solo pianists, or in other small groups. Men from fairly respectable backgrounds, including Jelly Roll Morton and Sidney Bechet (● p. 42), worked there in secret, not wanting their families to know. (Morton's grandmother discovered the truth, however, and slung her grandson, then only fifteen, out of their house.) Other notable musicians who started their careers in Storyville include King Oliver (● p. 48) and Louis Armstrong (● p. 56). Many famous early jazz compositions took their titles from streets in the region ("Basin Street Blues"), or from the names of specific establishments ("Mahogany Hall Stomp" was Armstrong's tribute to Lulu White's sporting house).

Storyville was a haven particularly for ragtime pianists. According to Clarence Williams (● p. 56), the "professors" who entertained clients on honky-tonk instruments sometimes doubled as pimps, conveniently observing professional activities as they played. Two of the best-known pianists were Kid Ross at Lulu White's (one of the most lavishly appointed venues of all, catering for the affluent and priding itself on Miss Lulu's "lifelong study of music and literature"), and Tony Jackson at Gypsy Schaeffer's. Morton recalled that Jackson's "Naked Dance" was a ragtime favorite, played at a rapid tempo to accompany the girls' nude dancing on a small stage while onlookers sipped champagne.

In 1917, Storyville was closed down following pressure from the US Navy. The closure was one factor encouraging musicians to migrate northward to Chicago (● p. 64) in search of work, although an exodus from the South had already been in progress for some time because of increasing economic depression in the region. Storyville's mythical status as the colorful progenitor of early jazz has probably led to its importance having been over-stressed: much fine music was developed at more salubrious establishments elsewhere in the city and, indeed, elsewhere in America.

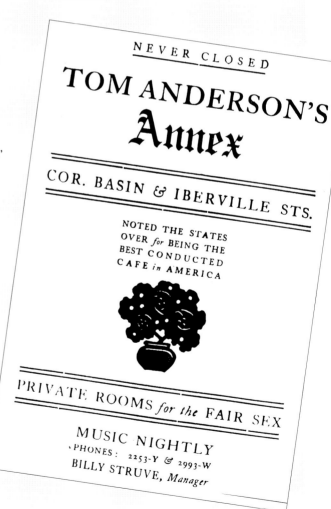

NEVER CLOSED

TOM ANDERSON'S *Annex*

COR. BASIN & IBERVILLE STS.

NOTED THE STATES OVER *for* BEING THE BEST CONDUCTED CAFE *in* AMERICA

PRIVATE ROOMS *for the* FAIR SEX

MUSIC NIGHTLY

PHONES: 2253-Y & 2993-W

BILLY STRUVE, *Manager*

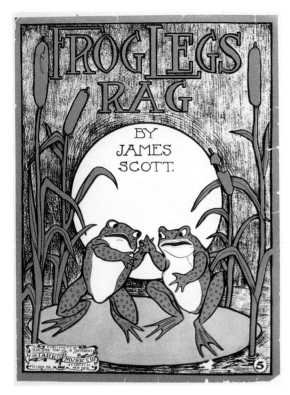

Above The front cover of James Scott's *Frog Leg's Rag*, published by John Stark in 1906.

Debussy Discovers Ragtime

The development of classical music in the nineteenth century was dominated by composers working in Germany and Austria, and was seen by many at the turn of the century to have reached its height in the operas of Richard Wagner. Although in his youth Claude Debussy (1862–1918) had been an ardent admirer of Wagner's music, the French composer eventually broke away from Austro-German musical techniques by cultivating an innovative style of musical impressionism. In the process, he laid the foundations for the extraordinary diversity in composition that characterizes twentieth-century music.

Debussy probably heard RAGTIME when the famous band led by John Philip Sousa appeared at the 1900 Paris Exposition as part of a European tour. The crisp clarity of the idiom must have appealed to Debussy's growing sense of anti-romanticism, and he went on to emulate the ragtime style in three piano pieces. The best known of these is "Golliwog's Cakewalk" (part of his *Children's Corner* suite, completed in 1908), which includes an incongruous quotation from Wagner's opera *Tristan und Isolde*. Debussy returned to the ragtime style in two later piano preludes: "Minstrels" (1910) and "General Lavine - excentric [*sic*]" (1913), the latter inspired by the antics of a clown from the Médrano Circus. Debussy's music, and that of his younger contemporary Maurice Ravel, came in turn to influence a later generation of jazz musicians. The advanced harmonies of French impressionism, which included the emphasis of attractive 7th, 9th and 11th chords in unconventional ways, became the staple harmonic vocabulary of both big-band and BOP idioms (● p. 96), while Debussy's pioneering MODAL techniques exerted a major influence on the work of Miles Davis and Bill Evans in the 1950s (● p. 146).

Right Debussy, photographed in 1910 outside his home in the Avenue des Bois, Paris.

WORLD EVENTS

1906
- Mount Vesuvius erupts, Pompeii
- San Francisco and Chile earthquakes
- British suffragettes imprisoned
- Deaths of Paul Cézanne and Henrik Ibsen

1907
- British reject proposal for Channel Tunnel
- Death of Edvard Grieg
- Rudyard Kipling receives Nobel Prize for Literature
- First wireless broadcast of classical music, New York

1908
- Alcohol banned in North Carolina and Georgia, USA
- Assassination of King Carlos I of Portugal
- Death of Nikolai Rimsky-Korsakov

1909
- Alcohol banned in Tennessee, USA
- Louis Blériot flies across English Channel
- Joan of Arc canonized
- Robert Peary reaches North Pole

The First Legend of Jazz: Buddy Bolden

The figure of Buddy Bolden, the cornetist who is reputed to have been the most influential of the early jazz musicians, is shrouded in mystery: only one photograph of him survives (above). He was committed to the state lunatic asylum in Jackson, Louisiana, in 1907 for smashing a jug on his mother-in-law's head, and he died in the same institution in 1931 – never having recorded his performances for posterity.

A builder by trade, Bolden had devoted his energies almost entirely to music by the turn of the century (retaining, however, some strength for his inveterate womanizing and carousing, and for the alcoholism that led to his mental breakdown). His ensemble of six instrumentalists reflected the standard FRONT LINE and RHYTHM SECTION format of early New Orleans groups (● p. 37).

Bolden is said to have imbued the RAGTIME style with elements borrowed from the rougher, improvised BLUES, and to have developed the improvised melodic embellishments so characteristic of New Orleans jazz. He played at such a piercingly loud volume, it reportedly caused parts of his instrument to eject themselves into mid-air.

Bolden's manner of playing was later reproduced by his protégé Bunk Johnson during the 1940s revival of early jazz styles (● p. 116), although by then it must have been virtually impossible to strip away the accumulated musical developments of four decades and achieve a truly authentic imitation.

1908

18 December First performance of French composer Claude Debussy's piano suite *Children's Corner*, which emulates the RAGTIME idiom in its "Golliwog's Cakewalk."

● Scott Joplin, his relationship with Stark deteriorating, publishes his *Pineapple Rag* with the Seminary Music Co. in New York. He also issues his *School of Ragtime: Six Exercises for Piano* this year. ● George Botsford composes his NOVELTY *Black and White Rag*, published in New York by Remick. In the 1970s, it becomes a hit as the theme tune to the BBC-television snooker program *Pot Black*, in a virtuoso arrangement by Winifred Atwell. ● Freddie Keppard begins to take his New Orleans band on tour. Other early jazz figures becoming prominent at around this time include cornetist Joe "King" Oliver (● p. 48), also based in New Orleans.

1909

15 June The Victor Dance Band records Botsford's *Black and White Rag* in New York.

● The band of the US Marines records Joplin's *Maple Leaf Rag*. Joplin publishes *Solace: a Mexican Serenade* in New York. ● Ragtime publication and the output of instruments from piano manufacturers both peak. ● Charles Ives completes his Piano Sonata No. 1, incorporating an outrageously jazzy section. This prophetic work, in which jazz elements are surrealistically distorted, is not performed in public until 1949.

Below The first page of Debussy's rag-influenced "Golliwog's Cakewalk," clearly showing the "oom-pah" figurations in the left hand and syncopated melody in the right.

1910-13

The Impact of the Blues

The blues, widely disseminated by the work of W. C. Handy, strengthens its influence on early jazz as the popularity of ragtime begins to decline.

1910

● John Stark moves his company back to St. Louis from New York. ● Scott Joplin's *Pineapple Rag* is issued as a song, with lyrics by Joe Snyder. ● King Oliver plays professionally in STORYVILLE. ● James Reese Europe (● p. 41) founds the Clef Club, an association for black musicians based in New York. ● Claude Debussy again emulates the RAGTIME style in "Minstrels" (*Préludes pour piano*, Book II).

1911

May Scott Joplin publishes, at his own expense, his ragtime opera *Treemonisha* in New York.

7 June Irving Berlin's song "Alexander's Ragtime Band," published by Ted Snyder and Co. (● p. 29), is recorded in New York. It is a phenomenal success, but is detested by classic ragtime composers for what they see as its commercial dilution of the idiom. ● Trombonist Kid Ory and clarinetist Sidney Bechet (● p. 42), among other musicians based in New Orleans, begin to establish their reputations.

Above An advertisement for James Reese Europe's Clef Club, founded in 1910 to promote the interests of black musicians.

Right Jim Europe attempts to conduct members of his Clef Club Orchestra (who seem to have no intention of playing!) in a publicity shot dating from c. 1914. The cluster of posed banjos in the foreground is notable.

W.C. Handy and the Blues

Right, below W. C. Handy at the piano in later life. Almost blinded in a subway accident in 1943, he died in 1958 – the year in which Nat King Cole portrayed him in the Paramount biopic *St. Louis Blues*.

Unlike RAGTIME, the blues was IMPROVISED music and did not initially circulate in printed form. The genre ultimately derived from plantation songs, and may be considered a secular counterpart of the SPIRITUALS popularized in the black church at around the same time. Originally sung unaccompanied, the CALL-AND-RESPONSE patterns typical of slave music were soon incorporated in the genre by the trading of melodic phrases between a solo voice and a single accompanying instrument, usually guitar (a format retained in the modern country blues).

By the turn of the century, a typical blues would be based on a melancholy text organized in verses of three lines (of which the first two were identical, and the third rhymed with them). The following example comes from a blues song recorded in the 1930s by Robert Johnson, one of the finest singers to hail from the Mississippi Delta:

I got stones in my pathway and my road seems dark at night,
I got stones in my pathway and my road seems dark at night,
I have pains in my heart, they have taken my appetite.

Other examples, such as those regularly sung by Bessie Smith (● p. 66), were more light-hearted, and often featured extensive sexual innuendo and a broad vein of comedy.

Since no examples of blues singing were recorded until the 1920s, it is impossible to reach definite conclusions about the genre's stylistic origins. It seems incontrovertible, however, that the improvised vocal melody would from the outset have been characterized by BLUE NOTES (● p. 19). These probably inspired the simple harmonies that later became standardized as the TWELVE-BAR chord progression fundamental to much later jazz, since these chords are often extended to include the blue dominant-seventh notes.

The first published examples of the blues were copyrighted by the bandleader W. C. Handy, who issued his *Memphis Blues* in 1912 and *St. Louis Blues* two years later. Handy's pre-composed piano accompaniments, replacing the improvised guitar parts of live blues performances, show how the blues and ragtime styles were already beginning to merge in anticipation of the birth of jazz. During the 1920s, the blues became a recognized sub-genre of jazz through the wide circulation of recordings made by singers such as Mamie Smith (● p. 44), Ma Rainey (● p. 53) and Bessie Smith, who earned herself the nickname "Empress of the Blues." It also spawned the development of the BOOGIE-WOOGIE style of piano playing, which enjoyed a popular revival in the 1940s.

1912

August W. C. Handy publishes his *Memphis Blues: a Southern Rag*, which begins to popularize the blues.

● Jerome H. Remick publishes an important anthology of orchestrated ragtime. ● Singer Bessie Smith joins F. S. Wolcott's "Rabbit Foot Minstrels." ● Kid Ory is leading his own band in New Orleans, where Armand Piron succeeds Freddie Keppard as leader of the Olympia Orchestra and hires King Oliver. ● James P. Johnson, later to become the "Father of Stride Piano" (● p. 46), turns professional and plays as a cinema pianist at the Nickelette in New York. ● Drummer Louis Mitchell forms his Southern Symphony Quintet in New York. ● Recordings are made of calypso music from Trinidad.

WORLD EVENTS

1910
- Marie Curie isolates radium
- Eruption of Mount Etna, Sicily
- Death of Leo Tolstoy, Mark Twain and King Edward VII

1911
- Civil War in Mexico
- Roald Amundsen reaches South Pole
- Italy at war with Turkey
- Death of Gustav Mahler

1912
- Sinking of the *Titanic*
- Unrest in the Balkans
- First Pathé newsreels
- Deaths of August Strindberg and Jules Massenet

1913
- Balkan wars escalate
- Igor Stravinsky composes *The Rite of Spring*

"Those parades were really tremendous things. The drums would start off, the trumpets and trombones rolling into something like Stars and Stripes ... You see, whenever a parade would get to another district the enemy would be waiting at the dividing line. If the parade crossed that line it meant a fight, a terrible fight ... Sometimes it would require a couple of ambulances to pick up the people that was maybe cut or shot occasionally ... And [there was] always plenty to eat and drink, especially for the men in the band, and with bands like Happy Galloway's, Manuel Perez's and Buddy Bolden's [● p. 25] we had the best ragtime music in the world. There was so many jobs for musicians in these parades that musicians didn't ever like to leave New Orleans."

Jelly Roll Morton

1913

New Year's Day Twelve-year-old Louis Armstrong is arrested for firing a shot in the air during a fit of high spirits in New Orleans.

29 December James Reese Europe records ragtime arrangements in New York with his Society Orchestra, which becomes the first black ensemble to record.

● Freddie Keppard takes his Original Creole Orchestra on tour. ● Mamie Smith starts singing in New York clubs. ● As the popularity of ragtime begins to dwindle, Artie Matthews publishes his first *Pastime Rag* and Luckey Roberts composes his *Junk Man Rag*. ● Canon Newboldt of St. Paul's Cathedral, London, preaches that ragtime is "indecent . . . suggestive of evil and destructive of modesty." ● The word "jaz" [*sic*] appears in print for the first time. In an article published in the *San Francisco Bulletin*, it is defined as "anything that takes manliness or effort or energy or activity or strength of soul."

Marching Bands

New Orleans at the turn of the century was a flourishing hub of musical activity. Predominant among black ensembles were the celebrated marching bands, which provided music for funeral ceremonies and other outdoor events. Many early jazz musicians gained their formative musical experiences by playing in these groups, which offered one of the few sources of paid employment to black musicians.

A typical band comprised cornets, trombones, clarinets, tubas and drums. Not surprisingly, these

Below The arrow indicates the young Louis Armstrong, participating in the brass band of the Colored Waifs' Home in New Orleans in c. 1913.

Tin Pan Alley

By the last decade of the nineteenth century, New York had become the powerful center of the music-publishing industry in the United States. The publishers, whose premises were largely concentrated on "Tin Pan Alley" (28th Street), were quick to capitalize on the growing popularity of VAUDEVILLE. They employed song PLUGGERS to promote their recent merchandise, and from the 1920s onward they fostered the fashion for musical comedies on Broadway. Both George Gershwin and Irving Berlin started their careers as humble song pluggers before going on to establish themselves as two of the finest popular songwriters of their era, alongside Jerome Kern and Cole Porter. All four composers contributed innumerable STANDARDS to the jazz repertoire.

Relations between jazz musicians and the publishers of Tin Pan Alley were not always cordial, however. Berlin's hit song "Alexander's Ragtime Band" (● p. 26) was disliked by RAGTIME composers, in spite (or perhaps because) of its popularity; and Kern heartily detested attempts to "jazz up" his songs (● p. 55), commenting that "no author would permit pirated editions of his work in which his phraseology and punctuation were changed." For impoverished jazz musicians, Tin Pan Alley often provided a welcome source of immediate income: it was by no means uncommon for musicians to compose a song or two in a taxi en route to a publisher's, the manuscript ready on arrival for an instant sale.

Right Front cover of Irving Berlin's hit song "Alexander's Ragtime Band", published in 1911.

instruments (all cheaply available second-hand) were soon favored in the make-up of early jazz ensembles. Somber music accompanied the procession to the cemetery, but an exuberant version of RAGTIME – a style itself originally based on marches (● p. 20) – would be performed on the return trip and at the prolonged feasting afterward.

Right The Onward Brass Band in New Orleans, c. 1913. From 1903 to 1930 this celebrated ensemble was led by cornetist and cigar-maker Manuel Perez (far left), who also played at Storyville's Mahogany Hall.

1914-16
On the Verge of Jazz

Ragtime enjoys its final flowering in a spate of recordings on piano rolls, while a white band from New Orleans takes Chicago by storm and ushers in the jazz craze.

Below The teenage George Gershwin during his time as a song plugger at Remick's publishing house.

Right The premises of Jerome H. Remick & Co. on Tin Pan Alley, where Gershwin worked between 1914 and 1917.

Opposite Although composed in 1905, Morton did not copyright his *Jelly Roll Blues* until 1915.

1914

● Louis Mitchell's Southern Symphony Quintet visits London to play their version of RAGTIME. They return to England in the following year after a tour of the USA. ● Fifteen-year-old George Gershwin leaves the New York High School for Commerce and begins work for Jerome H. Remick's publishing firm on Tin Pan Alley for $15 per week. His activities as a "song plugger" lead to a deep empathy for popular song styles. ● W. C. Handy publishes his *St. Louis Blues* and *Yellow Dog Rag*. The latter was originally entitled *Yellow Dog Blues*, an indication of the interchangeability of the two genre labels in this period. ● Edward Kennedy "Duke" Ellington composes his *Soda Fountain Rag*. ● James P. Johnson hears Eubie Blake play in Atlantic City, New Jersey. ● The *Ragtime Review* begins monthly publication.

1915

15 September Jelly Roll Morton publishes *Jelly Roll Blues*, the first work in a genuine jazz style to appear in print. Morton claims publication is necessary to introduce the new idiom to musicians outside New Orleans.

● In New Orleans, clarinetists Jimmie Noone and Johnny Dodds begin to make their names. ● Scott Joplin stages his ragtime opera, *Treemonisha,* in Harlem at his own expense, and receives only a lukewarm response. ● Luckey Roberts composes his tango *Spanish Venus*, an early example of what Morton terms the "Latin tinge" in jazz (● p. 114). ● Joseph Lamb composes his romantic *Ragtime Nightingale*, a piece that demonstrates ragtime's indebtedness to nineteenth-century classical piano music. ● John Stark issues his orchestral anthology *Standard High-Class Rags*. ● Joe Jordan plays ragtime in London.

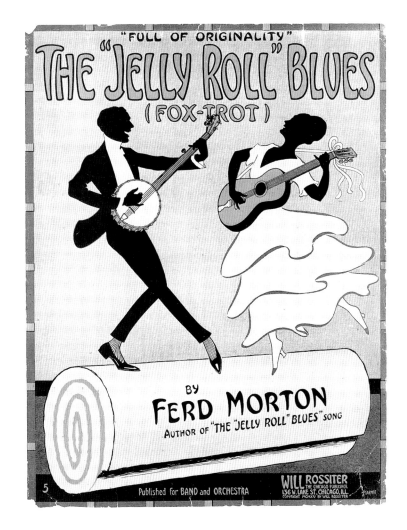

1916

3 March Johnny Stein's Dixie Jass Band appears at Schiller's Café on East 31st Street, Chicago. Stein is deposed as leader in June, whereupon the group renames itself the Original Dixieland Jass Band under cornetist Nick LaRocca (● p. 37).

1 May Stein's Dixie Jass band is reviewed in the *Chicago Herald*.

9 October The Chicago Piano Players' Social Club holds a ragtime CUTTING CONTEST and ball.

● Scott Joplin embarks on a substantial series of recordings on PIANO ROLLS, including *Maple Leaf Rag*. Nervous illness following the failure of *Treemonisha* forces him to enter Manhattan State Hospital for treatment. ● Luckey Roberts makes his recording debut, becoming the first black artist to record in the STRIDE style. ● James P. Johnson begins cutting piano rolls for the Aeolian Company in New York.

Rags on Rolls

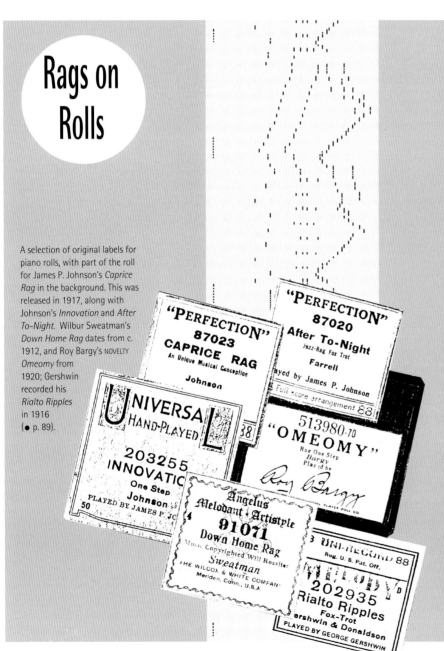

A selection of original labels for piano rolls, with part of the roll for James P. Johnson's *Caprice Rag* in the background. This was released in 1917, along with Johnson's *Innovation* and *After To-Night*. Wilbur Sweatman's *Down Home Rag* dates from c. 1912, and Roy Bargy's NOVELTY *Omeomy* from 1920; Gershwin recorded his *Rialto Ripples* in 1916 (● p. 89).

Recording technology before the advent of the electrical process in the 1920s was a primitive affair. Performers played into a large horn that transmitted the vibrations of their music directly to a needle cutting a groove on a wax master (a revolving cylinder or rotating disc). This process, developed independently by Thomas Edison and Alexander Graham Bell in the 1880s, resulted in recordings of wildly varying quality and limited sensitivity to dynamic contrasts.

Pianists generally preferred to record using the medium of the piano roll, which became popular at the turn of the century. A live performance at the keyboard was recorded as a series of perforations on a roll of paper, which could then be "read" by a special player-piano (i.e., pianola), which converted the pattern on the roll into a close approximation of the original mechanical action of the keys. Numerous RAGTIME pieces were preserved in this manner, including the only known recordings by Scott Joplin (● p. 21). The clattering action of the pianola was well suited to the reproduction of fast, virtuosic pieces, and this may have been one factor behind the development of a more exciting ragtime style, which left the restrained "classic" ragtime of Joplin and his associates far behind and culminated in the exuberant music of the Harlem STRIDE school.

A piano roll did not necessarily provide a faithful reproduction of a genuine live performance, however. Technicians could easily add extra notes in the workshop and, in some extreme cases, the entire "performance" could be fabricated without the use of a keyboard. The pianola system rapidly declined after the arrival of electrical recording in 1925 (● p. 59), when performers such as James P. Johnson (● p. 46) abandoned the old method in favor of live studio recordings.

WORLD EVENTS

1914

- Assassination of Archduke Ferdinand and beginning of World War I
- Foundation of American Society of Composers, Authors and Publishers

1915

- Gallipoli campaign
- Nurse Edith Cavell shot by Germans
- Deaths of Rupert Brooke and Alexander Scriabin

1916

- Battles of the Somme and Verdun
- Bombing of Paris and Constantinople
- Easter Rising staged in Dublin
- Deaths of Henry James, Max Reger and Enrique Granados (whose ship is torpedoed)

The Trumpet Family

Many might argue, with some justification, that the trumpet has been the most influential instrument in the history of jazz (pianists would doubtless disagree). Certainly the predominance of the trumpet – and its mellower cousin, the cornet – in the New Orleans marching bands (● p. 28) allowed it to assume the principal melodic role in early jazz ensembles. The earliest jazz practitioners, such as Buddy Bolden (● p. 25), stimulated the development of novel performance techniques that had scarcely been dreamt of during the trumpet's limited treatment in classical music. Jazz trumpeters employed a variety of contrasting timbres for expressive effect, including the GROWL and experimentation with a variety of MUTES, first undertaken by King Oliver (● p. 48). The instrument's range dramatically increased, and in the work of Louis Armstrong (● p. 56) it showed itself capable of dazzling virtuosity.

The size of the trumpet section in the big bands of the 1930s and 1940s swelled to four or five. Meanwhile, solo performers such as Roy Eldridge followed on from Armstrong's example and cultivated increasingly rapid figurations and piercingly high notes, both characteristics of BE-BOP trumpet playing epitomized in the work of Dizzy Gillespie (● p. 219). Aware of the natural agility of the competing saxophone, trumpeters did their best to keep up with the escalating pace of jazz in the later 1940s and 1950s, until Miles Davis (● p. 216) turned away from vacuous pyrotechnics to espouse a restrained, emotionally neutral idiom characterized by an absence of VIBRATO. This development influenced the emergence of COOL jazz (● p. 120), and in particular the playing of Chet Baker (● p. 210). Davis also introduced the haunting sound of the HARMON MUTE, which was later adopted by many other soloists.

Also important was the flugelhorn, a relative of the bugle with a range identical to that of the cornet. Although used in jazz as early as the 1930s, the flugelhorn's mellow tone came into its own during the boom in COOL jazz in the 1950s, when both Miles Davis and Chet Baker temporarily adopted it. Perhaps the most impressive exponent of the instrument was Thad Jones, who led one of the most exciting big bands of the 1960s (● p. 163) and whose popular composition "A Child is Born" derived much of its character from the rich and expressive tone of his instrument.

There have been few influential developments in trumpet technique since the 1960s, although Don Cherry's use of a tiny "pocket" trumpet is noteworthy.

Right A modern trumpet in B♭ (front), with its close cousins the cornet (right) and flugelhorn (left).

1917–1929

From New Orleans to the East Coast

An exodus of musicians from old New Orleans spreads jazz throughout the USA, first to Chicago and then New York, while some enterprising performers cross the Atlantic to stimulate the growing European demand for the new music.

Jelly Roll Morton's Red Hot Peppers, photographed in Chicago in 1926 (l. to r.): Andrew Hilaire (drums), Kid Ory (trombone), George Mitchell (cornet), Johnny Lindsay (bass), Morton (piano), Johnny St. Cyr (banjo) and Omer Simeon (clarinet).

1917

All that Jazz

The spectacular success of the first jazz record, cut by the Original Dixieland Jazz Band from New Orleans, threatens to sweep ragtime aside.

27 January The Original Dixieland Jass Band, a white group from New Orleans, performs in Manhattan.

30 January The Original Dixieland Jass Band records two sides in a trial session for Columbia. The company declines to issue the tunes, which would have been the first recorded jazz.

February Louis Mitchell's Syncopating Sextette appears in Glasgow. His Seven Spades appear in London later in the year.

2 February The word "jazz" (often spelled "jass" in these early years) appears in print in *The New York Times*.

26 February The Original Dixieland Jass Band records "Livery Stable Blues" and "Dixieland Jass Band One-step" in the studios of Victor. Further recordings follow in **August**, **September** and **November**.

March George Gershwin leaves Remick & Co. to work on Broadway.

7 March Victor issues the two sides recorded by the Original Dixieland Jass Band in February. These are the first jazz recordings to be made available to the public, and the witty farmyard-animal imitations in "Livery Stable Blues" help the release to become an instant commercial success.

The Original Dixieland Jass Band, Chicago 1917: Henry Ragas (piano), Larry Shields (clarinet), Eddie Edwards (trombone), Nick LaRocca (cornet) and Tony Sbarbaro (drums).

Down South in Dixie

Left The New Orleans Rhythm Kings, Chicago 1923. At the extreme right is Voltaire de Faut (C-melody saxophone), who recorded a fine duet with Jelly Roll Morton in May 1925. Morton, although not in this photograph, played piano for N.O.R.K. recordings made in July 1923.

The first band to make recordings billed as "jazz" was in many ways untypical of early groups, not least because it comprised five white men under the leadership of cornetist Nick LaRocca. The quintet hailed from New Orleans and derived its style from the music played there by black ensembles, achieving a rapid rise to prominence through spirited performances which incorporated novelty instrumental effects such as animal imitations. The group's success was an early (and by no means the only) example of the white commercialization of black music, and their recordings appear embarrassingly crude alongside the finesse of comparable black groups who recorded in the early 1920s.

Firmly based on the sectionalized structure and syncopated march rhythms of ragtime, with increasing use of the TWELVE-BAR BLUES progression, the New Orleans ensemble style is correctly termed "Dixieland" only when performed by white groups (the term derives from the nickname "Dixie," used to describe the southern secessionist states in the Civil War). Dixieland music sometimes incorporated improvised BREAKS, an important development away from the PRE-COMPOSED nature of ragtime. The normal arrangement included three solo melody instruments – cornet, clarinet and trombone – that simultaneously performed different embellished versions of the melody. This elaboration constituted another notable departure from traditional ragtime. The melodic embellishments were supported by a RHYTHM SECTION – a bass instrument (tuba or double bass), harmony instrument (banjo, guitar or piano) and simple drum kit (typically bass drum, side drum and suspended cymbal).

White groups were generally less adept at handling improvisation, BLUE NOTES and SWUNG RHYTHM than their black counterparts, although the New Orleans Rhythm Kings (who made recordings in 1922–25) represented a tangible improvement on the primitive idiom of the Original Dixieland Jazz Band. Both groups had disbanded by 1925, by which time black ensembles had gained the ascendancy they merited.

Jass or Jazz?

The exact etymology of the word "jazz" (which first appeared in print in a San Francisco newspaper in 1913) is impossible to establish, but its early connotations were undoubtedly sexual. The most likely derivation is from "orgasm," which in slang usage was shortened to "jasm." The word "jass" had become synonymous with fornication, and its original application to the new musical genre was decidedly uncomplimentary (e.g.,"that godawful jass music"). Around 1915, several bands provocatively adopted the expletive in their names, and it immediately caught on. Legend has it that the Original Dixieland Jass Band changed the spelling because pranksters often deleted the letter *j* from their posters!

The following alternative (and less convincing) etymological derivations have been proposed:

- jasmine (the practice of adding it to perfumes in New Orleans led to the phrase "jassing it up")
- *jaser* (a verb in the French dialect spoken in Louisiana, meaning "to chatter")
- *yas* or *jasi* (African words for acting energetically, or out of character)
- Jas. or Chas. (i.e., abbreviations for James and Charles)
- Jasper (a famous dancing slave in New Orleans in the 1820s)
- Jasbo (referring to Jasbo Brown, a black musician in Chicago)

Right The front cover of a Victor Records catalog issued in March 1917 lists the variety of spellings to which the word "jazz" was subjected in these early years.

WORLD EVENTS

16 March Czar Nicholas II abdicates, Russia

6 April US enters World War I

31 July Third battle for Ypres

26 September Death of Edgar Degas

6 November Passchendaele captured by British and Canadian forces

7 November Lenin's Bolsheviks assume power in Russia after October Revolution

10 December The Vatican forbids Roman Catholics to dance the tango

1 April Death of Scott Joplin (● p. 21) in New York.

18 May Erik Satie's ballet *Parade*, based on a scenario by Jean Cocteau (with set designs by Picasso), is given its first performance in Paris by Diaghilev's Ballets Russes. The score uses the ragtime idiom and quotes from a song by Irving Berlin in a section depicting "a little American girl."

21 September W. C. Handy's Orchestra of Memphis embarks on a series of recordings in New York, including (on **25 September**) their interpretation of "Livery Stable Blues."

"The word [jazz] never lost its association with those New Orleans bordellos. In the 1920s I used to try to convince Fletcher Henderson that we ought to call what we were doing 'Negro music.' But it's too late for that now."

Duke Ellington, 1976

Left Costume designs by Pablo Picasso for Erik Satie's ballet *Parade,* first staged in 1917.

12 November The US Navy closes down the red-light district of STORYVILLE, New Orleans. Many ragtime and jazz musicians leave the city to seek employment elsewhere.

● Clarinetist Sidney Bechet settles in Chicago and plays with King Oliver and Freddie Keppard.

1918

Ragtime Goes Abroad

Already outmoded in the US, ragtime enjoys a final flowering in Europe and influences classical composer Igor Stravinsky.

February–March James Reese Europe tours twenty-five French cities with "The Hellfighters," the RAGTIME band of the 369th US Infantry.

25 March The Original Dixieland Jazz Band (● p. 37) records four sides in New York, including Nick LaRocca's hit "Tiger Rag." They make further recordings later in the year.

28 September First performance of Russian composer Igor Stravinsky's music-theater piece *The Soldier's Tale*, which includes a movement entitled "Ragtime" (● p. 43).

November Louis Armstrong (● p. 56) begins work in bands performing on the Mississippi riverboats, including a famous group led by Fate Marable that performs on vessels sailing out of St. Louis. In this year Armstrong also replaces King Oliver (who moves to Chicago) in Kid Ory's band, based in New Orleans.

December The Louisiana Five record on the Emerson label in New York.

● Jelly Roll Morton (● p. 45), who is working in California, copyrights his *Frog-i-More Rag*.

Above Louis Armstrong (third from right) in Fate Marable's band on the steamboat S. S. Capital, St. Louis 1919. Marable is seated at the keyboard (third from left); to his right is Johnny St. Cyr, who would later play banjo in groups led by King Oliver and Armstrong along with drummer Baby Dodds (extreme right).

Right Giant Mississippi steamships, with their floating ballrooms, provided an important employment opportunity for early black jazz bands.

Europe in Europe

As the jazz craze took hold at the end of World War I, the RAGTIME style enjoyed its final heyday at the hands of James Reese Europe (1881–1919). His early career was spent as a director of musical comedies in New York, where he promoted the work of the ragtime songwriter Ernest Hogan (● p. 16) and formed the Clef Club, one of the first associations specifically designed to cater to the interests of black musicians. His Society Orchestra, which included violins and mandolins, made history as the first black group to make recordings (in 1913), and it performed colorful and witty orchestrated versions of popular RAGS, MARCHES and CAKEWALKS. Europe's work is especially notable for its unusual and expressive instrumentation that foreshadows later developments in jazz.

Jim Europe's fame spread to Europe when he crossed the Atlantic on tour with the all-black military band of the 369th US Infantry ("The Hellfighters"), which met with great success when it played in French cities during a six-week period in February and March 1918. An equally successful tour of America was brutally curtailed in the following year when Europe was stabbed to death by his drummer in circumstances that remain obscure.

Right Jim Europe hired singer Noble Sissle and ragtime pianist Eubie Blake as members of his Society Orchestra during World War I. Sissle and Blake were later responsible for the hit show *Shuffle Along* (● p. 47).

1919

Jazz on Tour

Dixieland causes a sensation in London. The jazz craze soon sweeps across Europe, where New Orleans clarinetist Sidney Bechet goes on tour and stays for three years.

> "The best qualification for a jazzist is to have no knowledge of music and no musical ability beyond that of making noises either on piano, or clarinet, or cornet or trap drum."

Review of the Original Dixieland Jazz Band's London show in the *Performer*, 10 April 1919

20 January Drummer Sonny Greer first plays with Duke Ellington (● p. 62), and remains with him until 1951. Ellington later declares, "Greer was not the world's best reader of music, but he was the world's best percussion reactor. When he heard a ping he responded with the most apropos pong."

7 April The Original Dixieland Jazz Band (● p. 37) performs at London's Hippodrome, where they are soon sacked. They move on to the Palladium and a nine-month spell at the Hammersmith Palais, and make an appearance before King George V at Buckingham Palace.

10 May James Reese Europe is killed in the middle of a high-profile national tour of the US. This year, his band records more than twenty sides in New York.

26 May *La La Lucille*, George Gershwin's first full-length musical comedy, opens at the Henry Miller Theater, New York.

June Will Marion Cook tours Europe with his Southern Syncopated Orchestra, having hired Sidney Bechet in Chicago before their departure. Bechet decides to remain in Europe.

October Swiss conductor Ernest Ansermet, who has heard Bechet perform in London, describes him as a "genius" in an article published in the *Revue Romande*.

8 November First performance of Igor Stravinsky's *Piano-Rag-Music* for solo piano.

29 December All VAUDEVILLE theaters are closed in the Soviet Union, following a decree from the Council of People's Commissars stating that light music is a corrupting influence.

Below Sidney Bechet, pioneer of the soprano saxophone, pictured here in the late 1940s.

Bechet Abroad

> "When you're really playing ragtime [i.e. jazz], you're feeling it out, you're playing to the other parts, you're waiting to understand what the other man's doing, and then you're going with his feeling, adding what you have of your feeling."
>
> Sidney Bechet, *Treat it Gentle*, 1960

Clarinetist Sidney Bechet was one of the legendary figures of New Orleans jazz, and one of the music's most wayward and idiosyncratic personalities. Sceptical about the importance of STORYVILLE as a catalyst in the music's origins (● p. 23), he recalled that outdoor parties and CUTTING CONTESTS in New Orleans were more significant occasions on which musicians traded creative ideas.

Bechet played with Will Marion Cook in Chicago and New York before embarking on a tour of Europe in 1919 with Cook's Southern Syncopated Orchestra. It was while in London that he bought himself a soprano saxophone, which became his preferred instrument. His playing was distinguished by an unusually intense VIBRATO, and a gift for appealing melodic invention. Deported from England after a brawl, he worked briefly in France before returning to the US in 1922. Two years later he enjoyed a spell playing with Duke Ellington's orchestra, during which he influenced the emerging talent of alto saxophonist Johnny Hodges.

In 1925 Bechet moved to Paris (● p. 59), where he served an eleven-month prison sentence following a firearms incident in 1929. With the rise of the new SWING music in the 1930s, his talent seemed in danger of being eclipsed by changing fashions, but he continued to make musical innovations, including a novel attempt to record as a one-man band (● p. 99).

Stravinsky's "Stolen" Rags

The Russian composer Igor Stravinsky, a self-styled musical "kleptomaniac" whose genius could transform almost any compositional source material into a highly original work of art, began to borrow from RAGTIME in 1918 when he included a ragtime-style dance in his music-theater piece *The Soldier's Tale*. Stravinsky's friend, the Swiss conductor Ernest Ansermet, had visited the US two years before and brought back the sheet music for various RAGS, and it was Ansermet's glowing reports of Sidney Bechet's clarinet playing in London in 1919 that stimulated Stravinsky to compose his *Three Pieces for Clarinet* in 1919.

Stravinsky wrote two more works in this period that were heavily influenced by ragtime. His *Piano-Rag-Music* for solo piano, conceived for Artur Rubinstein in 1919, demonstrates how the CROSS-RHYTHMS and OSTINATOS typical of ragtime complemented Stravinsky's own compositional preoccupations at the time. In *Ragtime for Eleven Instruments*, first performed in 1920 (● p. 44) his unorthodox instrumental ensemble included the distinctive cimbalom, a folk instrument from eastern Europe played with hammers, which was used by the composer to represent the clattering of a honky-tonk piano.

Stravinsky was for a time interested in mechanical pianos, and in 1945 he composed his *Ebony Concerto* for Woody Herman in emulation of the big-band style then fashionable.

Above The Original Dixieland Jazz Band appeared on the stage of the London Palladium on 12 April 1919.

The timely revival of early jazz styles in the late 1940s rescued him from a slide into oblivion, and he was again hailed as one of the giants of New Orleans jazz. A triumphant reception in Paris at the 1949 Salle Pleyel Jazz Festival (● p. 121) inspired him to move back to Europe in 1951 to spend his remaining eight years in France.

In his autobiography, Bechet provided a vivid description of an attempt by the French critic Hugues Panassié (● p. 80) to record hot jazz in New York in around 1938. Apparently unaware that jazz musicians tend not to give of their best early in the morning after the night before, Panassié was surprised when the musicians rolled into the studio obviously inebriated:

"Tommy [Ladnier, on trumpet], he showed up dead drunk. James P. Johnson, he just stretched himself on the piano and passed out. Some of the musicianers [*sic*] didn't know how many fingers they'd got on each hand . . . Tommy knew the records weren't what they could have been and he wanted to say something to appease Panassié, who was sitting in the corner holding his head – something he thinks will fit the occasion. So he pulled himself up and called out '*Vive la France*' and then fell almost flat on his face."

Left Picasso's front-cover design for the piano reduction of Stravinsky's *Ragtime for Eleven Instruments*.

WORLD EVENTS

5 January Nazi Party formed, Germany

17 January Pianist Ignacy Paderewski becomes Prime Minister of Poland

23 February Mussolini forms Italian Fascist Party

15 June Alcock and Brown fly the Atlantic non-stop

28 June Treaty of Versailles signed

27 July Chicago race riots

3 December Death of Pierre Auguste Renoir

1920

Branching Out From Dixie

Mamie Smith's recording debut marks the start of a widespread demand for female blues singers, while Paul Whiteman's band begins to be renowned for its successful brand of white dance music.

January The Original Dixieland Jazz Band (● p. 37) records in London.

27 April First performance of Igor Stravinsky's *Ragtime for Eleven Instruments* at the Aeolian Hall, London, conducted by British composer Arthur Bliss. Stravinsky's score features a front cover designed by Picasso.

10 August Mamie Smith records "Crazy Blues" for Okeh in New York; it is the first BLUES to be cut by a black singer. She goes on to record further blues sides in the autumn.

● In Chicago King Oliver forms his own band, which will later become the famous Creole Jazz Band. ● Bandleader Paul Whiteman makes his first recordings in New York. His disc coupling "Whispering" and "Japanese Sandman" goes on to sell over one million copies. ● John Stark publishes the last of Artie Matthews' five *Pastime Rags*. ● James P. Johnson (● p. 46) meets George Gershwin (● p. 89), and later reports that they enjoy "lots of talks about our ambitions to do great music on American themes."

Left Mamie Smith and her Jazz Hounds in 1920, with stride pianist Willie "The Lion" Smith at the keyboard.

Mister Jelly Roll

Right Jelly Roll Morton poses for a New York publicity shot in 1929, just before his music was finally eclipsed by the popularity of the fashionable swing bands.

WORLD EVENTS

16 January Prohibition comes into effect in America

25 January Death of Amadeo Modigliani

February Escalation of Russian Civil War

28 August Nineteenth Amendment guarantees women the right to vote, USA

2 October Death of Max Bruch

15 November Gustav Holst's *The Planets* first performed

Right US Government officials disposing of illicit alcohol during the 1920s.

For jazz to develop from its tentative beginnings into an intellectually satisfying and commercially viable art form, two things were needed by musicians: an ability to create varied and coherent musical structures, and a keen business instinct. Ferdinand "Jelly Roll" Morton (whose nickname apparently referred to part of his anatomy) combined both attributes at a crucial stage in the music's evolution. A product of STORYVILLE, he began his career as a brothel pianist and later branched out into pimping and managing a hotel, a casino and a boxing agency. The height of his musical achievements came in the mid-1920s when he worked and recorded in Chicago, enjoying the firm support of the Melrose brothers (his white publishers).

In 1926 Morton founded his finest group, The Red Hot Peppers, consisting of a standard New Orleans instrumentation (● p. 37) in which the piano was a featured solo instrument. The band was unusually well organized, with its members receiving regular fees for both recordings and rehearsals (the latter were by all accounts rigorous, and resulted in committed performances that displayed keen attention to every detail of the music). Morton's compositions were mostly based on the sectionalized structure of RAGTIME, and achieved a pleasing balance between passages for the full band using the COUNTERPOINT typical of the New Orleans style, as well as solo CHORUSES and BREAKS. In addition to being a STRIDE pianist of considerable accomplishment, Morton also promoted his talents as a singer and would later claim that he was one of the earliest exponents of both BLUES and SCAT vocal styles.

At the end of the 1920s, when the SWING music of the big bands rapidly swept the New Orleans style aside, Morton lost his position of ascendancy. His career was revived in 1938 by Alan Lomax, who edited his memoirs and encouraged him to make a series of historically valuable retrospective recordings for the Library of Congress in Washington, D.C. While Morton's music may seem today to lack some of the improvisational spontaneity of later jazz styles, his importance as the first musician to approach jazz from an intellectual point of view and to seek to improve its artistic standing is incalculable. And his flamboyant personality and repeated attempts to claim sole responsibility for the early development of jazz proved legendary.

"In your broadcast of March 26, 1938, you introduced W. C. Handy [● p. 27] as the originator of jazz . . . and blues. By this announcement you have done me a great injustice . . . It is evidently known, beyond contradiction, that New Orleans is the cradle of jazz, and I, myself, happened to be the creator in the year 1902."

Jelly Roll Morton, letter to Robert Ripley, 1938

1921
Striding Ahead

The Harlem "stride" school of piano playing grows in popularity, preserving a clear link with the outmoded ragtime style but delighting in greater virtuosity and jazziness.

January The town of Zion, llinois, bans jazz performances, considering the music to be a sinful pursuit.

20 April RAGTIME pianist Tony Jackson (● p. 23) dies in Chicago.

June King Oliver (● p. 48) takes his band to San Francisco, where they remain until December.

18 October James P. Johnson records the first version of his STRIDE solo *Carolina Shout*, which later has an enormous influence on major figures such as Fats Waller (● p. 105) and Duke Ellington (● p. 62).

Harlem Stride

When Jelly Roll Morton (● p. 45) made his historic retrospective recordings in 1938, he demonstrated how he habitually jazzed up Scott Joplin's *Maple Leaf Rag* during his early years in New Orleans. This tendency to elaborate existing rags by adding melodic embellishments and increasing the tempo was further encouraged during the 1910s by the popularity of PIANO ROLLS, and was much lamented by the composers of "classic" ragtime. It led to a brand of piano jazz referred to as the Harlem "stride" school, named after its principal center of development (the black enclave of New York City) and the characteristic "striding" motion of its left-hand split chords. Although in this technique and in its sectionalized structure the new style remained indebted to ragtime models, it was considerably "jazzier" than ragtime in its increased use of BLUE NOTES, IMPROVISATION and SWUNG RHYTHM.

Stride pianists developed a formidable skill, especially impressive in the accuracy of their leaping left hands, and considered themselves to be the élite of the jazz world. They dressed well (homburgs and cigars were *de rigeur*, even while playing) and were often well educated in classical music, which influenced their compositions. Willie "The Lion" Smith, for instance, wrote stride pieces with impressionistic titles reflecting his knowledge of piano music by Grieg and Debussy (● p. 24). All jazz

Above This uncharacteristically somber portrait of James P. Johnson, taken in 1921, scarcely reflects the infectious effervescence and virtuosity of the "stride" piano style he perfected in the 1920s.

pianists before the development of BE-BOP in the 1940s were initially schooled in the stride style, which remains the most technically challenging of all jazz keyboard idioms and continues to be promoted by performers such as Dick Hyman and Ralph Sutton.

The greatest of the first generation of stride pianists was undoubtedly James P. Johnson, universally known as "The Father of Stride Piano" and best remembered as the composer of the catchy "Charleston" (● p. 58). His most influential piece was *Carolina Shout*, which the young Duke Ellington attempted to learn by slowing down his pianola's mechanism in order to copy the fingering patterns preserved on a piano roll made by its composer in 1918. Johnson's protégé, Thomas "Fats" Waller, learned *Carolina Shout* in a similar way and went on to ensure that the popularity of the stride style continued into the 1930s.

For his part, Johnson became increasingly preoccupied with the composition of ambitious (and now largely forgotten) concert works in a SYMPHONIC JAZZ idiom, including the "Negro Rhapsody" for piano and orchestra premiered by Waller at Carnegie Hall (● p. 65) in 1928, and a *Harlem Symphony* (1932). Unlike many of his contemporaries, however, Johnson adapted his jazz style to changing fashions with some success and continued to record and compose stage shows well into the 1940s.

● Singer Mamie Smith continues her prolific output in the recording studio, cutting nearly thirty sides in this year alone. ● Fletcher Henderson (● p. 71) becomes musical director of Harry Pace's Black Swan Record Company in Harlem, the first label to be run by black entrepreneurs. ● Eubie Blake and Noble Sissle stage their show *Shuffle Along*, which runs for 504 performances on Broadway. Blake also records his *Charleston Rag* under the title *Sounds of Africa*. ● James Scott publishes a RAG with a title designed to draw attention to the improvisational liberties increasingly taken by pianists: *Don't Jazz Me Rag – I'm Music*. ● Zez Confrey scores a hit with his piano NOVELTY, *Kitten on the Keys*.

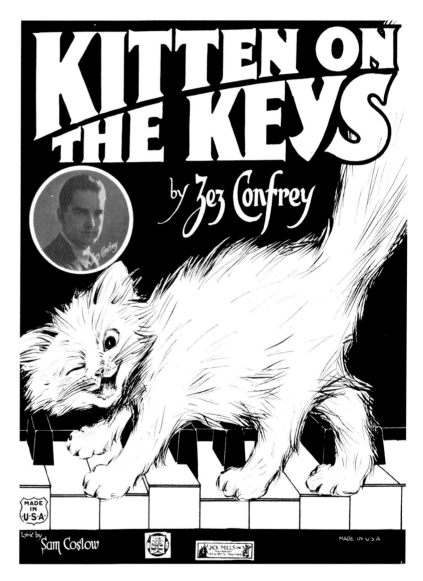

Above, top left The program for a performance of Blake's and Sissle's *Shuffle Along* in January 1922.

Above Zez Confrey (inset) appeared with Paul Whiteman's band at the famous 1924 concert which launched Gershwin's *Rhapsody in Blue* (● p. 55).

WORLD EVENTS

9 February End of Russo–Polish War

Spring Crisis over German post-war reparations

4 May French army enters the Ruhr

29 July Hitler elected leader of Nazi Party

2 August Death of Enrico Caruso

4 October Russia refused entry to League of Nations

16 December Death of Camille Saint-Saëns

1922

King Oliver in Chicago

King Oliver and Kid Ory establish their reputations in Chicago and Los Angeles as ragtime suffers its death throes.

24 January A private performance is mounted in Chelsea, London, of William Walton's entertainment *Façade*. Setting the nonsense poetry of Edith Sitwell to jazzy music, the production creates a scandal in the English capital.

Spring Kid Ory's Sunshine Orchestra makes its first recordings under the name Spikes' Seven Pods of Pepper in Los Angeles. The two sides issued ("Ory's Creole Trombone" and "Society Blues") are the first to be cut by a black ensemble playing in the New Orleans style.

July King Oliver invites Louis Armstrong (● p. 56) to join his Creole Jazz Band, which is now playing at Chicago's Lincoln Gardens.

> "As Oliver's recordings . . . recede further into the historical past, each succeeding generation will undoubtedly find it harder to relate to them. Forty years or so of solo-oriented jazz make it difficult for people to understand the collective music-making conception the Creole Jazz Band represented, and of course the antique sound of the old acoustical Gennett, Okeh and Paramount recordings is strange to modern ears. For me they have a lovely sound all their own, as nostalgic and personal as the sound of a Model T."
>
> Gunther Schuller, 1968

Right King Oliver (third from left), pictured with his Creole Jazz Band in San Francisco on 12 June 1921. Louis Armstrong joined the band in the following year, and in 1924 married its pianist, Lil Hardin (fourth from left).

The King of Creole Jazz

In the summer of 1922 at Chicago's Lincoln Gardens cornetist Joe "King" Oliver and his Creole Jazz Band brought the New Orleans style of small-ensemble jazz to its first artistic high point. The following April, they began recording their fine performances for posterity. Oliver's early days in STORYVILLE were typical of many first-generation jazz musicians, as was his migration northward in search of more rewarding work. By the time of his first recordings, he had assembled an impressive line-up of New Orleans performers. The FRONT LINE comprised Oliver (first cornet), Louis Armstrong (second cornet), Johnny Dodds (clarinet) and Honoré Dutrey (trombone), who together created splendid examples of the decorative COUNTERPOINT

essential to the New Orleans style. This quartet was supported by a solid RHYTHM SECTION made up of Lil Hardin (piano), Baby Dodds (drums) and Bill Johnson (banjo).

The Creole Jazz Band's success proved to be short-lived: the Dodds brothers quit in 1924, and Armstrong (married to Lil Hardin that year) soon followed suit. In 1927, in an attempt to adapt his output to the growing popularity of big-band jazz, Oliver formed a larger group in New York that met with little success. He made his last recordings in 1931 and died in oblivion seven years later.

In his brief moment of glory, however, Oliver accomplished two lasting achievements. He developed the timbral potential of the cornet and trumpet by

Below A sketch by Jean Cocteau celebrating *Le Boeuf sur le Toit*, the jazz club which opened in Paris at the end of 1921 and was soon frequented by composers of the stature of Satie and Ravel.

WORLD EVENTS

18 March Mahatma Gandhi imprisoned

29 July Greeks threaten to invade Constantinople

18 October Foundation of BBC

23 October Isadora Duncan's suggestive dancing banned in Boston

31 October Mussolini seizes power in Rome

● Discovery of Tutankhamen's tomb, Egypt

● James Joyce's novel *Ulysses*

experimenting with various forms of MUTE and other novel techniques, and his solos (notably that in "Dippermouth Blues," which extended across three CHORUSES) exerted a strong influence on the trumpeters who followed him – in particular Bubber Miley, who developed certain aspects of Oliver's playing into Duke Ellington's famous "jungle" style (● p. 63). In addition, Oliver brought the style of New Orleans ensemble jazz to such a peak of refinement that it became difficult to see how the music could continue to progress in the same direction. Not surprisingly, the subsequent virtuosity and improvisational brilliance of Armstrong and the sophisticated orchestrations of the big bands soon took jazz along new and contrasting paths.

29 August The New Orleans Rhythm Kings make their first recordings at Gennett's Richmond studios under the name Friar's Society Orchestra. Their repertoire includes several numbers made famous by the Original Dixieland Jazz Band (● p. 37).

21 October Fats Waller (● p. 105) makes his first recordings.

● William "Count" Basie (● p. 86) records his first piano solos. ● Mamie Smith records a further twenty sides this year. Her band, the Jazz Hounds, now includes saxophonist Coleman Hawkins, whom she meets on a trip to Kansas City. ● Europe's first jazz club, *Le Boeuf sur le Toit* ("The Bull on the Roof"), opens in Paris. ● As RAGTIME is supplanted by the new jazz craze, John Stark's ragtime publishing house goes out of business. ● German classical composer Paul Hindemith mimics ragtime and popular dance music in his solo piano work, *Suite "1922."*

1923
First Flowering

Fine recordings by black artists start to dominate the market and set new performance standards. The craze for the vocal blues intensifies, and French composer Milhaud breaks controversial new ground by adapting jazz for a classical ballet score.

16 February Bessie Smith (● p. 66) cuts her first recording, "Down-hearted Blues," in New York. It sells over three-quarters of a million copies within six months and she signs a nine-year contract with Columbia.

5 and **6 April** King Oliver's Creole Jazz Band (● p. 48), now appearing at Chicago's Lincoln Gardens, makes its first recordings. These include "Dippermouth Blues," and are cut at the Gennett Studios in Richmond, Indiana. The band includes Louis Armstrong (second cornet), the Dodds brothers (clarinet and drums) and Armstrong's wife Lil Hardin (piano).

Above The Gennett recording studio at Richmond was in reality a glorified railway shed. Attempted takes were frequently interrupted by the noise of passing freight trains.

Right Founded in 1917, the Gennett company had issued no fewer than 6000 recordings by the end of 1926. "Wolverine Blues" was cut in the Richmond studio on 13 March 1923 and "Canal Street Blues" on 6 April.

Left Bessie Smith, arguably the greatest of the female blues singers.

Race to Record

The success of the early Original Dixieland Jazz Band recordings did not immediately establish a new market within the recording industry. The full commercial potential of jazz discs was only realized in 1920 when Mamie Smith's best-selling sides revealed an extensive black audience who (contrary to popular white belief) could evidently afford gramophones. From 1921, so-called RACE RECORDS of jazz performances were aimed exclusively at black consumers. This divisive categorization persisted until World War II, although in practice many fine recordings by black artists had been circulated in general recording catalogues since the 1920s.

In 1923 there was a sudden increase in both the quality and quantity of jazz recordings, as many great black performers entered the recording studio for the first time. Among them were Bessie Smith, King Oliver, Sidney Bechet, Bennie Moten, Freddie Keppard, Louis Armstrong and Jelly Roll Morton. Their performances were preserved through the "acoustic" process (● p. 32). Problems of balance were enormous, and it is likely that in some areas (especially drumming, which was all but curtailed in the studio) these tracks differed significantly from live renderings; when European musicians attempted to copy the early recordings, these eccentricities were faithfully reproduced. After 1925 the widespread adoption of electrical recording techniques, in which an amplified electrical input from a microphone was transmitted to the cutting needle, revolutionized the industry and allowed recordings to be made on location.

Right Freddie Keppard in Chicago, c. 1918. Along with King Oliver, Keppard was one of the most influential and widely travelled of the early jazz cornetists.

22 and **23 June** King Oliver's band records seven sides for the Okeh label of the General Phonograph Corporation. Eight more Okeh sides follow in **October**.

Summer Fletcher Henderson (● p. 71) forms the Fletcher Henderson Orchestra and opens at the Club Alabam in the Nora Bayes Theater, West 44th Street, New York City.

17 July Having settled in Chicago in May, Jelly Roll Morton makes several recordings at the Gennett studios with the New Orleans Rhythm Kings, and as solo pianist in "King Porter Stomp" and (on **18 July**) "Grandpa's Spells."

30 July Sidney Bechet makes his first extant recordings with pianist Clarence Williams, who has also engaged Bessie Smith.

September Pianist Bennie Moten makes his first recordings for Okeh with a six-piece band from Kansas City.

Autumn Bandleader Elmer Snowden's Washingtonians open at the Kentucky Club on Broadway, with Duke Ellington as pianist. Its line-up soon expands with the addition of "Tricky Sam" Nanton (trombone) and Bubber Miley (trumpet).

White Labels, Black Music

The Victor company manufactured recordings of John Philip Sousa's band (● p. 20) and James Reese Europe's ragtime orchestra (● p. 28) early in the century and went on to issue the first Original Dixieland Jazz Band sides in 1917. With these successes, Victor stole the limelight from their rivals at Columbia. But it was Columbia who soon capitalized on the growing demand for recorded jazz by producing several series of RACE RECORDS from 1923 onward. These two labels dominated record production in later years: Victor recorded Jelly Roll Morton in 1926 and Duke Ellington in 1927 before being taken over by the Radio Corporation of America (RCA) in 1929. Meanwhile, Columbia, controlled from 1938 by the Columbia Broadcasting System (CBS), secured an international market for the big bands of the swing era and made a millionaire out of Miles Davis in the 1960s.

But in these pioneering years it was the small, independent labels that did most to promote the new music. The Okeh label shot to prominence by issuing the Mamie Smith record in 1920, and set up an extensive race series in 1921 that issued recordings by King Oliver, Louis Armstrong and Bennie Moten before it became part of Columbia in 1926. The two Gennett studios in Chicago and Richmond, Indiana (the latter a notoriously cramped shed next to a railway line: ● p. 50) recorded the New Orleans

Rhythm Kings in 1922 and added Jelly Roll Morton and King Oliver to their race catalogue in the following year. The Paramount label issued race records by Ma Rainey, King Oliver and Freddie Keppard, and the Vocalion company (a subsidiary of New York's Aeolian piano manufacturers) established a race series in 1926, marketing performances by Duke Ellington and King Oliver.

Below Trumpeter Wingy Manone (sitting on piano) recording with the San Sue Strutters for Okeh in Chicago in 1925.

Right Set design by Léger for Milhaud's jazz-inspired ballet *La Création du Monde* (1923).

Above Catalogs of "race records" issued by Victor (1929) and Okeh (1926).

25 October Darius Milhaud's ballet *La Création du Monde* opens in Paris with set designs by Fernand Léger. Based on black folklore, the work is heavily indebted to jazz and boldly synthesizes elements borrowed from baroque COUNTERPOINT and the BLUES.

November Columbia launches its first RACE RECORDS, including sides by King Oliver and Bessie Smith.

December Singer Ma Rainey records eight blues sides in Chicago for Paramount Records.

● James P. Johnson (● p. 46) visits London as director of a touring musical revue. In this same year, his first Broadway musical, *Runnin' Wild*, completes 213 performances and contains the hit number "Charleston" (● p. 58). ● French composer Maurice Ravel begins work on his Violin Sonata, which includes a movement entitled "Blues."

Above and right Representative labels from discs manufactured by Victor and Okeh.

WORLD EVENTS

4 January First network radio broadcast, USA

11 January French and Belgian forces occupy the Ruhr

31 August Italy occupies Corfu

1 September Earthquake in Tokyo kills 100,000

29 October Mustafa Kemal forms first Turkish Republic

11 November Hitler arrested after failed Munich *Putsch*

1924

Jazz in the Concert Hall

George Gershwin and Paul Whiteman collaborate on Rhapsody in Blue, a pioneering excursion into the realms of "symphonic jazz," which is adopted by other American classical composers in an energetic wave of nationalism.

February The Dodds brothers quit King Oliver's Creole Jazz Band (● p. 48), having discovered that Oliver has been retaining their earnings. Louis Armstrong (● p. 56) marries the band's pianist, Lil Hardin.

12 February First performance of George Gershwin's *Rhapsody in Blue* at New York's Aeolian Hall, with the composer at the piano and the Paul Whiteman band accompanying. It is billed as "An Experiment in Modern Music," and the phenomenal success of this "jazz concerto" stimulates other composers to cultivate an American nationalist idiom often labelled SYMPHONIC JAZZ.

18 February Bix Beiderbecke's recording debut, with The Wolverines, at the Gennett studios.

June Louis and Lil Armstrong quit King Oliver's band.

Summer Fletcher Henderson's orchestra (● p. 71) moves to the Roseland Ballroom, New York. ● Count Basie (● p. 86) joins the New York group Katie Krippen and Her Kiddies (with whom Fats Waller has recently appeared) in the touring show *Hippity Hop* on the Columbia burlesque circuit. He earns $40 per week, an amount that is soon doubled.

7 October Louis Armstrong makes his first recording with the Henderson Orchestra.

November Duke Ellington (● p. 62) makes his first recordings as leader of The Washingtonians.

December Jelly Roll Morton (● p. 45) records a duet version of "King Porter Stomp" with King Oliver.

Left George Gershwin at the piano, c. 1925. Looking on is Walter Damrosch, who conducted the first performances of Gershwin's Piano Concerto in 1925 and *An American in Paris* in 1928.

Below King Oliver's Creole Jazz Band, 1923 (l. to r.): Johnny Dodds (clarinet), Baby Dodds (drums), Honoré Dutrey (trombone), Louis Armstrong (cornet), Joe Oliver (cornet), Lil Hardin (piano) and Johnny St Cyr (banjo).

WORLD EVENTS

21 January Lenin dies, USSR

6 April Fascists win Italian general election

4 November Gabriel Fauré dies

29 November Giacomo Puccini dies

● Cecil B. de Mille's film *The Ten Commandments*

● The British Empire Exhibition results in the construction of Wembley Stadium, London

An Experiment in Modern Music

The ragtime craze had inspired several European composers to experiment with styles that attempted to fuse elements from popular and classical music, but it was not until the mid-1920s that American composers began to emulate their example by exploring a creative synthesis between the new "hot" jazz and art music. The concept of jazz for the concert hall was promoted by the bandleader Paul Whiteman, whose polished orchestrations later formed the basis for the big-band arrangements of the swing era.

In 1923 Whiteman asked George Gershwin (● p. 89) to compose something for a concert promoting American music to be held at the Aeolian Hall, New York, on Lincoln's birthday (12 February 1924). Having virtually forgotten about the request, it was only when Gershwin read in the *New York Tribune* that Rachmaninov would be at the concert and that George Gershwin was "reported to be at work on a jazz concerto" that he was spurred into action with only five weeks remaining before the event. He later commented that the resulting *Rhapsody in Blue* was conceived "as a sort of musical kaleidoscope of America – of our vast melting pot, of our incomparable national pep, our blues, our metropolitan madness." Legend has it that the score was still unfinished on the day of the concert and that Gershwin improvised large sections of the solo piano part.

Some critics found *Rhapsody in Blue* crude, but reluctantly admitted its claim to originality. The work's phenomenal success stimulated widespread interest in the new genre of SYMPHONIC JAZZ, and Gershwin went on to produce finer specimens such as *An American in Paris* (1928) and the opera *Porgy and Bess* (1935). He clearly saw symphonic jazz as the strongly nationalistic musical style for which American classical composers had long been searching.

When Aaron Copland returned from his studies in Paris, he immediately followed up Gershwin's lead with a succession of jazz-inspired works, including *Music for the Theater* (1925) and a Piano Concerto (1927). In an article entitled "Jazz Structure and Influence" published in 1927, Copland predicted that jazz might become "the substance not only of the American composer's foxtrots and Charlestons, but of his lullabies and nocturnes." Copland later moved away from an overtly jazzy style (although he composed a Clarinet Concerto for Benny Goodman [● p. 84] in 1950), but his brash and exciting early works directly influenced his protégé Leonard Bernstein, who brought the symphonic jazz trend to a new peak of sophistication with his Symphony No. 2 (1949) and *Prelude, Fugue and Riffs* (1955).

PAUL WHITEMAN
... AND HIS ..
PALAIS ROYAL ORCHESTRA

WILL OFFER

An Experiment in Modern Music

ASSISTED BY

ZEZ CONFREY *and* GEORGE GERSHWIN

New Typically American Compositions by VICTOR HERBERT, IRVING BERLIN and GEORGE GERSHWIN will be played for the first time.

AEOLIAN CONCERT HALL
ENTRANCE AND BOX OFFICE   34 WEST 43rd STREET

Tuesday, February 12, 1924

Lincoln's Birthday, at 3 P.M. *From 55c to $2.20*
Tickets on Sale Now!

Victor Records Exclusively
Chickering Pianos   Buescher Band Instruments

Above Paul Whiteman and his Orchestra posing for a publicity shot in January 1938.

Left The poster announcing the "New Typically American Compositions," which were performed in Whiteman's "Experiment in Modern Music" on 12 February 1924.

1 December Gershwin's musical *Lady, Be Good!*, his first with lyrics provided entirely by his brother Ira, opens at the Liberty Theater. Among its hits later to become jazz STANDARDS are the title song and "Fascinatin' Rhythm."

22 December Sidney Bechet (● p. 42) and Louis Armstrong record Clarence Williams' composition "Cake-walking Babies from Home" in New York for Gennett. Their group, the Red Onion Jazz Babies, is named after a New Orleans club.

● Jerome Kern, worried that hit songs from his musical *Sitting Pretty* would be distorted in jazz improvisations, describes jazz as a "debasement of all music."
● Belgian lawyer and critic Robert Goffin (● p. 75) organizes jazz parties in Brussels.

1925

Satchmo

Louis "Satchmo" Armstrong brings the early jazz style to its climax in a series of innovative recordings featuring virtuoso improvisations. Discs achieve better sound quality through developments in electrical recording techniques.

8 January Louis Armstrong and Sidney Bechet (● p. 42) re-record "Cake-Walking Babies" for Okeh with Clarence Williams' Blue Five (● p. 53).

14 January Bessie Smith (● p. 66) and Louis Armstrong record their celebrated version of W. C. Handy's "St. Louis Blues" for Columbia in New York.

May Jelly Roll Morton (● p. 45) records a duet improvisation on his "Wolverine Blues" with clarinetist Voltaire de Faut, Chicago.

29 May Fletcher Henderson (● p. 71) and Armstrong record "Sugarfoot Stomp," Don Redman's big-band arrangement of King Oliver's "Dippermouth Blues," in New York.

Louis Armstrong: Hot Five and Seven

Louis Armstrong (dubbed "Satchmo," i.e., satchel-mouth) began as a cornetist in early bands led by Kid Ory in New Orleans (1918), King Oliver in Chicago (1922–4) and Fletcher Henderson in New York (1924) before returning to Chicago in 1925 to form his own Hot Five. This group, known as the Hot Seven when tuba and drums were added, recorded prolifically on the Okeh label, and their technical brilliance exerted a profound influence on the development of jazz.

By 1925 Armstrong had changed from playing cornet to the brighter trumpet, and shown himself to be equally accomplished as a singer. Among the best

"Louis Armstrong would improvise on the same theme for a full half hour, taking twenty choruses in a row. Often he would be quite motionless as he played or sang – his eyes closed, like a man carried out of the world; tears would roll down his cheeks. His imagination seemed inexhaustible; for each new chorus he had new ideas more beautiful than those he had produced for the preceding chorus. As he went along, his improvisation grew hotter, his style became more and more simple – until at the end there was nothing but the endless repetition of one fragment of melody – or even a single note insistently sounded and executed with cataclysmic intonations."

Hugues Panassié, *Le Jazz Hot* (1934)

WORLD EVENTS

3 January Mussolini commences dictatorship in Italy

14 February Germany lifts ban on Nazi Party

25 March First electrical recording of classical music by pianist Alfred Cortot for the Victor Company, USA

April Paris Exposition des Arts Décoratifs launches art deco style

1 July Erik Satie dies

8 August Ku Klux Klan march in Washington, DC

1 December France, Germany, Italy and the UK sign the Treaty of Locarno

3 December Border established between Northern Ireland and the Irish Free State

● F. Scott Fitzgerald's novel *The Great Gatsby*

Right Armstrong (at the piano) with his Hot Five in 1925, during the time of their early recordings. The other members of the group are (l. to r.): Johnny St Cyr (banjo), Johnny Dodds (reeds), Kid Ory (trombone) and Lil Hardin-Armstrong (pianist).

Left Louis Armstrong in 1933. Taken in London during his European tour (● p. 76), the picture captures this singular performer's sense of humor and inimitable style.

known Hot Five and Seven recordings are "Heebie Jeebies" (1926), an early example of SCAT singing, and "West End Blues" (1928), with its virtuoso introductory trumpet cadenza and impressive TRUMPET STYLE piano solo by Earl Hines (● p. 124) . In 1928 Armstrong and Hines also collaborated in a duet recording of "Weather Bird," demonstrating an instinctive rapport between the two men that is unparalleled either before or since.

Armstrong was the first great innovator in jazz. He was responsible for the increased prominence of IMPROVISATION and he developed the concept of an extended improvised solo (i.e., CHORUS) based on the CHORD CHANGES of a song, always shaping his extemporized melodic lines with an innate sense of proportion and growth. In earlier jazz forms such as Dixieland (● p. 37), improvisation was confined to brief two-bar BREAKS between phrases: after Armstrong, the melodic ingenuity of the soloist assumed an unprecedented importance.

He considerably expanded trumpet technique, hitting notes higher than any played before and employing tricks such as the RIP for added excitement. He was the first in jazz to demonstrate consistent

LICKS: apart from the rip, he frequently ended long notes with a rich vibrato and tended to terminate phrases with characteristic melodic formulae. His singing was as innovative as his playing, his vocal improvisations shaped with the same instinctive sense of melodic structuring. And in his unwavering grasp of SWING he generated rhythmic excitement like no one before him.

In the 1930s Armstrong was based in New York and appeared as a highly paid featured soloist with various big bands. When he joined the books of hard-hitting agent Joe Glaser in 1935, his sell-out to the lucrative world of popular song and Hollywood films seemed complete. Many lamented what they saw as a defection to commercial interests and regretted his abandonment of fundamental artistic values. Miles Davis, while admiring Armstrong's playing, found his habitual impersonation of a grinning black minstrel racially unacceptable. In 1947 Armstrong formed his "All Stars" and began to record again in the New Orleans style, which was then enjoying a revival. He also embarked on a series of high-profile international trips organized by the US State Department, which led to a new nickname: "Ambassador Satch."

The Girl of the straight legs. "It's a pity you don't Charleston, Audrey. Your knees are simply made for it."

Above Robj porcelain figures of jazz musicians, *c.* 1925.

Above, right Inspired by the growing craze for dancing the Charleston, a 1925 *Punch* cartoon satirizes the dance's knock-kneed stance.

Below A New York dancing competition devoted to the Charleston during 1926. Composed by James P. Johnson, the original "Charleston" melody had featured in the hit stage show *Runnin' Wild* three years before.

June James P. Johnson (● p. 46) cuts a piano roll of his most famous composition, "Charleston (South Carolina)," a hit number from his Broadway musical *Runnin' Wild*. First recorded in 1923 and dedicated to the sailors from Charleston who attended Johnson's performances, the piece becomes highly popular worldwide as a lively dance that epitomizes the epoch for subsequent generations.

Above The first page of the autograph manuscript of Aaron Copland's *Music for the Theater* (1925). The concert in which this work was first performed also included Darius Milhaud's *Ballad* for piano and orchestra, with Milhaud himself appearing as soloist. The Milhaud-Copland pairing was entirely appropriate, since both composers were early pioneers of symphonic jazz.

12 November Having quit the Fletcher Henderson Orchestra and moved back to Chicago, Louis Armstrong makes his first recording with his Hot Five for Okeh.

20 November Aaron Copland's jazzy score *Music for the Theater* is performed in Boston. Just returned to America after a spell of compositional study in Paris, Copland is anxious to cultivate a distinctively American musical style.

3 December Premiere of George Gershwin's Piano Concerto in F Major in New York. The score is a more substantial and satisfying investigation of SYMPHONIC JAZZ than *Rhapsody in Blue*, but does not achieve the widespread popularity of the earlier work.

● Introduction of electrical recordings, in which a microphone and electrical amplification are employed. ● The Original Dixieland Jazz Band (● p. 37) disbands. ● Fats Waller (● p. 105) gives lessons in jazz organ playing (for accompanying silent films) to a twenty-one-year-old Count Basie (● p. 86) on the Wurlitzer pipe organ at Harlem's Lincoln Theater. ● The *Revue Nègre* (with a band that includes Sidney Bechet) visits Paris, where its star dancer Josephine Baker subsequently remains to join the *Folies-Bergères*. ● F. Scott Fitzgerald writes "The Children of Jazz" (*Tales of the Jazz Age*).

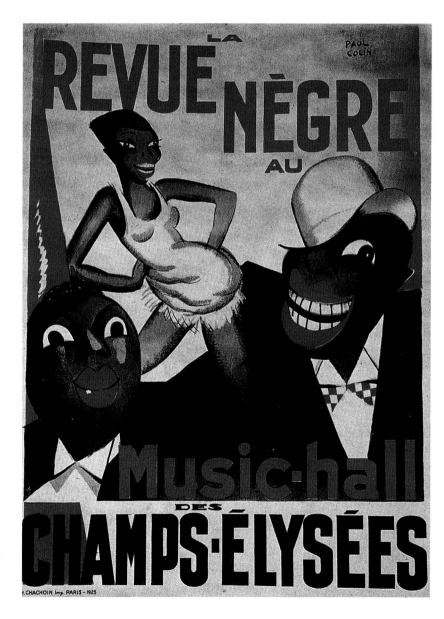

Right Poster by Paul Colin for the *Revue Nègre*, staged in Paris in 1925 and starring erotic dancer Josephine Baker. Racial stereotyping continued to persist in artworks associated with black American jazz, both in the USA and Europe.

1926
The New Virtuosity

Louis Armstrong's spellbinding talents continue to flourish, while the compositional skills of Jelly Roll Morton raise the art of jazz to a new intellectual level.

January *The Melody Maker and British Metronome* magazine begins publication in London.

28 February Louis Armstrong records his first song, "Heebie Jeebies," pioneering the use of SCAT singing and propelling his Hot Five to stardom. In this year, he switches from cornet to trumpet.

14 May Fletcher Henderson's band records "The Stampede" in New York, featuring tenor saxophonist Coleman Hawkins.

Autumn Bix Beiderbecke (● p. 72) joins the Jean Goldkette orchestra.

15 and **21 September** In Chicago Jelly Roll Morton's Red Hot Peppers (● p. 34) record some of their finest sides, including "Black Bottom Stomp" and "Dead Man Blues." Members of his band receive $5 per rehearsal and $15 per take. Further recordings are made on **16 December**, including "Grandpa's Spells."

November Fats Waller (● p. 105) records organ solos in New York.

● Paul Whiteman and his orchestra tour Europe to promote George Gershwin's *Rhapsody in Blue* (● p. 55). ● Sidney Bechet plays in Moscow with Benny Peyton's Jazz Kings. ● Duke Ellington hires trombonist Joe "Tricky Sam" Nanton, who models his GROWL style on Bubber Miley's innovations in trumpet playing. Ellington records with The Washingtonians, later restyled The Kentucky Club Orchestra. ● A. Coeuroy and André Schaeffner publish their book *Le jazz* in Paris, the first critical monograph on the subject to appear in print.

Above King Oliver and his Creole Jazz Band "tailgating" in State Street, Chicago, to promote their Okeh recording of "Dippermouth Blues" in 1923.

Trombone

As a stalwart member of the New Orleans marching bands (● p. 28), the trombone was assured a prominent place in jazz from the outset. It was quickly adopted as part of the three-strong FRONT LINE and used in melodic flourishes alongside the clarinet and trumpet. The early "tailgate" style of trombone playing (so called because the trombonist would stand at the rear of an open truck when the band was mobile) was championed by Kid Ory and characterized by robust GLISSANDOS made possible by the instrument's slide mechanism, which also permitted effective pitch-bending of BLUE NOTES.

The number of trombones in SWING bands increased from one in the 1920s to no fewer than four by the 1940s, thus allowing arrangers to introduce more complex harmonies in their brass writing. Big bands led by solo trombonists include those of Glenn Miller

Scat

The precise origins of scat singing are unknown, although it almost certainly thrived in New Orleans long before either Jelly Roll Morton or Louis Armstrong first employed it. Morton, with characteristic conceit, claimed to have invented the technique, even though Armstrong was the first to record it (and is said by some to have hit upon the style by accident when he dropped his sheet music in rehearsal but continued to sing *ex tempore*).

Armstrong's celebrated "Heebie Jeebies" (recorded in 1926) is an early but fine example of the use of nonsense syllables in an improvised vocal line, which is the essential characteristic of scat: the voice, in effect, becomes another instrument when divorced from meaningful words, and can even be used to imitate the melodic style of instrumental improvisations.

(● p. 107), Tommy Dorsey and Jack Teagarden.

The valve trombone is operated by a mechanism similar to that found on the trumpet. It was promoted as an instrument of supple lyricism and considerable agility by Juan Tizol (who played with Duke Ellington's orchestra between 1929 and 1944), and by Bob Brookmeyer in the 1950s. The slide trombone's technical difficulties did not, however, prevent it from achieving continued prominence in the BE-BOP and HARD BOP styles, thanks to the dexterity of musicians like J. J. Johnson and Kai Winding. Most jazz trombonists since then have remained somewhat conservative, although notable exceptions include the German player Albert Mangelsdorff – who exploits the avant-garde technique of MULTIPHONICS in which CHORDS are generated by singing notes into the mouthpiece while playing.

Above Trombonist Tommy Dorsey, who played with the Whiteman and Goldkette bands before teaming up with his clarinetist brother Jimmy to form the short-lived Dorsey Brothers Orchestra in 1934. The brothers were to collaborate again between 1953 and Tommy's death in 1956.

After Armstrong's popular success with the technique, it was promoted by bandleader Cab Calloway, and from the 1940s onward it was widely adopted as an ideal vehicle for vocal improvisations in the more angular melodies of BE-BOP. (It may have been a specific pair of scat nonsense syllables that christened the new style "be-bop.") The finest virtuoso of scat was without doubt Ella Fitzgerald (● p. 195), and the technique has remained popular to the present day in widely differing musical contexts.

1927-28

Harlem, Chicago and Kansas City

In the work of Duke Ellington, jazz achieves greater musical sophistication. Jean Goldkette and Paul Whiteman lead the finest white dance bands of the time, while Aaron Copland and George Gershwin produce masterpieces of symphonic jazz. Leading musicians converge on New York, the new capital of the jazz world.

Below The program cover for a typical Cotton Club show in 1938.

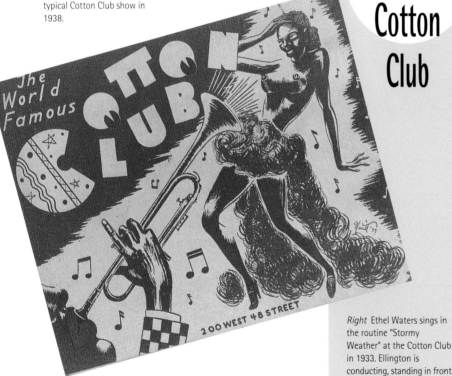

Duke Ellington at the Cotton Club

In 1923, Edward Kennedy "Duke" Ellington first began to make his mark in New York with his band The Washingtonians, which took its name from his home city. He soon assembled a remarkable corpus of talented instrumentalists, whose qualities he exploited not only by showcasing them in dynamic solo passages, but also by joining them in astonishingly varied and colorful combinations of a kind never before heard in jazz. These achievements, in addition to Ellington's expertise as an originator of intellectually satisfying musical structures, made him the most celebrated and critically acclaimed of all jazz composers.

Ellington's orchestra began its four-year residency at Harlem's famous Cotton Club in 1927, providing music for sumptuous stage routines in which exotically dressed black dancers performed for an

Right Ethel Waters sings in the routine "Stormy Weather" at the Cotton Club in 1933. Ellington is conducting, standing in front of Sonny Greer's impressive drum kit at rear left.

1927

28 January Premiere of Aaron Copland's jazz-influenced Piano Concerto, played by the composer and the Boston Symphony Orchestra under Serge Koussevitzky.

7 May Louis Armstrong (● p. 56) makes his first recordings with his Hot Seven (i.e., Hot Five plus drums and tuba).

June Jelly Roll Morton's Red Hot Peppers (● p. 34) continue their successful series of recordings in Chicago.

9 September Bix Beiderbecke (● p. 72) records his impressionistic piano solo *In a Mist*, reflecting the influence of Debussy (● p. 24).

18 September Jean Goldkette's orchestra is dissolved, forcing Beiderbecke to seek work elsewhere. He finds it in **November** with the Paul Whiteman band.

October Release of the first "talkie" motion picture, *The Jazz Singer*, starring Al Jolson.

4 December Duke Ellington begins his residency at the Cotton Club in Harlem, increasing the size of his band from six to eleven players. New names include Barney Bigard (clarinet) and Harry Carney (baritone saxophone). "Black and Tan Fantasy," "Creole Love Call" and "East St. Louis Toodle-oo" (the band's signature tune) are among the masterpieces recorded by Ellington this year.

Above, left Duke Ellington poses in c. 1931 with his famous orchestra, including saxophonists Johnny Hodges and Harry Carney (front row, second and third from right) and brass players Joe Nanton and Cootie Williams (back row, second and third from left).

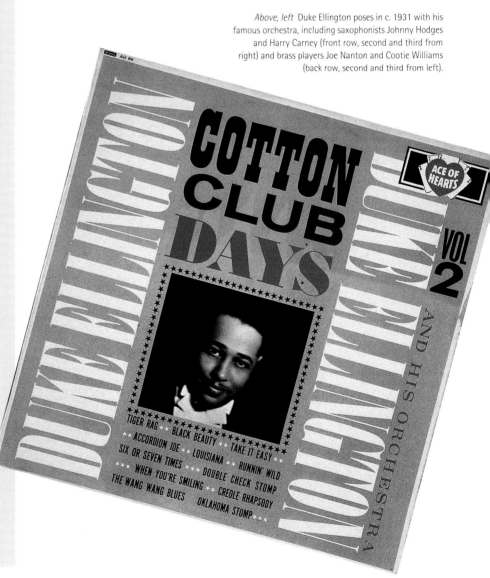

exclusively white audience. The band developed a new style of "jungle" music for these dances, which featured a GROWL technique of brass playing developed by trumpeter Bubber Miley and trombonist "Tricky Sam" Nanton. Ellington's other notable SIDEMEN in these early years were alto saxophonist Johnny Hodges (famous for his sensuous tone), baritone saxophonist Harry Carney (whose agility on his potentially ponderous instrument was phenomenal) and clarinetist Barney Bigard (who personified a direct link with old New Orleans). In 1929, the virtuoso Cootie Williams succeeded Miley as principal trumpet.

A succession of popular radio broadcasts from the Cotton Club brought Ellington national fame, and his name became known around the globe after the successes of "Mood Indigo" (1930) and "It Don't Mean a Thing (If it Ain't Got that Swing)" (1932). In 1933 he took his band on their first tour of Europe. By this time singer Cab Calloway had succeeded Ellington at the Cotton Club, and Calloway was in turn succeeded by Jimmie Lunceford in 1934. Racial unrest in Harlem in the following year forced the club to close down temporarily, but it re-opened in a different location in the autumn of 1936 and remained in business for a further four years. In the 1980s, the legendary venue inspired a movie by director Francis Ford Coppola (● p. 203).

Other important nightspots in Harlem during the heyday of the Cotton Club were Connie's Inn (which hosted performances by Louis Armstrong, Fletcher Henderson and Fats Waller between 1929 and 1931), Small's Paradise (haunt of STRIDE pianists Willie "The Lion" Smith and James P. Johnson) and the Savoy Ballroom (just one block away from the original Cotton Club on Lenox Avenue).

Kansas City

Jazz owed part of its origins to the RAGTIME music emanating from St. Louis at the turn of the century, and the state of Missouri again became important for the music's continuing evolution during the 1920s, when large ensembles in Kansas City began playing a distinctive brand of jazz. The style originated in the popular orchestrated versions of ragtime, but also benefitted from a mixture of BLUES elements alongside a new technique of repeated thematic fragments called the RIFF. This ultimately provided the foundation for the big-band music of the SWING era (● p. 71). Bennie Moten's band, which recorded between 1923 and 1932, and Walter Page's Blue Devils from Oklahoma City both featured the gifted young pianist Count Basie (● p. 86), who formed his own band from Moten's dispersed members and took New York by storm in 1936.

Later products of Kansas City include BOP giant Charlie Parker (● p. 136) and, more recently, FUSION guitarist Pat Metheny (● p. 198).

In 1995, director Robert Altman revisited the city (his own birthplace) to film a reconstruction of the heady period around 1934 when the swing style was emerging there. Altman assembled a pool of over twenty leading contemporary jazz musicians on the set of his Hey Hey Club to re-create the JAM SESSIONS of the era, and described the resulting movie, *Kansas City,* as "a jazz memory."

Left Poster advertising Bennie Moten's gig at the Golden Slipper in Dayton, Ohio, on 30 September 1930.

WORLD EVENTS

1927

24 March USA and UK use military force in China

21 May Charles Lindbergh makes solo flight across the Atlantic

14 September Isadora Duncan dies when her scarf is caught in the wheels of a car

25 November Eleven-year-old Yehudi Menuhin plays a concerto with the New York Symphony Orchestra

1928

11 January Death of Thomas Hardy

May Japanese troops in China

3 July First television sold, USA

12 August Death of Leoš Janáček

1 September King Zog becomes first monarch of Albania

15 September Alexander Fleming discovers penicillin

● D.H. Lawrence completes *Lady Chatterley's Lover*

Chicago

Chicago was beginning to lose its status as the focal point for jazz by the end of the 1920s. Many musicians from New Orleans and other southern cities had been migrating northward to the Windy City since the 1910s in search of employment, and by 1922 Chicago was home to such revered performers as Jelly Roll Morton, King Oliver and Louis Armstrong, who recorded many of their early masterpieces in the city's studios.

Important venues during the 1920s included the Apex Club on East 35th Street (which featured the music of New Orleans clarinetist Jimmie Noone from 1926), the Coliseum on East 15th Street (famous for

Right Earl Hines (seated at the piano) and his band pose behind their instruments at the Grand Terrace Café, Chicago, soon after he founded the ensemble in December 1928.

Below Bennie Moten (seated, right) shows a new arrangement to the young Count Basie at the Pearl Theater, Philadelphia, in c. 1931. Singer Jimmy Rushing stands between them.

December Louis Armstrong's Hot Five record "Hotter than That" and "Struttin' with some Barbeque" in Chicago.

● Russian pianist Leopold Teplitsky returns from the US with stocks of American jazz recordings, performing parts and instruments, and sets up "official" jazz activities in Leningrad on behalf of the Commissariat of Public Enlightenment. ● Jazz elements are used in two classical operas first performed in Germany during this year: Ernst Křenek's *Johnny Strikes Up* (Leipzig, 10 February) and Kurt Weill's *The Rise and Fall of the City of Mahagonny* (Baden-Baden, 17 July). ● Fats Waller (● p. 105) sells some of his compositions to Fletcher Henderson (● p. 71). Legend has it that Waller asks for, but does not receive, payment in the form of hamburgers (to which he is addicted).

1928

23 January Clarinetist Benny Goodman (● p. 84) makes his first recordings.

14 March Fletcher Henderson's band record their interpretation of Jelly Roll Morton's "King Porter Stomp," which becomes a hit under Goodman seven years later (● p. 82).

27 April James P. Johnson's *Yamekraw: a Negro Rhapsody* is performed at Carnegie Hall by his protégé Fats Waller and an orchestra conducted by W. C. Handy (● p. 27). The "Father of Stride Piano" devotes increasing energy to works for the concert hall.

May Alto saxophonist Johnny Hodges joins the Duke Ellington band.

28 June Louis Armstrong's Hot Five record "West End Blues," opening with a spectacular trumpet cadenza from Armstrong that is soon widely imitated.

July Count Basie (● p. 86) joins Walter Page's Blue Devils in Kansas City.

17 October Duke Ellington's Cotton Club orchestra records "The Mooche" in New York at one of six recording sessions held over the year.

5 December In Chicago Earl Hines and Louis Armstrong record their virtuosic duet "Weather Bird." Hines forms a big band at the Grand Terrace Café, which remains there under his leadership for ten years.

13 December First performance of George Gershwin's symphonic poem *An American in Paris*, New York.

● Belgian gyspy guitarist Django Reinhardt (● p. 75) loses the use of two fingers of his left hand in a caravan fire. ● Jelly Roll Morton and Louis Armstrong both move to New York.

hosting CUTTING CONTESTS between rival bands), the Dreamland Café, Friar's Inn, Lincoln Gardens and the Savoy Ballroom. Some of these were closely linked to local gangster organizations, and were heavily involved in the supply of illicit alcohol during Prohibition (1919–33). Figures such as the notorious Al Capone built empires through establishments known as "speakeasies," which sold bootleg liquor. Where there is alcohol, jazz is generally not far away, and a severe government clampdown on Chicago speakeasies in 1928 was one reason behind the new migration of musicians eastward to New York. By this time, the Big Apple was widely regarded as jazz's future city-of-opportunity.

Thanks to the tenacious efforts of performers such as Earl Hines (● p. 124), who remained for a decade at Chicago's Grand Terrace under the watchful eye of the Mafia, the city nevertheless remained firmly on the jazz map during the SWING era, and new venues sprang up in the 1940s that helped to promote the developing BOP style. Simultaneously, Chicago became one of the most important centers for the post-war growth of a powerful urban brand of BLUES, and in the 1960s the city again became prominent as the home of the radical FREE JAZZ (● p. 150).

Right Fletcher Henderson (extreme left) with his orchestra in 1927. Coleman Hawkins sits in the center of the front row.

1929

Empress of the Blues

Singer Bessie Smith, at the pinnacle of her career, appears in a Hollywood movie about W. C. Handy. Stride and boogie-woogie piano styles suffer a temporary setback with the murder of Pine Top Smith and the imprisonment of Fats Waller.

Above, left Bessie Smith, seen here in 1928. Her impassioned renderings of blues repertoire exerted a colossal influence on the next generation of jazz singers.

WORLD EVENTS

6 January Yugoslavia formed under King Alexander

14 February Valentine's Day Massacre, Chicago

16 May First Academy Awards Ceremony, Hollywood

19 August Death of Serge Diaghilev

24 October Wall Street stock market crash

● Cartoon characters Tin-Tin and Popeye created

28 January Duke Ellington's recording of "Tiger Rag" breaks new ground by lasting over six minutes and occupying both sides of a 78rpm disc.

1 March Fats Waller records some of his recent STRIDE compositions for solo piano, including "Handful of Keys." "Ain't Misbehavin'," from his hit stage show *Hot Chocolates,* featuring Louis Armstrong (who records the song on **22 July**), is recorded in a piano version on **2 August**. Waller is jailed this year for failing to keep up with his alimony payments. He also takes part in a mixed-race recording session at which he is forced to play behind a screen to segregate him from the white musicians.

15 March Twenty-four-year-old BOOGIE-WOOGIE pianist Pine Top Smith is shot dead during a fight at a performance in a masonic lodge in Chicago. His composition "Pine Top's Boogie Woogie" is the first known use of the term.

June Bessie Smith appears with an all-black cast in the Warner Brothers film *St. Louis Blues*, a biopic concerning the life of W. C. Handy (● p. 27), directed by Dudley Murphy. The musical direction is by Handy himself, supported by James P. Johnson's band (● p. 46).

October Count Basie (● p. 86) records in Chicago with Bennie Moten's band from Kansas City.

7 November Pianist Mary Lou Williams (● p. 196) records with Andy Kirk's Twelve Clouds of Joy in Kansas City.

29 November Cootie Williams replaces Bubber Miley in the Ellington band, which makes a short film entitled *Black and Tan Fantasy*. Puerto Rican valve trombonist Juan Tizol also joins the band this year.

● Sidney Bechet (● p. 42) is arrested in France following a shooting incident, and subsequently deported. ● The journal *Musik-Echo* is founded in Berlin. ● Jean Cocteau begins poetry readings with jazz accompaniment in Paris.

Bessie Smith

Bessie Smith's appearance in the 1929 film *St. Louis Blues* came at a time when she was one of the most prolific recording artists in New York. Like many vocalists, she had begun her career in MINSTREL SHOWS and VAUDEVILLE before branching out to combine her talents with many of the day's finest jazz instrumentalists. Her early successes through work for the Theater Owners' Booking Association (the acronym T.O.B.A. was alternatively rendered as "Tough on Black Asses") brought her to the attention of pianist Clarence Williams, with whom she recorded "Down-hearted Blues" in 1923. Further recordings with COMBOS led by Fletcher Henderson (● p. 71) and others followed, and her commercial success was secured by her popular stage shows *Harlem Frolics* and *Mississippi Days*.

Smith is today widely regarded as the finest jazz BLUES singer of all time. Her recordings, which spanned a period of some ten years, represent the first coherent attempt to import the spontaneous, often powerfully expressive style of raw blues singing into mainstream jazz. Her repertoire included examples of both the intensely melancholy and light-hearted blues styles

Left The original poster advertizing Bessie Smith's appearance in the 1929 Warner Brothers movie *St. Louis Blues.*

St. Louis Blues

Originally published in 1914, W. C. Handy's *St. Louis Blues* quickly became one of the most popular standards in the growing repertoire of jazz pieces based on the TWELVE-BAR BLUES. Bessie Smith and Louis Armstrong recorded their superb interpretation on 14 January 1925, with an understated chordal accompaniment provided on the harmonium by Fred Longshaw. The absence of drums, coupled with Longshaw's fluctuating pulse, allowed the soloists an unusual degree of expressive freedom as they spontaneously re-shaped Handy's simple theme, responding intuitively to each other's ideas.

Bessie's raw, earthy singing is a fine example of the so-called "dirty" tone so characteristic of female blues singers in the 1920s. Each of her two-measure phrases is followed by a two-measure answering phrase from Armstrong's cornet (a CALL-AND-RESPONSE pattern typical of much early jazz): Armstrong skilfully imitates the tone quality and pitch bending of the singer. Many more blue notes are sung and played than exist in Handy's printed score – especially that which flattens the third degree of the scale, repeatedly emphasized by Bessie to darken the mood.

The passionate spontaneity of this celebrated recording contrasts sharply with another interpretation cut in the same year by Paul Whiteman's dance orchestra, full of harmonic sophistication and colorful instrumentation but entirely PRE-COMPOSED. A few years later, Bessie Smith strengthened her association with Handy's tune when she performed it in the movie *St. Louis Blues* in June 1929, backed by a full choir and jazz band led by STRIDE pianist James P. Johnson.

(the latter often colored by heavy sexual innuendo). She developed a "dirty," GROWL tone that influenced many vocalists and instrumentalists, including Louis Armstrong (with whom she recorded a famous rendering of "St. Louis Blues" in 1925), Billie Holiday (p. 131) and the brass players of Duke Ellington's orchestra (p. 62).

Several factors combined to bring Smith's shining career to a sorry end. Her addiction to alcohol (a substance which, before it lost out to hard drugs, caused the premature demise of many musicians during Prohibition) coincided with a slump in the recording industry during the Depression. Her contract with Columbia lapsed in 1931 and was not renewed, and she made no recordings at all after 1933, although her singing continued to be well received in live performances.

On 25 September 1937 Smith was severely injured in an automobile accident and died within hours. The legend that she was refused admittance to a whites-only hospital, and expired before being admitted to an institution that accepted blacks, seems to have been concocted for political reasons.

Above Blues (1929), a painting by Archibald J. Motley Jr. (1891–1981)

1930-45
Swing

White musicians quickly capitalize on the success of black band arrangements to create a swinging style of jazzy dance music that will survive until the end of the Second World War and achieve global popularity.

Dorothy Dandridge dances atop Count Basie's piano in the movie *Hit Parade of 1943*, while his band nestles in a giant mock-up of a grand piano.

1930-31
Dance Bands

The suave, pre-composed music of white dance bands in New York begins to merge with the black big-band sound to create an exciting new style that becomes the pop music of the 1930s.

1930

9 October Louis Armstrong records "Body and Soul" in New York.

16 October Percussionist Lionel Hampton records his first vibraphone solo in a session with Louis Armstrong and decides to devote himself to this hitherto unexploited instrument.

17 October Duke Ellington's orchestra (● p. 62) records "Mood Indigo," one of nearly forty sides recorded by the band this year.

Though he started out as a drummer, Lionel Hampton recorded a vibraphone solo in 1930 and subsequently became this neglected instrument's first virtuoso. Invented during World War I and superficially similar to the xylophone, the vibraphone has metal bars laid out in a keyboard arrangement. Each bar is suspended

Left A modern Yamaha vibraphone. Note the instrument's sustaining pedal, and the tubular resonators increasing in size towards the bottom of the range.

above its own tubular resonator, which contains an electrically driven fan that produces an oscillating tone. Hampton promoted the vibraphone as a solo instrument in his work with the Benny Goodman Quartet (● p. 84), then went on to lead his own big band, which turned out to be the longest surviving ensemble in the history of jazz, remaining active into the 1980s.

Another notable exponent of the instrument was Red Norvo, who, in the 1940s and 1950s, demonstrated that it could be employed equally well in the widely differing styles of SWING, BE-BOP and WEST COAST. Milt Jackson gave the instrument an intellectual respectability in his intricate work with the Modern Jazz Quartet (● p. 128), and Gary Burton added further sophistication in the 1960s by developing the technique of holding two beaters in each hand and striking four notes simultaneously to make a chord.

All You Gotta Do is Swing

Below Lionel Hampton, who established the vibraphone as a jazz solo instrument in Benny Goodman's Quartet (1936–40) and went on to compose the wartime hit "Flying Home" in 1942.

Below The photograph on this LP reissue of Fletcher Henderson's music shows his band at Atlantic City in 1931, at the time when they were appearing at New York's Connie's Inn. In the back row are Coleman Hawkins (second from left) and Rex Stewart (fourth from left).

The big-band jazz that, in a diluted and commercialized form, became the pop music of the 1930s had essentially very little in common with the New Orleans style it supplanted. Some of the earliest practitioners originated in Kansas City (● p. 64) as part of a local development that climaxed in the definingly HOT sound of the Count Basie band (● p. 86). However, it was the popularity of the polished dance music being produced in New York that formed the backbone of the big-band style.

White dance bands had absorbed most of the important features of early jazz (principally BLUE NOTES, SYNCOPATION and SWUNG RHYTHM), but avoided extended IMPROVISATION in favor of a high degree of PRE-COMPOSITION – an essential ingredient where a large number of performers is involved. The elaborate improvised COUNTERPOINT of the New Orleans style gave way to a new technique, which soon became a cliché, of presenting a melody in a BLOCK-CHORD harmonization. These parallel harmonies would usually be assigned to a single instrumental family (i.e., reeds or brass), and might be rapidly traded from one group to the other in a pattern of RIFFS (yet another manifestation of the CALL-AND-RESPONSE concept).

The black pianist and arranger Fletcher Henderson created the finest dance music of his day and provided a model for much later swing music. Henderson's band appeared at Broadway's Club Alabam and then at the Roseland Ballroom in the mid-1920s, and for a time numbered Louis Armstrong (● p. 56) among its members. By 1927, the Henderson orchestra comprised three trumpets, two trombones, three saxophones (which could double on clarinets as required) and a standard four-piece RHYTHM SECTION. It was only when Benny Goodman (● p. 84) bought Henderson's arrangements for his own (white) band seven years later that the popularity of the swing style rapidly spread across America. The size of the big bands grew with their commercial success, so that by the 1940s a typical line-up might include four trumpets, three trombones and as many as five saxophones.

The work of Duke Ellington's orchestra (● pp. 62 and 183) from the late 1920s to the 1940s stands out as undoubtedly the most artistically satisfying example of the big-band style. While Ellington's music was rooted in the major technical innovations of the swing era, and included some of the most commercially successful compositions of the period – notably "It Don't Mean a Thing (If It Ain't got That Swing)" – his interest in pre-composed structures produced highly original and coherent musical forms capable of withstanding comparison with the output of the finest classical composers.

• Ted Lewis's DIXIELAND ensemble plays at the Kit Kat Restaurant, London, with Jimmy Dorsey (clarinet) and Muggsy Spanier (trumpet). • Paul Whiteman and his orchestra star in the movie *The King of Jazz* (Universal).

1931

20 January and **11 June** Duke Ellington again breaks with convention by recording two versions of his extended composition "Creole Rhapsody": each fills both sides of a 78rpm disc. Singer Ivie Anderson joins the band this year.

13 March Fats Waller (● p. 105) records "I'm Crazy 'bout my Baby."

6 August Bix Beiderbecke dies of pneumonia at the age of thirty-eight, New York.

17 September RCA demonstrates the first 33$\frac{1}{3}$ rpm long-playing disc.

4 November Buddy Bolden (● p. 25) dies, Jackson, Louisiana.

• Chick Webb's band is established at the Savoy Ballroom, Harlem. • Lil Hardin separates from Louis Armstrong and forms an all-female band. • French composer Maurice Ravel includes jazz elements in his Piano Concerto in G Major. • Hungarian composer Mátyás Seiber teaches jazz at the Hoch Conservatory, Frankfurt.

Left Bix Beiderbecke in the early 1920s: a musical genius driven to an early grave by alcoholism.

Bix and the Dance Bands

Right Bix (seated, center) at New York's Bronx Zoo in 1927, surrounded by other members of Jean Goldkette's dance band. The exotic instrument draped around the standing attendant is, in fact, a live snake!

Left Paul Whiteman and his orchestra as they appeared in the movie *The King of Jazz* (1930).

"The word jazz in its progress toward respectability has meant first sex, then dancing, then music. It is associated with a state of nervous stimulation..."

F. Scott Fitzgerald, *Echoes of the Jazz Age*, 1931

"It is my firm belief that what is still known as 'jazz' is going to play a considerable part in the serious music of the future ... The music of my race is something more than the American idiom. It is the result of our transplantation to American soil and was our reaction in the plantation days to the tyranny we endured. What we could not say openly we expressed in music."

Duke Ellington, "The Duke Steps Out," *Rhythm*, March 1931

Of the white dance bands that brought a diluted brand of jazz to a wider audience in the 1920s and helped to form the basis for the emerging big-band style, the most accomplished were those led by Jean Goldkette and Paul Whiteman. Goldkette had the good sense to employ the talented cornetist Bix Beiderbecke as a featured soloist. Beiderbecke was the first white performer to be widely regarded by black musicians as a genuine jazz talent. After an apprenticeship in the New Orleans style, he joined Goldkette in 1926, and then went to work with Paul Whiteman's orchestra in the following year. Beiderbecke left Whiteman in 1929 and played sporadically with the Dorsey brothers and other bands until his premature death two years later, which was accelerated by alcoholism – an all too frequent menace during the years of Prohibition.

Praised for his velvety tone and understated lyricism, Beiderbecke was in many ways the opposite of Louis Armstrong. His keen interest in classical music led him to compose a Debussy-inspired piano piece, *In a Mist* (1927), and in Whiteman he found a kindred spirit. There is no doubt that the increasing use of techniques from classical music by both Goldkette and Whiteman did much to stimulate a more sophisticated conception of jazz composition. From an early stage Whiteman also showed himself to be a pioneer of the hybrid SYMPHONIC JAZZ (● p. 55).

WORLD EVENTS
1930
18 February Planet Pluto discovered

2 March Death of D. H. Lawrence

29 March Chicago musicians oppose choice of American national anthem

4 May Gandhi arrested, India

14 September Nazi election successes

1931
23 January Death of Anna Pavlova

14 April Spain becomes Republic

1 May Empire State Building opened, New York

13 June German banks collapse

18 September Japan invades Manchuria

3 October Carl Nielsen dies

● Massive worldwide unemployment
● William Walton's oratorio *Belshazzar's Feast*

1932
Paris

France becomes the leading country in European jazz, producing the first critical books on the subject and launching the hugely successful Hot Club in Paris.

2 February Duke Ellington records "It Don't Mean a Thing (If it Ain't Got That Swing)," the first jazz composition with the word SWING in its title. In this year, he appears in a concert at Columbia University organized at the suggestion of the Australian composer Percy Grainger.

6 March Death of John Philip Sousa.

20 May Former Ellington trumpeter Bubber Miley dies, New York.

Summer Louis Armstrong's first tour to Europe includes a visit to London.

August Vocalist Adelaide Hall records with pianist Art Tatum (● p. 125) in New York.

9 December The Fletcher Henderson orchestra (● p. 71) records "New King Porter Stomp" for John Hammond in New York.

● Fats Waller (● p. 105) plays in Paris. ● Belgian lawyer Robert Goffin publishes his book *Aux Frontières du Jazz* in Paris. ● French critic Hugues Panassié (with Elwyn Dirants and Jacques Ozenfant) founds the Hot Club de France, Europe's first jazz club, in Paris.

Racial prejudices continue to mar objective musical criticism in the 1930s, as shown by the following bigoted response to Louis Armstrong's London appearance:

"Armstrong is the ugliest man I have ever seen on the music hall stage. He looks and behaves like an untrained gorilla. He might have come straight from some African jungle and then, after being taken to some slop tailors for a ready made dress suit, been put straight on the stage and told to 'sing'."

Hannen Swaffer, *Daily Herald* (25 July 1932)

WORLD EVENTS

2 January Japanese form a Manchurian Republic

28 January Japanese attack Shanghai

6 May President Doumer assassinated, France

June–August Nazi power escalates, Germany

12 August Monarchist coup, Seville

● Aldous Huxley's novel *Brave New World*
● Olympic Games in Los Angeles
● John Cockcroft splits the atom, Cambridge, UK

Le Hot Club de France

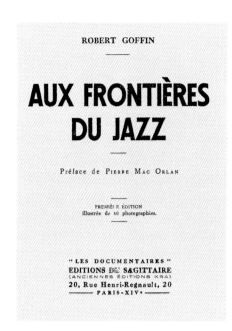

Left Belgian lawyer Robert Goffin published his ground-breaking book *Aux Frontières du Jazz* in Paris this year.

Below The Quintette du Hot Club de France in c. 1934, featuring the talents of Stephane Grappelli (extreme left) and Django Reinhardt (centre).

Right This fine study of Django Reinhardt, taken by William Gottlieb in the 1940s, clearly shows the guitarist's disfigured left hand.

In Paris in 1932, a group of like-minded jazz aficionados formed the Hot Club de France under the presidency of the French writer and critic Hugues Panassié, who also edited the club's influential journal (*Jazz-hot*) when it was launched in 1935. The Hot Club, the first organization of its kind in Europe, became famous after 1934 when it promoted its own jazz quintet (violin, three guitars and bass) featuring violinist Stephane Grappelli and guitarist Django Reinhardt. A wider circulation for the quintet's work was secured by the Swing record label, founded in 1937 by Panassié and Charles Delaunay (son of the painters Robert and Sonia). Swing also recorded the music of touring American musicians, such as saxophonists Coleman Hawkins and Benny Carter.

Apart from a separation during the war years when Reinhardt performed in occupied Europe while Grappelli remained in England (● p. 92), the two played together until Reinhardt's death in 1953. In temperament, they could hardly have been more different. Grappelli came from a comfortable middle-class background and initiated the use of the violin as a solo jazz instrument through dedicated hard work born of classical training. Reinhardt, on the other hand, hailed from Belgian gypsy stock (a fire in his caravan had crippled his left hand). He was an unpredictable and undisciplined genius, difficult to work with even at the best of times.

The instinctive musical rapport between the two men in performance was electrifying, and they generated a new brand of small-ensemble jazz at a time when big bands were at the height of fashion across the globe. Both players brought out qualities in their instruments never before seen in jazz, and exerted considerable influence on subsequent violinists and guitarists. Reinhardt's disability compelled him to play novel harmonies that might, arguably, not have been discovered had his fingers been capable of their full function. In the 1990s, the octogenarian Grappelli was still performing with as much verve as he had in his youth (and in much the same style), notably in partnership with British guitarist Martin Taylor – forty-eight years his junior.

1933

Satchmo and the Duke in Europe

European jazz is stimulated by visits from Louis Armstrong and Duke Ellington at a time when the Nazi Party in Germany seems bent on suppressing it. In America, singer Billie Holiday emerges just as Bessie Smith ends her recording career.

Above Guy Arnoux's *Couples Dancing to Jazz* (1920).

WORLD EVENTS

30 January Hitler becomes Chancellor of Germany

1 March Political arrests begin, Germany

4 March President Roosevelt initiates US economic recovery

20 March Establishment of Dachau concentration camp

1 April Jewish finances appropriated by Nazi government

4 July Gandhi imprisoned

5 December End of Prohibition, USA

● Ernest Schoedsack's movie *King Kong*

March The Berlin radio station Funkstunde bans jazz broadcasts in deference to Nazi-party doctrine.

21 March Art Tatum (● p. 125) records his first piano solo, "Tiger Rag," which is thought by some to be a piano duet.

2 June Duke Ellington and his orchestra sail from New York to Southampton to begin their first European tour, which includes a two-week appearance at the London Palladium and a visit to the Salle Pleyel, Paris. In **February**, the band records the Duke's most recent hit, "Sophisticated Lady."

July Louis Armstrong returns to London as part of his ongoing European tour.

15 July Trumpeter Freddie Keppard dies, Chicago.

24 November Bessie Smith (● p. 66) makes her last four recordings.

27 November Billie Holiday makes her first recording ("Your Mother's Son-in-Law") with Benny Goodman (● p. 84) for English Columbia, earning $35.

December A CUTTING CONTEST for tenor saxophonists in Kansas City (● p. 64) is won by Lester Young. Other contenders include Ben Webster, Herschel Evans and Coleman Hawkins.

● Eubie Blake and Noble Sissle take their show *Shuffle Along of 1933* on tour to Los Angeles, where it collapses and leaves seventeen-year-old pianist Nat "King" Cole (● p. 124) without a job. He finds one the following year with the Royal Dukes in Chicago, where he is influenced by Earl Hines at the Grand Terrace Café.

Left Billie Holiday, sporting her trademark gardenias in her hair (● p. 131).

Right The formidable Bessie Smith, pictured towards the end of her singing career in the 1930s – by which time sales of her recordings had reached several millions.

Jazzing in Europe

LONDON PALLADIUM ADJOINING OXFORD CIRCUS TUBE STATION

TWICE NIGHTLY AT 6.30 AND 9.0 P.M.	COMMENCING MONDAY, JUNE 12TH, 1933	MATINEES AT 2.30 WEDNESDAY & THURSDAY

JACK HYLTON PRESENTS (By Arrangement with MILLS-ROCKWELL Inc.)

DUKE ELLINGTON

FIRST TIME IN ENGLAND **AND HIS** CREATOR OF A NEW VOGUE IN DANCE MUSIC

FAMOUS ORCHESTRA

BESSIE Original Snake-Hips Girl **DUDLEY** | THREE World's Most Sensational Acrobatic Roller Skaters **WHIRLWINDS** SIXTEEN PALLADIUM GIRLS | BAILEY AND Rhapsody in Taps **DERBY**

SEVEN ROYAL **HINDUSTANS** | **MURRAY & MOONEY** | FRANK & BETTY **BOSTON**

RANDOLPH **SUTTON** | **LASSITER** BROTHERS One of America's Biggest Laughing Acts | CHEEKY CHAPPIE **MAX MILLER** | DE WOLF **METCALF** What! No! Rumba? **& FORD**

PRICES: 9d. to 5/- (Tax extra). Saturdays and Holidays, slight increase

Above Duke Ellington as he liked to appear in the 1930s: every bit as elegant and sophisticated as his highly acclaimed music.

On 19 January 1919, *The Times* in London, finally recognizing the existence of jazz, described the new music as "one of the many American peculiarities that threaten to make life a nightmare." Less than three months later, the Original Dixieland Jazz Band descended on the city fresh from their spectacular successes in Chicago and New York. They created a sensation: their appearance at the Hippodrome caused such a wildly enthusiastic response from the audience that they were immediately (and somewhat perversely) dismissed by the management. Undaunted, the band moved on to the Palladium (● p. 43) and Hammersmith Palais, and even performed for King George V at Buckingham Palace.

A burgeoning craze for hot dance music was intensified when Paul Whiteman visited England in 1923 and 1926, and when Louis Armstrong and Duke Ellington did so in 1932–33. Many British big bands enjoyed success during the 1930s, including one led by Jack Hylton, who persuaded Coleman Hawkins to

come to England in 1934. British short-sightedness soon began to rear its ugly head, however. The late 1920s brought vociferous demands for the jobs of native musicians to be protected from a feared invasion by immigrant Americans, and thus began the sorry tale of extensive anti-American action by the Musicians' Union that resulted in a regrettable musical insularity until horizons broadened in the 1950s (● pp. 85 and 135).

The situation was much more positive elsewhere in Europe. In France – the country in which Debussy, Satie and Stravinsky had all fallen under the spell of RAGTIME before 1918 – the arrival of the spectacularly erotic black dancer Josephine Baker (● p. 59) in the mid-1920s gave a new impetus to Parisian nightlife. Baker also visited Berlin in 1925 and 1927, and Paul Whiteman toured from Paris to Berlin in 1926 with *Rhapsody in Blue* (● p. 55). Jack Hylton appeared regularly in France and Germany in the late 1920s and early 1930s. An informal jazz festival was organized in 1932 in Belgium, where enthusiasts had been trying to emulate the New Orleans style for many years.

The arrival in Paris of major stars such as Fats Waller (in 1932), Duke Ellington (in 1933), and Louis Armstrong (in 1934) further intensified popular interest in American jazz, and with the foundation of the Hot Club de France (● p. 75) the position of Paris as the jazz capital of Europe was secured. It was here, not in America, that the first significant books on jazz were published: Hugues Panassié's *Le Jazz Hot* (1934) and Charles Delaunay's *Hot Discography* (1936). It was only the rise to power of Hitler's Nazi party (● p. 81) that threatened to impede the rapid progress of jazz throughout continental Europe.

1934
Stompin' At The Savoy

Chick Webb's band, with teenage vocalist Ella Fitzgerald, delights audiences in New York. Fletcher Henderson begins his association with Benny Goodman, who is unwittingly poised on the brink of international stardom.

30 March Coleman Hawkins arrives in England to work with Jack Hylton and his band, having quit Fletcher Henderson's orchestra earlier in the month. Lester Young becomes his temporary replacement.

18 May Drummer Chick Webb records "Stompin' at the Savoy" with his band. He soon employs sixteen-year-old vocalist Ella Fitzgerald (● p. 195), who wins two talent competitions in Harlem this year.

June Benny Goodman's band (● p. 84) opens at Billy Rose's Music Hall, New York.

July The journal *Down Beat: the Contemporary Music Magazine* is launched in Chicago.

Left Django Reinhardt (left) looks on in mock horror as Stephane Grappelli exchanges his violin for Reinhardt's guitar. This picture dates from 1948, some fourteen years after their first appearance with the Quintette du Hot Club de France in Paris.

Opposite, above CBS's LP reissue of classic Chick Webb recordings from the 1930s.

Right James P. Johnson (at the piano) with his Small's Paradise band, pictured in New York in 1934.

WORLD EVENTS

23 February Edward Elgar dies

23 May Outlaws Bonnie Parker and Clyde Barrow shot dead, USA

25 May Gustav Holst dies

May First Glyndebourne opera festival, UK

10 June Frederick Delius dies

23 June Italian troops invade Albania

25 July Nazi coup fails in Austria

19 August Hitler begins dictatorship

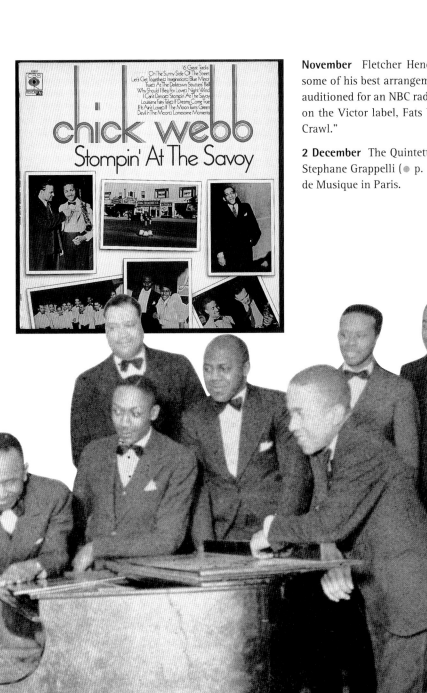

November Fletcher Henderson's band folds due to financial difficulties. He sells some of his best arrangements to Benny Goodman, whose band has just successfully auditioned for an NBC radio show. ● As part of his prolific series of piano recordings on the Victor label, Fats Waller (● p. 105) cuts "Honeysuckle Rose" and "Alligator Crawl."

2 December The Quintette du Hot Club de France, including Django Reinhardt and Stephane Grappelli (● p. 75), gives its first public performance at the Ecole Normale de Musique in Paris.

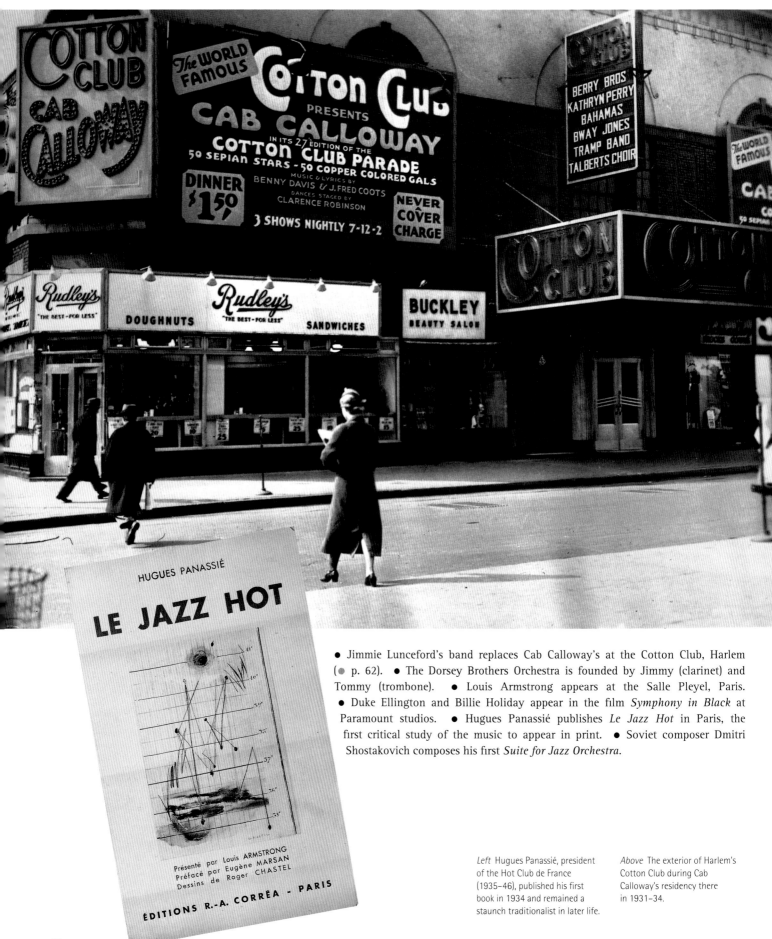

- Jimmie Lunceford's band replaces Cab Calloway's at the Cotton Club, Harlem (● p. 62). ● The Dorsey Brothers Orchestra is founded by Jimmy (clarinet) and Tommy (trombone). ● Louis Armstrong appears at the Salle Pleyel, Paris. ● Duke Ellington and Billie Holiday appear in the film *Symphony in Black* at Paramount studios. ● Hugues Panassié publishes *Le Jazz Hot* in Paris, the first critical study of the music to appear in print. ● Soviet composer Dmitri Shostakovich composes his first *Suite for Jazz Orchestra*.

Left Hugues Panassié, president of the Hot Club de France (1935–46), published his first book in 1934 and remained a staunch traditionalist in later life.

Above The exterior of Harlem's Cotton Club during Cab Calloway's residency there in 1931–34.

Jazz under the Nazis

Since its inception, jazz has been distinguished by a freedom of musical expression (sometimes politically symbolic) that ultimately derives from the performer's individuality. This essential trait was hardly likely to endear the music to the rulers of totalitarian regimes, which can function effectively only through the suppression of personal freedoms. In both Soviet Russia and Nazi Germany jazz came to be seriously discredited. In Hitler's Germany, it was perceived as the loathsome product of blacks and Jews, both ethnic groups that needed to be eradicated from society in order to preserve the purity of the Aryan master race. The fact that jazz was largely an American import made it even more distasteful to the Nazis, especially when the US joined the Allies fighting against Germany at the end of 1941.

The heady nightlife of Berlin in the 1920s, in which jazz played an important role, had attracted numerous foreign musicians (● p. 77). There were several German bands who imitated the style of "hot" recordings from America with some success, including multi-instrumentalist Stefan Weintraub and his Syncopators, who wisely failed to return to Germany from a world tour in 1933 when the Nazis came to power. In that year, propaganda minister Dr. Josef Goebbels set up the *Reichskulturkammer* to keep a watchful eye on cultural activities, and his control of broadcasting permitted him gradually to replace American-style jazz with an anodyne dance music designed to keep both public and troops happy. Meanwhile, Jewish musicians were increasingly prevented from plying their trade.

In 1937, Goebbels proclaimed that all music recorded by non-Aryan musicians was to be banned. Several regional authorities prohibited the live performance of jazz in 1938–39. The only authentic jazz on German airwaves featured in the notorious propaganda broadcasts by Lord Haw-Haw, where it was included solely as bait to entice listeners from enemy countries (● p. 96). Jazz nevertheless continued to be enjoyed covertly in Berlin, Leipzig (which opened an influential "Hot Club") and elsewhere. In Hamburg, the flamboyant "Swings" espoused both Anglo-American mannerisms and proscribed SWING music with courageous openness, and as a consequence many of them were sent to concentration camps. Favorite American numbers continued to be played wherever possible, however, often with their famous titles heavily disguised (in occupied Paris, for example, Gershwin's "Lady Be Good" was rendered as "Les Bigoudis," or "The Hair-Rollers"!). Even Luftwaffe pilots on bombing missions to England habitually tuned their radio receivers to the BBC's jazz broadcasts from London in an attempt to catch up on the outlawed music.

Jazz could be performed with greater ease in the Nazi-occupied countries of western Europe. In France, Belgium, Holland and Denmark regulations were sufficiently relaxed to permit recordings, which, although prohibited from sale in Germany, circulated freely in the country of origin. Thus Django Reinhardt (● p. 75) continued to promote his career in France, in spite of his anxieties concerning Nazi attempts to liquidate those of gypsy blood (● p. 104).

1935

Kings of Swing

Benny Goodman's spectacular success in Los Angeles creates a world market for big-band jazz. Symphonic jazz is further developed as a vehicle for American musical nationalism in Gershwin's folk opera Porgy and Bess.

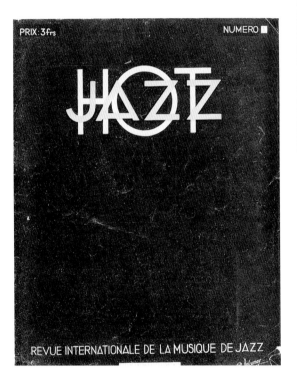

Above The journal *Jazz-hot*, first published in 1935 as the official organ of the Hot Club de France, was issued monthly until the beginning of World War II. Publication resumed in 1945, and from 1950 continued alongside the separate *Bulletin du Hot Club de France.*

March First publication of the journal *Jazz-hot: revue internationale de la musique de jazz*, Paris.

2 April Bennie Moten dies, Kansas City. Count Basie forms his Barons of Rhythm with members of Moten's band and the new group appears at the Club Reno, Kansas City.

April and **May** STRIDE pianist Willie "The Lion" Smith is rediscovered in a series of recordings for Decca, New York.

12 June Ella Fitzgerald (● p. 195) records "I'll Chase the Blues Away" and "Love and Kisses" with Chick Webb, in her first appearance on disc.

1 July Benny Goodman (● p. 84) records Jelly Roll Morton's "King Porter Stomp" in an arrangement by Fletcher Henderson (● p. 71). This month Goodman begins recording with a mixed-race trio that includes Teddy Wilson (piano) and Gene Krupa (drums).

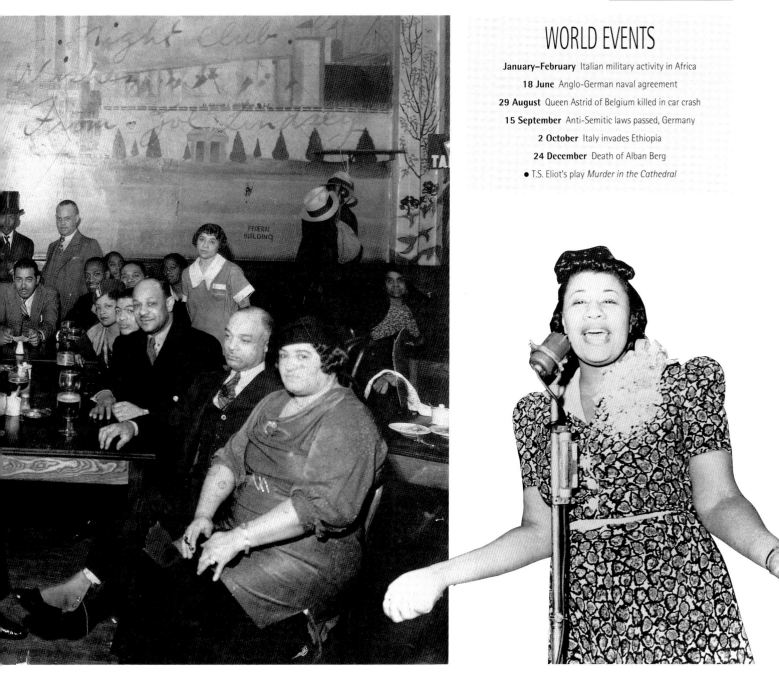

WORLD EVENTS

January–February Italian military activity in Africa

18 June Anglo-German naval agreement

29 August Queen Astrid of Belgium killed in car crash

15 September Anti-Semitic laws passed, Germany

2 October Italy invades Ethiopia

24 December Death of Alban Berg

● T.S. Eliot's play *Murder in the Cathedral*

Above A jazz party at Tony's Tavern, Chicago, on Valentine's Day 1935. Guests of honor are Duke Ellington and Louis Armstrong (fifth and sixth from left respectively).

Above, right Ella Fitzgerald at around the time she assumed the leadership of Chick Webb's band after the hunchback drummer's death in 1939.

2 and **31 July** Billie Holiday (● p. 131) records seven sides with Teddy Wilson in New York, including "What a Little Moonlight Can Do."

21 August Benny Goodman's American coast-to-coast tour climaxes with a sensationally successful performance at the Palomar Ballroom, Los Angeles, which intensifies public interest in the SWING-band style.

12 September Duke Ellington (● p. 62) records his second extended score, "Reminiscin' in Tempo," filling all four sides of two 78rpm discs.

Autumn Stephane Grappelli and Django Reinhardt (● p. 75) record together in Paris. ● Louis Armstrong, back in New York after his tours of Europe and now on the books of commercially aggressive agent Joe Glaser, re-enters the recording studio.

Populist and Classicist: Benny Goodman

A sudden decline in the fortunes of Fletcher Henderson's dance orchestra (● p. 71), when his tenor saxophonist Coleman Hawkins left to work for Jack Hylton in Britain, coincided with the meteoric rise to prominence of the twenty-five-year-old Jewish clarinetist Benny Goodman in 1934. Initially based in Chicago, Goodman moved to New York in 1928 – a year in which many notable musicians gravitated eastward to the Big Apple. He successfully auditioned for an NBC radio show in November 1934 with a newly formed big band and, at the suggestion of record producer John Hammond (● p. 209), Goodman bought a number of band arrangements from Henderson to augment his then meagre repertoire. The combination of Henderson's exciting and intricate orchestrations with the professionalism and commercial potential of Goodman's new band propelled big-band jazz into the limelight, and initiated a rage for SWING music that lasted well into the 1940s.

All this happened virtually overnight. In August 1935, after a dispiriting season in New York, Goodman took his band to California and played to a packed Palomar Ballroom in Los Angeles where the crowd went wild with excitement (as did those listening in to the live radio broadcast from the venue). Goodman instantly became a household name. He was dubbed the "King of Swing," and gained such nationwide prestige that he appeared at New York's Carnegie Hall (● p. 91) three years later. His band included flamboyant drummer Gene Krupa and agile trumpeter Harry James, both of whom left in 1938 to lead their own bands after personality clashes with the often intractable Goodman. Henderson joined the band as full-time staff arranger in 1939, and in the following year Goodman formed a new group that included guitarist Charlie Christian (● p. 98). He continued to produce big-band jazz of impeccable quality, and shrewdly hired BE-BOP soloists in the later 1940s when it seemed evident that jazz was moving in a new direction.

Alongside his cultivation of a polished big-band sound, Goodman worked with smaller groups that were prophetic of developments in jazz after World War II. In 1935 he set up a trio with Krupa on drums and the dexterous Teddy Wilson at the keyboard. Since Wilson was black and the other two members white, this was a bold statement in a period when mixed-race groups were still severely frowned upon in America. In the following year, the black vibraphonist Lionel Hampton (● p. 70) was added to the group to create a quartet.

Goodman was also the first jazz musician to pursue a parallel career in classical music, recording the Clarinet Quintet by Mozart in 1938 (● p. 91) and commissioning concert works from internationally distinguished composers such as Béla Bartók, Benjamin Britten, Paul Hindemith and Aaron Copland. That he was able to achieve all this remains an eloquent testament to his faultless technique, which has been the envy of every jazz clarinetist since.

Never easy to work with, Goodman had an absent-minded and sometimes irritable personality, and his inveterate musical perfectionism did not endear him to all his players. Pianist Jess Stacy recalled the leader's obsession with the accurate tuning of instruments, and even Goodman's own daughter declared that she was terrified of playing classical music for her father. He could also be devious: one of Goodman's star vocalists remained convinced that he had asked her to marry him just to ensure her continued commitment to the band at the height of her popular success.

Right Benny Goodman in the mid-1930s: the first performer to forge a dual career in jazz and the classics.

Left Benny Goodman and his quartet rehearse for a radio broadcast in 1938 (l. to r.): Lionel Hampton (vibraphone), Goodman (clarinet), Teddy Wilson (piano) and Gene Krupa (drums).

Below The cast assembles in Catfish Row to depart for a picnic in the original 1935 production of Gershwin's celebrated opera *Porgy and Bess* (Act 2 Scene 1). This scene includes the songs "I Got Plenty of Nuttin'" and "Bess, You is My Woman Now."

10 October George Gershwin's three-act opera *Porgy and Bess* opens at the Alvin Theater, New York; its plot, adapted from the novel by DuBose Heyward, is set among the black community of Charleston, South Carolina. Although not a striking success at first, the opera later becomes renowned as a landmark in the development of SYMPHONIC JAZZ and contributes a number of songs to the repertory of jazz STANDARDS.

12 October A meeting of German radio-station directors in Munich hears Nazi government plans for a total broadcasting ban on jazz.

● Britain's Ministry of Labour, under pressure from the Musicians' Union, decrees that American musicians are to be banned from appearing in the UK until mutually satisfactory terms are agreed with the American Federation of Musicians.

1936

Billie and Ella

The big-band era now in full swing, Count Basie injects a powerful blues flavor into the music. Recordings by young vocalists Billie Holiday and Ella Fitzgerald are soon heavily in demand.

January Count Basie signs a contract with Decca to record twenty-four sides per annum, for a yearly fee of $750 (with no royalties). Lester Young rejoins the Basie band this year after brief spells with Fletcher Henderson and others.

January–February A series of recordings in Chicago by Albert Ammons and Meade Lux Lewis heralds a revival of interest in BOOGIE-WOOGIE.

February Charlie Green, a jobbing trombonist who recorded with Bessie Smith, Fletcher Henderson and Chick Webb, dies from exposure on a Harlem street.

Right A bird's-eye view of Count Basie's band at the Apollo Theater, New York, in January 1939.

Below Basie's laconic and understated keyboard playing formed an effective contrast to the extrovert brilliance of his virtuoso big band.

The Count from New Jersey

In the spring of 1936, pianist William "Count" Basie was leading his Barons of Rhythm band at Club Reno in Kansas City (● p. 64). By happy chance, John Hammond (● p. 209) heard a broadcast from the venue and persuaded Basie to bring the band to New York, where its energetic "southwest" manner of playing soon enthralled audiences. Basie's early experience with Bennie Moten and Walter Page in Missouri had influenced his cultivation of a big-band style that was far more entrenched in the BLUES than that of his white competitors. His band's powerful sense of swing and greater improvisational spontaneity demonstrated how much jazzier a good black band could sound when compared with the polished but sometimes pedestrian performances of Goodman and others. Basie's orchestra exploited the WALKING BASS and characteristic rhythmic patterns of the SWING style to the full, creating an unfailing sense of musical momentum with techniques that could, however, all too easily become stale clichés.

A spell in 1937 at New York's Roseland Ballroom, former stomping ground of Fletcher Henderson, cemented the band's reputation. That same year it also recorded the hit tune "One o'clock Jump," which embodied a masterful treatment of a simple but catchy RIFF. Now expanded from its original nine members to no fewer than sixteen, the band included a formidable saxophone section that thrived on the creative tension between its two tenor players, Lester Young and the ill-fated Herschel Evans (● p. 92). Young espoused a light tone full of air and grace, while Evans was one of the most impassioned melodists of his generation. Basie himself contributed piano solos that seemed to leave their STRIDE origins far behind. This former protégé of Fats Waller (● p. 105) now began to rely on a bare minimum of notes, delivered with an unerring sense of timing and a delicacy of touch that at times sat oddly alongside the invigorating style of his band.

Clarinet

The clarinet was a favored instrument in New Orleans during the early days of jazz, flourishing both at the hands of untutored black musicians and through an extension of a European tradition of classical clarinet playing in which many Creole performers were schooled. The best of the latter, notably Sidney Bechet (● p. 42) and Barney Bigard (● p. 63), combined their considerable technical facility with a flair for the extemporized melodic embellishments characteristic of New Orleans jazz. This school of clarinet playing culminated in the fluent decorative improvising of later bandleader clarinetists, principally Artie Shaw and Benny Goodman (● p. 84).

During the SWING era, the clarinet gradually lost out to the growing popularity of the saxophone (● p. 193), both as a featured solo instrument and in big-band arrangements. For a time, reed players were expected to play both saxophone and clarinet, since both have similar single-reed mouthpieces and some shared fingering techniques (related to the "Boehm" system).

After the advent of BE-BOP, very few important clarinet soloists emerged. One exception was Buddy DeFranco, who met with a mixed critical reception. Rare ancillary instruments, such as the contrabass clarinet played by Anthony Braxton, were employed in the experimental FREE JAZZ of the 1960s (● p. 150) largely for their novelty value. At the hands of Eddie Daniels, however, the standard clarinet has more recently been revived as a versatile participant in the easy-going post-FUSION style produced on the GRP label (● p. 214).

Left Bandleader Artie Shaw, pictured here alongside a B♭ clarinet (left) and bass clarinet (right), the latter rare in jazz until the work of Eric Dolphy and others in the 1960s.

WORLD EVENTS

20 January King George V dies, UK

28 January Dmitri Shostakovich's opera *Lady Macbeth* banned by Stalin in USSR

26 February Volkswagen introduced, Germany

18 April Death of Ottorino Respighi

7 May Germany occupies the Rhineland

17 July Spanish Civil War begins

1 August Olympic Games open in Berlin

1 November Berlin and Rome form Axis

18 November General Franco established, Spain

10 December Abdication of Edward VIII, UK

17 March Nineteen-year-old Ella Fitzgerald stands in for Billie Holiday (her senior by only two years) with Teddy Wilson's band in a New York recording session.

30 June Billie Holiday and Teddy Wilson record "I Cried for You," which promptly sells fifteen thousand copies.

28 July Young pianist Nat King Cole (● p. 124) makes his first recordings with the Solid Swingers, a band led by his brother Eddie (on bass) in Chicago.

21 August Benny Goodman (● p. 84) adds vibraphonist Lionel Hampton (● p. 70) to his trio to record "Moonglow," the first in a celebrated series of quartet sessions.

9 October Count Basie records for Vocalion in Chicago at the instigation of John Hammond, who has heard the band's broadcasts from Kansas City.

● Duke Ellington (● p. 62) provides music for the Marx Brothers' movie *A Day at the Races*. ● In Paris Charles Delaunay publishes his book *Hot Discography*, the first jazz discography to appear in print. ● The English translation of Hugues Panassié's pioneering critical study *Le Jazz Hot* (● p. 80) is published in New York and London.

1937

The Nazi Ban

Virtually all imported jazz records are banned in Germany, in a year that sees the birth of the piano trio and the deaths of George Gershwin and Bessie Smith.

13 March Billie Holiday (● p. 131) makes her debut with Count Basie's band in Scranton, Pennsylvania. She stays with the group until early the following year, but contractual restrictions prevent her from recording with them.

28 April Coleman Hawkins records with Django Reinhardt (● p. 75) and Benny Carter in Paris.

14 May Duke Ellington records the exotic "Caravan," composed by his trombonist Juan Tizol. On **20 September**, he records his radical extended composition "Diminuendo and Crescendo in Blue," which is not successful until revived in 1956 (● p. 138).

June Count Basie's band (● p. 86) broadcasts from the Savoy Ballroom, Harlem, and appears at the Apollo Theater. On **7 July** they record "One o'clock Jump," which becomes their hit signature tune.

6 July Benny Goodman (● p. 84) records "Sing, Sing, Sing (With a Swing)" in Los Angeles, fusing the original Louis Prima tune with "Christopher Columbus" to create an extended piece that causes a sensation at Carnegie Hall (● p. 91) the following year.

Above Nat King Cole (far right) poses with his innovative piano trio.

WORLD EVENTS

26 April Germans bomb the Basque town of Guernica

6 May Airship *Hindenburg* explodes, New Jersey

12 May Coronation of King George VI, UK

28 July Japanese capture Peking

October Duke and Duchess of Windsor meet Hitler

8 November Japanese secure Shanghai

25 December Arturo Toscanini's inaugural concert with NBC Symphony Orchestra, USA

29 December Irish Free State renamed Eire

● Dmitri Shostakovich's Fifth Symphony

11 July George Gershwin dies from a brain tumor at the age of thirty-eight, in Hollywood.

September Nat King Cole (● p. 124) creates a new ensemble – the piano trio – by forming a group with Oscar Moore (guitar) and Wesley Prince (bass). The trio, based in Los Angeles, performs live for three years before committing their music to disc.

26 September Bessie Smith (● p. 66) dies from severe injuries in a motor accident.

December Nazi propaganda minister Josef Goebbels prohibits the sale of "non-Aryan" recordings in Germany, effectively outlawing all jazz recorded by black and Jewish artists. A list of proscribed compositions is circulated.

George Gershwin

Gershwin's untimely death in 1937 robbed the musical world of a unique talent. Unlike his compatriot Aaron Copland (● p. 55), Gershwin had approached the challenge of creating SYMPHONIC JAZZ from a grounding in popular rather than classical music, and had scored an early success with *Rhapsody in Blue* in 1924.

The son of immigrant Russian Jews (his real surname was Gershovitz), Gershwin began his career modestly at the age of fifteen by working as a song PLUGGER in a New York publishing house (● p. 31). He became a highly competent STRIDE pianist and recorded numerous piano rolls (● p. 32), but first found fame as a composer of popular musical comedies on Broadway, beginning with *La La Lucille* in 1919. Five years later, his older brother Ira joined him as librettist, usually adding words to themes George had already composed. Together they created a stream of brilliant songs that rapidly reached a wide international audience. The series of Broadway musicals on which they collaborated from 1924 onward spawned a number of independent hits, including "Fascinatin' Rhythm" (from *Lady, Be Good!*, 1924) and "I Got Rhythm" (from *Girl Crazy*, 1930).

Gershwin's "American folk opera," *Porgy and Bess* (● p. 85), although only achieving a limited success on Broadway in 1935, included several songs – "Summertime," "It Ain't Necessarily So," "I Got Plenty of Nuttin'" and "I Loves You, Porgy" – that became jazz STANDARDS. By this stage in Gershwin's career, the acclaim he had received in the concert hall with his ground-breaking symphonic jazz caused him to regard his work as a composer with more seriousness. For a time he even contemplated studying formally with French composer Maurice Ravel, who is reputed to have told Gershwin when they met, "Why be a second-rate Ravel when you can be a first-rate Gershwin?" Another report records that when Gershwin asked Ravel for lessons, the Frenchman replied with his own sly question: "How much do you earn from your composing?" When Gershwin revealed to Ravel the astronomical extent of his income, Ravel simply said "You teach me!"

Above, left George Gershwin at the piano.

Above, right "Rialto Ripples," which he co-composed with Will Donaldson, was recorded on piano roll by Gershwin in 1916.

1938

New Respectability

Benny Goodman's and John Hammond's concerts at Carnegie Hall raise jazz to the same social status as classical music. Jelly Roll Morton is discovered languishing in Washington, DC, and the early history of jazz begins to be documented in earnest.

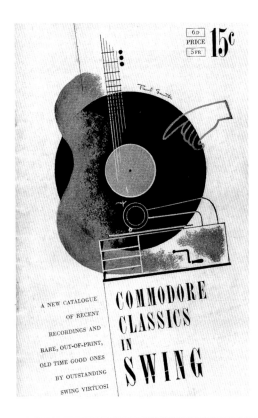

16 January Benny Goodman's band introduces jazz to New York's bastion of classical music, Carnegie Hall. The event, which is sold out, includes a sequence of pieces illustrating the history of jazz and a JAM SESSION involving musicians from the Benny Goodman (● p. 84), Duke Ellington (● p. 62) and Count Basie (● p. 86) bands. After the concert, the bands of Count Basie and Chick Webb compete informally at the Savoy Ballroom.

18 January Eddie Condon makes the first recordings on Milt Gabler's new Commodore record label (illustration, ● p. 224).

February Gene Krupa quits Benny Goodman to lead his own band.

March Art Tatum (● p. 125) plays in Soho, London.

10 April King Oliver (● p. 48) dies, Savannah, Georgia. He has made no recordings since 1931 and has spent two years in retirement, eking out a living as a pool-room janitor.

May–July Jelly Roll Morton (● p. 45), brought out of retirement by Alan Lomax, makes a historic series of retrospective recordings for the Library of Congress, Washington, D. C.

Far left Famous for recordings made by Billie Holiday, Coleman Hawkins and many musicians from Chicago in the 1940s, the Commodore label later benefited from reissue programs undertaken by Columbia, Telefunken and Mosaic.

Left Jelly Roll Morton in high spirits at the Jungle Club, Washington, in 1938.

WORLD EVENTS

12 March Germany annexes Austria

3 May Fascist summit, Rome

August–September Neville Chamberlain negotiates with Hitler

1 October Germany annexes Sudetenland

21 October Japanese capture Canton

9–10 November *Kristallnacht*: night of Nazi violence against Jews in Germany and Austria

● Walt Disney's cartoon *Snow White and the Seven Dwarfs*

Duke Ellington: Prelude to a Kiss

Duke Ellington's instrumental rendition of his song "Prelude to a Kiss" on 9 September 1938 encapsulated the composer's sophisticated artistry in a hauntingly beautiful three-minute composition. Deriving in style from the "mood" music that Ellington penned during his earlier Cotton Club days, the thirteen-piece orchestral arrangement perfectly absorbs each player's distinctive sonorities within the band's complex musical fabric.

Supported by the elusive chromatic harmony for which Ellington was famous, Lawrence Brown's expressive trombone melody threads its circuitous and unpredictable way through the rich orchestral backdrop. The theme is developed in a concentrated solo from Johnny Hodge's sensuous alto saxophone (complete with his trademark "smears"), a duet

Above Goodman's epoch-making appearance at Carnegie Hall in January 1938. His band includes Gene Krupa (drums, far left), who quit soon after to become a leader in his own right.

How to Get to Carnegie Hall

January 1938 marked a significant turning point in the history of jazz. Benny Goodman's appearance at New York's Carnegie Hall was the first occasion on which jazz was performed at a prestigious concert hall rather than in nightclubs and ballrooms. The event's sell-out success ensured that paying audiences would continue to enjoy professionally organized jazz concerts at classical venues in years to come. It is not surprising that this tradition was initiated by a white band: Goodman's mixed-race trio and quartet (● p. 84) could only be included in the program as a VAUDEVILLE-style interlude. But Goodman integrated

musicians from Count Basie's and Duke Ellington's black bands into the show, and from 1943 Ellington's orchestra itself made annual appearances at the historic venue, performing a series of large-scale "symphonic" works (● p. 104). Billie Holiday's two concerts at Carnegie Hall in 1948 (● p. 118) broke all their box-office records.

Goodman carefully organized his 1938 concert to demonstrate the historical evolution of jazz styles, and included a parody of the Original Dixieland Jazz Band's crude early recordings (● p. 37) along with a spirited tribute to Louis Armstrong (● p. 56), as well as a lengthy JAM SESSION on Fats Waller's "Honeysuckle Rose." (When asked how long he required for an intermission, the nonplussed Goodman replied, "How long does Mr Toscanini take?") Goodman's second appearance at Carnegie Hall, on 6 October 1939, with markedly different musicians, featured a light-hearted satirical interpretation of "T'ain't What You Do, It's the Way that You Do It" – which aped the styles of certain of his competitors – and his pseudo-Baroque hit "Bach Goes to Town."

In 1978, the sixty-nine-year-old Goodman fronted a much younger band in a concert at Carnegie Hall held to celebrate the fortieth anniversary of his original appearance. The program on that night included a powerful rendering of Jelly Roll Morton's "King Porter Stomp," in the same arrangement by Fletcher Henderson (● p. 71) that had become virtually the signature tune of the SWING era four decades earlier (● p. 82).

● ● ● ● ● ● ● ● ● ● ● ● ● ●

between Brown and baritone saxophonist Harry Carney and a solo from trumpeter Wallace Jones. Following the horn solos, the saxophone section inverts the theme, with the melody low in register and the accompanying chords floating high above.

Duke Ellington himself then takes center stage as piano soloist. In its use of parallel chord voicings – already heard in the introduction – his solo reveals the influence of impressionist composers such as Debussy. Interspersed with the piano phrases are parenthetical echoes and decorative paraphrases from the other instruments – a subtle and complex texture of a kind unique to Ellington's work in this period. Finally, Lawrence Brown's trombone returns the listener to the opening theme as this miniature masterpiece draws to its close.

24 July Artie Shaw's orchestra records its popular interpretation of Cole Porter's "Begin the Beguine" in New York.

August In Britain on tour, Fats Waller (● p. 105) appears in Glasgow. The Quintette du Hot Club de France records in London.

November Benny Goodman continues to develop his alternative career as a classical clarinetist by giving a recital in New York's Town Hall. This year he also records Mozart's Clarinet Quintet with the Budapest String Quartet and commissions Hungarian composer Béla Bartók to write his chamber work *Contrasts*.

15 December The Benny Goodman band records Alec Templeton's "Bach Goes to Town: Prelude and Fugue in Swing," a witty composition fusing Baroque CONTRAPUNTAL techniques with SWING.

23 December At Carnegie Hall, John Hammond (● p. 209) mounts a concert illustrating the history of jazz "From Spirituals to Swing," featuring BLUES pianists Pete Johnson, Albert Ammons and Meade Lux Lewis, Count Basie's band, the Benny Goodman sextet, Sidney Bechet (● p. 42) and James P. Johnson (● p. 46).

● Trumpeter Harry James quits Benny Goodman at the end of the year to form his own orchestra in Philadelphia. ● In New York, Winthrop Sargeant publishes his study *Jazz, Hot and Hybrid*, one of the earliest critical books on jazz in English.

1939

War

As big-band jazz, exemplified by Glenn Miller's polished performances, becomes the pop music of World War II, the tenor saxophone acquires a new prominence at the hands of Lester Young and Coleman Hawkins. The foundation of the Blue Note label inspires a revival of boogie-woogie and other blues-orientated styles.

February Stride pianist Willie "The Lion" Smith records eight of his compositions for Commodore, including "Echoes of Spring" and "Rippling Waters" which both reveal his debt to classical and impressionist composers.

9 February Herschel Evans dies from heart disease at the age of thirty in New York.

March A new band led by trombonist Glenn Miller (● p. 107) plays at the Glen Island Casino, New York. Moving on to play at Meadowbrook, New Jersey, the band becomes well known through regular radio broadcasts.

21 March Duke Ellington's orchestra records "Something to Live For" by Billy Strayhorn, with the composer appearing as pianist. It is the beginning of a long and fruitful association between the two men (● p. 183).

23 March Duke Ellington and his band sail to Le Havre for a concert tour of France, Holland and Denmark. Knowing of Hitler's antipathy toward jazz, they pass anxiously through Nazi Germany.

April Teddy Wilson leaves the Benny Goodman Quartet (● p. 84) to form his own big band.

4 April Glenn Miller records his "Moonlight Serenade."

20 April Billie Holiday (● p. 131) records the anti–racist song "Strange Fruit" with the Café Society band. With its graphic description of a lynching scene, it proves highly controversial and is banned by several radio stations.

16 June Bandleader Chick Webb dies, Baltimore, Maryland. His orchestra is taken over by his protegée Ella Fitzgerald (● p. 195), who leads it until 1942.

1 August Glenn Miller records the phenomenally successful "In the Mood." On the same day, guitarist Charlie Christian is hired by Benny Goodman (● p. 209).

3 September Britain's declaration of war on Nazi Germany finds the Quintette du Hot Club de France (● p. 75) on tour in London. All members of the group except Stephane Grappelli return to France and continue to perform there after the Nazi invasion in May 1940.

Saxophone: Body and Soul

When Coleman Hawkins ("Bean" to his associates) recorded his intense rendition of "Body and Soul" on 11 October 1939, he brought the saxophone's lyrical powers to a peak that, some would argue, has never been surpassed. By this time, the saxophone family had long been almost exclusively associated with jazz, although when invented in around 1840 by Adolphe Sax the instruments had been intended for classical music. Apart from a few cases of its use by composers such as Maurice Ravel, Alban Berg and Sergey Rachmaninov, the saxophone rarely appeared in the classical orchestra during the first half of the century. When George Gershwin (● p. 55) and Aaron Copland incorporated saxophones in the orchestration of their SYMPHONIC JAZZ scores in the 1920s, the instruments' blend of seductive warmth and brassiness – deriving from the combination of a single-reed mouthpiece and metal body – became indelibly associated with jazz.

Debate continues over precisely when the saxophone became an independent jazz solo instrument, but it appears prominently in numerous recordings from the early 1920s. Early players in New Orleans directly adapted clarinet style; many were proficient on both instruments (● p. 87). The finest exponent of this approach was Sidney Bechet (● p. 42), who promoted the Bb soprano saxophone in a series of recordings after 1923. Another New Orleans musician, Barney Bigard (● p. 63), adapted his clarinet-playing style for use on the Bb tenor saxophone, but it was not until Coleman Hawkins, Lester Young and Ben Webster that the tenor saxophone realized its full potential. From the lushness of Webster and lightness of Young to the later aggressive reediness of John Coltrane, an astonishing range of tone colors was revealed.

The Eb alto saxophone, on the other hand, had established itself as a solo voice at an early stage in the hands of Jimmy Dorsey and later in the elegant playing of Duke Ellington's saxophonist Johnny Hodges. The saxophone section in a typical big band of the SWING era comprised two altos, two tenors and a baritone; the work of Glenn Miller's saxophones is the

Right The record cover of Commodore's long-playing reissue of the piano compositions originally recorded by Willie "The Lion" Smith on 78s in 1939.

Below The two most widespread members of the saxophone family: tenor in B♭ (*left*) and alto in E♭ (*right*).

FL 30,003

COMMODORE PRESENTS

PIANO SOLOS BY WILLIE SMITH

ORIGINAL COMPOSITIONS

ECHOES OF SPRING
RIPPLING WATERS
PASSIONETTE
SNEAKAWAY
THE BOY AND THE BOAT
FADING STAR
FINGER BUSTER
MORNING AIR
CONCENTRATING
I'LL FOLLOW YOU

THE LION OF THE PIANO

COMMODORE 33⅓ RPM LONG PLAY

most striking example of the dense parallel harmonies they created. The baritone saxophone has been less popular as a solo instrument, although the work of Gerry Mulligan was an outstanding feature of the WEST COAST school from the 1950s. In Duke Ellington's orchestra, Harry Carney showed how the baritone was capable of a considerable fluency and delicacy.

After the innovations of Charlie Parker (● p. 136) in the 1940s, alto and/or tenor saxophone soloists became indispensable members of BOP and HARD BOP ensembles. Many players became proficient on more than one member of the saxophone family: John Coltrane (● p. 160) and Wayne Shorter played both tenor and soprano, Parker's disciple Sonny Stitt played the alto, tenor and baritone, and the soul-jazz performer Grover Washington, Jr., plays soprano, alto and tenor. The ethereal sonorities that the soprano instrument can deliver have, since the work of Shorter with Weather Report (● p. 174), become one of the most striking recent developments in saxophone playing.

5 September Lester Young records his "Lester Leaps In" with Count Basie (● p. 86) for Vocalion, New York.

11 October Coleman Hawkins records "Body and Soul" for Victor in New York, setting a new standard of improvisational sophistication for the saxophone. At the end of the year, a *Down Beat* readers' poll declares Hawkins the best tenor saxophonist.

November Artie Shaw suddenly retires, just one year after scoring a tremendous success with his "Begin the Beguine."

22 December Ma Rainey dies, Rome, Georgia.

● The Royal Air Force big band, "The Squadronaires," is formed in Britain to provide entertainment for servicemen. ● Drummer Art Blakey (● p. 138) appears with the Fletcher Henderson orchestra, shortly before Henderson disbands the group and joins Benny Goodman's big band as staff arranger. ● The Blue Note record company is founded by German emigrés Alfred Lion and Francis Wolff in New York. ● In New York, Frederic Ramsey and Charles Smith publish their book *Jazzmen: the Story of Hot Jazz Told in the Lives of the Men who Created it*, which promotes a new awareness of jazz history and helps revive DIXIELAND and RAGTIME in the 1940s.

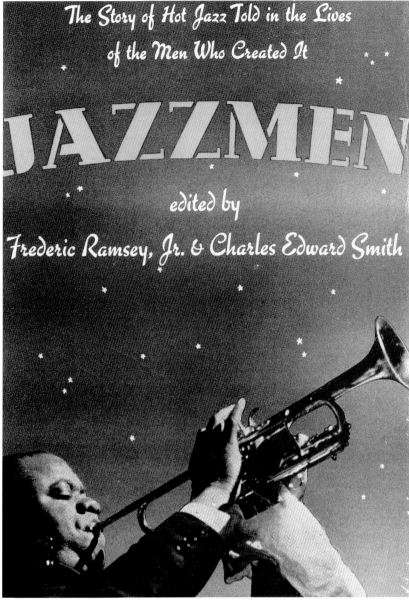

The Story of Hot Jazz Told in the Lives of the Men Who Created It

JAZZMEN

edited by

Frederic Ramsey, Jr. & Charles Edward Smith

Above The Royal Air Force "Squadronaires" performing at the Stoll Theatre in aid of the Musicians' Social and Benevolent Fund on 24 October 1943.

Left Tenor saxophonist Coleman Hawkins at the time of his hit "Body and Soul," which set a new standard of melodic lyricism.

Above Frederic Ramsey's and Charles Smith's book *Jazzmen* did much to foster public interest in the early history of jazz, which had been severely neglected until the late 1930s.

WORLD EVENTS

28 January Death of W. B. Yeats

28 March Spanish Civil War ends with Franco's capture of Madrid

March German army occupies Bohemia, Moravia, Slovakia and Lithuania

27 April Military conscription introduced in UK

30 April New York World's Fair

22 May Hitler and Mussolini agree their "Pact of Steel"

23 August USSR agrees a policy of non-aggression with Germany

1 September German troops invade Poland

3 September Britain and France declare war on Germany

17 December German battleship *Graf Spee* scuttled near Montevideo

- James Joyce finishes *Finnegans Wake*
- *Gone with the Wind* released

1940

Seeds of Revolution

A victim of its own success, big-band jazz becomes ever more diluted and commercialized. A new generation of performers evolve the be-bop style, which is ideally suited to smaller ensembles and destined to sweep the big bands aside.

January Lord Haw-Haw (the notorious wartime traitor, William Joyce) begins to make regular broadcasts of anti-British propaganda from Berlin. Jazz, which is now banned in Germany (● p. 81), is used in the broadcasts as bait to lure English-speaking listeners to tune in.

February Duke Ellington hires Ben Webster as tenor saxophonist. Ellington also records his masterpieces "Ko-Ko" (**6 March**), "Concerto for Cootie" (**15 March**) and "Cottontail" (**4 May**).

26 February Lionel Hampton's newly formed big band (● p. 70) records "Flying Home" in Chicago.

1 May Benny Goodman (● p. 84) performs Mozart's Clarinet Concerto under the direction of conductor Leopold Stokowski. In **July**, illness forces him to dissolve his band for three months.

Dropping Bombs

Although it seemed radical at the time, be-bop, or "bop," as it is usually abbreviated (the name was derived either from syllables commonly used in SCAT singing or from the off-beat accents of the drumming techniques characteristic of the style) was in many respects a logical development from the more conservative jazz of the early 1940s. Its most effective outlet was the small ensemble, which was more economically viable than the ailing big bands, but it retained the WALKING BASS, prominent use of RIFFS and some of the characteristic rhythmic patterns of the swing-band idiom.

Bop drummers such as Kenny Clarke and Max Roach adapted their accompaniments to create a high degree of unpredictability, injecting the music with powerful syncopated accents (especially on bass drum, a procedure known as "dropping bombs"). Latin rhythms also increasingly crept into the drumming, doubtless reflecting the influence of Dizzy Gillespie (● p. 114). Drummers now began to be promoted from merely keeping time to performing as full-fledged soloists. The FRONT-LINE instruments, principally trumpet and saxophone, improvised long and elaborate solos, typically framed by a UNISON statement of the HEAD theme (which was invariably pithy, highly syncopated and often fragmentary in nature). Solo melodic improvisations reached a peak of virtuosity, combining sheer speed with exciting dissonances, the notes sometimes passing by so rapidly that the traditional sense of SWUNG RHYTHM became an impossibility. As with the new drumming style, angularity and unpredictability were the order of the

day. Bop harmony, strikingly developed by Thelonious Monk, became a complex affair in which the TWELVE-BAR blues progression was supplemented with numerous additional and substitute chords.

In its formative years, the sometimes self-conscious complexity of bop served a clear extra-musical purpose: it discouraged a casual audience and allowed ensembles to exclude undesirable players, unversed as they were in the novel idiom, from participating in JAM SESSIONS. The motivation behind this aggressive stance (which often produced aggressive music) was largely political, since bop musicians wished to wrest the creative initiative back from the white performers who had scored such a considerable commercial success with big-band jazz – hence the boppers' preoccupation with IMPROVISATION and BLUES elements, both of which had been neglected by many popular white musicians. Players in the early bop groups emphasized their exclusivity by the wearing of

WORLD EVENTS

11 February USSR attacks Finland

9 April Germany invades Norway and Denmark

April–May Abortive British campaign in Norway

10 May Winston Churchill becomes Prime Minister, UK

15 May Holland falls to Germany

28 May Belgium falls to Germany

3 June Evacuation of British forces, Dunkirk

10 June Italy declares war on Britain and France

14 June Germans occupy Paris

June USSR invades Latvia, Estonia, Lithuania and Rumania

July Reciprocal bombing of English and German cities begins

Summer Battle of Britain

8 August Clarinetist Johnny Dodds dies, Chicago.

15 September *Down Beat* publishes a transcription of the first CHORUS from Coleman Hawkins' recording of "Body and Soul" (● p. 92).

November Cootie Williams leaves the Duke Ellington band, and is replaced by Ray Nance (trumpet/violin).

December Lester Young leaves Count Basie's band (● p. 86) to form his own small COMBO.

6 December Nat King Cole's trio (● p. 88) records "Gone with the Draft," a humorous song about conscription that soon becomes uncomfortably topical.

13 December Django Reinhardt (● p. 75) records "Nuages" in Nazi-occupied Paris.

● Under new management, Minton's Playhouse in New York becomes the venue for much exciting new jazz. Performers appearing here include pianist Thelonious Monk (● p. 154), trumpeter Dizzy Gillespie (● p. 219) and drummer Kenny Clarke.

● The American Society of Composers, Authors and Publishers issues a ban at the end of the year preventing the broadcast of ASCAP works (● p. 102). The boycott results in the growth of the rival organization Broadcast Music Incorporated (BMI).

Left Gillespie's *Ol'man Rebop* (with its early spelling of what would later become "be-bop") was an HMV LP reissue of ten sides cut in the period 1946–49.

Below, opposite Max Roach, resident drummer at Monroe's Uptown House, was a vital influence on the rhythmic sophistication of the emerging bop style.

Above Owner Teddy Hill (far right) poses outside his famous club with (l. to r.) house pianist Thelonious Monk and trumpeters Howard McGhee and Roy Eldridge.

goatees and berets (and, in Monk's case, a wide variety of silly hats) and by using "hip" language. In part, the eccentric image was intended to present bop practitioners as the new musical intellectuals, rather than purveyors of mindless dance music for the masses.

After Parker and Gillespie, the foremost advocates of the new style included saxophonist James Moody, who worked closely with Gillespie and helped take bop to Europe in the late 1940s. (Gillespie and Moody were renowned for the hilarious mock disagreements and brawls that they staged during performances.) Younger players, such as alto saxophonist Julian "Cannonball" Adderley, helped see bop safely through the changeable decades of the 1950s and 1960s, during which it sprang a stylistic offshoot – HARD BOP. Both idioms continued to be influential in the 1980s, largely due to the work of Art Blakey (● p. 138) and the historical awareness of Wynton Marsalis (● p. 196).

Minton's Playhouse

In 1938, saxophonist Henry Minton established a club on Harlem's West 118th Street in a rundown former dining room and engaged Thelonious Monk as house pianist in the following year. In 1940 the management of the venue passed to Teddy Hill, another saxophonist who had been in a band with James P. Johnson (● p. 46). Monk and resident drummer Kenny Clarke provided the backbone for a historic series of after-hours informal JAM SESSIONS with visiting instrumentalists that laid the foundations for the BE-BOP style, which soon spread throughout the jazz world and replace the outworn music of the big bands with an innovative and exciting musical language.

Two of the most prominent of the guest artists at Minton's were trumpeter Dizzy Gillespie (● p. 219), a former sideman of Teddy Hill's and pioneer of Latin jazz, and alto saxophonist Charlie Parker (● p. 136). In the early 1940s both men played in bands led by Earl Hines (● p. 124) and Billy Eckstine, in addition to pursuing their informal but vastly influential stylistic explorations at Minton's Playhouse (similar jam sessions were also conducted at Monroe's Uptown House on West 134th Street). Unfortunately, recording boycotts at the time meant that no bop numbers were recorded during its formative phase (● p. 103), although a few poor-quality private tape recordings of the seminal jam sessions afford a tantalizing glimpse of the atmosphere at Minton's and Monroe's, and reveal guitarist Charlie Christian (● p. 98) to have been a crucial influence on the development of the new style.

1941

Enter Bird

The be-bop revolution gathers pace with the emergence of alto saxophonist Charlie Parker, nicknamed "Bird" - one of the most prodigious and tragic figures in the history of jazz.

15 February In Los Angeles, Duke Ellington's band records Billy Strayhorn's "Take the 'A' Train," which is adopted as the band's new signature tune. Ellington's musical *Jump for Joy*, with a plot concerning the need for racial harmony, opens in Los Angeles this year.

April Trumpeter Roy Eldridge joins Gene Krupa's orchestra as featured soloist.

18 April Sidney Bechet (● p. 42) plays five different instruments to create one-man-band recordings of "The Sheik of Araby" and "Blues of Bechet," early examples of OVERDUBBING.

30 April Charlie Parker makes his first recording, "Swingmatism," with Jay McShann in Dallas. He begins to participate in the famous JAM SESSIONS at Minton's Playhouse (● p. 97), which result in the birth of the BE-BOP style.

May–June Pete Johnson and Albert Ammons continue their series of BOOGIE-WOOGIE recordings on the Blue Note label.

July End of ASCAP's broadcasting boycott (● p. 102).

10 July Jelly Roll Morton (● p. 45) dies, Los Angeles.

Above Charlie Christian's singular talent on electric guitar helped shape the distinctive style of bop melodic improvisations on all instruments.

Guitar

The short career of guitarist Charlie Christian, who died from tuberculosis in 1942, coincides with the instrument's evolution from its relatively insignificant role as a member of the RHYTHM SECTION to solo status. In traditional New Orleans jazz and dance bands of the late 1920s, the guitar had been only an occasional participant: the brighter, metallic sound of the BANJO was generally preferred to provide buoyant, strummed chords in the background, and perhaps contribute a spiky solo passage on occasion. The guitar gradually replaced the banjo in the early 1930s, partly because its comparatively delicate sonority made it a more appropriate partner to the double bass, which had quickly ousted the tuba as the supplier of the all-important bass line.

The dance bands of Whiteman and Goldkette (● p. 73) both employed Eddie Lang, the first guitarist to perform solos regularly. Lang died while having his tonsils removed in 1933, just as he was embarking on a promising career as Bing Crosby's accompanist. Lang also recorded duo sides in the late 1920s with violinist Joe Venuti (● p. 101), and it was a similar pairing of guitar and violin that was responsible for furthering the career of the most colorful early virtuoso of the guitar, Django Reinhardt (● p. 75). Both Lang and Reinhardt deserve credit for developing the instrument's melodic potential by learning how to improvise extended single lines, often at exceptionally fast speeds.

By the late 1930s, the first electrically amplified guitars had been launched in an attempt to combat the instrument's deficiencies: limited sustaining power and severely limited volume. Charlie Christian was the first guitarist to specialize in the amplified instrument, his expertise reaching a wider audience when he joined Benny Goodman's sextet in 1939. He went on to participate in the famous BE-BOP sessions at Minton's Playhouse, an experience that must have

WORLD EVENTS

February–March British army in Libya and Ethiopia

April German campaign in North Africa

6 April Germany invades Yugoslavia

22 June Germany invades Russia

12 July Anglo-Soviet agreement, Moscow

7 December Japanese bomb Pearl Harbor, Hawaii

8 December USA and UK declare war on Japan

11 December USA declares war on Germany and Italy

● Orson Welles directs and stars in *Citizen Kane*

Left The sheet music for Billy "Sweetpea" Strayhorn's perennially popular "Take the 'A' Train," recorded by Ellington in 1941.

Below Sidney Bechet indulging his taste for musical eccentricity at a one-man-band session in April 1941.

stimulated him to achieve new levels of fluency and rhythmic momentum through the seemingly endless melodic lines for which he was celebrated. Christian's innovations were taken still further by Wes Montgomery, whose career peaked in a series of recordings for Riverside around 1960. The impact of Montgomery's revolutionary left- and right-hand techniques continues to be felt in the melodic style of contemporary guitarists Pat Metheny (● p. 198) and Lee Ritenour.

The merging of jazz and rock styles in the late 1960s allowed the electric guitar and electric bass guitar to come into their own (● p. 127), but in the meantime the ACOUSTIC or semi-acoustic instrument continued to feature as a member of the rhythm section in both small and large ensembles. Fine rhythm-section playing was typified by Al Casey, stalwart guitarist of the popular COMBO Fats Waller and His Rhythm (● p. 105). The work of Barney Kessel and Herb Ellis in the 1950s showed how the instrument could move between accompanying and solo functions with ease, and both players successfully combined elements of the BOP and SWING styles.

In the 1960s, Joe Pass began to experiment with more complex textures, exploiting a phenomenal technical facility that enabled him to play melodic improvisations, supporting harmonies and independent bass lines simultaneously. His unaccompanied playing was, as a result, perhaps the richest and most satisfying of all guitarists, and his exquisite duets with Ella Fitzgerald showed him to be a consummate and sensitive accompanist.

7 August Billie Holiday (● p. 131) records "I Cover the Waterfront" in New York with Teddy Wilson and his orchestra.

October Radio stations in Nazi Germany begin broadcasting light dance music in an attempt to find a popular substitute for outlawed jazz.

● Stan Kenton (piano) founds his Artistry in Rhythm Orchestra in California.
● Charles Mingus (bass) plays with Louis Armstrong's band. (He is thrown out two years later for making anti-segregation remarks during a tour of southern states.)

99

1942
Industrial Action

The premature deaths of guitarist Charlie Christian and bass-player Jimmy Blanton deprive jazz of two blossoming talents in a year blighted by the onset of strike action by the major American musicians' union.

14 January Fats Waller (● p. 105) appears at Carnegie Hall (● p. 91), but his performance is adversely affected by alcohol.

2 March Charlie Christian dies at the age of twenty-five, New York.

April Twenty-three-year-old Leonard Bernstein appears as jazz pianist at the Fox and Hounds, Boston, with vocalist Eric Stein. The following year, Bernstein works on Tin Pan Alley (under the pseudonym Leonard Amber), producing published transcriptions of improvised solos by figures such as Coleman Hawkins and Earl Hines. ● The Nazi-controlled German Dance and Entertainment Orchestra begins work in Berlin.

11 June Trumpeter Bunk Johnson begins recording in New Orleans, marking the beginning of the revival of pre-SWING jazz styles.

30 July Duke Ellington's former bass player Jimmy Blanton dies of tuberculosis at the age of twenty-four, Los Angeles. This same summer, Barney Bigard (clarinet) and Ivie Anderson (vocals) leave the Duke Ellington Band.

Below, left The young Leonard Bernstein, who shot to international fame as a conductor in 1943 and later composed numerous works in a SYMPHONIC JAZZ idiom.

Below This 1942 radio broadcast in Hollywood, dedicated to US servicemen overseas, features (l. to r.): Dinah Shore, Spike Jones, Bob Burns, Count Basie, Lionel Hampton and Tommy Dorsey.

Left Ray Nance, who played both trumpet and violin in Duke Ellington's band for more than two decades.

Violin

Like the BANJO, the violin had been a popular instrument with slave musicians in the nineteenth century and was therefore a prominent participant in MINSTREL-SHOW ensembles. Violins (and sometimes cellos) featured in ragtime bands such as that led by James Reese Europe (● p. 41), and became staple members of white dance bands in the 1920s. The presence of violins is one superficial reason why the music of Paul Whiteman (● p. 73) sounds less jazzy than that of contemporaneous black bands, which tended to avoid the instrument.

Joe Venuti, who played with both Whiteman and Jean Goldkette, was one of the first violinists to achieve fame as a jazz soloist. On the other side of the Atlantic, Stephane Grappelli nurtured the instrument's capability for generating suave and sophisticated melodies. Both violinists played in celebrated duos alongside equally influential guitarists (● p. 98). Ray Nance's resourceful exploration of the violin's sonorous potential was a distinctive ingredient in Duke Ellington's orchestra from 1940 onward. The most influential violinist in recent years has been the classically trained French player Jean-Luc Ponty, who brought the instrument up to date by working with electronic techniques compatible with the demands of jazz-rock FUSION. More controversial has been the attempt of saxophonist Ornette Coleman (● p. 150) to originate a bizarre violin technique to supplement his equally self-taught trumpet playing.

WORLD EVENTS

January Japanese campaigns in East Indies, Malaya and Burma

3 June Battle of Midway, Pacific Ocean

25 June "Thousand Bomber" attack on Bremen, Germany

17 August US bombs Germany

13 September Germans attack Stalingrad, USSR

23 October Battle of El Alamein

● Humphrey Bogart and Ingrid Bergman star in *Casablanca*

1 August James Caesar Petrillo's American Federation of Musicians urges its members not to participate in studio recordings for record companies that fail to pay royalties to performers. Industrial action continues until the end of 1944, but V-discs (● p. 109), manufactured for supply to those on active service overseas, are exempted.

October Glenn Miller (● p. 107) dissolves his band and enlists as a captain in the US Army Air Force, where he forms a new service band.

Below Glenn Miller in his US Army Air Force uniform. Both Miller and clarinetist Artie Shaw led bands for the US services in the war, Shaw's Navy band performing throughout the Pacific theater in 1943 and Miller's visiting Europe in 1944.

Above James Caesar Petrillo (left), pictured here with Canadian musicians' union boss Walter C. Murdoch at a New York opera gala in October 1954.

Strike up the Ban

The gradual collapse of big-band jazz in the 1940s was accelerated by several factors, not least the general reaction against extravagance that affected all the arts after the calamaties of World War II. The war had also deprived many bands of their leading players through conscription into the armed forces, making it virtually impossible to maintain consistency of personnel. As if the severe wartime shortage of the shellac used in the manufacture of recordings were not problem enough, a series of disastrous strikes by several musicians' unions quickly struck the final nail in the coffin of the big bands.

The most powerful performing-rights organization in the USA during the 1930s was the American Society of Composers, Authors and Publishers (ASCAP), which collected and distributed royalties earned by its members. Increasing dissent over

October Eighteen-year-old singer Sarah Vaughan (● p. 123) wins a talent competition at Harlem's Apollo Theater with her rendition of "Body and Soul."

December Charlie Parker (● p. 136) joins Earl Hines's band, alongside Dizzy Gillespie (● p. 219).

● Eddie Condon's mixed-race band appears in a CBS television program. ● *Billboard* magazine publishes the first black record chart under the title "Harlem Hit Parade."

Above One of several Royal Air Force bands performs for the benefit of British servicemen in North Africa, c. 1942.

royalties payable on radio transmissions led to the formation of the rival Broadcast Music Inc. (BMI) and the decision by ASCAP to boycott radio broadcasts in 1940. Composers managed by ASCAP, including Duke Ellington, could not broadcast their own music until the dispute was resolved, and many resorted to broadcasting non-copyright tunes until the boycott ceased when a settlement was agreed in the summer of 1941.

Next came more prolonged industrial action against recording companies instigated by the American Federation of Musicians (AFM). Recordings were technically not licensed for broadcast in the 1930s, but the restriction had been widely ignored. In spite of its members' assertions that their livelihood had actually been improved by the enormous publicity brought by exposure on the airwaves, the AFM's

pugnacious leader James Caesar Petrillo insisted on strike action in August 1942. Record companies began to re-issue recordings made prior to the strike, but went on to reach agreements with the AFM by the end of 1944. In the meantime, vocalists such as Frank Sinatra and Bing Crosby (who were exempted from strike action) enjoyed a rise to prominence that would culminate in the modern phenomenon of the pop superstar. A renewed recording ban of shorter duration was enforced by the AFM in 1948.

In artistic terms, the most regrettable outcome of the recording bans was the fact that the formative process of the exciting new BE-BOP style in the early 1940s was not captured on disc. Charlie Parker, for example, did not begin recording in earnest until 1944, and most bop musicians were initially signed up by smaller independent labels such as Savoy and Dial.

1943

Black, Brown and Beige

Duke Ellington embarks on an ambitious series of annual concerts featuring extended symphonic-jazz scores. Fats Waller dies, and Art Tatum inherits his mantle as leading pianist.

Above HMV's long-play reissue of recorded extracts from Duke Ellington's *Black, Brown and Beige*, coupled with his later *Perfume Suite* (1963).

Above, right Ellington in 1943, surrounded by some of his staunchest sidemen (l. to r.): Nance, Stewart, Nanton, Carney, Hodges and Greer.

WORLD EVENTS

23 January British capture Tripoli

31 January Germans surrender at Stalingrad

28 March Death of Sergey Rachmaninov

12 May Germans surrender in Tunisia

16 May "Dambusters" raid by the RAF

21 June Michael Tippett imprisoned for conscientious objection, UK

26 July Mussolini resigns after Allied invasion of Sicily

3 September Allies land on mainland Italy

13 October Italy turns against Germany

23 January Duke Ellington's fifty-seven-minute work *Black, Brown and Beige* receives its first performance at Carnegie Hall (● p. 91), New York, and the proceeds are donated to the Russian war-relief fund. It meets with a mixed critical reception, but marks the start of Ellington's annual appearances at this prestigious venue (which cease after 1950). On 11 December the band, its line-up now expanded to include four trumpets, presents another large-scale work, *New World a-comin'*, at Carnegie Hall.

April Sarah Vaughan (● p. 123) joins Earl Hines's band as second pianist and singer, and soon after begins work with Billy Eckstine.

May Gene Krupa serves a short jail sentence for employing a minor in his band, but after his release he plays again with Benny Goodman (● p. 84) in **September**.

August Ben Webster quits Duke Ellington.

15 December Fats Waller dies during a rail journey to New York: his body is discovered at Kansas City station. Three days later, his former mentor James P. Johnson records "Blues for Fats."

29 December Singer Dinah Washington, currently with Lionel Hampton's band, records popular BLUES numbers in New York.

● Art Tatum (● p. 125) establishes a piano trio with Tiny Grimes (guitar) and Slam Stewart (bass), following the pioneering example of Nat King Cole. ● Glenn Miller (● p. 107) publishes a text-book guide to arranging music for big bands. ● Django Reinhardt (● p. 75), in panic at the news that the Nazis are sending gypsies to the gas chamber, attempts to reach Switzerland from occupied France. Stopped at the border, he is sent back without punishment by a German officer who is an admirer of jazz. ● In Germany, the Luftwaffe fits some of its Heinkel, Junkers and Messerschmitt fighter-bombers with a device nicknamed *Schräge Musik* ("slanting music," a slang term for the banned HOT jazz): two machine guns located on top of the aircraft, to be used in oblique attacks from beneath enemy bombers.

Fats Waller's death in December 1943, accelerated by his habitual over-indulgence, was a worldly exit fully in keeping with his flamboyant lifestyle. His clowning and infectious capers disguised a top-ranking musical genius whose importance lay in two distinct areas: the development of the STRIDE style of piano playing to its limits of virtuosity, and the promotion of jazz as a medium for refined popular entertainment.

The Harmful Little Armful

"My father [Fats Waller] had a unique system to reward inventiveness in improvisation.
Pop kept two bottles of gin on a table during the rehearsals. One bottle was for himself . . .
The other bottle was the 'encourager,' as he called it. When one of the band excelled in an improvisational section, Dad would stop the rehearsal, pour him a healthy shot of gin, and the two of them would toast each other."

Maurice Waller

Waller's early keyboard training was as a church organist, an experience that enabled him as a teenager to gain employment playing in cinemas and theaters in New York. (In later life he shocked the musical establishment by playing jazz on the organ of Notre Dame cathedral in Paris.) His skills as a pianist were fostered by James P. Johnson (● p. 46), whose piano concerto *Yamekraw* Waller performed at Carnegie Hall in 1928. Waller's astonishing keyboard facility and compositional fluency resulted in a steady succession of fine works for solo piano characterized by a combination of dazzling virtuosity and harmonic ingenuity, including *Smashing Thirds*, *Alligator Crawl* and *Handful of Keys*. Among his admirers was Al Capone, who allegedly had Waller kidnapped at gunpoint in Chicago in the mid-1920s, just to get him to play at the gangster's birthday party.

Waller's incomparable aptitude for songwriting was developed in collaboration with lyricist Andy Razaf, with whom he wrote numerous hits. Many of these began life in stage shows, including "Ain't Misbehavin'" – popularized by the vocal talents of Louis Armstrong (● p. 56), on whose gravelly tone Waller partly modelled his own singing voice. The peak of Waller's achievements came after 1934 in a series of recordings on the Victor label made with a versatile COMBO billed as "Fats Waller and His Rhythm." In this context he found full expression for his remarkable comic talents, interpreting his own songs with infectious wit and a strong dose of satire. Among the most celebrated numbers in his vast repertoire was "Honeysuckle Rose," which, along with many other Waller songs, became an indispensable STANDARD for later jazz musicians, not only in its original form, but as a harmonic skeleton on which other compositions were based.

As a keyboard technician, Waller formed an essential link between the first generation of STRIDE performers and the innovative work of later pianists such as Art Tatum (● p. 125) and Thelonious Monk (● p. 154).

Left Fats Waller: an infectiously high-spirited entertainer endowed with a prodigious keyboard technique.

1944

All-American All Stars

Pianist Thelonious Monk emerges as a composer of striking originality, as both be-bop and swing idioms are pursued side by side. The big-band movement suffers a major loss when Glenn Miller is declared missing, presumed dead.

18 January *Esquire* magazine holds an All-American All-Stars concert at the Metropolitan Opera House, New York, featuring Roy Eldridge, Art Tatum (● p. 125), Coleman Hawkins, Louis Armstrong (● p. 56), Jack Teagarden, Lionel Hampton (● p. 70), Barney Bigard and Billie Holiday (● p. 131).

April Trombonist Juan Tizol quits Duke Ellington to play with the Harry James orchestra.

July Producer Norman Granz initiates the series "Jazz at the Philharmonic" with concerts at the Los Angeles Philharmonic Auditorium. These popular touring JAM SESSIONS last until 1967.

22 August Trumpeter Cootie Williams makes the first recording of Thelonious Monk's "'Round about Midnight." Monk makes his first recordings, with the Coleman Hawkins Quartet, on **19 October**.

September Charlie Parker (● p. 136) leaves Billy Eckstine's band, where he has been playing alongside Dizzy Gillespie (● p. 219) since April. ● Eighteen-year-old Miles Davis (● p. 216) arrives in New York to attend the Juilliard School of Music. Inspired by Billy Eckstine's band (which he has recently heard at the Riviera Club in St. Louis), he soon falls in with Parker and Gillespie.

30 September Lester Young is drafted into the US Army, in the same year he is voted most popular tenor saxophonist by *Down Beat* and appears in the short film *Jammin' the Blues*.

November RCA Victor and Columbia finally agree to the demands of the American Federation of Musicians (● p. 103) and the recording ban is lifted.

November–December Pianist Erroll Garner records prolifically in New York, where he occasionally stands in for Art Tatum at the Three Deuces club.

December Duke Ellington (● p. 62) records extracts from his *Black, Brown and Beige* (● p. 104) for RCA.

15 December Glenn Miller, who has become a major in the US Army Air Force, is presumed dead after his aircraft disappears during a flight from London to liberated Paris.

● Pianist Oscar Peterson forms a piano trio along the lines of the famous examples led by his keyboard idols, Nat King Cole and Art Tatum (● p. 125). Cole's trio is voted Best Small COMBO of the year by *Down Beat*, an achievement they repeat in each of the next three years. They also win the similar *Metronome* poll annually from 1945 to 1948.

Left Billie Holiday and Art Tatum at the *Esquire* concert held at New York's Metropolitan Opera House in January 1944.

The Jazz Impresario: Norman Granz

Norman Granz's jazz empire began to take shape in 1944 with the mounting of his highly successful JAM SESSIONS at Los Angeles' Philharmonic Auditorium in aid of charity. Two years later the venue lent its name to Granz's roadshow, "Jazz at the Philharmonic," which took Oscar Peterson (● p. 162), Ella Fitzgerald (● p. 195), Charlie Parker (● p. 136), Dizzy Gillespie (● p. 219) and many other leading figures on worldwide tours. These ultimately resulted in some of the best recordings of live jazz ever issued.

Above Victory Boogie Woogie, one of the last paintings by Dutch abstract artist Piet Mondrian (1872–1944).

Glenn Miller: Wartime Serenade

Below Captain Glenn Miller consults with Marjorie Ochs in June 1943 about the radio show "I Sustain the Wings," mounted at Yale by the US Army Air Force's Technical Command.

Trombonist Glenn Miller, the name most inextricably associated with the SWING music of the war years, has remained one of the hardest jazz talents to assess. The popular image of the uniformed bandleader taking his music across the Atlantic to entertain his nation's servicemen must be seen in the wider context of a popularity that propelled his band into an enviable and longstanding position at the top of the US record charts. This success was maintained throughout the war, but sometimes at the expense of musical quality. Several commentators have argued, with reason, that Miller's brand of big-band jazz could be stilted, often failed to swing, and marked the parting of the ways between true jazz and the broader appeal of nascent pop music. Others have admired his cultivation of an immediately recognizable "sound world," based on a distinctive consistency of orchestration. The latter included his trademark techniques of doubling a clarinet melody with massed saxophones an octave lower, and employing four trombones for sonorous chordal backgrounds.

After working as a sideman for the Dorsey brothers in the mid-1930s, it took Miller several years to establish himself as a leader. In 1939 his second band appeared at New York's Glen Island Casino, where regular broadcasts secured him many young and enthusiastic fans. The same year brought two hit recordings, "In the Mood" and "Moonlight Serenade," the latter stylishly demonstrating the lengths to which the parallel harmonies of the swing style could be taken. Movie appearances by the band in 1941–42 significantly augmented their popular following.

Miller's career in the US Army Air Force began in 1942, when he formed a new band to entertain troops both at home and (in 1944) abroad. The band's visit to Britain, where they broadcast for the BBC, was rapturously received and did much to boost Allied morale. It was in December 1944, while flying ahead of his band to Paris, where they were scheduled to play, that his aircraft was lost without trace in bad weather.

● ● ● ● ● ● ● ● ● ● ● ● ●

Granz founded his record label Clef in 1946, which became incorporated into a bigger company, Verve, ten years later. A new label, named Pablo after the painter Picasso and adopting a design by the artist as its logo (● illustration, p. 189), was founded by Granz in 1973. It continued to promote the work of Jazz at the Philharmonic stars, and spawned a related label, Pablo Live, set up in 1977 to preserve live JAM SESSIONS (many recorded at the tenth Montreux Festival held in Switzerland in that same year), which remained Granz's speciality.

WORLD EVENTS

27 January End of Leningrad siege

April-May Soviet advances in Rumania and the Crimea

6 June Allied landings on Normandy beaches ("D-Day")

20 July Unsuccessful assassination attempt on Hitler

25 August Liberation of Paris

5 September Liberation of Brussels

11 September US Army crosses German border

16 December Ardennes campaign ("Battle of the Bulge")

1945

Restless Peace

Jazz becomes polarized between the continuing be-bop style, which receives new blood in the music of the young Miles Davis, and the conservative idiom championed by the revivalist movement.

Below At New York's Town Hall on 16 May 1945, the new bop style was celebrated by Charlie Parker and Dizzy Gillespie, accompanied by Curly Russell (bass) and Harold "Doc" West (drums).

9 January Dizzy Gillespie (● p. 219) records "Be-bop" in New York.

17 January Sidney Bechet (● p. 42) returns to New Orleans for the first time in twenty-five years and plays with Louis Armstrong (● p. 56) at the Municipal Auditorium.

1 February Lester Young, still in the US Army, is arrested for possession of marijuana and court-martialed. He spends the next ten months in detention and is then discharged.

24 July Duke Ellington (● p. 183) records his *Perfume Suite* (● illustration, p. 104), performed this year at Carnegie Hall.

September Bunk Johnson performs in New York during the ongoing revival of New Orleans jazz.

October Charlie Parker (● p. 136) hires nineteen-year-old trumpeter Miles Davis (● p. 216) to replace Dizzy Gillespie at the Three Deuces on 52nd Street, New York. Davis promptly abandons his studies at the Juilliard School to record with Parker's Ree Boppers.

26 November Charlie Parker records "Now's the Time" for Savoy in New York in his first session as leader: his ensemble includes Dizzy Gillespie (on piano, under the pseudonym "Hen Gates"), Miles Davis and Max Roach (drums). In December he plays with Gillespie in Los Angeles, and their quintet becomes the leading light of BE-BOP.

31 December Pianist Mary Lou Williams gives the first performance of her *Zodiac Suite* at New York's Town Hall.

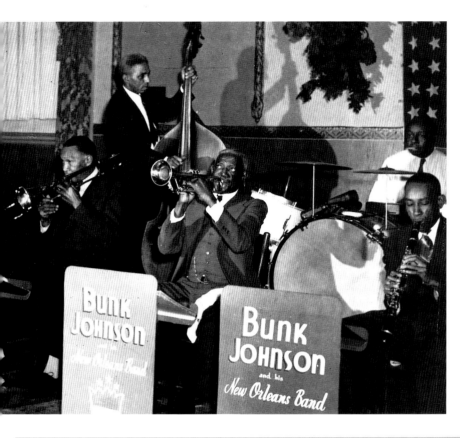

WORLD EVENTS

17 January Warsaw falls to USSR

13 February Budapest falls to USSR

7 March Cologne falls to Allies

12 April Death of President Roosevelt, USA

28 April Mussolini lynched

30 April Hitler commits suicide

2 May Berlin captured by Russian troops

7 May Total surrender of German forces

6 and 9 August US atomic bombs dropped on Hiroshima and Nagasaki

14 August Japan surrenders

15 September Composer Anton Webern accidentally shot dead by US military policeman, Austria

26 September Death of Béla Bartók

24 October United Nations founded

● Benjamin Britten's opera *Peter Grimes*

Left Members of Bunk Johnson's revivalist band performing at New York's Stuyvesant Casino in 1945.

Operation V-disc

The industrial action against record companies enforced by the American Federation of Musicians in 1942–4 (● p. 103) did not extend to recordings made as part of the war effort. Between October 1943 and 1949, more than nine hundred recordings were issued in the "V-disc" series (the "V" denoting "Victory"), exclusively for distribution to personnel of the US Army, Navy, Marine Corps and Coast Guard. The total number of copies circulated has been estimated at eight million. The AFM had only allowed the project to proceed on the strict understanding that no discs would be made commercially available, and in compliance with this demand Major Howard C. Bronson was appointed to oversee the destruction of the master discs after the war. Copies of the mass-produced discs survived in private ownership, however, and have been re-issued in CD compilations so that these historic musical documents might enjoy a renewed circulation.

The V-disc operation was managed by a team of experts who had formerly worked for major record companies and were thus able to source and re-issue recordings made before the imposition of the AFM ban. They also organized ad hoc groups of performers to make new recordings. Material circulated on V-discs included the legendary *Esquire* jazz performances at New York's Metropolitan Opera House in 1944 (● p. 106), for which Lionel Hampton's "Flying Home" was re-titled "Flying on a V-disc." Recordings of broadcasts were also issued, including radio interviews with famous musicians such as Louis Armstrong.

Above Although variable in musical quality, wartime V-discs are unique survivors from a period when all other new recordings of jazz were boycotted by industrial action.

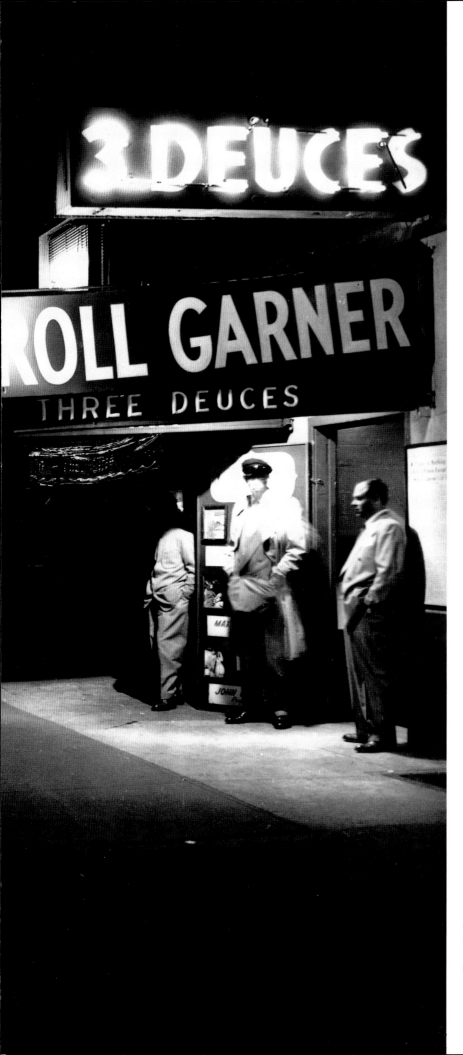

1946-58
Style and Idea

Jazz styles begin to diverge and co-exist: bop intensifies into hard bop, "cool" jazz is developed as its refreshing antidote, Latin jazz becomes increasingly popular and the "third stream" continues the synthetic ideal of symphonic jazz.

The Three Deuces club on New York's 52nd Street in the late 1940s, when "The Street" hosted the finest jazz performances in the world. Founded in 1937, the Three Deuces (like many neighboring establishments) became a strip joint in the early 1950s.

1946-47

The Latin Tinge

Dizzy Gillespie breaks new ground in the development of Afro-Latin and Afro-Cuban jazz. Stravinsky and Bernstein revitalize symphonic jazz, ragtime is revived, and musicians increasingly succumb to hard drugs.

1946

28 January Charlie Parker and Dizzy Gillespie play for Norman Granz's "Jazz at the Philharmonic" in Los Angeles. In this same month, Miles Davis plays with Parker at the Finale Club in Little Tokyo, Los Angeles.

31 January Django Reinhardt and Stephane Grappelli (● p. 75) are reunited after their wartime separation and record "Echoes of France" in London.

13 February The first concert performance of Leonard Bernstein's *Three Dance Episodes* (from his musical *On the Town*) takes place in San Francisco. The piece becomes popular as one of the jazziest of jazz-influenced orchestral scores.

16 February Billie Holiday's concert at New York's Town Hall is promoted as a "jazz *Lieder*" event in an attempt to acquire for jazz the status of concert music, the venue marking a significant contrast to the night-club scene.

25 March First performance of Igor Stravinsky's *Ebony Concerto*, a "jazz concerto grosso" written for Woody Herman's First Herd, at Carnegie Hall.

Drugs

WORLD EVENTS

1946

1 February Hungary becomes Republic

24 February President Perón assumes power, Argentina

2 June Italy becomes Republic

25 July US nuclear tests on Bikini Atoll

August Mao Tse-Tung revives Chinese Civil War

14 November Death of Manuel de Falla

15 November Indonesia gains independence from Holland

● Alfred Hitchcock's movie *Notorious*

1947

February–March Crisis in Palestine

20 July Dutch fight Indonesians in Java

15 August India and Pakistan gain independence from Britain

31 August Communists assume power, Hungary

● Arnold Schoenberg composes *A Survivor from Warsaw*
● Tennessee Williams' play *A Streetcar Named Desire*

Above A stunned Stan Getz peers from a police car in Seattle after attempting to steal narcotics from a drugstore in 1954 ("It's the craziest thing I've done," Getz later commented). Having fled from the scene of his crime empty-handed, he was apprehended after he telephoned the shop assistant to apologize for his folly.

Far right Musical and spiritual soulmates Billie Holiday and Lester Young unwind at Birdland in the late 1940s. Both their careers were affected by drug habits.

Billie Holiday's narcotics conviction in 1947 was but the tip of a depressing iceberg. Until the rock scene became a major forum for hard drugs in the 1960s, it was jazz that was inevitably associated with substance abuse.

A first resort for musicians had been illicit alcohol during Prohibition, a time when both cocaine and marijuana were also common. Military discipline during World War II was responsible for bringing some musicians' drug habits out into the open, as in the case of conscripted saxophonist Lester Young, who was busted for smoking marijuana (● p. 108). By the time of Charlie Parker's notorious heroin-induced breakdown in the late 1940s, hard drugs had become widely available at very low prices, and their consumption was almost universal among musicians. Some naively thought that if they consumed enough of the stuff, they would end up playing like Parker.

Above Bop pianist Bud Powell, pictured here in 1953, was one of several prominent musicians to receive electric shock treatment for personal problems.

28 March Miles Davis records with Charlie Parker's septet for Dial Records in Los Angeles; takes include "Ornithology" and "Night in Tunisia." Davis then rejoins Billy Eckstine's band.

20 July Trombonist Joe "Tricky Sam" Nanton dies, San Francisco.

29 July Charlie Parker is arrested on a (drug-related) arson charge after igniting his hotel bed and walking naked on the streets of Los Angeles. He is committed to Camarillo State Hospital for six months, where he receives electric-shock treatment.

● Arranger Don Redman tours Europe with a band that includes saxophonist Don Byas. ● Dizzy Gillespie forms a big band including John Lewis (future founder of the Modern Jazz Quartet) on piano and Kenny Clarke on drums. ● Pianist Luckey Roberts records RAGTIME numbers for Circle Records. Ragtime is on the verge of a major revival (● p. 116). ● Bud Powell, a leading keyboard exponent of the BE-BOP style, is sent by his mother to the Bellevue Hospital in New York, where he receives electric-shock treatment for mental instability. ● Norman Granz founds the Clef record label, which is later incorporated into Verve Records (● p. 106).

Many, including Billie Holiday (● p. 131), spent a high proportion of their earnings on heroin. Brushes with the law were frequent: Holiday was (with ridiculous insensitivity) arrested again on her hospital deathbed, and COOL trumpeter Chet Baker (● p. 210) served time in an Italian prison in 1960. Both Holiday and Thelonious Monk (● p. 154) lost their New York cabaret cards as a result of drug offenses, which meant they were barred from performing in nightclubs. Holiday's answer was to perform in prestigious venues such as New York's Carnegie Hall and Town Hall, eloquently demonstrating the hypocrisy of the system. (Cabaret cards were eventually abolished in 1967.)

Later musicians who battled against heroin addiction, with varying degrees of success, included John Coltrane and Miles Davis. A full list of players whose deaths were accelerated by their habit would be long and dispiriting, but a glance through the Biographical Index (● pp. 226-38) will graphically illustrate the seriously limited life-expectancy of jazz musicians whose careers peaked in the two decades following the BOP revolution.

> "Heroin was a major figure in the bop movement, as significant in shaping the music as Parker himself, because one after another it took away most of the leading figures."

James Lincoln Collier, *The Making of Jazz*, 1978

Left *Begin the Beguine*, painted in 1946 by German artist Max Beckmann (1884–1950), took its title from the hit version of Cole Porter's song recorded by Artie Shaw and his band in 1938.

Right The "Mambo King," Machito (far right), plays maracas alongside other members of his Afro-Latin band.

Jelly Roll Morton identified what he termed the "Latin tinge" in jazz during its very earliest years, when simple rhythmic characteristics of Latin American music were adopted in surprising contexts such as W. C. Handy's *St. Louis Blues* (published in 1914). It was the growing vogue for Latin American dances in the 1930s, however, that resulted in a more prominent presence of Latin rhythms and harmonies in jazz. Elements from Cuban music were promoted in a big-band context by "Machito" (Raúl Grillo), who formed an Afro-Latin band in New York in 1941.

Dizzy Gillespie's strong interest in the music during the same period was reflected in the large number of Latin-influenced BE-BOP compositions sporting Latin characteristics, including "Night in Tunisia" and "My Little Suede Shoes." In 1947, having experienced Afro-Cuban music at first hand (thanks to his friendship with Machito's onetime musical director, Mario Bauza), Gillespie formed his own Latinesque big band and co-composed "Manteca" with Chano Pozo, a conga player he had imported into his RHYTHM SECTION. The same year Gillespie produced "Cubana Be/Cubana Bop," its title suggesting the synthesis of bop and Latin idioms then taking place.

Also active in the development of big-band Latin jazz was the WEST COAST leader Stan Kenton, whose hit track "The Peanut Vendor" (recorded in December 1947) featured an authentic three-man Latin percussion team that featured Machito on maracas. The piece became popular once again in the UK during the 1970s after its over-exposure in a television advertising campaign for salted peanuts.

In the 1960s and 1970s, Brazilian music stole the initiative from Cuba and began to make a strong impact on jazz, first with the bossa nova craze – imported by jazz musicians of the stature of saxophonist Stan Getz (● p. 153) – and then with the effective adaptation of Brazilian vocal and percussion techniques as part of the burgeoning jazz-rock scene of the 1970s and 1980s.

Jazz Latin Style

1947

16 January Mississippi riverboat performer Fate Marable dies, St. Louis.

8 February Louis Armstrong (● p. 56) appears at Carnegie Hall (● p. 91) with Billie Holiday (● p. 131).

March Miles Davis records with Illinois Jacquet's band, New York.

8 May Miles Davis begins a series of recordings with Charlie Parker, with whom he is playing at the Three Deuces on 52nd Street, New York.

17 May Louis Armstrong introduces his new All Stars group at Town Hall, New York.

27 May Billie Holiday is convicted for possession of heroin in Philadelphia and sentenced to be detained for one year and one day in the Federal Reformatory for Women at Alderson, West Virginia. She receives time off for good behavior and is released on 16 March 1948.

14 August Miles Davis makes his first recordings as leader. His "All Stars" COMBO includes Charlie Parker, John Lewis (piano) and Max Roach (drums).

29 September Ella Fitzgerald (● p. 195) and Dizzy Gillespie appear in a sell-out concert at Carnegie Hall. The program includes Gillespie's "Cubana Be/Cubana Bop," an example of his flair for Afro-Cuban jazz; he records it in **December**, along with "Manteca."

October–November Thelonious Monk (● p. 154) records several of his compositions in New York, including "In Walked Bud" and "'Round About Midnight."

Below, left RCA Victor's LP reissue of popular tracks recorded by Louis Armstrong in the 1930s and 1940s.

Below, right Thelonious Monk made his recording début for Blue Note in the autumn of 1947.

Thelonious Monk: 'Round Midnight

The premier recording of Monk's "'Round Midnight" – or, to give it its full title, "'Round about Midnight" – was made by trumpeter Cootie Williams in August 1944, some three years before the BOP pianist entered the studio to record the composition for himself. With vibraphonist Milt Jackson, Dizzy Gillespie recorded a version for septet in Hollywood on 7 February 1946, also before Monk.

Not surprisingly, Monk's own interpretation, preserved in a New York studio on 21 November 1947 with a quintet including drummer Art Blakey, is far more innovative than its predecessors. Subtle allusions to the dreamy theme are introduced by alto saxophone, piano and trumpet in laid-back CALL-AND-RESPONSE before a brief unaccompanied bass link ushers in the full melody. Monk's typically spiky and angular piano technique here contrasts effectively with the sustained backing supplied by the horns, while complex added-note harmonies and sharp off-beat dissonances alternate with filigree cascades up and down the keyboard, many based on the whole-tone scale Monk borrowed from Debussy. Particularly expressive after so much chromaticism is the unexpected shift to a bright major chord in the final cadence of each thematic statement. Also striking is Monk's occasional playing of adjacent notes simultaneously to create stark "wrong note" effects.

"'Round Midnight" quickly became a favored standard, and with Gillespie's "Night in Tunisia" continues to be celebrated as one of the most harmonically inventive bop compositions. Notable among later interpretations are Bill Evans's multi–layered overdubbed version in *Conversations with Myself* (1963).

Reviving Ragtime

As the thirties came to a close, interest in the old genres of RAGTIME and New Orleans jazz blossomed. With the onset of the radical innovations of BE-BOP in the early 1940s (● p. 96), many conservative listeners and performers began to cultivate an exclusive interest in earlier, historic styles (and were uncharitably dubbed "moldy figs" by more progressive thinkers). Jelly Roll Morton's 1938 retrospective (● p. 90) was soon followed by the foundation of the Blue Note label in 1939, which stimulated Sidney Bechet to make new recordings in the traditional New Orleans style and prompted a popular revival of the BOOGIE-WOOGIE piano music that had been more or less dormant for a decade.

Trumpeter Bunk Johnson, who had known the mythical Buddy Bolden (● p. 25), was brought out of retirement in 1942 to become the leading practitioner of the revivalist movement. Trombonist Kid Ory (● p. 60) was re-discovered in the following year and participated in a series of radio broadcasts hosted by Orson Welles. In 1947, musicians schooled in both bop and traditional idioms competed against one another in a high-profile radio broadcast (● p. 117).

During this same period, books devoted to the historic figures of early jazz appeared. Titles included Frederic Ramsey's and Charles Smith's *Jazzmen* (1939), W. C. Handy's autobiography (1941), Rudi Blesh's and Harriet Janis's *They All Played Ragtime* (1950) and Alan Lomax's *Mister Jelly Roll* (1950).

Above Bunk Johnson (left) performs with famous blues singer Huddie "Leadbelly" Ledbetter, a convicted murderer who was pardoned and released from his Louisiana prison when he sang for the governor.

October–December Charlie Parker records numerous tracks for the Dial and Savoy labels in New York and Detroit.

● Woody Herman, Meade Lux Lewis, Louis Armstrong and Billie Holiday appear in the movie *New Orleans*. ● The Atlantic label is founded by the Turkish entrepreneur Ahmet Ertegun in New York. From 1955, he runs the company with his brother, Nesuhi Ertegun. ● Duke Ellington records as prolifically as ever, and continues his annual series of large-scale works at Carnegie Hall with the premiere of his new *Liberian Suite*. *The Deep South Suite* was heard at the venue in 1946; *The Tattooed Bride* follows in 1948. ● Coleman Hawkins bases his unaccompanied "Picasso" on "Body and Soul" (● p. 92). ● Drummer Art Blakey founds an octet called Jazz Messengers. ● Radio listeners in New York are treated to a contest between the new BE-BOP and old TRAD styles, promoted by Barry Ulanov and Rudi Blesh respectively. Performers illustrating the bop idiom include Charlie Parker and Dizzy Gillespie.

Left Woody Herman, whose virtuoso band inspired Igor Stravinsky to compose his *Ebony Concerto* in 1945.

Below Jazzing in the movies: Billie Holiday and Louis Armstrong in the 1947 film *New Orleans*.

1948

The First Jazz Festival

French jazz aficionados mount the first major festival in Nice. Bop earns itself an enthusiastic European following, while Miles Davis's nonet lays the foundation for new stylistic directions in America.

February Dizzy Gillespie (● p. 219) brings BE-BOP to Europe, appearing at the Nice Jazz Festival. Other participants include Louis Armstrong's All Stars, which Earl Hines (● p. 124) joins this year. Organized by Hugues Panassié and the Hot Club de France, the Nice event is the first international jazz festival.

March Billie Holiday sings two concerts at Carnegie Hall, and breaks their box-office records on both occasions.

21 June Columbia introduces microgroove discs made from vinyl, the first "long-playing" records to be marketed.

September Miles Davis (● p. 216) forms a nonet which appears for two weeks at The Royal Roost, Broadway, as a temporary replacement for Count Basie's band (● p. 86).

Autumn Benny Goodman (● p. 84) plays with his newly formed sextet and septet, in which he is reunited with pianist Teddy Wilson.

November Ben Webster rejoins Duke Ellington's orchestra.

December Miles Davis quits Charlie Parker and plays at New York's Onyx Club on 52nd Street. He has grown increasingly disillusioned with Parker, who earlier this

Drums

Jazz drumming originated as a unique synthesis of rhythmic patterns borrowed from the military march and from African tribal drumming, the greater complexity of the latter coming increasingly to the fore as the music developed. Primitive drum kits, in which a bass drum was played by a pedal mechanism so that the hands were left free to play cymbals and/or snare drum, were used in RAGTIME and theater orchestras early in the century. The influence of standard marching rhythms (known as the "rudiments") persisted in New Orleans jazz. Although the playing of drummers such as Tony Sbarbaro, of the Original Dixieland Jazz Band (● p. 37), may sound crude and stiff today, the DIXIELAND style added SYNCOPATION and, at the time, must have appeared strikingly novel. As jazz developed into the faster-tempo, more dance-orientated Chicago idiom of the 1920s, the drumming became more sophisticated, involving increased use of crisp suspended cymbal strokes as a form of punctuation and developing the "fill" technique (any short rhythmic formula used to fill brief gaps in the musical texture).

The pounding bass-drum playing of early jazz, often comprising one stroke per beat, gradually yielded to a subtler approach. In the late 1920s the invention of the "high-hat" (a pair of horizontally mounted cymbals opened and closed by a foot pedal) allowed rhythmic continuity to be maintained in the background. This rhythm was achieved with simple and unwavering "swing" patterns played on the high-hat with a single stick while the pedal opened and closed the cymbal plates on alternate beats. Drummer-bandleaders such as Gene Krupa and Chick Webb began to promote themselves as soloists in the 1930s, although the quality of their solos was distinctly variable and often relied more on a flamboyant visual impact than on imaginative rhythmic creations. Sonny Greer's work in Duke Ellington's orchestra (● p. 62) initiated the fashion for a "jungle" style of drumming involving ancillary instruments such as gongs, timpani, tom-toms and cymbals of different sizes.

In tandem with the rapid development of other musical parameters in the 1940s, BOP drumming introduced a refreshing liberation from typical rhythms. Although the "swing" figuration often persisted in the background (now transferred to a single "ride" cymbal), the bass drum and snare drum

A typical modern drum-kit, comprising "high-hat" cymbal (front), two suspended cymbals, pedal-operated bass drum (rear), side drum and three tom-toms of different sizes.

year gets them both fired from the Argyle Show Bar in Chicago when, too stoned to perform, Parker still insists on attempting to collect his fee. A union official orders him from his office at gunpoint. ● British Decca launches a subsidiary label, Capitol, to sell imported recordings made by Capitol in the US (founded in 1942).

2 December Dizzy Gillespie's Cuban drummer, Chano Pozo (● p. 114), is shot dead in Harlem.

15 December End of second recording ban by the American Federation of Musicians.

30 December Tenor saxophonist Stan Getz (● p. 153) performs an impressive solo in a recording of "Early Autumn" made by Woody Herman's Second Herd in Los Angeles.

● Duke Ellington and his orchestra tour Europe, with only part of the band appearing in London because of British union restrictions on appearances by American musicians (● p. 77). ● Art Blakey visits Africa to study native drumming techniques.

Left Stan Getz at around the time he recorded "Early Autumn" in 1946.

were used to supply unpredictable off-beat accentuation (● p. 96). At the hands of the Kenny Clarke and Max Roach, drum solos became more elaborate affairs on a par with those of the melodic instruments. Drum "fills" and accompaniments began closely to mirror and develop fragments of themes emerging in improvised sections, thus ensuring that the drummer became a far more integrated member of the ensemble. These trends were also reflected in the resourceful work of Buddy Rich (who led his own small groups and drummed for bandleader Harry James until 1966), and Roy Haynes (whose collaborators have ranged from Charlie Parker to Chick Corea).

Bop drumming reached its apogee in the intricate playing of Art Blakey (● p. 138), who studied African drumming in 1948–49 and developed a sophisticated technique of POLYMETER, in which pulses of different speeds are superimposed. The prodigious Tony Williams, in his work as a teenager with Miles Davis in the early 1960s, showed that Blakey's exhilarating approach could be taken to still higher levels of complexity.

The experimentation of the FREE JAZZ movement (● p. 150) led at times to the total abrogation of a regular pulse, but the craze for FUSION (● p. 170) in the 1970s concentrated on the heavy regular BACKBEATS of rock music that had been a feature of some HARD-BOP pieces since the late 1950s. Rock also influenced the use of quaver patterns in "straight" (i.e., not SWUNG) rhythm, and an extended kit in which multiple tom-toms and cymbals of graded pitches became commonplace. Electronic drums and the generation of computerized drum techniques have also contributed to the development of modern jazz (● p. 221).

Above Duke Ellington and Sonny Greer with the latter's impressive array of percussion, pictured at Chicago's Hotel Sherman in 1940. Notable exotica are the orchestral timpani (far right), five Chinese temple blocks (center), tubular bells (rear) and two gongs of different pitches mounted on tall stands for optimum visual impact.

WORLD EVENTS

30 January Assassination of Gandhi, New Delhi

25 February Communists gain control of Czechoslovakia

15 May British abandon Palestine

May Foundation of State of Israel

24 June USSR isolates Berlin, leading to massive airlift

29 July London hosts first Olympic Games since 1936

15 August Republic of South Korea instituted

● George Orwell's novel *1984*

1949

Migration to France

The first Festival International de Jazz in Paris seduces American players to the rapidly expanding European jazz scene. Back in the US, new developments in recording technology are set to revolutionize the music industry.

1 January To celebrate the lifting of the recording ban imposed by the American Federation of Musicians (● p. 103), RCA records the *Metronome All Stars* with musicians including Miles Davis (● p. 216), Dizzy Gillespie (● p. 219), Fats Navarro, J. J. Johnson, Kai Winding, Buddy DeFranco, Charlie Parker (● p. 136), Lennie Tristano and Shelly Manne under arranger/director Pete Rugolo. The union sets a three-hour limit to recording sessions; any work in addition to this is deemed to be overtime.

10 January 45 rpm and 33$^1/_3$ rpm discs introduced in the US.

21 January Miles Davis and Gil Evans record the first of three nonet sessions, eight tracks from which are issued as *Birth of the Cool* on the Capitol label in 1954.

8 April Premiere of Leonard Bernstein's Second Symphony, *The Age of Anxiety* (based on the poem by W. H. Auden), by the Boston Symphony Orchestra under Serge Koussevitzky. The Boston critic Cyrus Durgin describes the work's exhilarating scherzo ("The Masque") as "a marvellous distillation of the movement of jazz."

Right Miles Davis's nonet at a Capitol recording session on 21 January 1949. Davis is standing behind saxophonists Gerry Mulligan and Lee Konitz.

The epithet "cool" in jazz has no precise definition, being used as a loose opposite of HOT and embracing a wide range of styles. The intricate ensemble arrangements by Gil Evans, inspired by Claude Thornhill's orchestra and recorded by Miles Davis's nonet in 1949–50 after the band appeared at The Royal Roost on Broadway, were issued with the prophetic title *The Birth of the Cool* in 1954. These influential tracks were later seen to epitomize certain aspects common in all later "cool" jazz: emotional restraint (achieved partly through an avoidance of "expressive" playing techniques such as VIBRATO), and a harmonic and contrapuntal sophistication made possible by more PRE-COMPOSITION and therefore less IMPROVISATION. Although the Davis nonet continued to demonstrate its debt to BOP, the subsequent evolution of "cool" jazz represented a sometimes self-conscious turning away from the highly charged and spontaneously virtuosic atmosphere of the BOP style.

Participating in Davis's nonet were saxophonists Gerry Mulligan and Lee Konitz, who went on to spearhead their own WEST COAST "cool school" (● p. 134). The term "cool" has also been applied to the tightly organized music of John Lewis's Modern Jazz Quartet (● p. 128), and to the refined piano styles of George Shearing and Dave Brubeck (● p. 188).

Right Charles Delaunay's Jazz Festival was held in Paris in 1949, 1952 and 1954 at the Salle Pleyel. A second Paris Festival ran for four years in the late 1960s, and today's Paris event was instituted in 1980.

FESTIVAL INTERNATIONAL 1949 JAZZ

CH. DELAUNAY

Below French and American musicians rehearse for the first Paris Jazz Festival in May 1949. The line-up includes US tenor saxophonist Don Byas (second from left), whose emigration to France in 1946 was followed by many of his American colleagues who were attracted to the energy and freedom of the European jazz scene.

May The first Festival International de Jazz held in Paris features appearances by Charlie Parker, Dizzy Gillespie, Sidney Bechet, Miles Davis and Kenny Clarke. The reception they are given is so positive that Bechet and Clarke decide to settle in Europe, while Davis returns to the US thoroughly disillusioned with the American jazz scene.

Right 15 December 1949: the scene at Birdland, the nightclub named after Charlie Parker, on its opening night. Performing at the venue are (l. to r.): Max Kaminsky (trumpet), Lester Young (tenor saxophone), "Hot Lips" Page (trumpet), Charlie "Yardbird" Parker (alto saxophone) and blind pianist Lennie Tristano.

Below Charlie Parker warms up before going on stage at the Paris Jazz Festival in May 1949.

16 May Lennie Tristano's recordings *Digression* and *Intuition* constitute an early experiment in free ensemble IMPROVISATION.

7 July One of the earliest jazz legends, trumpeter Bunk Johnson, dies in Los Angeles.

September Norman Granz pairs Canadian pianist Oscar Peterson and bassist Ray Brown for a "Jazz at the Philharmonic" concert at Carnegie Hall. The two men later work together in Peterson's two famous piano trios (1951–66). ● Dave Brubeck (● p. 134) records in San Francisco with his piano trio and experimental Jazz Workshop Ensemble octet.

15 December The club Birdland, named after Charlie "Bird" Parker (● p. 136), opens on Broadway.

Christmas Day Charlie Parker appears at Carnegie Hall.

● New Jazz and Prestige record labels founded by Bob Weinstock in New York.
● Stan Kenton and his twenty-piece orchestra play their PROGRESSIVE JAZZ at Carnegie Hall.

Sassy

Sarah Vaughan (nicknamed "Sassy" for her sharp tongue) began a five-year Columbia contract in 1949, cutting over twenty tracks in one year. Seven years before, she won an amateur talent competition at New York's Apollo Theater, which secured her first engagements with pianist Earl Hines (● p. 124) and singer Billy Eckstine. Endowed with one of the richest voices in jazz, Vaughan combined an almost operatic power with a phenomenal variety of color and an unusually wide range: she could instantly switch from deep huskiness to brilliant high notes with ease, and her tone could veer from the lushly romantic to the bitterly ironic within a single phrase.

Although her widespread popularity depended largely on interpretations of sentimental BALLADS, she was a brilliant (if sparing) exponent of SCAT (● p. 61) and knew how to adapt her melodic shapes to the harmonic demands of the BOP style (● p. 96). From the 1950s her career followed parallel paths, her recordings divided between commercially oriented popular song (often with saccharine background strings) and more compelling virtuoso interpretations of STANDARDS with some of the finest jazz musicians of the time.

Right Sarah Vaughan's beauty and stunning artistry won her an enthusiastic popular following in the 1940s. She is seen here performing during a tour of Britain in 1954.

WORLD EVENTS

18 April Republic of Eire established

23 May (West) German Federal Republic established

27 July Maiden flight of the world's first jet passenger aircraft, the De Havilland Comet.

8 September Death of Richard Strauss

1 October People's Republic of China founded by Chairman Mao Tse-tung

7 October (East) German Democratic Republic established

16 October End of Civil War in Greece

30 December Vietnam achieves independence from France

● Movie version of Leonard Bernstein's musical *On the Town* wins two Oscars

1950

Parker in Scandinavia

Charlie Parker tours Sweden and Benny Goodman crosses the Atlantic, stimulating a growing appreciation of jazz in northern Europe.

Below Charlie Parker performing in Sweden in November 1950.

March Oscar Peterson (● p. 162) makes his debut recordings in New York. Over the next four decades he becomes one of the most prolific recording artists of all time.

18–19 May Sarah Vaughan (● p. 123) records in New York with Miles Davis (● p. 216) as sideman.

June Charlie Parker (● p. 136) and Thelonious Monk (● p. 154) record together in New York. Their sessions include interpretations of "Bloomdido" and "My Melancholy Baby."

7 July Trumpeter Fats Navarro dies of tuberculosis at the age of twenty-six, New York.

Summer Miles Davis, Art Blakey (● p. 138), Dexter Gordon and Charlie Parker are apprehended at Los Angeles's Burbank Airport for possession of drugs, but they are later acquitted. Thelonious Monk is subsequently arrested for possession and banned from appearing in New York nightclubs for the next six years.

November Charlie Parker tours Sweden.

6 November Benny Goodman (● p. 84) and the NBC Symphony Orchestra give the

WORLD EVENTS

12 January Death of George Orwell

3 April Death of Kurt Weill

8 March Soviet Union declares its nuclear weaponry

28 June North Korean forces enter Seoul and provoke Korean War

26 September Liberation of Seoul by UN troops

24 October Chinese invade Tibet

2 November Death of George Bernard Shaw

November–December Chinese army repels UN forces in Korea

Pianists

After the untimely death of Fats Waller (● p. 105) in 1943, three performers independently continued to augment the potential of the piano as one of the most versatile of jazz instruments. Their innovations were influential on two younger players who began to establish themselves in the early 1950s – Oscar Peterson and Erroll Garner.

Below Earl Hines, here sporting the trademark hat and cigar of early jazz pianists, was the first performer to break significantly away from the stride style.

Earl Hines first revealed his talents during early work with Louis Armstrong (● p. 57) in the late 1920s. His TRUMPET STYLE of playing was the first tangible departure from the post-ragtime STRIDE idiom, cultivating a right-hand melodic technique more directly comparable to that of FRONT-LINE melody instruments, and using octave doublings to emphasize certain passages. Hines also possessed the crucial ability to make his often florid embellishments seem an essential part of the melody, in contrast to the superficial decorative patterns of so many performers. In his 1951 recording of Waller's "Honeysuckle Rose" with Armstrong's All Stars, for example, he deploys a glittering array of GLISSANDI and trills that wittily merge into various parts of the theme. Hines also deserves credit for furthering the role of the piano as a featured instrument in big-band jazz during his Chicago years (● p. 64).

Nat "King" Cole, who was strongly influenced by Hines's rhythmic sophistication, created an altogether new jazz medium in the shape of the piano

By Alan Lomax
Drawings by David Stone Martin

first performance of Aaron Copland's Clarinet Concerto, New York. This year Goodman also goes on a European tour with trumpeter Roy Eldridge.

● Erroll Garner composes his piano solo "Misty" (soon to become a STANDARD) on a flight from San Francisco to Denver, but does not record it until 1954. ● Pianist Ahmad Jamal founds his first trio with Ray Crawford (guitar) and Eddie Calhoun (bass). ● Both the Count Basie (● p. 86) and Dizzy Gillespie orchestras are experiencing financial difficulties and forced to disband. Basie forms a new small COMBO that includes Clark Terry (trumpet) and Buddy Rich (drums). ● Members of the Willesden Music Makers' Club are taken to court for organizing the illegal entry to, and performances in, Britain of Sidney Bechet in November 1949, and Coleman Hawkins in December 1949. Legislation prompted by the demands of the British Musicians' Union has effectively banned American musicians from appearing in the UK since 1935 (● p. 85), and is not repealed for another four years (● p. 135). ● Two important books are published in New York: Alan Lomax's *Mister Jelly Roll*, based on the memoirs of Jelly Roll Morton (● p. 45), and Rudi Blesh's and Harriet Janis's *They All Played Ragtime*.

Left Jelly Roll Morton's colorful memoirs are a vivid, if sometimes unreliable, account of early New Orleans jazz.

Below Dizzy Gillespie, pictured before his adoption of a trumpet with its bell bent upwards (● p. 219).

trio. Originally a combination of piano, guitar and bass (● p. 88), the trio format provided a buoyant backing for Cole's suave singing and explored novel textures such as closely interlocking figurations played simultaneously by piano and guitar. Although Cole was a gifted pianist, his success as a vocalist was destined to sidetrack him from further innovation at the keyboard. His trio disbanded in 1951 as he became increasingly involved in popular broadcasting (he had his own cult television show in 1956). But the trio medium proved to be one of the most enduring ensemble formats in jazz, later acquiring a greater rhythmic drive when Oscar Peterson replaced the guitarist with a drummer in 1958.

Art Tatum, virtually blind from birth, modelled his own trio on the original Cole format in 1943. Endowed with the most prodigious technical facility of any jazz pianist, Tatum was held in awe by his contemporaries, who habitually referred to him as "God." His style was deeply rooted in the STRIDE school, especially its virtuoso manifestation at the hands of Fats Waller. Tatum's left-hand figurations became infinitely more flexible, however, sometimes only hinting at an underlying stride motion. His harmonic vocabulary was the most sophisticated yet seen in jazz, and it allowed him to explore revelatory new approaches to well-worn traditional themes. Rhythmic surprises and complexities of texture both reached a high point in Tatum's work, and his sheer technical perfection made any performance an exciting experience. Unlike Hines, however, his abilities sometimes led him to display his technical accomplishments merely for their own sake.

1951

Modern Jazz

Pianist John Lewis begins work with a group soon to become the influential Modern Jazz Quartet. Meanwhile, Charlie Parker's professionalism deteriorates and the young Miles Davis emerges from his shadow.

Left Lennie Tristano, voted Musician of the Year by *Metronome* in 1947, smoothed out the rhythmic irregularities of bop in his highly intellectual brand of cool jazz.

January Duke Ellington's *Harlem Suite* is performed at New York's Metropolitan Opera House. Johnny Hodges (alto saxophone) and Sonny Greer (drums) both quit the orchestra in **February**, the latter after twenty-seven years' membership.

17 January Miles Davis records in New York with Charlie Parker and resumes his gigs at Birdland.

30 January Earl Hines (● p. 124) makes a live recording with Louis Armstrong's All Stars at a concert in Pasadena, and soon after quits the band.

March Cab Calloway draws attention to the growing drug problem in jazz in an article published in *Ebony Magazine*.

July Charlie Parker loses his cabaret card because of involvement with narcotics, and is unable to play in New York nightclubs. On his birthday, **29 August**, he is informed that the American Federation of Musicians is considering investigating his erratic behavior. In spite of the popularity of his performances with string accompaniment, he is in growing financial debt to his agent.

5 October The Miles Davis All Stars record their first long-playing album for Prestige.

30 October Blind pianist Lennie Tristano records *Ju-Ju*, an early experiment in OVERDUBBING. This year he forms a jazz conservatory in New York with the help of Lee Konitz (alto saxophone) and Warne Marsh (tenor saxophone).

12 December Formerly married to vibraphonist Red Norvo (● p. 70), singer Mildred Bailey dies in Poughkeepsie, New York. The couple had been dubbed "Mr and Mrs Swing."

● Pianist Dave Brubeck (● p. 188) forms his first quartet, with alto saxophonist Paul Desmond. ● John Lewis forms a quartet with Milt Jackson (vibraphone), Ray Brown (bass) and Kenny Clarke (drums) under the name Milt Jackson Quartet (● p. 128). ● Trumpeter Chet Baker (● p. 210) is court-martialed for desertion from the US Army due to mental instability. ● Sidney Bechet emigrates to France. ● Eleven-year-old pianist Herbie Hancock (● p. 201) performs a Mozart concerto with the Chicago Symphony Orchestra. ● Alex North composes a jazz score for Elia Kazan's film *A Streetcar Named Desire*, starring Vivien Leigh and Marlon Brando (● p. 141).

WORLD EVENTS

14 March UN troops take Seoul, Korean War

May London's South Bank complex opened in Festival of Britain

11 September Igor Stravinsky's opera *The Rake's Progress* first performed, Venice

● Film version of George Gershwin's *An American in Paris* wins Oscar for Best Picture

● J.D. Salinger's novel *The Catcher in the Rye*

Electric Bass

In 1951 Leo Fender's musical-instrument company developed its "Precision" four-string electric bass guitar, a highly marketable innovation that borrowed the electrical amplification of six-string guitars, first introduced with the Gibson company's pioneering 1936 model. The Fender Precision Bass® was only a guitar by virtue of the horizontal manner in which it was played: it is more accurate to consider the instrument as a direct descendant of the double bass, with which it shares the tuning system for its four strings. On some later models, the "frets" characteristic of the guitar fingerboard (metal strips indicating where the left-hand fingers should be placed) were omitted so that the playing technique became much closer to that of the double bass. Designed to be both more portable and louder than a conventional string bass, the electric version was readily accepted as a practicable alternative capable of injecting new vitality into the lowest layer of the musical texture.

Although it quickly became a staple member of rock bands and has continued to dominate the pop and rock scene, the electric bass was promoted by several prominent jazz musicians during the 1950s. Lionel Hampton's bass player, Monk Montgomery, adopted the instrument almost immediately, but it was not until the boom in jazz-rock FUSION (● p. 170) that the electric bass came into its own in the jazz world. Some players fluctuated (and have continued to fluctuate) between ACOUSTIC and electric bass, while others were trained solely on the electric model from the beginning of their careers. The instrument's penetrating, rich tone and considerable power made it an ideal vehicle for conveying the potent RIFF patterns that characterized the bass part in a typical fusion piece, while making an obvious aural reference to the color of rock music and rhythm'n'blues.

One of the most intriguing coincidences in jazz history is the fact that many prominent masters of the electric bass were born in 1951, the year of its launch. These include Stanley Clarke, who tried out a succession of different instruments before settling on electric bass, with which he made a memorable

contribution to the often hard-driving sound of Chick Corea's fusion group Return to Forever (● p. 178) in the 1970s. Clarke's exact contemporary Jaco Pastorius provided a solid bass support for Joe Zawinul's rival fusion band Weather Report (● p. 174) at the peak of its popularity in 1976–82, developing techniques of stunning flexibility and inventiveness that included chordal playing, harmonics and GLISSANDI. (His predecessor in Weather Report was Alphonso Johnson, who was also born in 1951.) Miles Davis's electric bassist, Michael Henderson, was another 1951 arrival, as was Mark Egan, who succeeded his teacher, Pastorius, in Pat Metheny's fusion group (● p. 198) in 1978.

Since the 1970s, the electric bass and six-string electric guitar have also occasionally been employed by composers of classical music in a not entirely successful attempt to bridge the cultural gap between pop music and the concert hall.

Above and right The Fender Precision Bass®, seen here with an advertisement for the same company's Broadcaster electric guitar, revolutionized the sound of jazz when it came into widespread use in the 1960s.

1952

West Coast travels East

Leonard Bernstein directs a critical investigation into the tension between bop and traditional styles as Duke Ellington celebrates twenty-five years in the music business. The new West Coast "cool" school begins to make its presence felt in New York.

Left Members of Jazz at the Philharmonic rehearse in Stockholm on 27 March 1952 (l. to r.): Ella Fitzgerald, Oscar Peterson, Roy Eldridge and Max Roach.

WORLD EVENTS

6 February Death of George VI, UK

26 July Death of Evita Perón, Argentina

3 October First British nuclear-weapons test

4 November Dwight Eisenhower elected President, USA

● Columbia University establishes a studio for electronic music
● Samuel Beckett's play *Waiting for Godot*
● Jackson Pollock's abstract expressionist paintings cause controversy

22 and 28 January Charlie Parker (● p. 136) records sessions with string backing and Latin repertoire for Mercury (Verve).

24 February Charlie Parker receives an award from *Down Beat* for best alto saxophonist on a New York television program in which he jams with Dizzy Gillespie (● p. 219).

March Norman Granz's "Jazz at the Philharmonic" (● p. 106) tours Sweden with Lester Young, Roy Eldridge and Max Roach. Louis Armstrong also visits Europe this year.

March–April Dizzy Gillespie records numerous tracks in Paris.

April Charles Mingus (● p. 190) and Max Roach found the record label Debut, which remains in business until 1957.

Spring Carnegie Hall mounts a concert devoted to Californian jazz (● p. 134), featuring Chet Baker (● p. 210), Gerry Mulligan and Paul Desmond. Mulligan and Baker form a new quartet, notable for its exclusion of the piano.

May Charlie Parker plays with Chet Baker in Los Angeles, where he participates in a JAM SESSION for "Jazz at the Philharmonic." This summer, Parker gets himself further in debt with his agent and faces union fines for unprofessional conduct.

9 May Miles Davis (● p. 216) records for Blue Note, in a year in which he is increasingly afflicted by his drug habit.

Opposite, above Chet Baker (trumpet) and Gerry Mulligan (baritone sax) in action with their popular quartet in September 1952.

John Lewis and MJQ

Miles Davis's nonet of 1949 (● p. 120) fully utilized the many talents of BOP pianist John Lewis, a skilled arranger and thoughtful composer. Lewis's keyboard technique was characterized by a sensitive delicacy unusual in the bop idiom that prevailed at the time. After working with Charlie Parker, Illinois Jacquet and Lester Young, Lewis joined vibraphonist Milt Jackson's quartet in 1951 alongside two fellow sidemen from Dizzy Gillespie's big band – bassist Ray Brown and drummer Kenny Clarke.

The group soon gained an enormous popular following and adopted the name Modern Jazz Quartet in 1952, the year in which Percy Heath succeeded Brown on double bass. Connie Kay replaced Clarke two years later, and the Lewis-Jackson-Heath-Kay combination endured for two memorable decades. When the group finally disbanded in 1974, the break-up proved to be only temporary, and in 1981 the acclaimed quartet re-formed for a tour of Japan (● p. 196).

13 June Leonard Bernstein organizes a Festival of Creative Arts at Brandeis University, Waltham (near Boston), and hosts a high-powered symposium on jazz that debates the conflict of BE-BOP with traditional idioms, illustrated by comparative improvisations on the same STANDARDS. Performers include Miles Davis, John Lewis and Charles Mingus.

2 September Gerry Mulligan's quartet records "My Funny Valentine."

14 November Duke Ellington's 25th Anniversary is celebrated in two concerts at Carnegie Hall, with a prestigious line-up that includes Billie Holiday (● p. 131), Charlie Parker, Dizzy Gillespie and Stan Getz (● p. 153).

22 December Milt Jackson and John Lewis rename their group the Modern Jazz Quartet, and record for Prestige with a new bass player, Percy Heath.

29 December Bandleader and SWING innovator Fletcher Henderson (● p. 71) dies, New York. Large crowds attend his funeral in Harlem.

● Avant-garde American composer John Cage creates his *Collage*, in which forty-two jazz records are played simultaneously.

The Modern Jazz Quartet Plays *No Sun in Venice*
Original Film Score by John Lewis

Under Lewis's musical direction, MJQ evolved an intellectually satisfying brand of bop that won many admirers in the concert hall but was criticized by some jazz purists for an approach that was too COOL and seemed to cater primarily to the tastes of classical music lovers. Lewis's use of classical methods of composition, most notably the strict COUNTERPOINT of the Baroque era (evident in MJQ's extraordinary soundtrack to the 1957 film *No Sun in Venice*, ● p. 141), was symptomatic of his frustration with the simplicity and frequent predictability of bop's musical forms. Bop pieces had invariably followed the same pattern: a statement of the theme (HEAD), a succession

of improvised variations, and a further statement of the unadulterated theme by way of conclusion. Lewis composed elaborate structures of thematic complexity and textural variety in which bop improvisation remained an essential ingredient. In doing so, he achieved a satisfying hybrid style. Not surprisingly, only a few of his pieces were adopted by other jazz musicians, although "Django" – a tribute to Django Reinhardt (● p. 75) – continues to be re-interpreted as a favorite STANDARD.

However much the purists continue to lament Lewis's clear nods in the direction of a classically oriented audience, his distinctive music introduced many new listeners to jazz who might not otherwise have been drawn toward it. His thorough exploration of a possible synthesis between classical and jazz idioms, much of it concentrated in the production of so-called THIRD-STREAM music, was an important artistic breakthrough that exerted a strong influence on the future course of the music's development.

Above Vibraphonist Milt Jackson, shown here playing in Woody Herman's band at Birdland in June 1950, teamed up with John Lewis in the following year to launch the highly successful Modern Jazz Quartet.

Left Album cover for the Atlantic soundtrack recording of MJQ's score to the movie *No Sun in Venice* (1957), featuring a painting by Turner of the Grand Canal.

1953

Reviving the Big Bands

Trumpeter Chet Baker becomes the star of West Coast jazz. Count Basie and Benny Goodman are both back at the helm of new big bands after post-war austerity put the large ensemble out of fashion.

Above Lionel Hampton's band made a timely tour to Europe in 1953 when the big-band sound was enjoying a popular revival.

5 February Charlie Parker (● p. 136) visits Montreal for a television appearance. He later returns to Canada for a concert at Toronto's Massey Hall on **15 May** alongside Bud Powell, Dizzy Gillespie, Charles Mingus and Max Roach. Back in Montreal in **October**, he is reported to the American Federation of Musicians for allegedly throwing together an inferior band at the last minute.

9 February Dizzy Gillespie appears at the Salle Pleyel, Paris, where he makes a live recording.

2 March Dave Brubeck's quartet (● p. 188) records their album *Jazz at Oberlin* at Oberlin College, part of a series of highly acclaimed appearances at American university campuses.

16 May Gypsy guitarist and original Hot Club de France musician Django Reinhardt (● p. 75) dies, Fontainebleau, France.

June Charlie Parker appears at the Hi-Hat Club, Boston.

24 June André Previn, working as a film-music arranger and jazz pianist in Hollywood, records an album of Fats Waller STANDARDS in Los Angeles.

August *Down Beat* introduces its first Critics' Poll, in which Chet Baker (● p. 210) wins the "New Star" award.

Autumn–Winter Miles Davis (● p. 216) plays in Detroit.

21 November Larry Shields, former clarinetist with the Original Dixieland Jazz Band (● p. 37), dies in Los Angeles.

2 December Pianist Mary Lou Williams (● illustration, p. 196) records with tenor saxophonist Don Byas in Paris, where Byas has lived since 1946.

12 December Count Basie's new big band records the long-playing album *Dance Session* in New York.

● Benny Goodman's re-formed band goes on tour with Louis Armstrong's All Stars (● p. 57). A serious clash of temperaments between the two leaders precipitates Goodman's nervous breakdown. ● Teddy Wilson tours to England, "Jazz at the Philharmonic" appears in London, and Lionel Hampton's band (● p. 70) visits Europe. ● Valve trombonist Bob Brookmeyer replaces Chet Baker in Gerry Mulligan's WEST COAST quartet (● p. 134). ● The Sydney Jazz Club opens in Australia.

Flute

In June 1953, tenor saxophonist Frank Wess joined Count Basie's big band. Wess also played the flute, and Basie soon began to promote this instrument as a new element in jazz. The innovation was adopted by various WEST COAST bands during the 1950s, a movement reflected in Gil Evans's inclusion of flute parts in the orchestral arrangements he undertook for Miles Davis in 1958 (● p. 142). By this time, big-band saxophonists were habitually doubling up as flautists and Herbie Mann emerged as the foremost soloist on the instrument (winning the *Down Beat* flute poll, a category established in 1956, for thirteen consecutive years). But the most significant exponent of the flute was Eric Dolphy, who supported Ornette Coleman in his exploration of FREE JAZZ in the early 1960s

In 1952 and 1953, Billie Holiday gradually returned to the performance circuit after several years of serious disruption to her career caused by drug addiction (● p. 115). "Lady Day" – the nickname was coined by her soulmate, tenor saxophonist Lester Young, whom she in turn dubbed "Pres" ("President") – never recaptured the superior vocal quality of her youthful performances in the 1930s, but her singing retained its affecting idiosyncracies. Through a series of European tours and American television appearances she remained a high-profile figure until her final breakdown and death in 1959 (● p. 146). Her sartorial trademarks were a gardenia in her hair (● p. 76) and long white gloves: the gardenia was a holdover from the time when she accidentally burnt her hair with a curling iron immediately before a performance and hid the damage with a flower, while the gloves elegantly covered the telltale needle marks on her arms.

Few would argue against the widely held view that Holiday was the finest jazz vocalist of all time. Self-taught, Holiday sang from instinctive musicality, and her Harlem performances in 1933 quickly attracted the attention of producer John Hammond (● p. 209). Her early success also led to work with Teddy Wilson and Benny Goodman (● p. 84), and she made a dazzling series of recordings with both musicians. Moving on to collaborate with band leaders of the stature of Count Basie (● p. 86) and Artie Shaw, Holiday became renowned for her uncanny ability to re-compose well-known tunes as she went along: a melody would never be sung in its usual form, but would be altered on the spur of the moment to produce memorable variations that were often a considerable improvement on the original.

Holiday's singing voice was, by her own admission, modeled squarely on that of Louis Armstrong (● p. 56), but it exuded a captivating blend of vulnerability and sexuality that has never been equalled. Deft virtuoso showpieces such as "What a Little Moonlight Can Do" (1935) were gradually replaced in her repertoire by more tender ballads, and in 1939 she unwittingly gained notoriety with her powerful anti-lynching song "Strange Fruit" (● p. 92). In the later 1940s, she appeared at Carnegie Hall (● p. 118) in triumph after undertaking a drug rehabilitation program, but she was continually dogged by a succession of exploitative husbands, unhappy bisexual affairs and a self-destructiveness that brought her life to an untimely close.

Above Billie Holiday's instinctive re-shaping of familiar melodies made her one of the most spontaneously lyrical of all jazz artists.

Lady Day

(● p. 150) and went on to work with Charles Mingus.

Later flautists tended to polarize at either the avant-garde or commercial end of the stylistic spectrum. Like Dolphy's, Roland Kirk's flute-playing was subservient to his proficiency on a variety of other wind instruments (● illustration, p. 13). However, unlike Dolphy, Kirk played lesser-known varieties of the flute family, including nose flutes and a homemade "black puzzle flute." These produced a sonorous contrast to his unique and bizarre method of playing three different saxophones simultaneously! In another vein, Dave Valentin, who records for GRP (● p. 214), is a slick technician whose easy-going melodic style is worlds apart from Kirk and other innovators of the 1960s and 1970s.

1954

East and West

Major European tours by American stars coincide with the growing popularity of the "cool school" on the West Coast. Charlie Parker attempts suicide and begins a tragic final decline that leads to his premature death in 1955.

9 January A concert in Stockholm begins Billie Holiday's first European tour, which includes visits to Scandinavia, France, Germany, Switzerland and England.

18 January Charlie Parker (● p. 136) plays at the Hi-Hat Club, Boston, and makes the first of several radio broadcasts from the venue with "Symphony Sid" Torin as master of ceremonies.

February Miles Davis (● p. 216) returns to New York after spending five months playing in Detroit. He records two albums in New Jersey for the Prestige label: *Walkin'* (**29 April**) and *Miles Davis and the Modern Jazz Giants* (**Christmas Eve**), the latter with Thelonious Monk (● p. 154) and Milt Jackson (● p. 129).

15 February In Los Angeles, the Chet Baker Quartet (● p. 210), at the height of its popularity, records STANDARDS including "My Funny Valentine" and "But Not for Me."

March Count Basie's first European tour takes his band to Copenhagen, Stockholm, Amsterdam, Brussels, France, Germany and Switzerland.

Left Chet Baker with members of his sextet at a recording session in 1954. His West Coast colleagues are tenor saxophonist Jack Montrose (center) and alto saxophonist Herb Geller (right).

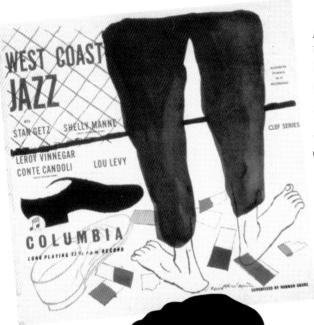

April The Dave Brubeck Quartet (● p. 188) records *Jazz Goes to College* at the Universities of Ohio and Michigan. Brubeck's photograph appears on the cover of *Time* magazine this year.

17 May Drummer Shelly Manne records his album *West Coast Sound* in Los Angeles.

1 June Saxophonist Gerry Mulligan (● p. 134) appears at the Paris Jazz Festival.

17 July The first American jazz festival is organized in Newport, Rhode Island, by George Wein.

Left Recorded in Los Angeles in August 1955, Stan Getz's album *West Coast Jazz* was a success for Columbia and one of many "cool" recordings issued in the mid-1950s.

Below Count Basie enjoying the adulation of female admirers in Paris on 4 March 1954.

Left Dave Brubeck, seen here in 1957, studied classical techniques with French composer Darius Milhaud, a noted pioneer of SYMPHONIC JAZZ (● p. 53).

Jazz West Coast

1954 was a good year for the West Coast style, with Chet Baker and Gerry Mulligan both achieving fame and Dave Brubeck appearing on the cover of *Time* magazine. Based in California, the West Coast school took its initial inspiration from Miles Davis's *Birth of the Cool* (1949), to which baritone saxophonist Gerry Mulligan contributed several arrangements. In 1952 Mulligan formed a quartet in Los Angeles with Chet Baker (trumpet), Bob Whitlock (bass) and Chico Hamilton (drums). The group played jazz that showed a considerable degree of emotional restraint, the overriding characteristic of the COOL school (as it was immediately dubbed). Baker based his playing (without VIBRATO) on that of Davis, and cultivated an understated directness both on his trumpet and in his crooning, seductive singing voice, which, together with his handsome looks, rapidly made him a popular idol. Like most other prominent West Coast players, these musicians were white, and their relaxed idiom became familiar on numerous Hollywood soundtracks.

The most successful cool pianist was undoubtedly the enduringly popular Dave Brubeck, who remained based in California. Brubeck received a thorough grounding in classical music, which left its mark on his jazz compositions in their frequent use of advanced harmonies, elaborate structures and complex or irregular METERS. The most famous example of the last is the experiment with quintuple time in his quartet's 1959 recording of "Take Five," a catchy and now ubiquitous number written by the group's saxophonist, Paul Desmond, who also recorded with Mulligan in this period.

The cool style was not restricted to the West Coast, however: a number of skilled performers promoted it in New York. East Coast exponents include the expatriate English pianist George Shearing (who was blind from birth), and the versatile saxophonist Stan Getz (● p. 153). The influence of Lester Young inspired Getz to develop a highly melodic style of improvisation that was so distinctive it earned him the nickname "The Sound." His gift for memorable lyricism was developed through the valuable experience of playing in famous SWING bands, including those led by Benny Goodman (● p. 84), Woody Herman and Stan Kenton. Kenton's band gained notoriety for promoting a sometimes pretentious PROGRESSIVE JAZZ that was often censured by critics. In the 1950s the group featured an impressive number of future West Coast and cool–school players, including saxophonists Lee Konitz and Art Pepper, and drummer Shelly Manne.

August Charlie Parker, in deteriorating health and depressed by the death of his daughter on 7 March, attempts suicide.

24 August J. J. Johnson and Kai Winding form a trombone duo and record their launch album, *Jay and Kai.*

September Parker is admitted to Bellevue Hospital, New York. After his discharge in October, poverty forces him to pawn his saxophone.

31 October Charles Mingus (● p. 190) makes his first recording with members of his newly founded Jazz Composers' Workshop.

23 December John Lewis, with the Modern Jazz Quartet, records his composition "Django" in memory of guitarist Django Reinhardt (● p. 75), who died in 1953.

● Anthony Mann's film *The Glenn Miller Story,* starring James Stewart as Miller, dramatizes the late bandleader's life and reconstructs his musical arrangements. Among the participating jazz stars are Louis Armstrong, Gene Krupa and Barney Bigard. The movie receives Oscar nominations for script and music direction. ● British musicians' union laws restricting the appearance of American performers in the UK are relaxed. ● Gene Krupa and Cozy Cole found a school for jazz drummers. ● Louis Armstrong publishes his autobiography, *Satchmo: My Life in New Orleans.*

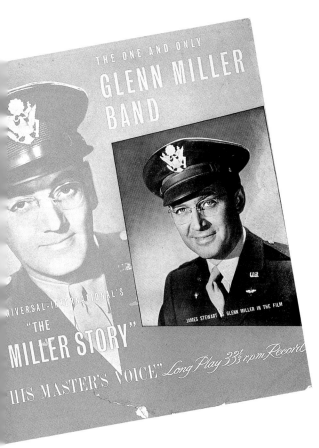

Above The sleeve notes for this 1955 HMV album of original Miller hits inspired by the movie *The Glenn Miller Story* proclaimed: "the Miller music to be heard in the picture is a re-creation by a present-day band and, however well done, nothing can match the supremacy of the original."

Below Satchmo's interpretations of STANDARDS by W. C. Handy were recorded in June 1954.

1955

Disaster at Birdland

Parker's career comes to a tragic end. The jazz scene begins to be dominated by small groups led by Miles Davis, Art Blakey and Charles Mingus.

4–5 March Charlie Parker plays his last two gigs at Birdland, with Kenny Dorham, Bud Powell, Charles Mingus (● p. 190) and Art Blakey (● p. 138). The second night is disastrous, largely because of Powell's severe inebriation. As Powell staggers off stage in mid-gig, Mingus tells the audience: "Please don't associate me with any of this. This is not jazz: these people are sick."

12 March After lying seriously ill for three days in the New York hotel suite of Baroness Pannonica ("Nica") de Koenigswarter, a patroness of jazz musicians, Parker dies while watching Tommy Dorsey's television show. Causes of death are registered as lobar pneumonia and cirrhosis of the liver.

May A memorial concert for Charlie Parker (lasting four hours) is held at Carnegie Hall (● p. 91).

Left Charlie Parker in full melodic flight at Birdland in 1950.

Right The famous club named after Parker, seen here in 1956, was opened on Broadway in December 1949 (● p. 122).

Opposite An innovator since the 1920s, Earl "Fatha" Hines was still producing fresh-sounding unaccompanied jazz piano in the mid-1950s.

Bird

The year 1955 witnessed the sad final days of one of jazz's most revered and legendary figures, Charlie "Yardbird" Parker. Parker (whose nickname derived from his penchant for fried chicken) began to develop his career in 1939 when he moved from Kansas City to New York. There he sought to escape the clichés of the SWING style by cultivating a novel kind of improvisation in which DISSONANT notes were deliberately emphasized. Under the influence of guitarist Charlie Christian (● p. 98), Parker combined this approach with an intelligent use of LICKS to create a new style of playing known as "formulaic improvisation," in which lengthy melodic paragraphs were constructed using a handful of basic note-patterns, while subtle dislocated rhythms and angular leaps kept the listener guessing about the music's direction.

From 1942 to 1945 Parker played alongside Dizzy Gillespie (● p. 219) in successful big bands led by Earl Hines (● p. 124) and Billy Eckstine. When Parker and Gillespie joined forces with Kenny Clarke and Thelonious Monk at Minton's Playhouse in Harlem for a series of JAM SESSIONS (● p. 97), Parker's musical experiments became absorbed into the new BOP style as one of its essential ingredients. His music gained more widespread exposure in 1945, both in New York and Los Angeles, but most of the following year was spent in a sanatorium, and his professionalism was continually compromised by escalating drug addiction and alcoholism.

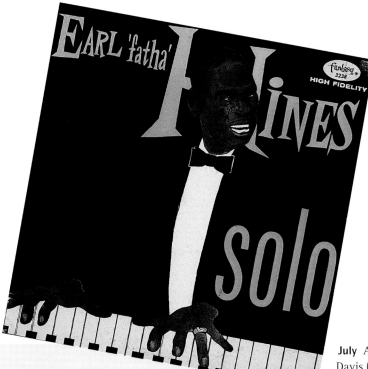

WORLD EVENTS

18 April Death of Albert Einstein

14 May Warsaw Pact agreed

18 July Disneyland opens, Los Angeles

12 August Death of Thomas Mann

- Bill Haley's hit song "Rock Around the Clock"
- Tennessee Williams's play *Cat on a Hot Tin Roof*
- Pierre Boulez's composition *Le Marteau sans maître*

In 1951 he lost his cabaret card, and three years later he attempted suicide (● p. 135). Even when sober, his behavior was pathologically adolescent. Miles Davis described Parker's deterioration toward the end of 1948: "I didn't like whites walking into the club where we were playing just to see Bird act a fool, thinking that he might do something stupid, anything for a laugh . . . It was embarrassing." One musical consequence of Bird's boyish high spirits was his habit of quoting well-known melodies in incongruous musical contexts, as with the sudden intrusion of the jaunty English folk song "Country Gardens" at the conclusion of his 1951 recording of the otherwise lyrical "Lover Man."

In spite of the commercial success of his recordings with saccharine string accompaniment in the period 1947–52, the roots of Parker's innovation remained controversial. He regarded bop as a fundamental departure from the techniques of earlier jazz, although many (including Gillespie) hotly disagreed and preferred to view the new style as a logical continuation of traditional musical values. For all his self-conscious modernism, Parker's compositions were mostly based on the TWELVE-BAR BLUES and tended to use a limited range of harmonies. At his peak in 1947–48, his ensembles provided a bop schooling for several major talents, such as Miles Davis, and no subsequent saxophonist – or, indeed, other instrumentalist – could escape entirely from his colossal influence.

In 1988, serious jazz enthusiast Clint Eastwood directed *Bird*, a moving film portrayal of Parker's final years, using the saxophonist's original recordings as the basis for his soundtrack (● p. 211).

July Artists who appear at the second Newport Jazz Festival include Miles Davis (● p. 216), Louis Armstrong (● p. 56), Count Basie (● p. 86), Woody Herman, Dave Brubeck (● p. 188), Gerry Mulligan (● p. 134) and Thelonious Monk (● p. 154).

August Johnny Hodges rejoins Duke Ellington's band after an absence of four years. In this year, Ellington's *Night Creature* is performed at Carnegie Hall with a full symphony orchestra (the broadcasting orchestra, Symphony of the Air).

12 August Bassist Oscar Pettiford records his *Bohemia after Dark*, making use of the rhythms of native American Indians.

September Chet Baker embarks on a seven-month trip to Europe that includes appearances in Iceland and England.

16 October Leonard Bernstein's television program "The World of Jazz" (ABC) features the conductor singing a BLUES version of iambic-pentameter couplets from Shakespeare's *Macbeth* and declaring that BOP is "the real beginning of serious American music." The program includes the first performance of Bernstein's *Prelude, Fugue and Riffs*, given by Benny Goodman; the score was originally composed for Woody Herman in 1949.

October–November Miles Davis makes his first recordings with a new quintet including John Coltrane (tenor saxophone), his second choice when Sonny Rollins proves to be unavailable. The RHYTHM SECTION comprises Red Garland (piano), Paul Chambers (bass) and Philly Joe Jones (drums). George Avakian buys Davis out of his Prestige contract, securing him as a Columbia artist who will receive $4000 for his first recording on the new label.

November Art Blakey records at the Café Bohemia, New York, with his definitive Jazz Messengers: Horace Silver (piano), Hank Mobley (tenor saxophone) and Kenny Dorham (trumpet). In this year, alto saxophonist Julian "Cannonball" Adderley makes his New York debut at the same venue.

17 November James P. Johnson, the "Father of Stride Piano," dies, New York.

● Pianist Lennie Tristano conducts further experiments in OVERDUBBING on the Atlantic label. ● Charles Mingus founds a "Jazz Workshop" ensemble, for which he composes music communicated to the players by dictation rather than notation. ● Release of the movie *The Benny Goodman Story*, featuring Steve Allen as Goodman, with appearances by Harry James and Gene Krupa.

1956

Ellington at Newport

A thrilling live performance at Newport throws the Duke Ellington orchestra back into the limelight. Hard bop establishes itself in the US as the sound of the day, while British traditionalist Humphrey Lyttleton enters the UK pop charts.

30 January Charles Mingus (● p. 190) records his album *Pithecanthropus Erectus* for Atlantic, breaking new ground in free ensemble improvisation.

22 June Sonny Rollins records *Saxophone Colossus*, New York.

26 June Trumpeter Clifford Brown, who has fronted a quintet with Max Roach for the past two years, is killed in a car crash at the age of twenty-five.

July Duke Ellington's popularity is spectacularly rekindled by a performance at the Newport Jazz Festival of "Diminuendo and Crescendo in Blue," featuring a searing 27-CHORUS saxophone solo by Paul Gonsalves. Ellington appears on the cover of *Time* magazine, and the Columbia release of the Newport performance becomes his best-selling record.

September After anthologizing the works of Cole Porter and Rodgers and Hart, Ella Fitzgerald (● p. 195) continues her "songbook" series for Verve by recording a collection of songs by Duke Ellington in Los Angeles. Irving Berlin is given the same treatment in 1958, George Gershwin (● p. 89) in 1959, Jerome Kern in 1963, and Johnny Mercer in 1964.

11 September Pianist Art Tatum (● p. 125) and saxophonist Ben Webster record together in Los Angeles for Norman Granz (● p. 106).

Below Ella Fitzgerald's maturing talents were showcased in the impressive "songbook" recordings preserved by Verve in the 1950s and 1960s.

Bop Hardens

Right The strong rhythmic drive and melodic appeal of Art Blakey's Jazz Messengers defined the hard-bop sound of the late 1950s.

"Hard bop," a phrase often used to describe a style that emerged from the aftermath of the bop revolution, is one of those terms in jazz that is rarely given a precise definition. In one sense, the powerful rhythmic drive and sometimes aggressive virtuosity of improvisations by the next generation of performers was indeed "hard," and this intensity provided the *lingua franca* of modern jazz. But in other respects "hard bop" represented a move in somewhat different stylistic directions, reflecting a refreshing emphasis on simplified blues elements and making clear references to the music of the black church. The latter trend in 1950s and 1960s jazz is otherwise known as "soul" or "funk," though neither of these labels should be confused with their modern pop equivalents. Of vital importance in disseminating this new music was the Blue Note record label (● p. 166), which flourished throughout both decades.

Drummer Art Blakey helped spearhead the movement with the foundation of his second "Jazz Messengers" group in 1955. In company with pianist Horace Silver, trumpeter Kenny Dorham and tenor

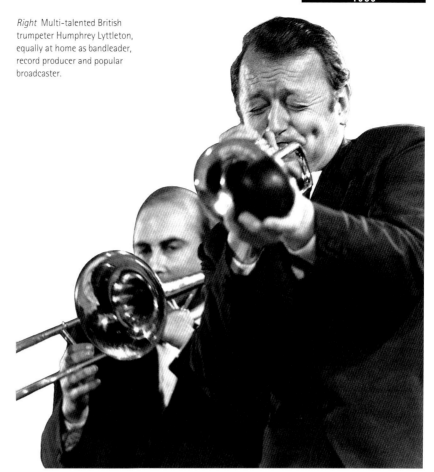

Right Multi-talented British trumpeter Humphrey Lyttleton, equally at home as bandleader, record producer and popular broadcaster.

saxophonist Hank Mobley, Blakey promoted a down-to-earth style replete with appealing, bluesy melodies and an infectious rhythmic drive. Among the many talents who served their apprenticeship in Blakey's Jazz Messengers over the years were trumpeters Donald Byrd (● p. 12) and Lee Morgan, whose hard-bop composition "The Sidewinder" was a hit on his Blue Note album of the same name in 1964 (● p. 158).

The fluctuating membership of Blakey's long-lasting enterprise later included pianist Keith Jarrett (● p. 185), saxophonist Wayne Shorter and prodigious young trumpeter Wynton Marsalis (● p. 196). The Messengers were re-assembled for a Blue Note promotion in 1985 and for Blakey's seventieth-birthday celebrations in 1989 (● p. 212), almost exactly one year before his death.

October Miles Davis (● p. 216) completes his Prestige contract by recording the four quintet albums *Workin'*, *Relaxin'*, *Cookin'* and *Steamin'*. He then leaves for a short tour of Paris, Amsterdam and Stockholm. John Coltrane (● p. 160) quits the group for a year to seek a cure for his drug addiction: he is temporarily replaced by Sonny Rollins.

5 November Art Tatum dies, Los Angeles. ● NBC launches its *Nat King Cole Show* on television. Cole is heckled by racists during a live performance in Birmingham, Alabama, this year.

26 November Tommy Dorsey dies, Greenwich, Connecticut.

November–December Trumpeter Lee Morgan cuts his first sides as leader for the Blue Note (● p. 166) and Savoy labels.

12–13 December Art Blakey records his album *Hard Bop*.

● At the invitation of the US State Department, Dizzy Gillespie (● p. 219) becomes an "ambassador of jazz" and forms a new big band to tour the eastern Mediterranean, the Middle East, Pakistan and South America. ● Horace Silver leaves Art Blakey's Jazz Messengers. ● Pianist Ahmad Jamal's recording of "On Green Dolphin Street," a theme from a 1947 film starring Lana Turner, exerts a strong influence on Miles Davis (● p. 142). ● Trumpeter Humphrey Lyttleton's "Bad Penny Blues" reaches the top twenty in the UK charts. ● European tours by Louis Armstrong (who also visits Africa), Jazz at the Philharmonic, and Stan Kenton's orchestra. ● In New York, French author and former jazz violinist André Hodeir publishes his book *Jazz: its Evolution and Essence,* a revised translation of his *Hommes et problèmes du jazz* (Paris, 1954). ● Billie Holiday (● p. 131) publishes her autobiography *Lady Sings the Blues*, ghost-written by William Dufty. ● Louis Armstrong appears in the movie *High Society.*

1957

Cinema and Third Stream

Jazz reaches a mass audience through the medium of film, and simultaneously achieves a new intellectual high point in the "third stream" initiative, which seeks to unite jazz with elements of classical music.

Right Sleeve design for John Coltrane's *Blue Train*, showing the saxophonist in characteristically pensive mood.

BLUE TRAIN · john coltrane · blue note 1577

Below French actress Jeanne Moreau, star of Louis Malle's thriller *Lift to the Scaffold*, borrows Miles Davis's trumpet during a publicity photo-shoot for the movie.

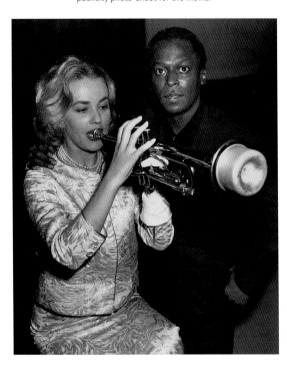

March Max Roach and Sonny Rollins record *Jazz in 3/4 Time*, an early attempt to break away from the ubiquitous 4/4 METER.

4 April John Lewis's Modern Jazz Quartet (● p. 128) provide a score to the film *Sait-on jamais* (titled in English *No Sun in Venice*), which is recorded by Atlantic. They perform the score live at New York's Town Hall on **12 May**, and during an extensive tour of Europe in the autumn.

May Miles Davis collaborates with arranger Gil Evans on the album *Miles Ahead*. ● Gerry Mulligan tours Sweden.

14–15 May Thelonious Monk (● p. 154) records with Art Blakey's Jazz Messengers (● p. 138) for Atlantic in New York.

12 June Clarinetist and bandleader Jimmy Dorsey dies, New York.

July–August Charles Mingus (● p. 190) records *Tijuana Moods*, an idiosyncratic and spirited reinterpretation of Latin elements.

19 August Leonard Bernstein's jazz musical *West Side Story* is staged in Washington, D. C. It transfers to New York on **26 September**.

15 September John Coltrane (● p. 160) records his sextet album *Blue Train* for Blue Note, New York.

18 September Louis Armstrong causes controversy by speaking out against President Eisenhower's administration during a prolonged spell of racial violence attendant on an initiative (launched in May) to end segregation in American schools.

4 December In Paris, Miles Davis records a score to Louis Malle's thriller *L'Ascenseur pour l'échafaud* (*Lift to the Scaffold*); his local quintet includes Pierre Michelot on bass and Kenny Clarke, who emigrated to Europe the previous year, on drums. Back in New York, Davis's line–up includes Cannonball Adderley on alto saxophone; John Coltrane rejoins them to form a sextet.

8 December Billie Holiday performs "Fine and Mellow" in a live television broadcast.

● Brandeis University (● p. 129) commissions THIRD STREAM works from Charles Mingus, Gunther Schuller, George Russell and Harold Shapero. ● The US State Department continues to promote wide-ranging jazz tours by sending Benny Goodman (● p. 84) to the Far East. ● Former New York waitress Carla Borg marries Canadian pianist Paul Bley, who encourages her to develop her compositional talents. ● Pianist Erroll Garner begins to perform under a pink spotlight. ● Pianist and arranger Toshiko Akiyoshi wins a poll in *Down Beat* and receives her award at Berklee College, Boston, alongside Duke Ellington, who is presented with a "Hall of Fame" award.

WORLD EVENTS

16 January Death of Arturo Toscanini

20 September Death of Jean Sibelius

4 October USSR launches first Sputnik satellite

5 December Dutch ejected from Indonesia

● Boris Pasternak's novel *Dr. Zhivago* wins Nobel Prize; USSR forbids him to accept.

● David Lean's film *Bridge on the River Kwai* wins Oscar for Best Picture

Jazz at the Movies

By the late 1950s, movie audiences had grown accustomed to the sound of jazz in film soundtracks, to numerous cameo appearances on camera by star instrumentalists and singers, and to the occasional biopic devoted to the life of an especially celebrated musician. However, jazz music in films had been strictly confined to "diegetic" situations: music heard by the film's characters themselves, whether played by a band in full view on the studio set, or issuing from a prop radio or phonograph. All that was changed with Alex North's background score for the 1951 film version of Tennessee Williams' play *A Streetcar Named Desire*. Imbued with a strong jazz flavor, the music helped create a sultry atmosphere and began a fashion in many later scores for employing jazz to accompany scenes of sleaze or corruption. At the same time, COOL jazz featured more prominently in films as "aural wallpaper," and with so many cool musicians based on the west coast, this trend produced welcome employment opportunities in Hollywood, though they were mostly reserved for white musicians.

Two unusual and influential jazz film scores were recorded in 1957. Miles Davis found himself in Paris, where he improvised a soundtrack to Louis Malle's thriller *L'Ascenseur pour l'échafaud* (*Lift to the Scaffold*), which in some respects looks forward in style to the MODAL jazz he pioneered soon afterward (● p. 146). Meanwhile, John Lewis and his Modern Jazz Quartet provided a score for another French film, Roger Vadim's *Sait-on jamais* (*No Sun in Venice*), which, in its use of sophisticated PRE-COMPOSED structures and pseudo-Baroque COUNTERPOINT (p. 129), could hardly have been more contrasted to Davis's instinctive effort. Both musicians went on to

produce other notable film scores, Lewis scoring *Odds Against Tomorrow* in 1959 and Davis contributing music to the boxing epic *Jack Johnson* in 1970.

The following chronological list gives a few highlights of the numerous soundtracks created by leading jazz practitioners (and, in the unusual case of Herrmann's *Taxi Driver*, by a non-jazz composer who turned to the idiom late in his distinguished Hollywood career):

Leonard Bernstein: *On the Waterfront* (1954)+
Henry Mancini: *Touch of Evil* (1958)
Chris Barber: *Look Back in Anger* (1959)
Duke Ellington: *Anatomy of a Murder* (1959)
Charles Mingus: *Shadows* (1959)
Duke Ellington: *Paris Blues* (1961)+
John Dankworth: *The Servant* (1963)
Chico Hamilton: *Repulsion* (1965)
Herbie Hancock: *Blow-Up* (1966)
Sonny Rollins: *Alfie* (1966)
Neal Hefti: *The Odd Couple* (1967)
Quincy Jones: *In Cold Blood* (1967)*
Gato Barbieri: *Last Tango in Paris* (1972)
Herbie Hancock: *Death Wish* (1974)
Bernard Herrmann: *Taxi Driver* (1975)+
Oscar Peterson: *The Silent Partner* (1978)
Pat Metheny and Lyle Mays: *The Falcon and the Snowman* (1984)
Herbie Hancock: *Round Midnight* (1986)*
Miles Davis: *Siesta* (1987)
Dave Grusin: *The Fabulous Baker Boys* (1989)
Dave Grusin: *The Firm* (1993)+

[* Academy Award for Best Original Score]
[+ Academy Award Nomination for Best Original Score]

Below A beaming Herbie Hancock displays the Oscar he received for his soundtrack to *Round Midnight* in March 1987.

Musicians in the Movies

Films depicting the lives and work of jazz musicians include:

● *The Fabulous Dorseys* (1947), featuring the Dorsey brothers

● *The Glenn Miller Story* (1954), starring James Stewart

● *The Benny Goodman Story* (1954), starring Steve Allen

● *St. Louis Blues* (1958), starring Nat King Cole as W. C. Handy

● *The Gene Krupa Story* (1959), starring Sal Mineo

● *Lady Sings the Blues* (1972), starring Diana Ross as Billie Holiday

● *Bird* (1988), starring Forest Whitaker as Charlie Parker

1958

Jazz Messengers

Art Blakey promotes hard bop in Europe, innovative modal techniques are perfected by Bill Evans and Miles Davis, and a major new festival is established in California.

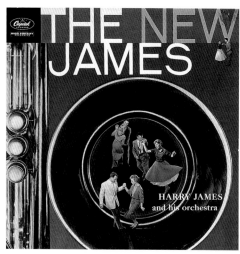

Above The Harry James Orchestra gained a popular following with its post-Basie swinging big-band sound in the 1950s.

"I think a movement in jazz is beginning away from the conventional string of chords, and a return to emphasis on melodic rather than harmonic variations. There will be fewer chords but infinite possibilities as to what to do with them."

Miles Davis, December 1958

WORLD EVENTS

1 January European Economic Community established

February Munich air disaster decimates Manchester United soccer team

29 March Pablo Picasso's mural *The Fall of Icarus* unveiled, UNESCO, Paris

26 August Death of Ralph Vaughan Williams

- Boeing 707 jet revolutionizes air travel
- Hovercraft invented

Third Stream

The interest in SYMPHONIC JAZZ stimulated by Paul Whiteman's collaborations with Gershwin and others in the 1920s (● p. 55) remained strong throughout the 1930s and 1940s, influencing classical composers and jazz musicians alike. From the desire to unite elements of art-music and jazz emerged various synthetic styles – some laying themselves open to charges of pretentiousness, such as that promoted by Stan Kenton's west coast Innovations in Modern Music band.

When critic and jazz scholar Gunther Schuller (a French horn player with the orchestra of New York's Metropolitan Opera) invented the term "third stream" while at Brandeis University in 1957, he intended it to signify a wholesome union between high art and jazz. However, many purists in both camps regarded the trend with unwarranted and self-protective cynicism. Schuller produced a stream of model third-stream compositions for widely varied instrumental groups (including full orchestra), and he collaborated with the like-minded John Lewis (● p. 128), one of the more successful jazz practitioners to espouse classical compositional techniques. In 1960 Lewis's Modern Jazz Quartet recorded Schuller's *Concertino* for jazz quartet and orchestra on the Atlantic label. Other musicians who made notable contributions to the third-stream movement were Charles Mingus (● p. 190), Anthony Braxton and pianist Ran Blake, who broadened the definition to embrace the use of musical material from non-Western cultures.

9 January Critic Barry Ulanov speaks out against sexism in jazz by publishing an article in *Down Beat* entitled "Women in Jazz: Do They Belong?"

February Sonny Rollins records his *Freedom Suite* with Oscar Pettiford and Max Roach; the sleeve notes attack continuing racism in America.

March Dave Brubeck's quartet tours Denmark, while Oscar Peterson (● p. 162) appears at the Concertgebouw, Amsterdam.

28 March Early blues bandleader W. C. Handy dies, New York. Nat King Cole portrays the "Father of the Blues" (● p. 27) in a feature-film tribute entitled *St. Louis Blues*; its cast also includes singers Cab Calloway, Ella Fitzgerald and Mahalia Jackson.

2–3 April Miles Davis's sextet (● p. 140) records *Milestones*, which includes an early example of MODAL jazz.

26 May Miles Davis records "On Green Dolphin Street" (● p. 139) with pianist Bill Evans (● p. 156).

July–August Miles Davis and Gil Evans record large-ensemble arrangements of STANDARDS from George Gershwin's opera *Porgy and Bess* (● p. 85).

30 October Art Blakey's Jazz Messengers (● p. 138) record *Moanin'* for Blue Note, a defining album in the HARD BOP style.

The barriers between modern classical music and jazz were more spectacularly broken down by the controversial avant-garde performers of the early 1960s (● p. 150), by which time the third stream seemed more in the nature of a luxurious anachronism than a potent musical force. For many listeners, Duke Ellington's achievements many decades before (● p. 62), combining considerable intellectual sophistication with an uncompromised jazz idiom, had seemed a more worthwhile synthesis.

> "'Third stream' describes the theoretical merging of two souls into one, those of jazz and European composed music. The unrequited love on both sides for the most incompatible characteristics of the other has resulted in many illicit encounters, and quite a few bastard offspring . . ."
>
> Brian Priestley, 1995

Right The formidable Gunther Schuller (seen here conducting at London's Barbican Centre in 1991): composer, jazz historian and music educator.

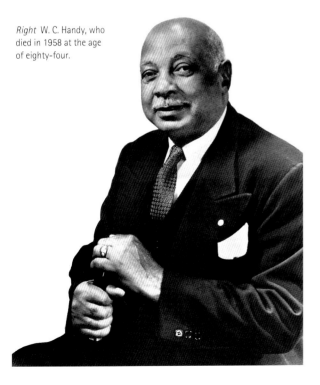

Right W. C. Handy, who died in 1958 at the age of eighty-four.

October The first annual Monterey Jazz Festival is mounted by Ralph J. Gleason in California. ● Billie Holiday's second tour of Europe takes her to France and Italy and includes an appearance in a small hall at La Scala opera house, Milan.

November Art Blakey and his Jazz Messengers appear in Paris a few weeks after Blakey records *Holiday for Skins* for three jazz drummers and seven Latin percussionists.

15 December Bill Evans records *Everybody Digs Bill Evans*, including the influential MODAL track "Peace Piece."

● Duke Ellington (● p. 183) appears before Queen Elizabeth II at the Leeds Festival during his first trip to England for twenty-five years. He commemorates the occasion the next year by recording *The Queen's Suite* in a limited edition of one disc, which is sent to Buckingham Palace. ● Stan Getz (● p. 153) and Oscar Pettiford emigrate to Europe, both settling in Copenhagen: Getz's wife is Danish. ● More US State Department tours take Woody Herman to South America, Dave Brubeck to the Middle East and Indian subcontinent, and Jack Teagarden to the Far East. ● Harold "Duke" Dejan forms his Olympia Brass Band in New Orleans, re-capturing the flavor of the city's early processional music (● p. 28). ● Antonio Carlos Jobim, director of Odeon Records, launches the BOSSA NOVA craze by recording João Gilberto's "Chega de Saudade."

1959-69

The Birth of Modern Jazz

During the 1960s, a drastic upheaval of jazz styles matched the instability equally evident in other art forms. Harmonic innovation and structural freedom caused jazz audiences to dwindle, until Miles Davis introduced a spectacularly successful hybrid jazz-rock style at the end of the decade.

Jacob Lawrence's painting *Cabaret* (1962).

1959
Giant Steps

In a year during which jazz is deprived of some of its most enduringly popular talents (Lester Young, Billie Holiday and Sidney Bechet), its stylistic development strides ahead with the innovations of modal and free jazz.

February Louis Armstrong (● p. 56) plays at the Nordstrandhallen, Norway.

14 February Drummer Baby Dodds dies in Chicago.

28 February Thelonious Monk (● p. 154) appears at New York's Town Hall.

1 March Miles Davis records *Kind of Blue*, pioneering the technique of MODAL JAZZ, and creating one of the finest spontaneously improvised albums of all time.

15 March Tenor saxophonist Lester Young dies in New York.

4 May Saxophonist John Coltrane (● p. 160) records *Giant Steps* in New York.

14 May Saxophonist/clarinetist Sidney Bechet dies in Paris.

22 May Ornette Coleman (● p. 150) records *The Shape of Jazz to Come* in New York.

12 June Billie Holiday (● p. 131) is arrested in hospital for possession of narcotics; she dies on **17 July** of cirrhosis of the liver with multiple complications.

Summer Duke Ellington (● p. 183) composes his first complete film score, for the courtroom drama *Anatomy of a Murder*, starring James Stewart. The film includes a brief cameo appearance by Ellington, who performs a piano duet with Stewart at a restaurant.

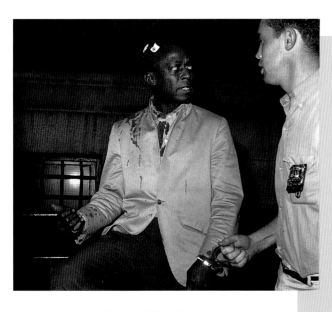

Left Miles Davis "resisting arrest" in August 1959, an instance of alleged police brutality and racism that gained rapid and widespread publicity.

WORLD EVENTS

2 January Fidel Castro assumes power in Cuba

8 January Columbia and Princeton Universities receive Rockefeller grant to establish a center for electronic music

3 February Death of Buddy Holly

18 March Hawaii joins USA

9 April Death of Frank Lloyd Wright

26 April Panama invaded by Cuban forces

22 September China barred from joining UN

September First cassette tapes launched in US

14 December Archbishop Makarios becomes first President of Cyprus

● William Wyler's movie *Ben Hur* costs $4 million

Changing Modes

Until the late 1950s all jazz performances were based on pre-set sequences of CHORDS, referred to by musicians as the CHANGES (i.e., changes of harmony). These harmonic sequences might be borrowed from well-known songs (STANDARDS), or be newly composed. In either case, a performance would normally begin with a statement of the original theme as a HEAD, and be followed by a series of solo IMPROVISATIONS based on repetitions of the song's underlying harmonies (each solo being termed – rather confusingly – a CHORUS). A final statement of the HEAD would bring the piece to a close. From the 1920s to the 1940s, the chordal vocabulary of jazz increased in complexity through the importation of more advanced harmonies (mostly borrowed from modern classical music), but the underlying structural principle of the "changes" remained constant.

This process was revised when Miles Davis (● p. 216), John Coltrane (● p. 160), Bill Evans (● p. 156) and others began to base some of their improvisations on SCALES rather than on chords. These were not the overworked major and minor scales familiar in earlier popular or classical music: they were the MODES, which had provided the basis for music in medieval and renaissance times and which had been resurrected by composers such as Debussy (● p. 24) at the turn of the twentieth century. Instead of constructing a sequence of familiar chords, progressive jazz musicians now based large stretches of music on the limited pitches of a single mode. Contrast might be created by switching abruptly to a

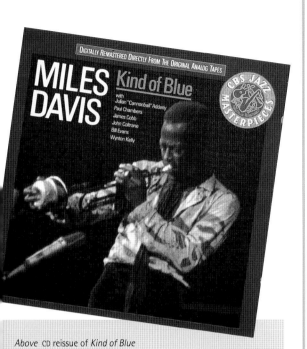

The Dave Brubeck Quartet: Blue Rondo à la Turk

Brubeck's album *Time Out* (1959) is a fine illustration of two of the pianist's most important characteristics: his debt to classical music and his rhythmic originality. "Blue Rondo à la Turk" acknowledges the classics in its rondo structure (a form in which repetitions of a main theme are interspersed with contrasting episodes) and in its emulation of the pseudo-oriental flavour of Mozart's famous *Turkish Rondo*.

"Blue Rondo" uses an unconventional irregular METER, subdividing the nine beats of each measure into a 2+2+2+3 pattern instead of the more conventional 3+3+3. Departing from normal jazz textures, Brubeck has all the instruments play this pattern simultaneously to intensify the effect. The opening section builds to a thrilling climax in which percussively dissonant piano chords suggest the influence of twentieth-century classical masters such as Bartók and Stravinsky. Then, in a delicious moment of unpredictability, the music sideslips effortlessly into a bluesy and swinging four-beat tempo. This attempt to establish a conventional jazz idiom is checked three times with brief interruptions by the edgy 2+2+2+3 rondo theme before the music finally settles into a TWELVE-BAR BLUES.

Alto saxophonist Paul Desmond improvises four twelve-bar CHORUSES with his inimitable polished tone, then Brubeck offers a carefully controlled piano solo: the thicker chordal voicings of its central section (choruses 2 and 3) are symmetrically framed by sparse right-hand melodic work in the two outer sections (choruses 1 and 4). Desmond re-enters – as if to embark on another leisurely saxophone solo – but the irregular rondo theme makes three further sudden interruptions and emerges into a recapitulation of the opening section.

different mode in a later section of the piece. Famous early examples of this practice are heard in Miles Davis's 1958 album *Milestones*, and in certain tracks of the seminal *Kind of Blue* (1959).

The new modal approach had two important stylistic effects. First, the soloists were able to achieve more flexible melodic improvisations, being freed from the confines of strict harmonic schemes. Second, the essentially "static" nature of modal music (as opposed to the "dynamic" sense of progression created by the tension and relaxation inherent in any good sequence of chords) led to a contemplative mood in which pieces might be protracted to sometimes inordinate length.

Two further techniques emerged from modal jazz during the 1960s. As a compromise between the strict application of modes and more conventional harmonic schemes, pieces might be built up from repetitions of just two different chords (which rapidly became a sometimes irritating cliché). Then, with the emergence of jazz-rock FUSION in the late 1960s and early 1970s (● p. 170), long stretches of modal music were animated by successions of RIFFS, often provided by the FUNKY electric bass guitar.

12 August Dave Brubeck (● p. 188) and his Quartet record *Time Out*, which includes Paul Desmond's hit "Take Five." ● Miles Davis is assaulted by police outside Birdland on Broadway in New York (where his sextet is playing), having been told to move on. Photographs of him, bloodstained and handcuffed to a police officer, appear in the next day's newspapers; he is later cleared of all charges.

Autumn Ornette Coleman plays FREE JAZZ at the Five Spot, New York.

October John Lewis (● p. 128) composes music for the movie *Odds Against Tomorrow* and records it with the Modern Jazz Quartet.

● Ronnie Scott opens his jazz club on London's Gerrard Street. ● Gene Krupa's life story is celebrated in the Hollywood biopic *The Gene Krupa Story* (released in Europe as *Drum Crazy*). ● Oscar Peterson (● p. 162) forms a trio with Ray Brown (bass) and Ed Thigpen (drums). ● Trumpeter Chet Baker is arrested in Harlem on a narcotics charge and moves to Europe. He remains there until 1964, as does pianist Bud Powell. ● Wayne Shorter joins Art Blakey's Jazz Messengers. ● Charles Mingus (● p. 190) provides music for John Cassavetes' movie *Shadows*.

1960

The Freedom Principle

European appearances by mainstream American musicians are now commonplace, as a radical new avant-garde "free" jazz begins to assert itself stateside.

Above The abstraction of the sleeve design for Cecil Taylor's Blue Note album *Unit Structures* (1966) reflected the esoteric nature of the music Taylor had been producing since the early 1960s.

WORLD EVENTS

4 May Albert Camus killed in a car crash

11 June Benjamin Britten's opera *A Midsummer Night's Dream* premieres, Aldeburgh, UK

9 November John F. Kennedy elected President, USA

- Laser beams demonstrated
- Federico Fellini's film *La Dolce Vita*
- Alfred Hitchcock's film *Psycho*

9 January The Metropol Jazzhus opens in Oslo, hosting a performance by Stan Getz (● p. 153) on **1 April**.

January–February Dave Brubeck's quartet (● p. 188) records selections from Bernstein's *West Side Story* (● p. 140).

February John Coltrane (● p. 160) purchases his first soprano saxophone.

13 February Ella Fitzgerald (● p. 195) records live on tour in Berlin.

10–11 March Declaring that "flamenco is the Spanish counterpart of our BLUES," Miles Davis completes his album *Sketches of Spain* with Gil Evans, then embarks on a European tour, which includes a visit to London. John Coltrane quits again, and is replaced by Sonny Stitt on the British leg of the trip.

April The Modern Jazz Quartet (● p. 128) tours Scandinavia, then returns to New York to make an album with orchestral accompaniment in **June**.

2 April Bud Powell appears in Essen, West Germany.

June Crowd disturbances interrupt the Seventh Newport Jazz Festival. Charles Mingus (● p. 190) mounts an alternative event at nearby Cliff Walk Manor Hotel in **July**.

June–July John Coltrane and Don Cherry collaborate on the album *The Avant-Garde*, under the influence of innovative saxophonist Ornette Coleman (● p. 150).

August–September Max Roach records his album *We Insist!: Freedom Now Suite*, with a line-up that includes Coleman Hawkins.

8 September Bassist Oscar Pettiford dies in Copenhagen, two years after his emigration to Europe.

METROPOL JAZZ

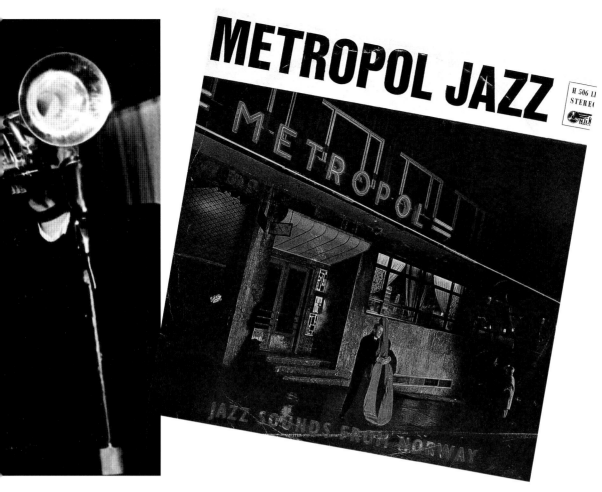

H 506 LI
STEREO

Opposite, left Gerhard Aspheim (left) and Eovind Salberg perform at Oslo's Metropol Jazzhus, opened on 9 January 1960.

Left The Metropol quickly established itself as a premier European jazz venue, attracting US performers of the calibre of Stan Getz within months of its opening.

Below Don Cherry, leading light of the jazz avant-garde, improvises on his notorious "pocket" trumpet.

Land of the Free

Whereas MODAL jazz (● p. 146) had been only a mild departure from the harmonic and melodic basis of earlier jazz styles, a movement that began to flourish in the early 1960s represented what many commentators saw as the final abrogation of conventional musical values in the interests of artistic gimmickry. The social context for the iconoclastic "free jazz" movement is crucially important, for the trend intensified alongside increasingly heated civil rights protests. The new generation of black musicians was angry, and espoused musical freedom as a potent symbol for the liberation of the black community from oppression. In some respects, the social significance of jazz had come full circle, and returned to its very earliest preoccupations.

The leading light of the 1960s avant-garde was Ornette Coleman, a controversial figure who sometimes played a white plastic alto saxophone. Self-taught, he was ridiculed by many and was branded as an exponent of "anti-jazz," a term also applied by critics such as John Tynan and Leonard Feather to the later work of John Coltrane (● p. 160) and the achievements of newcomer Don Cherry (who played a miniscule "pocket" trumpet). Cherry collaborated with Coleman on *The Shape of Jazz to Come* in 1959, and the new movement was christened with the appearance of their album *Free Jazz* in the following year. This venture, an astonishingly radical extended improvisation for octet, exerted a palpable influence on Coltrane's *Ascension* (1965), but was otherwise treated with derision in most quarters.

While Coleman disappeared into a self-imposed retirement in 1962, pianist Cecil Taylor continued to develop his own unique brand of "free" (but in essence often highly disciplined) jazz. His album *Unit Structures* (1966: illustration, p. 148) was characterized by musical textures of such unorthodox complexity that to all intents and purposes it sounded closer to experimental art music than to jazz.

Avant-garde techniques were simultaneously proving to be little more than a minority interest in the field of classical music, and the failure of the free jazz movement to reach a wide audience is not surprising. Many musicians, alienated (some by design) from the jazz mainstream, organized themselves into collectives in the early 1960s to promote their artistic creeds in an environment where commercial success was not an overriding concern. The best known of these was the Chicago-based Association for the Advancement of Creative Musicians, founded in 1966, which three years later spawned the influential Art Ensemble of Chicago. This group, like many other free jazz artists, later found a more receptive audience in Europe, where free jazz thrived in the late 1960s and early 1970s.

Right A civil rights demonstration in April 1960 takes place outside department stores accused of racial discrimination in Little Rock, Arkansas, which had experienced serious race riots three years before.

Far right Passengers travelling on a Greyhound bus look on in amazement as their vehicle is set ablaze by a white racist mob in May 1961 at Anniston, Alabama.

Above Eric Dolphy, a talented multi-instrumentalist who played bass clarinet on Ornette Coleman's ground-breaking album *Free Jazz*.

September Duke Ellington's *Suite Thursday* (inspired by John Steinbeck's novel *Sweet Thursday*) is performed at the Monterey Jazz Festival. This year Ellington spends two months in Paris, where he composes a film score to *Paris Blues*, in which he appears alongside Louis Armstrong and Paul Newman. With Billy Strayhorn, he arranges suites based on Tchaikovsky's ballet *The Nutcracker* and Grieg's *Peer Gynt*.

October John Coltrane records *My Favorite Things* with his new quartet. The group also records *Coltrane's Sound* and *Coltrane Plays the Blues*.

12–13 October Pianist Cecil Taylor and tenor saxophonist Archie Shepp record *The World of Cecil Taylor*.

20 October Back in the US after an appearance in Antibes in **July**, Charles Mingus and Eric Dolphy record an interpretation of Mingus's "What Love," featuring avant-garde instrumental voice imitations. Recorded during the same sessions, the complex "Fables of Faubus" dramatizes the notorious attempts by the Governor of Arkansas to resist the abolition of segregation.

November Gerry Mulligan (● p. 134) plays in Milan and Berlin. In this year, he makes an acting appearance in the movie *The Subterraneans*, which features a score composed by André Previn. ● Saxophonist Joe Harriott, a Jamaican emigré, records *Free Form* in London.

2 November Drummer Shelly Manne opens his own club, "Shelly's Manne-Hole," in Los Angeles.

December Ornette Coleman records his octet album *Free Jazz*, an extended avant-garde improvisation issued with Jackson Pollock's *White Light* as its cover design.

● Chet Baker is arrested in Italy on a drug charge. ● Stan Tracey becomes house pianist at Ronnie Scott's jazz club in London, a position he holds for the next seven years. ● Sidney Bechet's autobiography, *Treat it Gentle*, is published posthumously.

1961

The Duke Meets the Count

Duke Ellington and Count Basie join forces in the recording studio for the first time. Free jazz is savagely attacked by critics, and Stan Getz's return to the US helps launch a craze for bossa nova.

January Stan Getz leaves Copenhagen and returns to the US.

2 January Art Blakey takes his Jazz Messengers (● p. 138) to perform in Tokyo. Other musicians who visit Japan this year include Oscar Peterson (● p. 162) and Ella Fitzgerald (● p. 195).

22 February Nick LaRocca, onetime leader of the Original Dixieland Jazz Band (● p. 37), dies in New Orleans.

4 March Dizzy Gillespie appears at Carnegie Hall.

14–22 April Miles Davis records live at San Francisco's Black Hawk: the resulting albums are spliced together from different takes and are marred by inconsistent speeds.

May Thelonious Monk (● p. 154) tours England, France, Switzerland and Sweden.

11 May Don Micheal attacks Ornette Coleman's album *This is Our Music* in a savage review for *Down Beat*. Coleman's avant-garde quartet (● p. 150) disbands this year.

Double Bass

Jazz double-bass playing progressed from its primitive function in RAGTIME orchestras and early New Orleans groups, where the instrument merely emphasized the main beats of the prevailing march rhythm, to a much more flexible role in the big bands of the SWING era. The familiar WALKING BASS was an essential feature of both swing music and the BOP style that succeeded it. Its continued use represented both an increase in melodic interest in the lowest part of the music's texture and the new importance of the bass line in maintaining rhythmic momentum.

As bands grew larger, the double bass became less audible. One attempt to combat this problem was the evolution of the "slap" pizzicato, which causes the string to rebound off the instrument's fingerboard with a sharp, percussive noise. Ultimately, the inability of the double bass to compete with louder instruments on equal terms was a significant factor behind the rise in popularity of the electric bass guitar in the 1970s (● p. 127), although the introduction of metal strings and electric amplification on the ACOUSTIC instrument partly alleviated the problem.

In spite of its inherent drawbacks, many players retained a preference for the conventional double bass. Both Ray Brown and Charles Mingus (● p. 190) successfully adapted bop improvisation techniques for the instrument, and by the 1940s it had become a solo voice in its own right. Scott LaFaro (● p. 153), Gary Peacock and Niels-Henning Ørsted Pederson revealed the double bass's surprising capability for virtuosity by playing the instrument in the high register with a dexterity more typical of guitarists. Technical flexibility continues to characterize the work of contemporary bass players such as Dave Holland (famed for his speed of execution), Charlie Haden (a sideman of Ornette Coleman who has become an important leader in his own right) and Charnett Moffett.

Right Virtuoso Danish bass player Niels-Henning Ørsted Pederson, staunch sideman to Oscar Peterson in the 1970s and 1980s.

When versatile tenor saxophonist Stan Getz left Denmark and returned to the US in January 1961, he already enjoyed a reputation as one of the finest melodists in jazz. He served a solid swing-style apprenticeship in the bands of Stan Kenton, Benny Goodman and Woody Herman in the 1940s and produced a popular lyrical interpretation of "Early Autumn" in a recording cut in 1948. These achievements led to his first work as a leader in 1949. Thereafter Getz remained refreshingly aloof from current stylistic "schools," although his 1950s work increasingly revealed its debt to the fashionable COOL approach.

Getz's homecoming after his brief European interlude brought him renewed fame when he began to concentrate on the growing fashion for BOSSA NOVA ("new tendency"). This supremely marketable blend of laid-back Brazilian exoticism and sophisticated WEST COAST jazz scored its first success in 1962 when Getz collaborated with guitarist Charlie Byrd in the recording *Jazz Samba* (● p. 154), which won a Grammy award. The biggest bossa nova triumph was recorded by Getz with the husband-and-wife team of Astrud and João Gilberto in 1963. "The Girl from Ipanema" became a major hit when re-released as a single in the following year and has been cited as one of the five most-played songs of all time.

Both native Brazilians, the Gilbertos injected considerable authenticity into the style, as did Rio-born pianist Antonio Carlos Jobim. The latter had launched the new craze with his own record company back in 1958, and his song "Desafinado" was featured on the Getz–Byrd *Jazz Samba* release.

Stan Getz and the Bossa Nova

Right Stan Getz pauses for a photo-opportunity while boarding a Scandinavian Airlines jet at Copenhagen in 1958, bound for Frankfurt. Getz lived in Denmark between 1958 and 1961.

Brazilian music continues to exert a strong influence on modern jazz, especially in the seductive melodic style of the more popularly orientated FUSION groups such as that led by Pat Metheny (● p. 198) and those promoted by the GRP label (● p. 214).

19 May Miles Davis and Gil Evans appear at a Carnegie Hall concert for the African Research Foundation, during which Max Roach stages an anti-racist protest.

25 May John Coltrane (● p. 160) records *Olé Coltrane* with Freddie Hubbard and Eric Dolphy.

6 July Duke Ellington and Count Basie record *The First Time: The Duke Meets the Count*, featuring music from Ellington's recent score to the movie *Paris Blues* (● p. 151). ● Scott LaFaro, Bill Evans' prodigious bass player, is killed in a car accident at the age of twenty-five in Geneva, New York. A few days earlier, the Bill Evans Trio (● p. 156) recorded two live albums at the Village Vanguard, Greenwich, that are widely considered to be among the finest of their kind.

September Saxophonist Eric Dolphy tours Denmark.

23 November John Tynan, associate editor of *Down Beat*, brands the recent work of John Coltrane and Eric Dolphy as "anti-jazz."

● After riots in the previous year, the Newport Jazz Festival is cancelled and subsequently relocates to New York. ● Billie Holiday (● p. 131) is posthumously elected a member of *Down Beat*'s "Hall of Fame." ● Philip Larkin begins work as *Daily Telegraph* jazz critic this year.

1962

Through the Iron Curtain

The eccentric Thelonious Monk becomes a household name as his performances receive high critical acclaim. Mainstream American jazz musicians appear in the Soviet Union for the first time, and European jazz benefits from the active presence of Bud Powell and Dexter Gordon.

Left Cootie Williams, who returned to the Ellington fold in 1962.

WORLD EVENTS

25 May New Coventry Cathedral consecrated, UK; Britten's *War Requiem* commissioned in celebration

5 August Death of Marilyn Monroe

6 August Death of William Faulkner

October Cuban missile crisis

● Opening of Lincoln Center for Performing Arts, New York

● Alexander Solzhenitsyn's novel *One Day in the Life of Ivan Denisovich*

February Stan Getz (● p. 153) and Charlie Byrd record "Desafinado" in Washington and start a craze for BOSSA NOVA, on which Getz capitalizes by mounting an ambitious big-band session recorded in **August**.

24 March Bandleader Jean Goldkette dies, Santa Barbara, California.

28 May Herbie Hancock (● p. 201) records his first album as leader, *Takin' Off*.

July Benny Goodman (● p. 84) and pianist Teddy Wilson visit the Soviet Union under the auspices of the US State Department, forming part of the first group of American jazz musicians ever to appear in the country.

August Count Basie's band (● p. 86) tours Sweden.

September Trumpeter Cootie Williams rejoins the Duke Ellington orchestra after an absence of twenty-two years. ● Dexter Gordon tours to London and decides to remain in Europe (he settles in Copenhagen and does not return to the US until 1977). In **November** he appears at Oslo's Metropol Jazzhus, which has already hosted an appearance by Bud Powell on **1 September**. Powell also plays in Stockholm, Copenhagen and Paris this year.

17 September Duke Ellington records *Money Jungle* with Max Roach and Charles Mingus (● p. 190), showing his awareness of ongoing stylistic trends in jazz.

26 September Duke Ellington records with John Coltrane (● p. 160) in New York.

October Tenor saxophonist Archie Shepp, recently departed from Cecil Taylor (● p. 151), records his first album with a new quartet featuring trumpeter Bill Dixon.

12 October Charles Mingus fronts a big band at New York's Town Hall.

November A bossa-nova concert is mounted at Carnegie Hall.

23 November Cecil Taylor records live at the Café Montmartre, Copenhagen.

Thelonious Monk: Wrong Notes and Silly Hats

Thelonious Monk's popularity was at its height in 1962, when he was awarded a high-profile recording contract by Columbia. Perhaps *the* quintessential BOP musician, Monk presented an image of arty bohemian eccentricity with his trademark hats and awkward stage presence. His seemingly clumsy piano playing masked a very real compositional talent; in his way, he was just as influential on younger musicians as Charlie Parker (● p. 136), his sometime collaborator at Minton's Playhouse (● p. 97).

Initially eclipsed by the rapid success of his pupil Bud Powell, Monk made his first recordings with Coleman Hawkins's small ensembles in the closing stages of World War II. Engagements with Dizzy Gillespie (● p. 219) and Duke Ellington's former trumpeter Cootie Williams led to the latter's recording in 1944 of what remains Monk's best-known composition, "'Round Midnight" (● p. 116). A steady series of sessions for Blue Note (1947–52), Prestige (1952–55) and Riverside (1955–61) gradually cemented Monk's reputation as an originator of harmonically daring pieces showing a flair for

Right Benny Goodman entertains a delighted young audience in Red Square, Moscow, in the summer of 1962.

December Dave Brubeck (p. 188) on tour in Amsterdam.

15–16 December Oscar Peterson's trio (p. 162) record their BLUES-based album *Night Train* in Chicago.

● Guitarist Joe Pass, recently discharged from a drug rehabilitation center, names his first recording, *Sounds of Synanon*, after the institution.

idiosyncratic yet catchy melodies. His collaborations in 1957 with Art Blakey (p. 140) and John Coltrane propelled him into the limelight for the first time, and an appearance with a ten-strong band at New York's Town Hall in 1959 received critical acclaim. He became famous both at home and in Europe, where he had first appeared at the 1954 Paris Jazz Festival and where he toured widely in 1961. Three years later, his international status was confirmed by an appearance on the cover of *Time* magazine and a tour of Japan.

It is often claimed that Monk's distinctive piano style was rooted in the STRIDE idiom, but this tended to show itself only in his rendering of slow ballads. At a

faster tempo, his playing was often muscular and dominated by a stiff finger-technique that produced percussive sonorities. Unlike most bop performers, he employed a bare minimum of notes, frequently studding his improvised solos with pregnant silences that kept the audience in suspense as to his next move: abrupt cascades based on Debussy's whole-tone scale were a favorite device. According to the individual listener's sympathies, his playing could be described as either crudely inept, or replete with emotional significance and a laudable economy of musical material. The most memorable description of his keyboard style has undoubtedly been Philip Larkin's likening it to a "*faux-naif* elephant dance."

Though Monk's playing was controversial, his compositions continue to receive almost universal praise for their originality and memorability. Alongside "'Round Midnight," other Monk pieces that have established themselves in the repertoire of STANDARDS include "Straight, No Chaser," "Epistrophy," "Blue Monk," "In Walked Bud," "Rhythm-a-Ning" and "Evidence."

Left Thelonious Monk's eccentric image and apparent lack of a fluent keyboard technique belied his serious musical philosophy and significant compositional innovations.

1963-64

Technology and Spirituality

Highly varied studio sessions by Bill Evans, John Coltrane and Charles Mingus break new ground in recording techniques and achieve considerable expressive power.

1963

20 January Charles Mingus (● p. 190) records *The Black Saint and the Sinner Lady*, one of the finest experiments in extended structure of its time, in which post-Ellington sophistication meets OVERDUBBING techniques and free improvisation.

January–February Bill Evans records his solo album *Conversations with Myself*, on which three separate keyboard parts are superimposed by overdubbing.

February Coleman Hawkins appears at the Metropol Jazzhus, Oslo.

22 February Dave Brubeck (● p. 188) appears at Carnegie Hall.

May Dexter Gordon records in Paris. ● Thelonious Monk (● p. 154) makes live recordings in Tokyo.

26 July Miles Davis appears with seventeen-year-old drummer prodigy Tony Williams in Antibes. Williams now forms part of Davis's new quintet – featuring George Coleman (tenor saxophone), Herbie Hancock (piano) and Ron Carter (bass) – which recorded *Seven Steps to Heaven* in New York in **May**.

6 September Duke Ellington (● p. 183) embarks on a tour arranged by the US State Department. His itinerary includes Syria, Jordan, Jerusalem, Beirut, Afghanistan, India, Ceylon, Pakistan, Iran, Iraq, Kuwait, Turkey, Cyprus, Egypt and Greece. The tour is abandoned after the assassination of President John F. Kennedy on **22 November**.

Left This expressive sketch of Bill Evans was drawn by Norwegian jazz critic Randi Hultin.

Everybody Digs Bill Evans

BOP piano playing quickly ran itself into a stylistic rut when second-rate pianists found themselves unable to achieve the individuality of Thelonious Monk (● p. 154) or Bud Powell. Mechanical, fragmented improvised melodies in the right hand were invariably supported by spiky and seemingly random chords in the left (a type of accompaniment known as "comping"), and it all sounded much the same.

Bill Evans proved himself to be practically the single-handed savior of modern jazz piano when he emerged from working with Charles Mingus and Miles Davis in the late 1950s to establish himself as a strongly individual talent. His interest in MODAL techniques was demonstrated by the track "Peace

Piece" on his album *Everybody Digs Bill Evans* in 1958, and was intensified the following year by his collaboration with Davis on the seminal project *Kind of Blue* (● p. 146). Modal techniques, stemming ultimately from Evans's awareness of the music of classical French composers such as Debussy (● p. 24) and Satie, became part of an unusually rich harmonic vocabulary that allowed him to escape from the clichés of other bop pianists. Arguably his finest work was recorded in 1959–61 with a trio featuring bassist Scott LaFaro and drummer Paul Motian. This ensemble, which benefitted from an outstanding instinctive rapport between the three men, was cruelly curtailed by LaFaro's untimely death (● p. 153).

Evans's most important and influential attribute was his innate lyricism, which added a vein of sensitivity and expressiveness into jazz at a time when it was most in need of it. Unlike some other COOL performers, Evans combined his relaxed musical intimacy with sophisticated compositional and improvisational techniques that never allowed the listener to lapse into complacency. His work was widely emulated in Europe in the 1970s, and had a decisive impact on later American pianists such as Keith Jarrett (● p. 185) and Lyle Mays (● p. 211).

Left Tony Williams was the youngest and most virtuosic jazz drummer of the decade. He is seen here playing with Miles Davis in London in the late 1960s.

821 984-2

Above Polygram/Verve reissued Evans's boldly original *Conversations with Myself* on CD in 1984.

Over-dubbing

and contrapuntal ingenuity. He repeated the experiment with a second album, *Further Conversations with Myself*, in 1967. However, his was not the first such venture: it had been inspired by Lennie Tristano's *Ju-Ju* (recorded in 1951 but not released until 1971), and *Requiem* (1955), a radical project in which the master tape was played back at increased speed to create a disconcerting timbre.

All this technological wizardry was made possible by the introduction of magnetic tape, which rapidly supplanted the old electrical recording method (● p. 59) in the late 1940s. In addition to its multi-tracking possibilities (which later extended to the provision of twenty-four individual tracks on a two-inch tape), magnetic tape could be easily cut, spliced and re-mixed to create seemingly endless artistic possibilities. Creative overdubbing and editing techniques were pioneered by Charles Mingus, notably in his album *The Black Saint and the Sinner Lady* (also recorded in 1963), and by Miles Davis in collaboration with his Columbia producer, Teo Macero, from 1968 onward.

Bill Evans's solo album *Conversations with Myself* (1963) was a bold experiment in "overdubbing," a technique otherwise known as multi-track recording, which allowed him to accompany himself by adding two further tracks to his original take. Evans's compositional skill produced textures of great fluidity that were shot through with harmonic resourcefulness

WORLD EVENTS

1963

30 January Death of Francis Poulenc

28 August Martin Luther King addresses civil rights rally, Washington, DC

31 August Death of Georges Braque

11 October Death of Jean Cocteau

22 November President Kennedy assassinated, Dallas, Texas

● National Theatre opens, London

1964

June Nelson Mandela begins life sentence, South Africa

14 October Martin Luther King receives Nobel Peace Prize

15 October Death of Cole Porter

● Film musical *My Fair Lady* receives Oscar for Best Picture
● Stanley Kubrick's film *Dr. Strangelove*
● The Beatles appear in the film *A Hard Day's Night*

Autumn Sonny Rollins plays in Stuttgart, Germany.

November John Coltrane's "Alabama" is inspired by the fate of four black children killed in a church bombing incident.

14 December Dinah Washington dies in Detroit of an accidental drug overdose.

21 December Lee Morgan records his best-selling HARD-BOP hit *The Sidewinder* for Blue Note.

● Count Basie's band tours to Japan.

1964

15 January Trombonist and singer Jack Teagarden dies, New Orleans.

12 February The Miles Davis Quintet performs at New York's Philharmonic Hall. The event spawns the album *My Funny Valentine*, one of the greatest of all live jazz recordings. After the group's appearance in Tokyo in **July**, Wayne Shorter replaces George Coleman as tenor saxophonist. The group attends the Berlin Festival in **September**.

Far left, opposite Hard-bop trumpeter Lee Morgan, pictured here in London in 1961. He scored a major success with *The Sidewinder* in 1964, but his career was brutally curtailed by a bullet in 1972 (● p. 179).

Below Meade Lux Lewis, the Chicago pianist who spent the post-war years on the West Coast, died in a road accident in 1964 at the age of fifty-nine.

Above Dinah Washington performs in Los Angeles in 1959, four years before her untimely death. Her vocal artistry straddled the gospel, popular and jazz styles.

25 February Saxophonist Eric Dolphy records *Out to Lunch* for Blue Note with a quintet that includes Freddie Hubbard and Tony Williams. Dolphy shows his versatility by playing both bass clarinet and flute.

March Trumpeter Clark Terry and valve-trombonist Bob Brookmeyer begin a three-year series of recordings together.

3 March Chet Baker (● p. 210) is deported from Germany to the USA.

April Charles Mingus and Eric Dolphy perform in Amsterdam, Paris, Wuppertal and Stuttgart.

7 June BOOGIE-WOOGIE pianist Meade Lux Lewis is killed in a car accident, Minneapolis.

29 June Eric Dolphy dies from a heart attack in Berlin during his European tour with Charles Mingus.

A Love Supreme: John Coltrane

Above, opposite The somber sleeve for Coltrane's album *A Love Supreme*, on which the other musicians taking part were not credited – perhaps so as not to dilute the sense that this was a single artist's ultimate spiritual statement.

Below Coltrane in action at the Concertgebouw, Amsterdam, on 2 December 1962.

Few performers straddled the apparent gulf between HARD BOP and the avant-garde with the conviction of tenor saxophonist John Coltrane. A solid bop apprenticeship with Dizzy Gillespie (● p. 219) in 1949–51 laid the foundations for his improvising technique, but it was not until he joined Miles Davis's famous quintet (● p. 137) in 1955 that his uncompromising musical personality began to assert itself. Unlike Davis, however, Coltrane's improvisations often comprised strings of notes delivered at a frenetic speed that sometimes conflicted with the underlying chords (an approach aptly described by critic Ira Gitler as "sheets of sound").

Coltrane's own quartet – featuring the talents of pianist McCoy Tyner, bassist Jimmy Garrison and drummer Elvin Jones – was established by 1961 and survived until the year before his death in 1967. By then, Coltrane had begun to associate himself with the FREE JAZZ movement, absorbing Ornette Coleman's experiments into his own octet album *Ascension* (1965), and working with leading innovators such as saxophonists Eric Dolphy and Pharoah Sanders. Sanders and Archie Shepp were primarily responsible for furthering the aggressive tone representative of Coltrane's playing at its most powerful, a sound that became a prominent feature of the avant-garde in the later 1960s.

Coltrane emerged from a drug-related personal crisis in 1957 with a heightened sense of spirituality and a strong religious fervor. His deliverance from self-destruction was celebrated in the 1964 recording *A Love Supreme*, a landmark in the development of the "concept" album, which connected as much with white hippies of the time as it did with black civil rights activists. In the first track, "Acknowledgement," a four-note instrumental motif is reiterated to saturation point, and then is explained when the quartet sings it to the four syllables of the album's title. The fourth and final track is an ambitious "Psalm" in which the saxophonist improvises, in a suitably declamatory style, an instrumental interpretation of his own poem of praise and thanksgiving printed in the sleeve notes.

Coltrane had as great an influence on younger tenor saxophonists as Charlie Parker did on subsequent alto players, especially in terms of tone production. The impact of his playing was immediately evident in the 1960s and has continued without significant interruption to affect the work of musicians up to and including recent figures such as Mike Brecker, Courtney Pine and Branford Marsalis.

"Not merely loved, not merely idolized, [Coltrane] came to be revered as a saint, a mystic being whose simple presence on earth, some of his worshippers believed, would set the world straight. One writer, Frank Kofsky, wrote his name in for vice president during the 1964 elections. Another placed him in a pantheon along with Muhammed and Jesus. Yet another, Joachim Berendt, claimed that there emanated from him 'a hymnic power of love' . . . John Coltrane, in sum, was seen – and still is seen by many – not merely as a great jazz musician, but as a spiritual leader on a level with the founders of the world's great religions."

James Lincoln Collier, 1978

A Love Supreme/John Coltrane

June–July Duke Ellington's first tour to Japan. In **September**, he records selections from the film *Mary Poppins* in Chicago.

June–August Dexter Gordon makes a series of recordings in Copenhagen.

September Charles Mingus presents his large-scale *Meditations on Integration* at the Monterey Jazz Festival.

9 September Avant-garde tenor saxophonist Albert Ayler (● p. 164) records his album *Ghosts* in Copenhagen.

October Blind multi-instrumentalist Roland Kirk performs at Stockholm's first "Newport in Europe" festival, held in the city's Johanneshov Ice Stadium.

26 October Horace Silver records *Song for My Father* for Blue Note.

7 November Pianist Erroll Garner appears at the Concertgebouw, Amsterdam.

30 November Arranger Don Redman dies, New York.

9 December John Coltrane records his album *A Love Supreme*, a spiritual statement about his recovery from drug addiction. It sells hundreds of thousands of copies through canny marketing.

● British saxophonist/composer John Dankworth and his wife, singer Cleo Laine, record their album *Shakespeare and All That Jazz*, setting the bard's texts to music that veers between lyricism and playful eccentricity. ● The classic Benny Goodman Quartet (● p. 84) of the 1930s re-forms to record *Together Again!* for RCA. ● The Jazz Composers' Guild is formed in New York to promote avant-garde jazz.

Right Duke Ellington's and Billy Strayhorn's *Far East Suite* (recorded in 1966) was a musical celebration of the band's visits to India and the Middle East in 1963, and to Japan in 1964.

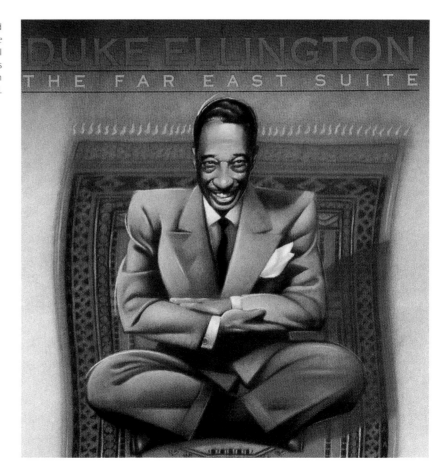

1965

'Trane Ascendant

John Coltrane joins the avant-garde with his album Ascension, *while Duke Ellington's spirituality is revealed in a very different musical idiom. Ben Webster emigrates to Europe, and Wayne Shorter makes his mark with the Miles Davis Quintet.*

20–22 January Miles Davis records the album *E.S.P.* in Los Angeles with a quintet featuring Wayne Shorter alongside Herbie Hancock (● p. 201), Ron Carter and Tony Williams.

January–February Ben Webster, now settled in Copenhagen, is active in Denmark and Norway.

15 February Nat King Cole (● p. 124) dies of cancer at the age of forty-seven, Santa Monica, California.

March Stan Getz (● p. 153) performs in Vancouver, British Columbia.

17 March Herbie Hancock records *Maiden Voyage* with his colleagues in Davis's rhythm section and trumpeter Freddie Hubbard. The album's title track demonstrates a sophisticated application of MODAL techniques.

25 March Stan Tracey's quartet records the suite *Under Milk Wood* in London. The work is inspired by the writings of Welsh poet and playwright Dylan Thomas.

20 June A Pittsburgh piano workshop showcases the talents of Mary Lou Williams and Earl Hines (both closely associated with the city), alongside Duke Ellington and Willie "The Lion" Smith.

28 June John Coltrane (● p. 160) records *Ascension*, a bold experiment in collective improvisation loosely modeled on the spirit of Ornette Coleman's *Free Jazz* (● p. 150). The work is issued in two versions due to Coltrane's indecision about which take he prefers.

Left Oscar Peterson's prodigious keyboard technique and musical sensitivity have delighted audiences across the globe since he first came to prominence in the 1950s.

Oscar Peterson

Canadian pianist Oscar Peterson, one of the most prolific recording artists of all time, acquired his phenomenal technical fluency after spending ten hours a day practising Chopin's *Etudes* in his youth. With a solid classical technique behind him, Peterson set about emulating characteristics of the jazz pianists he admired, most notably the dexterity and harmonic ingenuity of Art Tatum and the melodic appeal of Nat King Cole (● pp. 124–5). These features were amalgamated into a distinctive keyboard style that alternated attractive melodies and glittering virtuoso passages, and was distinguished by sensitive and inventive accompanying behind the solo work of other instrumentalists.

Peterson came to prominence in the USA following an appearance at Carnegie Hall in 1949, after which he became a stalwart member of Norman Granz's touring venture "Jazz at the Philharmonic" (● p. 106). His preferred medium was the piano trio, a format he

RCA VICTOR

DUKE ELLINGTON'S
CONCERT OF SACRED MUSIC

Duke Ellington pays tribute in music, song and dance. "Every man prays in his own language," he insists, "and there is no language that God does not understand."

Recorded by the Ellington Orchestra, Brock Peters and others, at the New York Fifth Avenue Presbyterian Church.

Above This LP release of Duke Ellington's *Concert of Sacred Music* shows the scene at the second performance of the work in New York's Fifth Avenue Presbyterian Church on Boxing Day 1965.

July Fresh from a concert at Newport shared with Archie Shepp, Coltrane travels to Paris and Antibes.

21 August Thelonious Monk (● p. 154) records live in Montreal, where, four days later, Oscar Peterson also plays.

September Albert and Donald Ayler (● p. 164) record *Spirits Rejoice*, featuring Call Cobbs in a rare jazz use of the harpsichord. ● Dizzy Gillespie and Charles Mingus are the stars of this year's Monterey Jazz Festival.

16 September The Grace Cathedral, San Francisco, hosts the first of Duke Ellington's "Sacred Concerts" under the title *In the Beginning, God*. It is repeated on **26 December** at the Presbyterian Church on Fifth Avenue, New York, and then receives over fifty further performances. The Pulitzer Prize Committee declines to accept a proposal to award a citation to Ellington.

6 November Pianist Clarence Williams dies, New York.

December Trumpeter Thad Jones and drummer Mel Lewis found a rehearsal orchestra that blossoms into one of the finest big bands working in a post-Basie idiom.

● Ornette Coleman emerges from two years of retirement to appear at the Village Vanguard, Greenwich, and also plays at the Golden Circle in Stockholm. ● Two important organizations are formed to promote the interests of the jazz avant-garde: the Association for the Advancement of Creative Musicians, founded in Chicago by Muhal Richard Abrams, and the Underground Musicians Artists Association, on the West Coast. ● The first annual Ragtime Festival is held in St. Louis, Missouri. ● The Blue Note label is taken over by Liberty Records (● p. 167) this year.

inherited directly from Cole and Tatum, in which the additional instruments were originally a guitar (Herb Ellis) and double bass (Ray Brown). In 1958, he substituted a drummer (Ed Thigpen) for the guitarist to create a group capable of greater rhythmic drive. This innovation prompted the pianist's style to move closer to the prevailing HARD BOP idiom of the day. After a spell devoted to solo concerts in the early 1970s, Peterson formed a new trio, with Danish bassist Niels-Henning Ørsted Pederson (● p. 152) and British drummer Martin Drew, that became popular in the UK through its studio performances in the BBC television series *Oscar Peterson's Piano Party*.

Peterson plays a special Bösendorfer grand piano, which he takes on tour with him. This instrument features additional keys at the bottom of the keyboard that allow bass lines to be extended below the normal register. When not in use, these extra keys are intended to be hidden by a hinged cover, so as not to distort the pianist's normal perspective. On one memorable occasion at London's Royal Festival Hall when Peterson was sharing a gig with Count Basie, he left the stage having forgotten to cover up the extra bass notes. When Basie came onstage to play a STRIDE solo on Peterson's unusual piano, he stunned himself (and the audience) by missing every single bass note. Basie was not amused.

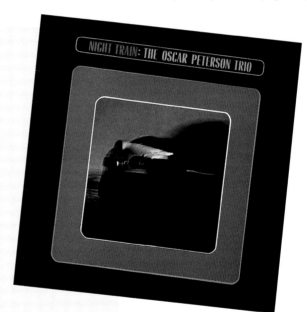

Above The Oscar Peterson Trio's celebration of the blues: *Night Train* (Verve, 1962).

OTHER EVENTS

4 January Death of T. S. Eliot

February–March Intensified US offensives in Vietnam

18 March First spacewalk (by Alexei Leonov)

11 August Thirty-four killed in Los Angeles race riots

27 August Death of Le Corbusier

● Film musical *The Sound of Music* receives Oscar for Best Picture

● First performance of Charles Ives's Symphony No. 4

1966

Greenwich Village

The Village Vanguard, in New York's Greenwich Village, cements its reputation as a leading venue by hosting the Jones-Lewis big band. The increasingly international nature of jazz takes John Coltrane and Duke Ellington to Japan, Earl Hines to Russia and many other American musicians to Europe.

Witches, Devils, Spirits and Ghosts

Saxophonist Albert Ayler had only been recording for four years in 1966, but in that short time he had acquired a reputation as a singular talent among the new wave of avant-garde musicians. Often collaborating with his brother Donald (trumpet), Ayler specialized in small-ensemble work characterized by the absence of a pianist – a feature inherited directly from the music of Ornette Coleman (● p. 150).

Under the influence of Coleman's and Cecil Taylor's radical attitudes to harmony, rhythm and texture, Ayler developed a remarkably free approach to improvisation that was most notable for its abandonment of regular METERS and even of recognizable tempos. As in much avant-garde jazz, Ayler seemed at times not to know when to stop playing (the same failing was openly confessed by Coltrane in his later years), and many of his improvisations lasted well beyond the limits of audience endurance.

Early work in Scandinavia in 1962 was followed by a mixed reception back in the USA, where, as in the case of Coleman, Ayler's provocative music led some critics to claim that he lacked a basic technical competence on his instrument. Coleman had been criticized for showing no apparent awareness of the history of jazz styles, but the Ayler brothers forestalled such criticism by absorbing elements culled directly from revered New Orleans traditions (funeral music, marches and folksongs). Brief snatches of simple melody would emerge from chaotic group improvisation like a breath of fresh air, only to be swallowed up again in another burst of frenzied and complex musical activity. The foundations for this sometimes bizarre style were laid in a series of idiosyncratic recordings, including two albums from 1964 – *Witches and Devils* and *Spiritual Unity*, the latter featuring Ayler's composition "Ghosts" – and *Spirits Rejoice* (1965).

In the few years before his untimely death, which occurred in circumstances sufficiently ambiguous to make him a cult figure (● p. 175), Ayler returned to his roots in rhythm'n'blues and appeared to have jumped back off the avant-garde bandwagon. As with many musicians tempted by the allure of commercially viable genres, he faced accusations of having "sold out." But avant-garde jazz was destined to remain essentially a minority interest, and many of the finest performers who subscribed to its artistic tenets found it necessary to earn their daily bread by other means.

Left The Ayler brothers in New York, 1966: Albert (left) and Donald (right).

WORLD EVENTS

30 July England wins soccer's World Cup, London

31 July Race riots in New York, Cleveland and Chicago

13 August Cultural Revolution, China

16 September Samuel Barber's *Antony and Cleopatra* opens new Metropolitan Opera House, New York

12 October Gunther Schuller's opera *The Visitation*, based on a work by Franz Kafka, is performed, Hamburg, Germany

- Truman Capote's novel *In Cold Blood*
- Dolby hi-fi noise-reduction system introduced

Right Thelonious Monk's protégé Bud Powell (seen here in Paris in 1960 at the height of his powers) returned to the USA in 1964, whereupon severe psychological and health problems forced him into retirement – and, soon after, an early grave.

Below Trumpeter and bandleader Thad Jones, here assuming the less familiar role of percussionist.

26 January Sonny Rollins records themes from his soundtrack to the British movie *Alfie*, starring Michael Caine.

February Thad Jones and Mel Lewis debut with their new big band at the Village Vanguard, a long-standing gig that lasts until the 1980s.

April Duke Ellington attends the World Festival of Negro Arts held at Dakar, Senegal. This year, Ellington also tours Japan and visits France and England, where his *First Sacred Concert* (● p. 163) is performed in Coventry Cathedral. Back home, he receives the President's Gold Medal of Honor from Lyndon Johnson.

May Earl Hines (● p. 124) plays in London.

19 May Cecil Taylor (● p. 150) records his complex *Unit Structures* (● p. 148) with an unorthodox ensemble that includes an oboe. His avant-garde style comes closer to the sound of contemporary classical composers than to jazz.

22 July John Coltrane (● p. 160) records live during a tour of Japan.

31 July Pianist Bud Powell dies, New York.

July–August Earl Hines takes his band to the Soviet Union on a US State Department goodwill tour.

4–7 August An international jazz festival is held in Molde, Norway.

24–25 October The Miles Davis Quintet (● p. 137) records *Miles Smiles*, the trumpeter's musical style reaching out for more abstraction while retaining powerful rhythmic momentum and strong BLUES elements.

November Albert Ayler tours Germany and France.

19–21 December The Duke Ellington orchestra records *The Far East Suite*, celebrating its recent State Department tours to the Middle East (● p. 161).

● Pianist Bill Evans plays in Denmark and at Oslo's Munch Museum. ● Louis Armstrong (● p. 56) appears as "Sweet Daddy Willie Ferguson" in the movie *A Man Called Adam*.

1967
Ends and Beginnings

In a year that brings the deaths of numerous influential talents, attention turns increasingly toward the burgeoning rock scene.

February John Coltrane (● p. 160) makes his last recordings, *Interstellar Space* and *Expression*.

20 February Duke Ellington performs his *First Sacred Concert* (● p. 163) at Great St. Mary's Church, Cambridge, UK.

March–April Earl Hines (● p. 124) and Roy Eldridge take a large group on tour to Europe.

23 March BOOGIE-WOOGIE pianist Pete Johnson dies, Buffalo, New York.

27 April Ben Webster records in London with trumpeter Bill Coleman.

May Saxophonist Charles Lloyd tours the Soviet Union and records live in Tallinn.

31 May Billy Strayhorn, Duke Ellington's co-composer (● p. 183), dies in New York. In **August** Ellington records Strayhorn's compositions on an album, *And His Mother Called Him Bill*, dedicated to his memory.

May–July The Miles Davis Quintet records the albums *Sorcerer* and *Nefertiti*. Most of the former and the title track of the latter are composed by Wayne Shorter.

BLUE LIGHTS VOLUME 2 1597
Artist KENNY BURRELL
Cover Design by REID MILES & ANDY WARHOL

WORLD EVENTS

27 January Apollo space crew killed in launchpad fire, Houston, Texas

6 March Death of Zoltán Kodály

5 June Six-Day War, Middle East

29 November Karlheinz Stockhausen's electronic *Hymnen* performed in Cologne

● First heart-transplant operation

● Mike Leigh receives Best Director Oscar for *The Graduate*, popularizing the songs of Simon and Garfunkel

Blue Note: Anatomy of a Record Label

Left One of a pair of related sleeve designs produced for Blue Note records by artist Andy Warhol in 1958.

"Hot jazz ... is expression and communication, a musical and social manifestation, and Blue Note records are concerned with identifying its impulse, not its sensational and commercial adornments."

Launch catalog for Blue Note, 1939

In 1967 Alfred Lion retired from his position at the helm of Blue Note, the influential record label he founded in New York twenty-eight years earlier (● p. 94). The label made its name during a revival of interest in early jazz by putting its faith in Sidney Bechet (● p. 42), then a neglected figure, who recorded a quintet version of Gershwin's "Summertime" for Lion in June 1939. The sudden craze for BOOGIE-WOOGIE piano in the wake of John Hammond's Carnegie Hall concert in the previous year prompted Lion to promote the work of Meade "Lux" Lewis, Albert Ammons and Pete Johnson – with considerable commercial success. Other major traditionalists who were signed up by Blue Note in the 1940s included dixieland trumpeter Bill Davison, pianists James P. Johnson (● p. 46) and Earl Hines (● p. 124), and Cab Calloway's tenor saxophonist, Ike Quebec.

Quebec served as the label's A&R (Artists and Repertoire) man in the late 1940s. He persuaded Lion and his partner, Francis Wolff, to back recordings in the new BOP style. This initiative resulted in Thelonious Monk's famous sessions in 1947–52, and those cut by Bud Powell in 1949–51 and Miles Davis in 1952–53. Blue Note's commitment to BOP soon led naturally enough to a close involvement with the development of HARD BOP. By that time, the talents of recording engineer Rudy van Gelder, who was also employed by Prestige and Savoy, had earned all three labels a reputation for producing some of the finest mono sounds in the business. Blue Note issued an unrivaled selection of seminal hard-bop and SOUL-jazz recordings in the late 1950s and 1960s, including the best-known albums by drummer Art

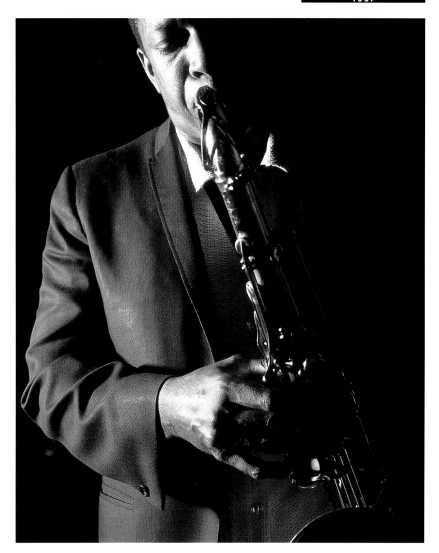

Right John Coltrane, who died in 1967 after attracting a cult following.

Blakey (● p. 138), trumpeters Lee Morgan and Freddie Hubbard, and pianist Horace Silver. Important new additions to the Blue Note catalog in the 1960s were Herbie Hancock and Wayne Shorter, both members of Davis's second great quintet who used the label to establish themselves as leaders in their own right.

Blue Note's importance was by no means confined to the consistently high quality of the music it preserved. The label paid musicians for rehearsals, a policy almost as unusual in the 1950s as it had been for Jelly Roll Morton in the 1920s, which undoubtedly had a beneficial effect on performance standards. And the recordings themselves were issued in striking sleeves (● pp. 148 and 168), designed by Reid Miles and often featuring photographs by Francis Wolff himself.

Bought by Liberty in 1963 and again by EMI in 1980, Blue Note's more recent work has included a firm commitment to the reissue of its earlier classic recordings, as well as fostering a new generation of traditional players under its subsidiary label Forecast. Michael Cuscuna first set this policy in motion in the mid-1970s, and has more recently issued much important Blue Note material (including the complete Monk sessions) under the aegis of his Californian company, Mosaic.

July The first Montreux Jazz Festival is mounted in Switzerland at Montreux Casino. ● In a potent sign of changing musical fashions, *Down Beat* announces that it will henceforth devote attention to rock music as well as jazz.

17 July John Coltrane dies from liver disease aged forty, New York.

20–21 July Dexter Gordon records in Copenhagen.

9 August Bill Evans records *Further Conversations with Myself* (● p. 157).

7 September Former Duke Ellington trumpeter Rex Stewart dies, Los Angeles.

December The Dave Brubeck Quartet disbands after a quarter of a century together.

29 December Bandleader Paul Whiteman dies, Doylestown, Pennsylvania.

● Trumpeter Lester Bowie forms the Art Ensemble of Chicago. ● Mayor John Lindsay abolishes the New York cabaret card, which musicians formerly had to acquire in order to appear at nightclubs. Such a card was refused to Billie Holiday when she applied for it after her prison term (● p. 113), and Thelonious Monk and Charlie Parker (● p. 126) both had their cards confiscated. ● Duke Ellington receives an Honorary Doctorate of Music from Yale University. ● Herbie Hancock (● p. 201) supplies a score for the trendy British film *Blow-Up*, directed by Michelangelo Antonioni and starring David Hemmings and Vanessa Redgrave. ● Frith Street becomes the new location for Ronnie Scott's famous London jazz club, founded in 1959.

1968

New Talents

Herbie Hancock and Chick Corea are the leading lights of modern jazz piano, both having served apprenticeships with Miles Davis. The free-jazz movement receives a boost from the impressive work of Anthony Braxton and Carla Bley.

Below CD reissue of Hancock's *Speak Like a Child*, exemplifying the striking sleeve designs for which Blue Note records were celebrated.

WORLD EVENTS

4 April Martin Luther King assassinated, Memphis, Tennessee

May Student protests in Paris

21 August Soviet invasion of Czechoslovakia

10 October Premiere of Luciano Berio's *Sinfonia*, New York

● Film musical *Oliver!* wins Best Picture Oscar

● London Bridge dismantled and shipped to Arizona

A Nordic Front

19 January First performance of Duke Ellington's *Second Sacred Concert* before an audience of seven thousand at the Cathedral of St. John the Divine, New York. Further performances are mounted in San Francisco, Paris, Stockholm, Barcelona and Orange, France.

5 February STRIDE pianist Luckey Roberts dies, New York.

23 February Vibraphonist Gary Burton appears at Carnegie Hall.

9 and **11 March** Herbie Hancock (● p. 201) records the album *Speak Like a Child* for Blue Note with a sextet including Thad Jones and bassist Ron Carter.

6 June Alto saxophonist Phil Woods records live at the Ninth Ljubljana Jazz Festival, Yugoslavia.

15 June Guitarist Wes Montgomery dies, Indianapolis, Indiana. His album *A Day in the Life*, recorded in 1967, is the year's best-selling jazz LP.

July Cecil Taylor (● p. 150) records *Praxis* in Italy.

August Herbie Hancock quits the Miles Davis Quintet.

September Chick Corea (● p. 178) and bassist Dave Holland join Miles Davis to replace Herbie Hancock and Ron Carter in the final recording session for the album *Filles de Kilimanjaro*.

1 September Duke Ellington visits South America, performing in Brazil, Argentina, Uruguay and Chile.

The European audience for jazz remained small outside France and England during the SWING era, although musicians in Scandinavia began to copy American styles as early as the 1930s. Danish violinist Svend Asmussen emulated the work of Joe Venuti (● p. 101) and accompanied Fats Waller when he visited Copenhagen in 1938, while Minneapolis-born violinist Leon Abbey appeared at the city's Hollaenderbyen restaurant the same year. Abbey also played at Oslo's Saga-Cinema and Stockholm's Nojesfaltet amusement park in the late 1930s, and Asmussen took his own brand of jazz to Stockholm's China Theater in 1942.

Sweden became an important center for the emerging European BOP movement in 1948, when Dizzy Gillespie's big band toured the country and influenced emerging Swedish saxophonists Lars Gullin and Arne Domnérus. Domnérus participated in the seminal 1949 Paris Jazz Festival (● p. 122), and Gullin distinguished himself in 1954 as the first European musician to head a *Down Beat* poll. Around this time Gullin began to absorb the new COOL style of Miles Davis and others. When Stan Getz (● p. 153) emigrated to Denmark in 1958, he brought a further influx of cool techniques with him.

In the 1960s, Scandinavian jazz venues became some of the most stimulating nightspots in Europe, hosting performances by high-ranking American musicians, many of them expatriates. The most prominent venues were Oslo's Metropol Jazzhus (opened in 1960) and Stockholm's Golden Circle, where Ornette Coleman (● p. 150) recorded in 1965. The initiative passed to Copenhagen in 1976 with the reopening of the Montmartre Jazzhus (founded in the 1950s), which secured residencies by Dexter Gordon and Thad Jones and fostered the growing European FREE-JAZZ movement. International awareness of Danish jazz has largely been fostered by the impressive work of bass player Niels-Henning Ørsted Pedersen (● p. 152), who made his name as a member of Oscar Peterson's trio.

Norwegian jazz grew in importance during the 1970s, thanks largely to the tireless endeavors of critic Randi Hultin, whose energy and enthusiasm attracted a stream of American musicians to Oslo. Native talents included bassist Arild Andersen, who collaborated with free-jazz trumpeter Don Cherry in 1968 and then with saxophonist Jan Garbarek in the early 1970s. Garbarek, a leading name on the ECM label (● p. 177), allied himself to a new synthetic jazz idiom that made considerable use of Scandinavian folk elements. This distinctively North European jazz style had already been pioneered by Swedish trumpeter Bengt-Arne Wallin in his album *Old Folklore in Swedish Modern* (1962), and by Finnish baritone saxophonist Seppo Paakkunainen and his group, Karelia.

For details of current international jazz festivals in Scandinavia, see the Reference Section.

Left Autograph manuscript of *Randi's Rag*, a personal tribute to Norwegian jazz critic Randi Hultin composed by stride pianist Eubie Blake (● p. 200) in 1974 at the age of ninety-one.

25–26 October Ronnie Scott records live at his London club.

Autumn Artists appearing at the Newport Jazz Festival in **June** undertake an extensive tour to Europe and appear at London's "Jazz Expo '68." Musicians involved include Dave Brubeck, Gary Burton, Benny Carter, Dizzy Gillespie, Earl Hines and Gerry Mulligan.

● Saxophonist Anthony Braxton, a member of the Chicago Association for the Advancement of Creative Musicians, now forms his own Creative Construction Company, records a mammoth solo performance in his double-album *For Alto Saxophone* and collaborates with other AACM members in *Three Compositions of New Jazz*. ● Chet Baker is mugged by a gang of drug addicts in San Francisco and loses several of his teeth. He is unable to play for two years. ● Flugelhorn player Art Farmer moves to Vienna, where he plays with the Austrian Radio Orchestra. ● The Black Artists Group is formed in St. Louis along the lines of early avant-garde collectives (● p. 150). ● Carla Bley's Jazz Composers Orchestra Association forms the New Music Distribution Service to disseminate its recordings. ● Saxophonist Joe Harriott (● p. 151) and violinist John Mayer form a double quintet in London to record music synthesizing elements of jazz and Indian music with a ten-piece ensemble comprising six jazzmen and four Indian players. ● Gunther Schuller completes his book *Early Jazz*, the first critical and analytical study of the music's origins and development.

Left Ronnie Scott's world-famous jazz club on London's Frith Street, premises it has occupied since 1967. A fine tenor saxophonist in his own right, Scott allegedly took his own life in 1996 after suffering from severe depressive illness for many years.

1969

New Horizons

Spectacularly rescued from dwindling public interest by the arrival of jazz-rock fusion, jazz is now an approved academic pursuit in US universities and its history is celebrated at The White House.

Right A late photograph of Coleman Hawkins, a supremely lyrical master of swing-style saxophone who died in 1969.

4 January Bassist Paul Chambers dies from tuberculosis.

18 February Miles Davis records his album *In a Silent Way* in New York.

April Pianist Herbie Hancock records *The Prisoner* for Blue Note.

29 April President Nixon holds a seventieth-birthday party for Duke Ellington at The White House, awarding him the Medal of Freedom. Jazz celebrities attending the event include Ellington's mentor Willie "The Lion" Smith, Dave Brubeck, Earl Hines and Clark Terry.

19 May Tenor saxophonist Coleman Hawkins dies.

26 May is proclaimed Duke Ellington Day in the State of New York.

12 August The Art Ensemble of Chicago records in Paris, where Don Cherry also appears this year.

19–21 August Miles Davis records his album *Bitches Brew* (● p. 172) in New York.

September The University of California at Berkeley stages an international symposium on the work of Duke Ellington.

October Miles Davis is wounded in a Brooklyn shooting incident.

November Duke Ellington appears in Manchester and Bristol. This year he also tours Eastern Europe and the West Indies.

● Manfred Eicher founds the record label ECM (Edition of Contemporary Music) in Cologne (● p. 177), which soon establishes an innovative house style synthesizing FREE JAZZ and jazz-rock FUSION. ● Drummer Tony Williams forms Lifetime with John McLaughlin (guitar) and Larry Young (organ).

Right President Richard Nixon addresses the assembled company at his White House party to celebrate Duke Ellington's seventieth birthday.

WORLD EVENTS

2 March Concorde's maiden flight

17 March Mrs Golda Meir becomes Premier of Israel

8 June US government pledges gradual withdrawal from Vietnam

21 July First moon landing

15 August British troops sent to Belfast

1 September Colonel Gaddafi siezes power in Libya

● Woodstock festival of pop music, US
● Philip Roth, *Portnoy's Complaint*
● Mario Puzo, *The Godfather*

Birth of Fusion

"Jazz as we know it is dead."

Front cover, *Down Beat*, 5 October 1967

Although the 1960s brought many exciting innovations in jazz, the decade also saw one of its greatest crises as a new generation of young listeners were seduced away by the mass appeal of the blossoming pop and rock industry. Jazz had grown increasingly respectable since the 1940s, and could no longer represent the heady spirit of rebellion it had championed in bygone years. Once a music associated with sex, illicit alcohol and (later) drugs, jazz now seemed almost squeaky clean. (Significantly, rock rapidly succeeded jazz not only as a more popular music but also as the core of the escalating 1960s drug scene.)

Much worse, or so it seemed at the time, jazz was becoming increasingly characterized by an esoteric intellectualism guaranteed to alienate even its most devoted adherents. The gritty, avant-garde experiments perpetrated by the likes of Ornette Coleman (● p. 150), Cecil Taylor and Albert Ayler (● p. 164) never achieved the global popularity of the catchy numbers the Beatles manufactured with such tuneful ease. Even jazz stars of the magnitude of Miles Davis and John Coltrane (● p. 160) found themselves performing to half-empty venues in the mid-1960s.

The solution, which remains controversial among jazz aficionados, was a classic case of "if you can't beat 'em, join 'em." The Columbia label, concerned that Miles Davis's album sales were dwindling, boldly suggested that they cash in on the rock craze. Davis accordingly produced two albums in 1969 that launched a new concept of jazz-rock FUSION: *In a Silent Way* and *Bitches Brew*. The latter went on to distinguish itself as one of the best-selling jazz albums of all time, thus vindicating Columbia's policy – at least in commercial terms. The new music unashamedly borrowed two prominent features from rock: a bias toward electronic and amplified sounds (principally electric bass guitar with electric piano and/or synthesizers), and non-swinging rhythmic patterns characterized by emphatic BACKBEATS. The traditional WALKING BASS disappeared, replaced by syncopated bass RIFFS that could be repeated at length.

Later developments in FUSION (and other CROSSOVER ventures) were made by a clutch of talented sidemen who participated in Davis's 1969 recordings. These included keyboard players Chick Corea (● p. 178), Herbie Hancock (● p. 201) and Joe Zawinul (● p. 174), drummer Tony Williams (● p. 157) and British guitarist John McLaughlin (● p. 179).

"Miles hears and what he hears he paints with. When he sees he hears, eyes are just an aid to hearing if you think of it that way. It's all in there, the beauty, the terror and the love, the sheer humanity of life in this incredible electric world which is so full of distortion that it can be beautiful and frightening in the same instant."

Ralph J. Gleason, sleeve note to *Bitches Brew*, 1969

Right Miles Davis at Tanglewood, 18 August 1970. Compare his attire to the conventional dress of his earlier career (● p. 146).

171

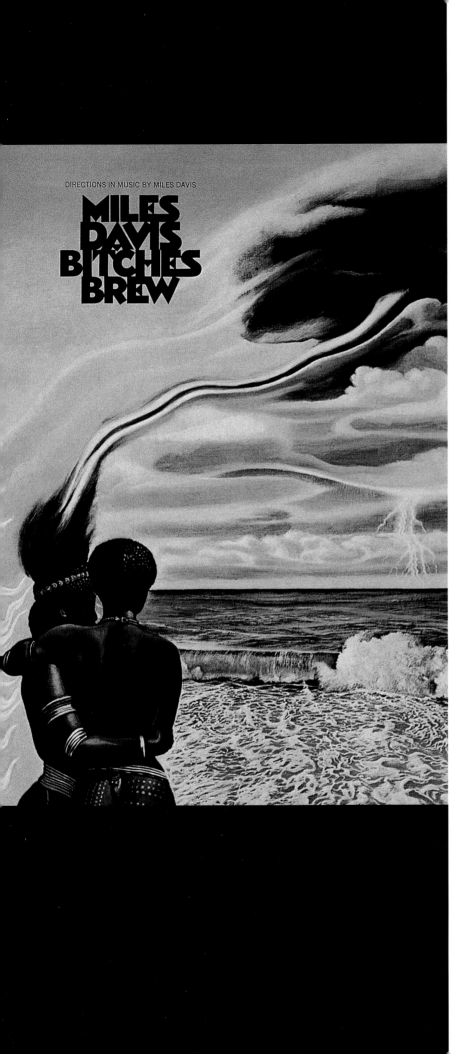

1970-95

Innovation and Reaction

Jazz-rock fusion wins itself a vast new audience in the 1970s, but the next decade is one of stylistic indecision: traditional jazz styles are resurrected, the avant-garde movement acquires a renewed impetus, and European jazz begins to explore novel crossover idioms.

Miles Davis's aggressive fusion double-album *Bitches Brew*, released by Columbia in 1970, proved to be one of the best selling and most influential recordings in jazz history.

1970
Forecast Unsettled

Keyboard players Joe Zawinul and Chick Corea are poised to take American jazz into a new electronic realm. In Britain, Ian Carr and Tony Oxley continue the surge of creative energy already initiated by John McLaughlin.

January British trumpeter Ian Carr records his first album, *Electric Rock*, with his jazz-rock group Nucleus in London. They go on to win a major prize at the Montreux Jazz Festival this year, as well as appearing at the festival in Newport.

7 February British drummer Tony Oxley records *Four Compositions for Sextet* in London.

February–June The Art Ensemble of Chicago undertakes a series of recording sessions in Paris.

March Miles Davis (● p. 216) is arrested when a police officer attempting to move him away from a restricted parking zone notices he is carrying brass knuckles for protection. He spends a night in a police cell and is fined for not possessing a vehicle registration.

April Miles Davis's double album *Bitches Brew* (● p. 172) is released. It meets with phenomenal commercial success and initiates jazz-rock FUSION as the jazz style of the future. Davis begins work on his movie score to the boxing epic *Jack Johnson*.

The astonishing speed with which jazz styles were changing as the new decade began was aptly summarized by the name of a new FUSION group founded in December 1970: Weather Report. The band was the brainchild of Austrian-born keyboard player Joe Zawinul and saxophonist Wayner Shorter, both of whom had served as sidemen to Miles Davis during his recent stylistic crisis (● p. 170). Weather Report soon became one of the most influential groups in the history of jazz. It survived until 1986, producing on average one album per year on the Columbia label (which began reissuing its work on CD in 1990). During the band's sixteen-year career, its members included some of the most significant younger talents of the fusion boom, notably Jaco Pastorius (electric bass) and drummers Alex Acuña, Steve Gadd and Peter Erskine.

Like Chick Corea in his work with Return to Forever, Zawinul's fusion style promoted infectious dance rhythms and enticing melodies that were a sharp contrast to the provocative and adventurous approach taken by Miles Davis in *Bitches Brew*.

Right Weather Report's best-selling album *Heavy Weather* (1976) spawned a pop hit by Manhattan Transfer.

Far right Wayne Shorter co-led Weather Report with Joe Zawinul, and developed an ethereal tone on soprano saxophone that exerted a major influence on fusion players.

Weather Report

Zawinul's expertise with synthesizers resulted in fresh and sophisticated musical textures, and in its first two years the band began to absorb significant rock influences (although Zawinul later objected to the comparison, commenting that rhythm'n'blues had a more potent impact on his work). The album *Heavy Weather* scored a major success in 1976, realizing phenomenal sales that were only eclipsed by Manhattan Transfer's subsequent pop vocalization of the album's most famous track, "Birdland."

Weather Report's most impressive achievement was its ability to synthesize diverse musical elements into a coherent and immediately recognizable style, presenting its music in a commercially viable format

WORLD EVENTS

2 February Death of Bertrand Russell

25 February Death of Mark Rothko

April Apollo 13 crew stranded in space

30 April US Army in Cambodia

18 September Jimi Hendrix dies from drug overdose

4 October Janis Joplin dies from drug overdose

● Columbia introduces quadrophonic discs
● Glenda Jackson wins Best Actress Oscar for Ken Russell's
Women in Love

Right Albert Ayler, whose body was discovered in a New York waterway in November 1970. Widely misunderstood, his music attempted to unite traditional New Orleans elements with progressive avant-garde techniques.

without compromising artistic standards. The striking sleeve designs of their LPs may have been closer to the pop market than to those of mainstream jazz records, but the group could just as happily work in an avant-garde idiom as in a more superficially "popular" style. Snatches of banal yet catchy melodies were disrupted by a skillful application of unpredictable rhythms and unexpected harmonies so that themes always sounded fresh and original, even where the individual ingredients might be clichéd. Subtle and sensitive use of electronic tones, real-life sound effects and free improvisation were amalgamated with sometimes strictly PRE-COMPOSED structures to create music that appealed (like all great music) to both heart and mind.

7 April Chick Corea's trio records *The Song of Singing* for Blue Note, an eclectic album that includes perhaps the most satisfying and musical of all experiments with ATONAL jazz.

11 May Duke Ellington's celebrated alto saxophonist Johnny Hodges dies, New York.

June Keith Jarrett (● p. 185) joins Miles Davis's group, playing electric organ.

25 June Duke Ellington's ballet *The River* is performed by the American Ballet Theater at the State Theater, New York.

Summer Bill Evans (● p. 156) plays at the Kongsberg Jazz Festival, Norway.

23–23 September Soprano and tenor saxophonist Jan Garbarek records *Afric Pepperbird* in Oslo for ECM (● p. 177). He visits the USA with the aid of a Norwegian government grant this year.

October Chick Corea and Dave Holland quit Miles Davis, later forming the group Circle with drummer Barry Altschul and saxophonist Anthony Braxton. ● Thelonious Monk (● p. 154) appears in Tokyo.

November Charles Mingus and Sun Ra record in Berlin.

24 November is proclaimed Duke Ellington Day in New Mexico.

25 November Saxophonist Albert Ayler's body is recovered from New York's East River after he has been missing for three weeks. Whether his drowning was self-inflicted or an act of homicide is never established.

● Joshua Rifkin records Scott Joplin's piano RAGS for the Nonesuch label. ● Max Roach refuses to record in the USA as a protest against exploitation of musicians. His protest lasts until 1976. ● Poet and *Daily Telegraph* jazz critic Philip Larkin publishes his collected jazz criticism in London under the title *All What Jazz: a Record Diary, 1961–8.*

1971

Death of a Legend

Louis Armstrong dies one month before his seventieth birthday and is internationally mourned. Jazz-rock fusion gathers momentum with the music of Weather Report and the Mahavishnu Orchestra.

January British tenor saxophonist Tony Coe (the performer of Henry Mancini's famous *Pink Panther* theme) records with compatriot Brian Lemon's piano trio in London.

February Anthony Braxton records in London.

16–17 February Joe Zawinul's new FUSION group Weather Report (● p. 174) records *Orange Lady* in New York.

21 February Circle (● p. 175) tours to Paris, where the quartet's concert is recorded by ECM.

12 April Pianist Wynton Kelly dies, Toronto.

21–22 April Chick Corea (● p. 178) records two sets of *Piano Improvisations* in Oslo for ECM.

12 June Vibraphonist Gary Burton records in Tokyo. This year he also collaborates with Keith Jarrett (● p. 185).

6 July Louis Armstrong dies, New York. Three weeks later, his first wife, Lil Hardin Armstrong (● p. 48) dies of a heart attack.

"[Armstrong's] style of improvisation would seem to have combined the highest reaches of instrumental virtuosity with the most tensely disciplined melodic structure and the most spontaneous emotional expression, all of which in one man you must admit to be pretty rare."

Virgil Thomson, 1981

Above Louis Armstrong lying in state in the summer of 1971.

Right One year before his death, "Satchmo" was pictured on the steps of his home at Queen's, London Island. His impromptu music-making with black youngsters recalled images of his own humble musical beginnings at New Orleans' Colored Waifs' Home (● p. 28).

ECM and the New European Jazz

As several leading members of the American avant-garde migrated to Europe in the late 1960s, European musicians grew more confident in developing a new brand of jazz that departed from the hegemony of orthodox American styles. One of the most enduring successes borne on this new wave of independence was that of the Edition of Contemporary Music, a record label established in Cologne by bassist Manfred Eicher in 1969. Initially linked to the FREE-JAZZ movement, ECM seduced many cutting-edge American musicians into its studios during the 1970s, including pianists Keith Jarrett (● p. 185) and Chick Corea (● p. 178), vibraphonist Gary Burton and guitarist Pat Metheny (● p. 198).

The unique house sound cultivated by ECM, which has in more recent years become diluted, was the first European jazz style to have had a perceptible influence on the development of American jazz. Beginning with an unlikely but artistically successful amalgamation of free jazz and jazz-rock FUSION, ECM went on to encourage ACOUSTIC recordings at a time when electronic techniques prevailed. More important, at least as far as native European musicians were concerned, was the label's commitment to an innovative mixture of jazz-rock and folk music, which continued to produce some of the freshest sounds in jazz into the 1980s.

The linchpin of ECM's jazz-folk ventures was the Norwegian saxophonist Jan Garbarek, who used plaintive and sometimes plangent tones on soprano saxophone to evoke the atmosphere of Scandinavian landscapes in prolonged MODAL improvisations. Varied and equally striking soundscapes were created by German bassist Eberhard Weber, who, together with his pianist Rainer Brüninghaus, often collaborated on the label with Garbarek in the 1980s. Pat Metheny's early albums with ECM (1975–84) absorbed reminiscences of American country music into the house style, and provided a sound basis for his later explorations of free jazz and jazz-rock.

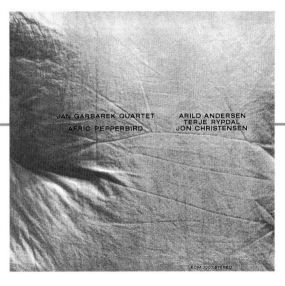

JAN GARBAREK QUARTET
AFRIC PEPPERBIRD
ARILD ANDERSEN
TERJE RYPDAL
JON CHRISTENSEN

ECM 1007 STEREO

Jazz critic Martin Williams reviews Charles Mingus's autobiography and concludes:

"Beneath the armor of destructive (if thoroughly understandable) self-pity, there is a man who seems compelled to ask the world to hurt and misuse him, and who therefore shows the world his (and its) shadow side. And beneath that man is a being in torment who protests his accomplishments in music and his conflicting heritage as an American mulatto but who seems unable really to believe in them or to take confidence in them or take heart from them, and accept his place as an American musician. The Gods have indeed looked with favor upon those complex and gifted men who, like Ellington, discover, accept, and live out their destinies from the beginning."

Right Jan Garbarek's album *Afric Pepperbird*, recorded with an all-Norwegian quartet, was the first release on Manfred Eicher's ECM label in 1970.

July Miles Davis plays four concerts to a sparse audience in New York, during a difficult year in which he is taken to court for breach of contract, pursued by tax inspectors and served with an $11,000 bill for repairs to his Lamborghini (one of his several prized sports cars).

14 August John McLaughlin's newly formed Mahavishnu Orchestra records *The Inner Mounting Flame* in New York.

September Duke Ellington (● p. 183) visits the Soviet Union for a five-week tour of major cities. On the way home in **October**, his orchestra visits the UK, appearing in Bristol and Birmingham.

November Thelonious Monk (● p. 154) records extensively in London, where Miles Davis appears at the Royal Festival Hall.

December Sun Ra's Arkestra is on tour in Cairo.

● Jack DeJohnette and Keith Jarrett quit Miles Davis. ● Charles Mingus (● p. 190) publishes his autobiography, *Beneath the Underdog*.

WORLD EVENTS

6 April Death of Igor Stravinsky

July Color television relay of US astronauts driving on moon's surface

26 December US aircraft bomb North Vietnam

● Stanley Kubrick's film *A Clockwork Orange* banned in UK
● Andy Warhol exhibition at Tate Gallery, London

1972
The Old and the New

Scott Joplin's opera Treemonisha *(1911–15) receives a long overdue professional performance, while the frontiers of jazz-rock fusion are broadened by the continuing work of Chick Corea and Joe Zawinul.*

Left Chick Corea, who typified the new stylistic versatility of jazz musicians in the 1970s.

Chick Corea and Return to Forever

"What I am striving for is incorporating the discipline and beauty of the symphony orchestra and classical composers – the subtlety and beauty of harmony, melody and form – with the looseness and rhythmic dancing quality of jazz and more folky musics."

Chick Corea, interviewed in *Down Beat*, 1974

The stylistic implications of Miles Davis's pioneering FUSION album *Bitches Brew* (● p. 171) were later fully explored by two keyboard players featured on that release: Joe Zawinul, who founded Weather Report (● p. 174) in 1970, and Chick Corea. Already established as a virtuoso ACOUSTIC pianist with a wide-ranging approach before his encounter with Davis, Corea became renowned in the early 1970s not only as the leading exponent of electronic keyboards but as the founder of the fusion group Return to Forever in 1972. The band went through several personnel changes during the rest of the decade, moving from a Latin-tinged flavor in the earlier years to a heavier rock style. Stalwart members included Stanley Clarke (electric bass), Al Di Meola (electric guitar) and Lenny White (drums) – performers whose stunning virtuosity was a perfect match for Corea's own technical dexterity. The group's success coincided with Corea's deep involvement in L. Ron Hubbard's cult of Scientology, which promotes the concept of clearing away the mental constraints that prevent direct communication.

Corea has always been a resourceful composer, and the music he created with Return to Forever was

January Joe Zawinul's Weather Report (● p. 174) records the album *I Sing the Body Electric*.

2–3 February Chick Corea records his debut album with FUSION group Return to Forever.

4 February Charles Mingus (● p. 190) appears at the Philharmonic Hall, New York.

19 February HARD-BOP trumpeter Lee Morgan is shot dead at Slug's jazz club, New York, by his former mistress Helen More.

June Miles Davis (● p. 216) records *On the Corner*.

17 July marks the beginning of Duke Ellington Week in the Sate of Wisconsin. Ellington tours the Far East this year.

October Miles Davis is involved in an automobile accident that leaves him with both legs broken.

● Thelonious Monk begins a ten-year period of retirement at the home of jazz patron Baroness Nica de Koenigswarter (● p. 136). ● Saxophonist Ornette Coleman's *Skies of America* for jazz quartet and orchestra is performed by the London Symphony Orchestra. ● Scott Joplin's opera *Treemonisha* (● p. 21) receives its first professional staged performance at the Memorial Arts Center, Atlanta, Georgia. ● Billie Holiday's autobiography *Lady Sings the Blues* (ghost-written by William Dufty in 1956) is made into a film by director Sidney Fury, with Diana Ross starring as Holiday. ● John McLaughlin records *Birds of Fire* and *Love Devotion Surrender* with his Mahavishnu Orchestra.

Left British-born guitarist John McLaughlin moved to New York in 1969 and made a vital contribution to the emerging fusion movement.

distinguished by an entirely characteristic concern for structural variety. As a result, the band's achievements are some of the most cogent and enduring of the fusion era. Its POLYTONAL harmonies and intricately woven textures reflect an intellectual approach to jazz composition quite unlike Davis's intuitive originality, and its material was sufficiently memorable for several pieces to become STANDARDS in their own right.

Corea played a number of electronic keyboard instruments, including the Fender Rhodes ELECTRIC PIANO (with its distinctive metallic timbre that today sounds dated) and a variety of SYNTHESIZERS (● p. 193). Yet he continued to perform on a conventional acoustic piano and integrated the instrument into an otherwise electronic rock-influenced context. After Return to Forever disbanded in 1980, Corea returned once more to the reputable territory of acoustic jazz in a succession of fine trio and quartet sessions, and appeared alongside performers of the stature of Herbie Hancock (● p. 201) and Gary Burton. In the mid-1980s he recorded classical music and composed a Piano Concerto, but he then inspired a fusion revival with his new Elektric Band (● p. 205), which signed with the popular GRP label (● p. 214).

Above Return to Forever's album *No Mystery* (1975) featured compositions by all members of the group, and tempered their formerly aggressive rock sonorities with the addition of Corea's delicate acoustic piano.

WORLD EVENTS

30 January British troops kill thirteen in Northern Ireland shootings

17 February UK decides to join European Economic Community

May Strategic Arms Limitations Treaty (SALT) limits US and Soviet nuclear weapons

28 May Death of Duke of Windsor (formerly Edward VIII)

5 September Eleven Israelis murdered by Arab terrorists at Munich Olympics

November Final US bombing campaign against North Vietnam

● Andrew Lloyd Webber's rock opera *Jesus Christ Superstar*

1973-74

Headhunters

Herbie Hancock scores a major fusion success with Headhunters. Free jazz expands in Europe, and the deaths of Ben Webster and Duke Ellington mark the end of a mainstream era.

1973

January Bill Evans (● p. 156) performs in Tokyo, where Cecil Taylor and Sarah Vaughan appear later this year.

23 January Trombonist Kid Ory dies, Honolulu.

23 February Miles Davis is arrested at his home for possessing cocaine and an unlicensed handgun and is later fined $1000. In this year, the trumpeter's already wide musical horizons broaden further through a growing interest in the avant-garde music of Karlheinz Stockhausen.

18 April STRIDE pianist Willie "The Lion" Smith dies, New York.

Summer Gil Evans, moving on from his earlier post-Ellington style of PRE-COMPOSED band music (● p. 120), joins the electronic bandwagon with his album *Svengali*.

20 September Tenor saxophonist Ben Webster dies in Amsterdam, two weeks after appearing at his last gig.

16 October Drummer Gene Krupa dies, Yonkers, New York.

24 October Duke Ellington's *Third Sacred Concert* ("The Majesty of God") is performed at Westminster Abbey, London. His autobiography, *Music is My Mistress,* is published this year.

27–28 November Jan Garbarek records his version of Jim Pepper's *Witchi-Tai-To* in Oslo for ECM (● p. 177).

31 December John McLaughlin's first Mahavishnu Orchestra disbands after recording the album *Between Nothingness and Eternity.*

DEDICATED TO JAMES BROWN AND HIS MANDOLIN CLUB

THE ENTERTAINER

BY

SCOTT JOPLIN

COMPOSER OF

MAPLE LEAF RAG
SUNFLOWER SLOW DRAG
PEACHERINE RAG
SWIPESY CAKE WALK
THE STRENUOUS LIFE (RAG)
THE RAGTIME DANCE (SONG)
ETC., ETC..

A RAG TIME TWO STEP

50

JOHN STARK & SON
SHEET MUSIC PUBLISHERS
ST. LOUIS

Joplin Triumphant

By the end of the 1960s, the ancient RAGTIME art of Scott Joplin (● p. 21) seemed a world away from the social and stylistic preoccupations of contemporary jazz. In one of the most astounding turnarounds in the history of music, ragtime found itself propelled back into the limelight during the early 1970s, and even entered the pop charts.

Three factors created this entirely unpredictable situation. One influence was Joplin's opera *Treemonisha*, which had its first professional performance in 1972 (● p. 179) and won its composer a posthumous Pulitzer Prize when recorded four years later. A second ragtime-related success was the Oscar-winning movie *The Sting*, which made an overnight hit of Joplin's ragtime two-step *The Entertainer* in 1973. Lastly, and of least interest to the wider listening public, pianist Joshua Rifkin began a series of "authentic" recordings of ragtime pieces, reconstructing the restrained, unadorned manner of presentation Joplin had ceaselessly championed. By treating the music with a musicological respect normally reserved for the work of classical composers, Rifkin's performances seemed to bestow on Joplin's legacy that aura of classicism for which America's first great black composer had always yearned.

Made famous once again in the 1970s by the movie The Sting (right), Joplin's The Entertainer (left) was in fact an anachronism in this context: the film was set in the 1930s when old-fashioned ragtime had sunk into virtual oblivion.

December In Los Angeles, Joe Pass records his solo-guitar album *Virtuoso*, the first disc to be issued by the new Pablo label established by Norman Granz (● p. 106).
● German bassist Eberhard Weber records his album *The Colors of Chloe* for ECM, with a group featuring pianist Rainer Brüninghaus.

● Herbie Hancock (● p. 201) records his jazz-rock album *Headhunters* in San Francisco with multi-instrumentalist Bennie Maupin, bassist Paul Jackson, drummer Harvey Mason and percussionist Bill Summers. Achieving widespread popularity through the use of down-to-earth funky elements, it immediately breaks all sales records for jazz. ● The comedy thriller *The Sting*, starring Robert Redford and Paul Newman, is a smash hit at the box office, and promotes wider public awareness of the RAGTIME music of Scott Joplin by using the composer's piano rags in its soundtrack. The movie's score is arranged by the combined talents of Marvin Hamlisch and Gunther Schuller, who goes on to reconstruct ragtime arrangements from *The Red Back Book* (1915), which he performs with the New England Conservatory Ragtime Ensemble. ● Dizzy Gillespie (● p. 219) arranges a comeback appearance for Chet Baker (● p. 210) after a temporary retirement.

1974

February Soprano saxophonist Steve Lacy performs in Paris, appearing later in the year in Italy and Holland.

March Thad Jones and Mel Lewis take their big band (● p. 163) to Tokyo.

April The Akiyoshi–Tabackin big band records in Los Angeles. Formed in Hollywood last year by pianist Toshiko Akiyoshi and her second husband, saxophonist Lew Tabackin, the group forges a reputation for sophisticated arrangements and vivid instrumental colorings. ● Jan Garbarek and Keith Jarrett (● p. 185) record together in Norway.

14 May Paul Gonsalves (● p. 138) dies, London.

Above Willie "The Lion" Smith playing at the Newport Festival in 1971, two years before his death. He still sports the trademark hat and cigar of the 1920s stride pianists.

Above Hancock's funky album *Headhunters* included the track "Chameleon," which became a chart hit.

May John McLaughlin reforms an eleven-strong Mahavishnu Orchestra.

24 May Duke Ellington dies, New York.

29 May Anthony Braxton performs in Denmark, in a busy year in which he also visits London and Toronto.

4 July Stephane Grappelli (● p. 75) and Earl Hines (● p. 124) perform together in London.

Summer Chick Corea and Return to Forever (● p. 178) record their fusion album, *Where Have I Known You Before?*

August Herbie Hancock records the soundtrack to Michael Winner's violent movie *Death Wish*, starring Charles Bronson.

October Dutch saxophonist Willem Breuker records with his unorthodox Kollectief orchestra; he is soon regarded as one of the leading lights of the European avant-garde.

8 October Baritone saxophonist Harry Carney dies, New York.

November Oscar Peterson (● p. 162) visits the Soviet Union.

25 November The Modern Jazz Quartet (● p. 128) gives a final concert at New York's Lincoln Center before disbanding after over twenty years together, as Milt Jackson decides to pursue his own career. The group reforms in 1981 (● p. 196).

8 December French jazz critic Hugues Panassié (● p. 80) dies, Montauban.

● Count Basie (● p. 86) and his band make an amusing cameo appearance in Mel Brooks' comedy western *Blazing Saddles*. ● German author Ekkehard Jost publishes his book *Free Jazz* in Graz.

Above The eclectic music of Willem Breuker cultivated a bizarre mix of elements drawn from folk traditions and avant-garde free jazz.

Right The elder statesman of jazz: Edward Kennedy Ellington towards the end of his distinguished career.

WORLD EVENTS

1973

1 January UK becomes full member of European Economic Community

27 January End of Vietnam War

26 March Death of Noel Coward

8 April Death of Pablo Picasso

May Watergate scandal, USA

28 September Death of W. H. Auden

20 October Syndey Opera House opens

● Peter Schaffer's play *Equus*

1974

13 February Alexander Solzhenitsyn exiled by USSR

20 July Turkish forces invade Cyprus

8 August President Nixon resigns, USA

● David Hockney's paintings exhibited in Paris
● Tom Stoppard's play *Travesties*
● Sidney Lumet's film *Murder on the Orient Express*

The Ellington Phenomenon

Duke Ellington's death in 1974 at the age of seventy-five robbed the jazz world of arguably its greatest talent. Ellington was universally praised for creating memorable pieces in which complex techniques assimilated from classical music were inextricably fused with spontaneous jazz elements. In doing so he bridged the gap between nightclub and concert hall and has been regarded by many commentators as the finest American composer of all.

After departing from the Cotton Club (● p. 62), Ellington's band continued to flourish, thanks to its outstanding and unusually stable membership. In the 1930s, Ellington began to experiment with extended pieces and was the first jazz composer to attempt to break away from the structural limitations imposed by 78rpm discs (which could only accommodate a little over three minutes of music on each side).

Below The principal theme of Ellington's *First Sacred Concert*, in the hand of its composer.

"Reminiscing in Tempo" (1935), for example, occupied all four sides of two discs, and his large-scale "Diminuendo and Crescendo in Blue" sounded so avant-garde in 1937 that it only became popular nearly twenty years later (● p. 138).

His inspiration never flagging, Ellington created a steady stream of popular compositions showcasing the talents of valve-trombonist Juan Tizol, trumpeter Cootie Williams, saxophonists Ben Webster and Harry Carney, and (from 1939) the highly skilled arranger Billy Strayhorn. Strayhorn composed numerous pieces for the Ellington band, including its signature tune "Take the 'A' Train" (1941), and was as important as Ellington to its continuing success story until his death in 1967.

Ellington's ambitious extended jazz works had meanwhile crystallized in a series of performances at Carnegie Hall, commencing with *Black, Brown and Beige* in 1943 (● p. 104), which met with a mixed critical reception. Avoiding direct confrontation with the manifold artistic and technical difficulties involved in composing successful extended structures, Ellington's later large-scale ventures were invariably couched in the form of the suite (a succession of individual movements linked by common subject matter or similar musical material), for which the new medium of the long-playing disc was ideally suited.

Among the most notable examples to have originated in live performances were the three "Sacred Concerts" (1965, 1968 and 1973: see chronologies), and the *Far East Suite* (1966), inspired by Ellington's worldwide travels to exotic countries on behalf of the US State Department (● p. 161).

In 1973, Ellington published his autobiography *Music is My Mistress*. His book touchingly reminisces about the individual players whose talents and loyalty did much to secure the band its consistent success. It also reveals two preoccupations that greatly affected Ellington's character: his religious fervor, and his obsession with middle-class respectability – which resulted in a sometimes embarrassing deference to authority figures, notably the British monarchy (● p. 143). Yet these attributes may have been partly responsible for the refreshingly clean image of the Ellington orchestra, which survived the heroin-drenched BOP era with its reputation intact, while nevertheless responding artistically to the important stylistic developments introduced at the time.

After Ellington's death, the leadership of the band passed to his son Mercer, an accomplished trumpeter in his own right who composed the band's hit tune "Things Ain't What They Used to Be" in 1941. He took the orchestra to Europe in 1975 and 1977 and recorded spirited performances on various labels in the 1980s, including GRP (● p. 214). While not quite catching the unique sound quality of the legendary Ellingtonians of previous decades, digital technology has nonetheless imbued the Duke's perennial masterpieces with renewed vitality.

"In music, as you develop a theme or musical idea, there are many points at which direction must be decided, and any time I was in the throes of debate with myself, harmonically or melodically, I would turn to Billy Strayhorn. We would talk, and the whole world would come into focus ... He was not, as he was often referred to by many, my alter ego. Billy Strayhorn was my right arm, my left arm, all the eyes in the back of my head, my brainwaves in his head, and his in mine."

Duke Ellington, 1973

1975

Davis Bows Out

Miles Davis's poor health forces him into retirement while the fusion boom he initiated continues to flourish. Scott Joplin's posthumous reputation is strengthened by triumphant stagings of his opera in the US.

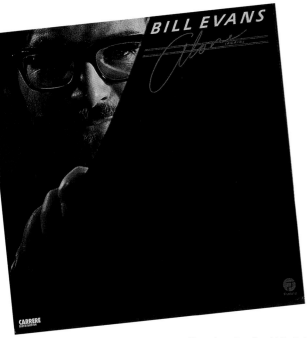

Above A master of sophisticated keyboard textures and musical sensitivity, Bill Evans continued to demonstrate the virtues of acoustic jazz piano in the midst of a rock-tinged decade.

WORLD EVENTS

21 May Barbara Hepworth killed in house fire, Cornwall

17 April Khmer Rouge takes control in Cambodia

April North Vietnam invades South Vietnam; Saigon evacuated by US

● Steven Spielberg's blockbuster film *Jaws*

January Tenor saxophonist Mike Brecker and his trumpeter brother, Randy, record together in New York. ● Chick Corea and Return to Forever (● p. 178) record *No Mystery*.

24 January Keith Jarrett makes a recording of a solo concert in Cologne for ECM (● p. 177).

February Miles Davis (● p. 216) appears in Japan, in spite of increasing ill health.

Spring French violinist Jean-Luc Ponty quits John McLaughlin's Mahavishnu Orchestra over a royalty dispute.

23 May Scott Joplin's opera *Treemonisha* (● p. 21) is staged in Houston under the direction of Gunther Schuller. According to the *New York Times*, "nobody applauded, they just yelled. Some even lost control and dashed onto the stage to join in." The work is equally successful when it opens on Broadway.

June Paul Desmond and Dave Brubeck (● p. 186) join forces on board the SS *Rotterdam*, recording for BBC television.

June–July Montreux continues to flourish as a center for excellence in jazz, hosting performances by Bill Evans, Dizzy Gillespie, Milt Jackson, Joe Pass, Oscar Peterson, Archie Shepp and Japanese saxophonist Sadao Watanabe.

July Miles Davis plays at the Newport Festival and, following a performance in Central Park in **August**, decides to retire. He contracts pneumonia and has a hip operation in **December**, and does not play in public for five years.

8 August Saxophonist Julian "Cannonball" Adderley dies, aged forty-six, Gary, Indiana.

September Eberhard Weber's group Colours records his richly textured album *Yellow Fields* for ECM.

December Bill Evans records his solo album *Alone (Again)* on the west coast. ● Guitarist Pat Metheny (● p. 198) records his first album *Bright Size Life* for ECM, supported by bassist Jaco Pastorius and drummer Bob Moses.

● Fourteen-year-old trumpet virtuoso Wynton Marsalis (● p. 196) performs Haydn's Trumpet Concerto with the New Orleans Symphony Orchestra. ● Alfred Hitchcock's former composer, Bernard Herrmann, writes a moody jazz score for Martin Scorsese's *Taxi Driver*, starring Robert De Niro. The theme is performed on the soundtrack by alto saxophonist Ronny Lang.

Jarrett in Cologne

"There was once a joke that in the year 2045 someone brought out a 'Best of Keith Jarrett' set in the currently fashionable laser-hologram/virtual reality format. It consisted of 87 LHVR diskettes. (There was an audiophile vinyl option, but you needed your own truck to take it home.)"

Richard Cook and Brian Morton, 1994

The ECM label (● p. 177) received a major boost in 1975 when its recording of pianist Keith Jarrett's live solo concert in Cologne became a best-seller: it has now sold over two million copies. The success of his first ECM album, *Facing You* (1971), spawned an eighteen-concert tour of Europe in 1973. As a result of that achievement Jarrett began a series of solo concerts in which he improvised colossal and richly varied extended pieces that demonstrated his absorption of jazz, classical, rock and country influences. Recordings of these performances at Bremen and Lausanne were released by ECM on a triple-LP set that was singled out as the best issue of 1974 by both *Down Beat* and *The New York Times*.

Jarrett's decision to concentrate on ACOUSTIC piano performances in the midst of the fusion boom's obsession with electronics may, in retrospect, be viewed as one of the most tenacious and significant musical gestures of the decade. In dividing his time between work in Europe and the USA, he also typified the increasingly global nature of modern jazz.

Since making his name in the 1970s, Jarrett has devoted his considerable energies to several clearly defined areas of activity: recordings of classical music (notably works by J. S. Bach in 1988 and Shostakovich in 1992); the composition of sometimes large-scale pieces for the concert hall; further extended solo improvisations on the Cologne model (in Germany in 1981, Paris in 1988 and London and Vienna in 1991); and a re-exploration of jazz STANDARDS with a trio featuring Gary Peacock (bass) and Jack DeJohnette (drums). His output extended to collaborations with Jan Garbarek (● p. 192), whose preoccupations with economy of musical material and haunting tones were well in accord with Jarrett's own thinking.

An unfortunate characteristic of Jarrett's performances is his tendency to sing along as he plays. With some pianists, notably Oscar Peterson (● p. 162), this habit can be infectiously high-spirited. But in the case of Jarrett, his wheedling and strained voice sometimes constitutes a serious distraction from the sensitive and musical nature of his keyboard playing, as in his trio's otherwise fine tribute to Miles Davis, *Bye Bye Blackbird* (ECM, 1991).

Below Keith Jarrett relaxes in the New York studios of Atlantic Records in 1971 under the watchful eye of his producer, George Avakian.

1976-78
Consolidation

In the wake of the fusion boom of the early 1970s, performers explore varied new musical directions and some return to earlier styles for inspiration.

1976

28 January Ray Nance, former violinist and trumpeter with Duke Ellington (● p. 101), dies in New York.

10 March Dave Brubeck celebrates the twenty-fifth anniversary of the formation of his quartet in a Michigan reunion with Paul Desmond (alto saxophone), Gene Wright (bass) and Joe Morello (drums).

June The Newport Jazz Festival hosts what is destined to be the last public performance by Thelonious Monk (● p. 154). Also at the Festival, Herbie Hancock (● p. 201) records live on **29 June** with his group VSOP.

July John McLaughlin disbands his second Mahavishnu Orchestra.

25 July Paul Bley appears in Japan and records live. Other artists visiting Japan this year include Keith Jarrett, Duke Jordan, Johnny Griffin, Milt Jackson, Hank Jones and Jim Hall.

August–September Charles Mingus (● p. 190) on tour in Europe.

Left Paul Desmond (left) and Dave Brubeck, whose popular quartet celebrated its twenty-fifth anniversary in 1976.

Japan

WORLD EVENTS

1976

20 July Viking space probe transmits pictures from Mars

25 July Philip Glass's minimalist opera *Einstein on the Beach* premieres in Avignon

2 November Jimmy Carter becomes the first Southerner to be elected US President since the Civil War

4 December Death of Benjamin Britten

- National Theatre opens, London
- Alex Haley's novel *Roots*
- US bicentennial celebrations

1977

27 March World's worst aviation disaster kills 582, Tenerife

12 August Test flight of US space shuttle

16 August Elvis Presley dies (or does he...?)

- Pompidou Centre opens, Paris
- George Lucas's movie blockbuster *Star Wars*

1978

17 March György Ligeti's opera *Le Grand Macabre* staged, Stockholm

April Revolution in Afghanistan

1 May Death of Aram Khachaturian

- Hit film musical *Grease*
- Michael Cimino's movie *The Deer Hunter* wins three Oscars

Jazz was initially slow to develop in Japan, a country that, until the Meiji Restoration of 1868, had been all but impervious to foreign cultural influences. Some early Western performers had spread the music to limited regions of Southeast Asia during the SWING era, but with the outbreak of World War II the Japanese authorities banned jazz completely with a totalitarian censorship directly analogous to the prohibitions in Nazi Germany (● p. 81) and the Soviet Union (● p. 207). After the cessation of global hostilities in 1945, however, a surge in imported American influences resulted in a sudden boom in indigenous Japanese jazz and a growing enthusiasm for the BOP style.

By the early 1950s, the Hot Club of Japan (founded in 1946) had begun to flourish and the climate was ripe for American star performers to undertake high-profile tours to prime locations in Tokyo and Osaka. Many such visits were sponsored by Norman Granz's "Jazz at the Philharmonic" (● p. 107) from 1953 onwards, and tours by artists of the stature of Miles Davis, John Coltrane, and Art Blakey had become commonplace in the mid-1960s. By the 1970s, Japanese jazz had acquired an exciting international flavor and the nation's capital frequently provided a meeting place for the finest performers in the world. In the 1980s and 1990s, enterprising Japanese record companies embarked on substantial programs of reissuing classic American recordings, which stimulated the growth of similar efforts in Europe and the United States.

Many Japanese performers have forged impressive reputations for themselves in the West, but none more successfully than pianist Toshiko Akiyoshi. A protégée of Oscar Peterson, Akiyoshi emigrated to the US in 1956 to study at Berklee College of Music in Boston. She worked with Charles Mingus (● p. 190) in the early 1960s, and by the early 1970s had become internationally renowned as one of the finest and most sophisticated big-band arrangers in the business. Saxophonist Sadao Watanabe, who assumed the leadership of Akiyoshi's quartet when she emigrated and who duly followed her to Berklee in 1962, also achieved world acclaim, and he is equally at home in post-BOP and jazz-rock FUSION idioms. The latter has proved to be more enduringly successful in Japan than FREE JAZZ, which has tended to be pursued more actively by expatriate Japanese performers working in Europe.

Above, left Born in Manchuria, pianist Toshiko Akiyoshi made her name in Japan in the early 1950s during the post-war boom in the Japanese jazz scene. Since moving to the USA, she has been active on both West and East Coasts.

Dave Brubeck's Silver Jubilee

In 1976 Dave Brubeck's famous quartet reunited to celebrate twenty-five years since its inception. The event drew attention once more to the Californian pianist's stature as one of the most popular and influential of the first generation of COOL performers. Unlike those other pioneers of cool, Miles Davis (● p. 120) and John Lewis (● p. 128), Brubeck had not served his musical apprenticeship in the BOP style. His training was primarily in classical music, and included lessons from expatriate French composer Darius Milhaud (who espoused the cause of SYMPHONIC JAZZ in the 1920s [● p. 53]). This classical stance allowed Brubeck to avoid the clichés of 1950s bop from the outset, and he went on to create jazz compositions that were highly original in both texture and structure. His music appealed to the listeners' intellect as much as their emotions without sacrificing melodic appeal, and became widely known during a series of much-publicized tours of American university campuses in the mid-1950s.

Brubeck's early work is best represented by his perennially popular album *Time Out* (1959), which featured the hit track "Take Five," written by his alto saxophonist Paul Desmond (● p. 186). This famous tune is cast entirely in bars containing five beats, an irregular METER much used in modern classical music but here making its jazz debut. Other tracks on the disc offered more complex attempts to break away from the 4/4 time ubiquitous in jazz, including "Blue Rondo à la Turk," which subdivided nine beats into the irregular pattern 2+2+2+3 (● p. 147).

Brubeck's definitive quartet disbanded in 1967 when Desmond quit and the leader decided to concentrate on the creation of concert works. His variously constituted jazz COMBOS in the 1970s sometimes featured the talents of his three sons (proficient on keyboards, trombone/bass guitar and drums), and critics formerly opposed to the apparent lack of swing in his early playing began to discern a greater sense of lyrical freedom as a new decade began and he appeared at the Newport and Concord Festivals (in 1980 and 1982 respectively).

Left CD reissue of Brubeck's *Time Out*, one of the most tuneful examples of 1950s cool jazz and the most rhythmically innovative recording of its time.

Weather Report: Black Market

The title track of Weather Report's album *Black Market* (1976) is a perfect illustration of the mixture of commercial appeal and sophistication so typical of early fusion music. It also celebrates the Afro-American heritage of the style, which the group's leader Joe Zawinul claimed to be of far greater significance than the white rock music that lent its name to jazz-rock.

The piece begins with the recorded sound of animated chatter in a black market-place, an overtly ethnic atmosphere that is heightened when the instruments enter with a persistent use of a pentatonic (i.e., five-note) scale. (Pentatonicism is common in many ethnic musics, and African pentatonicism may well have been responsible for the development of BLUE NOTES in early jazz.) The exuberant bass RIFF and Zawinul's cheerfully meandering synthesizer melody both adhere rigidly to the scale, a technique clearly influenced by Miles Davis's earlier MODAL experiments. A restatement of the theme is reinforced by the addition of a driving rock beat from Alex Acuña: in all, no fewer than three drummers are used on the track.

Just as the hypnotically revolving five-note patterns seem in danger of outstaying their welcome, the music launches into a passage of vibrant, complex harmonies enlivened by the unpredictable yet catchy syncopations typical of the style. As the rock accompaniment increases in intensity, Wayne Shorter plays a hard-edged soprano saxophone solo. Then, as the volume decreases, the bass-riff patterns gradually begin to suggest the pentatonic music of the opening. Yet the main theme fails to return, and the music merges into sound effects (thunderclaps and explosions suggestive of a fireworks display) as the piece fades away.

Right Roland Kirk (seen here in New York in 1967), who died in 1977. The ostensible gimmickry of his simultaneous playing on multiple instruments belied his genuine musicality and the high regard for mainstream jazz styles invariably revealed by his performances.

Above One of the live recordings from the 1977 Montreux Festival issued on the Pablo label, with its distinctive Picasso logo at top center.

9 September The Thad Jones–Mel Lewis big band plays in Munich.

15 September The Montmartre jazz club opens in Copenhagen (● p. 169).

October Lee Konitz records with a nonet that continues to reflect the influence of the COOL sound originally pioneered by Miles Davis and Gil Evans (● p. 120). This year Konitz makes two visits to London and an appearance in Rome.

December Ornette Coleman plays in Paris. The tenor saxophonist's comeback is further celebrated this month with the album *Dancing in Your Time*, revealing an absorption of FUSION influences in the use of electric guitars by his new group, Prime Time.

● Weather Report records their best-selling Columbia albums, *Black Market* and *Heavy Weather* (● p. 174). ● Scott Joplin receives a posthumous Pulitzer Prize as his opera *Treemonisha* is recorded for the first time

1977

2 January Pianist Erroll Garner dies, Los Angeles.

February Guitarist Pat Metheny records his ACOUSTIC album *Watercolours* for ECM with Lyle Mays (piano), Eberhard Weber (bass) and Danny Gottlieb (drums).

30 May Alto saxophonist Paul Desmond dies, New York.

July Count Basie's band, Dave Brubeck's new quartet and Dizzy Gillespie appear at the Montreux Jazz Festival. Many performances at the Festival are recorded live on Norman Granz's new label, Pablo.

Summer Charles Mingus again tours Europe, but the trip is blighted by his deteriorating health.

September The Monterey Jazz Festival celebrates its twentieth anniversary in California.

October Vibraphonist Lionel Hampton and baritone saxophonist Gerry Mulligan record together in New York.

Autumn Pianist Earl Hines makes a series of comeback recordings in Chicago and New Orleans.

November Sarah Vaughan records *I Love Brazil* in Rio de Janeiro.

5 December Multi-instrumentalist Roland Kirk dies, Bloomington, Indiana.

● Foundation of the eclectic World Saxophone Quartet by Hamiett Bluiett, Julius Hemphill, Oliver Lake and David Murray. ● Tenor saxophonist Scott Hamilton, aged twenty-three, records his debut album for Concord. The disc's title, *Scott Hamilton Is a Good Wind Who is Blowing Us No Ill*, borrows a phrase coined by critic Leonard Feather. Hamilton soon becomes a leading revivalist. ● Soprano saxophonist Steve Lacy is active in Italy, France, Switzerland and Germany. ● Drummer Kenny Clarke returns to the US from Europe, where he has lived for twenty-one years. ● Martin Scorsese directs his movie *New York, New York*, starring Robert De Niro as a saxophonist; his mimed playing is coached by tenor player Georgie Auld, a former sideman with Artie Shaw, Benny Goodman and Count Basie.

1978

March The Ganelin Trio (● p. 207) records *Strictly for Our Friends* in Moscow.

5 April Violinist Stephane Grappelli plays at New York's Carnegie Hall.

May The Art Ensemble of Chicago records in Germany.

Mingus and his Dynasty

Above Charles Mingus was equally important as a virtuoso bassist and provocative composer.

Charles Mingus made his last important recordings in 1977, bringing to a close a career marked by innovation, controversy and the grueling demands he constantly imposed on his distinguished sidemen. Although his exploration of advanced double-bass technique was itself notable (● p. 152), Mingus will be best remembered for the seriousness of his intellectual attitude to jazz. Such an approach paid dividends in the creation of intelligent and often challenging structures within a richly varied musical language. At times, he flirted with the avant-garde by verging on the brink of ATONALITY and total rhythmic freedom.

Highlights of his work in the 1950s include his colorful interpretation of Hispanic elements in *Tijuana Moods* (1957), an early example of the imaginative use of tape-editing to reduce the duration of the tracks. The project was in part a cathartic experience intended to dispel one of the bassist's habitual dark moods. "All the music in this album," Mingus wrote,

"was written during a very blue period of my life. I was minus a wife, and in flight to forget her with an unexpected dream in Tijuana . . . After finding myself with the sting of tequila, salt and lime in my mouth and burning my nostrils, I decided to benefit musically from this experience and set out to compose and re-create what I felt and saw around me. It included a strip tease ['Ysabel's Table Dance'] in one of the many local night clubs."

Less entertaining, if more prophetic musically, was the previous year's album *Pithecanthropus Erectus*, with its passages of free improvisation boldy foreshadowing the work of Ornette Coleman (● p. 150) and MODAL techniques looking ahead to Miles Davis (● p. 146). But many critics single out *The Black Saint and The Sinner Lady* (1963) as Mingus's most important work, not merely as an unusually early example of OVERDUBBING but for his conception of the album as one continual piece of music (the release was segmented into separate tracks at the behest of the nervous record company). Along with conquering technological limitations, here Mingus achieved a balance between spontaneity and orderly PRE-COMPOSITION only equalled in the work of Duke Ellington.

Mingus's importance in jazz history lies in his serious promotion of the work of other like-minded musicians through his own record label, Debut (founded in 1952), in his collaboration with the Jazz Composers' Workshop (which he formed in 1953), and in setting up a new festival at Newport during the official Festival's crisis period (● p. 148). Since his death in 1979, Mingus's artistic legacy has been promoted in performances by his widow's band, Mingus Dynasty (● p. 192) and, since 1991, by the Mingus Big Band in New York.

For critic Martin Williams's thoughts on the significance of Mingus's utterly depressing 1971 fantasy-autobiography, *Beneath the Underdog*, see ● p.177.

Right Blind pianist Lennie Tristano, who died in 1978, is here pictured playing at New York's Keynote in 1946 at around the time of his early collaboration with bop stars Charlie Parker and Dizzy Gillespie.

"I am a good composer with great possibilities and I made an easy success through jazz but it wasn't really success – jazz has too many strangling qualities for a composer . . . If music lovers knew the wealth of talent being wasted in the name of jazz they'd storm the managers' and bookers' offices and tell them they refuse to settle for the crap they're getting! How many jazz musicians would stay in the clubs if they could even make a living playing in parks and simple places without the big build-up that's now an absolute necessity for survival? Tote that Down Beat, win that poll, hope I get a mention before I'm too old! . . . If I want it right, Nat, guess I'll have to leave jazz – that word leaves room for too much fooling."

Charles Mingus to Nat Hentoff

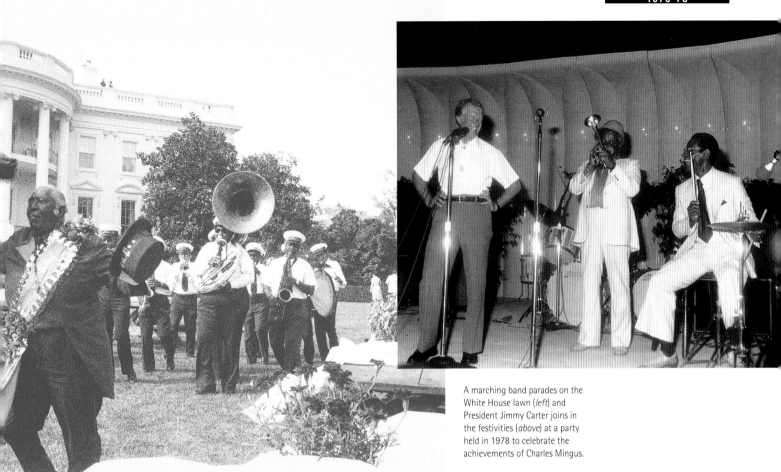

A marching band parades on the White House lawn (*left*) and President Jimmy Carter joins in the festivities (*above*) at a party held in 1978 to celebrate the achievements of Charles Mingus.

18 June   President Jimmy Carter hosts a jazz concert at the White House, Washington, D.C., in honor of Charles Mingus. Participants include Stan Getz (● p. 153), Dizzy Gillespie (● p. 219), Dexter Gordon and Max Roach.

11 August   Tenor saxophonist David Murray appears in London. Other American artists visiting the English capital this year include Phil Woods (**March**), Oscar Peterson (**October**) and Joe Pass (**November**).

14 August   Violinist Joe Venuti dies, Seattle, Washington.

September   Tenor saxophonist Johnny Griffin, who has lived in Europe since 1963, makes a rare US appearance at the Monterey Festival. He goes on to record in Berkeley with trumpeter Nat Adderley, brother of saxophonist Julian "Cannonball" Adderley. ● Don Cherry records *Codona* for ECM (● p. 177) with Collin Walcott (sitar and tablā) and Nana Vasconcelos (percussion). The album, inspired by Indian music, is a landmark in the crossover between jazz and ethnic music soon to be a strong feature of the 1980s (● p. 178).

23 September   Dexter Gordon plays at Carnegie Hall.

October   Chick Corea (● p. 178) and Gary Burton record *Duet* in Oregon, while Herbie Hancock (● p. 201) plays a series of concerts in Tokyo.

18 November   Pianist Lennie Tristano dies, New York.

28–29 December   Chet Baker (● p. 210) records in Paris.

● Drummer Peter Erskine joins Weather Report. ● The Cuban group Irakere promote Afro-Cuban jazz at the Newport and Montreux jazz festivals. ● Gil Evans appears at the Royal Festival Hall, London. ● Keyboard player Bob James scores a popular success with his FUSION theme to the American television comedy *Taxi*.

191

1979

The Mingus Legacy

Influential composer and virtuoso bassist Charles Mingus dies, aged fifty-six. Other leading performers join forces in small groups, some of which celebrate his work.

5 January Charles Mingus (● p. 190) dies, Cuernavaca, Mexico.

8 February In an interview published in *Down Beat*, Joe Zawinul argues that the music of his seminal FUSION group, Weather Report (● p. 174), is based more on (black) rhythm'n'blues than on (white) rock music.

March Drummer Jack DeJohnette collaborates with tenor saxophonist David Murray on the ECM album *Special Edition*, which becomes the name of a succession of small ensembles led by DeJohnette.

May Keith Jarrett (● p. 185) and Jan Garbarek record *Nude Ants* at the Village Vanguard, New York, for ECM.

9–10 July Mingus Dynasty, formed by Susan Graham Ungaro Mingus in memory of her late husband, records *Chair in the Sky*.

August Don Cherry (trumpet), Dewey Redman (tenor saxophone), Charlie Haden (bass) and Billy Higgins (drums) give a renewed boost to the FREE JAZZ movement with their album *Old and New Dreams*.

25 August Bandleader Stan Kenton (● p. 134) dies, Los Angeles.

● The Concord Jazz Festival features performances by Dave Brubeck (● p. 188), Ray Brown and Charlie Byrd.

Above Stan Kenton, whose controversial "progressive jazz" had been one of the few big-band styles to flourish after World War II.

Right Norwegian saxophonist Jan Garbarek (● p. 177), who recorded with Keith Jarrett in 1979.

Opposite Sonny Stitt (right), here seen in conversation with fellow saxophonist Red Holloway in London in 1980, developed Charlie Parker's style of improvisation to an unsurpassed peak of perfection.

Electrifying Jazz

The importation of electrically amplified and electronically generated sonorities in the 1970s revolutionized the sound of jazz. Initially inspired by the desire to cash in on the commercial success of rock music, the use of electronic technology later produced artistically satisfying creative results. In the case of the guitar, available in amplified versions since the late 1930s, the stylistic progression was a relatively smooth affair; this was equally true of the electric bass guitar (● p. 127), which first came into its own with the FUSION boom.

The earliest electric keyboard instrument to gain widespread acceptance in jazz was the electric organ, popularized (in its original Hammond model) by Fats Waller in the late 1930s before Jimmy Smith expanded the instrument's stylistic horizons in the 1950s and promoted its association with BLUES-based idioms. The organ remained popular until the early 1970s, when it was quickly supplanted by advancing technology. First came the electric piano which, as with the electric bass guitar, had originally been developed in the 1950s in an attempt to combat the ACOUSTIC instrument's perceived deficiences in both volume and portability. The most popular variety by far proved to be the Fender-Rhodes model, launched in 1965, which produced a bright, metallic sound characteristic of innumerable albums recorded in the 1970s. The most influential exponents were Chick Corea (● p. 178), Joe Zawinul (● p. 174) and Herbie Hancock (● p. 201), but part of the credit for its promotion must go to Miles Davis, who prompted all three keyboard players to explore the instrument's potential while working on his epoch-making early fusion albums in 1968–69 (● p. 171).

More radical in both technology and creative potential was the synthesizer. A source of experimentation by avant-garde classical musicians in the 1960s, it was favored because it offered seemingly limitless possibilities for unusual timbres. The first generation of synthesizers lacked today's digital technology, producing "source" sounds that were then modified by a variety of processing devices. Until the mid-1970s, only a single melodic line could be played, and the performance style was inevitably influenced by that used on the electric guitar. Paul Bley and Sun Ra were early advocates of the Moog synthesizer, which became available in a compact portable version (the "Minimoog") in 1970.

Zawinul, Hancock and Corea progressed from the electric piano to working with synthesizers after leaving Miles Davis and founding their own fusion bands in the early 1970s. The Oberheim company's development in 1974 of a device that could play more than one note at a time provided a timely stimulus to further experimentation, and resulted in the appearance of the "Polymoog" and a rash of comparable instruments manufactured by other companies. The advent of digital technology permitted players to use complex SAMPLING and SEQUENCING techniques, while introducing an impressive capacity for storing pre-arranged timbres. This new versatility culminated in the computerized and phenomenally capable Synclavier, used by Lyle Mays to create a stunning range of atmospheric effects in his work with Pat Metheny in the 1980s (● p. 211).

The keyboard is not the only mechanism capable of controlling a synthesizer, and alternative technologies have been evolved to allow guitarists (● p. 199), drummers (● p. 221) and even wind players to access the astonishing soundscapes made possible by this versatile invention. Both Akai and Yamaha launched so-called Electronic Wind Instruments in 1987, and in the same year saxophonist Mike Brecker featured the Akai model on his debut album for MCM/Impulse.

September Clarinetist Woody Herman takes part in the Monterey Jazz Festival.

17 October British trombonist Chris Barber records *Come Friday* in Germany.

28 October Chick Corea (● p. 178) and Gary Burton perform together in Zurich.

11 November Milt Jackson and Sonny Stitt record together in Milan.

26 November Pianist Bill Evans (● p. 156) makes his last major recordings in Paris.

● Pianist Horace Silver records his final album for Blue Note, *Silver'n'Strings*, ending a twenty-eight-year association with the label. ● Thad Jones quits drummer Mel Lewis, with whom he has led a superior big band for fourteen years (● p. 163), and moves to Denmark. The band continues to perform under Lewis's sole leadership. ● Manhattan Transfer's *Extensions* makes a pop hit of Joe Zawinul's "Birdland" (● p. 174). ● Dizzy Gillespie (● p. 219) and Al Fraser publish their book *To Be or Not to Bop*. Also published this year is William Gottlieb's *The Golden Age of Jazz*, a photographic collection of artists from the SWING and BOP eras.

1980

Complementary Pathways

As the new decade begins, performers once more polarize between classicism and post-fusion modernism.

Below Bill Evans, the most influential jazz pianist of the early 1960s, appearing at Ronnie Scott's London club in August 1980 shortly before his death.

29 May Pat Metheny (● p. 198) records *80/81* with saxophonists Mike Brecker and Dewey Redman, bassist Charlie Haden and drummer Jack DeJohnette.

June Soul-jazz saxophonist Grover Washington, Jr., records his album *Winelight*, including the hit song "Just the Two of Us." The disc wins two Grammy awards. ● Miles Davis (● p. 216) records *The Man with the Horn*, marking his return to the recording studio after five years of retirement.

27 June Clarinetist Barney Bigard dies, Culver City, California.

July Eighteen-year-old trumpeter Wynton Marsalis (● p. 196) records at Montreux with Art Blakey's Jazz Messengers (● p. 138). Meanwhile, Oscar Peterson (● p. 162) and Freddie Hubbard top the bill at Holland's North Sea Jazz Festival in The Hague.

Summer The Art Ensemble of Chicago is active in Germany and Italy.

15 September Pianist Bill Evans (● p. 156) dies, aged fifty-one, in New York. The date provides the title for a haunting memorial track on the Pat Metheny/Lyle Mays album *As Falls Wichita, So Falls Wichita Falls* (ECM).

October–November A new annual jazz festival is launched in Paris, with main events broadcast by Radio France.

15–16 November The Ganelin Trio (● p. 207) records in Leningrad.

Ella Fitzgerald, who received a Grammy award in 1980 at the age of sixty-two, had long been one of the most popular vocalists in jazz. While some listeners regretted the considerable refinement of her vocal technique, which could never match the raw emotional resonances of an artist such as Billie Holiday (● p. 131), many found that Fitzgerald's comforting sense of self-assurance and vocal agility combined to produce one of the most infectiously spirited sounds in all jazz.

Fitzgerald first came to public attention in the 1930s when, still a teenager, she was hired by drummer Chick Webb – a charismatic hunchback – to front his band at the Savoy Ballroom. On Webb's death in 1939, she assumed the leadership of the band (● p. 92), now famous for her interpretation of "A-tisket, A-tasket" recorded in the previous year. After the war, she was widely promoted by Norman Granz as part of his "Jazz at the Philharmonic" operation (● p. 106), and it was to Granz's label Verve that she defected from Decca in 1956. She recorded prolifically, and under the patronage of Verve she interpreted huge quantities of STANDARDS in Granz's ambitious "songbook" series, made between 1956 and 1964 (● p. 138) and now available as an eighteen-CD boxed set. As in the case of Sarah Vaughan, her recorded output reached a far wider audience than much mainstream jazz of the 1950s and 1960s. Since the rise of Frank Sinatra and others during the musicians' strikes of the early 1940s (● p. 103), singers have generally been welcomed more readily by the masses than instrumentalists.

Perhaps the finest SCAT singer (● p. 61) of all time, Fitzgerald delighted audiences with her textless improvisations on numbers such as Gershwin's "Lady Be Good" and Billy Strayhorn's "Take the 'A' Train." Her ability to imitate the pyrotechnics of BOP instrumentalists also allowed her to work alongside virtuoso performers in the context of small ensembles. She recorded classic performances alongside bassist

Ella Fitzgerald

Above The First Lady of Jazz: Ella Fitzgerald in 1959 at the height of her popularity.

Ray Brown (her husband from 1948 until 1952), Louis Armstrong (● p. 56), Oscar Peterson (● p. 162), Joe Pass and countless others. She was no stranger to big bands, either, collaborating memorably with Duke Ellington (● p. 62) in the late 1950s, and with Count Basie (● p. 86) as recently as 1990.

The First Lady of Jazz continued to perform well into her old age, but increasingly succumbed to the ravages of a heart condition and diabetes; complications from the latter resulted in the tragic amputation of both legs below the knee, which put her permanently into a wheelchair. She died on 14 June 1996 at the age of seventy-eight.

WORLD EVENTS

22 February Death of Oskar Kokoschka

August US film stars go on strike

4 November Ronald Reagan elected US President

8 December John Lennon murdered, New York

● Umberto Eco's novel *The Name of the Rose*

December Vibraphonist Mike Mainieri and tenor saxophonist Mike Brecker form the FUSION group Steps, which records in Tokyo.

● Guitarist Bill Frisell begins working with drummer Paul Motian, formerly a sideman with Bill Evans. ● The newly formed Savoy Sultans (who borrow their name from a SWING-era band) popularize a modern brand of swing at the Newport Festival and Kool Festival, the latter held at Waterloo Village, New Jersey. ● Danish guitarist Pierre Dørge forms his New Jungle Orchestra, which goes on to explore novel syntheses between traditional jazz, Ellingtonian jungle music, and various ethnic musical traditions (● p. 204). ● "Wild" Bill Davison brings his own variety of the old Chicago style to Carnegie Hall. ● Trumpeter Doc Cheatham, aged seventy-five, promotes traditional jazz in a regular Sunday gig at Greenwich Village's Sweet Basil club.

1981

Japan Moves Center Stage

As Miles Davis emerges from temporary retirement, he tours Japan in a year in which the country also hosts inspired performances by the reunited Modern Jazz Quartet, Wynton Marsalis and Herbie Hancock.

Above Pianist Mary Lou Williams, who died in 1981 at the age of seventy-one. Her *Zodiac Suite* was performed by the New York Philharmonic in 1946, but she is best remembered as an exceedingly versatile pianist and accomplished swing-band arranger.

29 January Drummer Cozy Cole dies, Columbus, Ohio.

28 May Pianist Mary Lou Williams dies, Durham, North Carolina.

5 July Miles Davis (● p. 216) appears at Avery Fisher Hall, New York, during the Newport Jazz Festival. The event marks his return to the live–performance circuit after a prolonged retirement caused by ill health.

September–October Miles Davis tours Japan with a group that includes Bill Evans (soprano saxophone) and Marcus Miller (bass). He earns $700,000 for eight appearances.

October The Modern Jazz Quartet is re-formed for a reunion concert in Tokyo as part of the Monterey Jazz Festival's tour to Japan; its members have spent seven years apart. The event is commemorated by their recording *Reunion at Budohkhan*.

● Wynton Marsalis leaves Art Blakey's Jazz Messengers and tours Japan with Miles Davis's former rhythm section: Herbie Hancock (piano), Ron Carter (bass) and Tony Williams (drums). He records with them for CBS and is signed up to record an album, *Wynton Marsalis,* as leader on the same label. ● Martial Solal composes his Concerto for Jazz Trio and Orchestra. ● Alto saxophonist David Sanborn records his album *Voyeur*, combining FUSION with popular funk. The track "All I Need is You," composed by bassist Marcus Miller, wins a Grammy Award.

WORLD EVENTS

12 April First US space-shuttle mission

April Race riots in Brixton, London

29 July Wedding of the Prince of Wales and Lady Diana Spencer

6 October Assassination of President Sadat of Egypt

13 December Poland declares martial law to quash trade union "Solidarity"

● Assassination attempts on US President Reagan and Pope John Paul II.

Wynton Marsalis

In 1981, at the age of nineteen, Wynton Marsalis entered the record books by becoming the first performer to sign recording contracts for both classical music and jazz simultaneously. Born in New Orleans in 1961, he had followed in the footsteps of his illustrious predecessors by playing in a marching band (at the age of eight) before acquiring a formidable instrumental technique that allowed him to play Haydn's Trumpet Concerto with the New Orleans Philharmonic Orchestra when he was only fourteen. His two careers developed in parallel through classical studies at New York's renowned Juilliard School and through membership of Art Blakey's equally renowned Jazz Messengers (● p. 138), which he joined in 1980. Four years later he again made history as the first artist to receive Grammy Awards for both classical and jazz recordings.

His rapid rise to prominence in the jazz world came when he joined the members of Miles Davis's formidable rhythm section from the 1960s – Herbie Hancock (● p. 201) on piano, Ron Carter on bass, and Tony Williams on drums – to play at the Newport Festival and tour Japan in 1981. The group also recorded for CBS with Hancock as leader. In 1983 Wynton's older brother Branford joined the group as tenor saxophonist and, under the name VSOP II, the quintet's debt to the 1960s Davis style became patently obvious. In the mid-1980s Marsalis formed his own quartet, and its performances of STANDARDS

Left A child prodigy who matured into one of the most spectacular talents of recent years, Wynton Marsalis has combined careers in classical music and jazz with equal success.

were soon hailed as the finest of the decade. From 1988 onward he devoted his attention to projects reclaiming the heritage of early jazz, whether the New Orleans style or the masterpieces of Duke Ellington. In the 1990s he made a name for himself as a fluent lecturer and music educator, skillfully presenting a series of television programs for children ("Marsalis on Music") that were given worldwide exposure.

Marsalis entered jazz at a time when it was seriously in need of a new, younger audience to sustain its development. His youthful, fresh image and precocious talents (backed up by marketing on the part of CBS/Sony rivaled only by their earlier promotion of Miles Davis) made him appear to be its timely savior. Outspoken against what he saw as the artistic sell-out of FUSION, Marsalis promoted the performance of live ACOUSTIC jazz firmly rooted in traditional musical values. As with many of jazz's most capable technicians, however, his consummate facility has sometimes encouraged him to stray into mere virtuosity for virtuosity's sake; and his exhortations on his definition of "real" (i.e., historically aware) jazz and its superiority to jazz-rock hybrid styles led to a temperamental clash with his idol Miles Davis, who in 1986 refused to allow him to play with his band in Vancouver. "I was never jealous of him," Miles said, but added in a fit of pique, "the more famous he became the more he started saying things – nasty, disrespectful things – about me, things I've never said about musicians who influenced me and who I had great respect for."

"I really liked Wynton when I first met him. He's still a nice young man, only confused. I knew he could play the hell out of classical music, and had great technical skills on the trumpet ... But you need more than that to play great jazz music, you need feelings and an understanding of life that you can only get from living, from experience."

Miles Davis, *The Autobiography* (1989)

"The first night we played [at Boston's Kix Club in spring 1981] ... One night, there was this little crippled black guy ... I was playing this blues, and he was sitting right in front of the stage. I played it to him because I knew that he knew what the blues were. Halfway through my solo, I looked into this guy's eyes, and he was crying. He reached up his withered arm, which was trembling, and with his shaking hand he touched my trumpet as though he was blessing it – and me."

Miles Davis, *The Autobiography* (1989)

1982

After Monk

Thelonious Monk's death inspires a rash of memorial tributes, and his compositions remain a core part of the standards repertoire.

17 February Thelonious Monk (● p. 154) dies, Weehawken, New Jersey. Entirely by coincidence, the new group Sphere (its name borrowed from Monk's middle name, and established to promote his music) is scheduled to record its first album *Four in One* on the same day.

20–21 February Oscar Peterson's trio (● p. 162) performs in Japan with guitarist Joe Pass and records a live Pablo double album, *Freedom Song*, partly inspired by the prolonged incarceration of Nelson Mandela in South Africa.

March Bassist Eberhard Weber records *Later That Evening* for ECM, with an ensemble including guitarist Bill Frisell and pianist Lyle Mays. ● Pianist Monty Alexander, a performer strongly influenced by Oscar Peterson, tours Japan and performs in Osaka and Tokyo. His trio features former Peterson sidemen, bassist Ray Brown and guitarist Herb Ellis.

23 March Sonny Greer, founder-drummer of the Ellington orchestra (● p. 119), dies in New York.

April Milt Jackson (● p. 129) makes several appearances at Ronnie Scott's London club, concentrating on STANDARDS by Thelonious Monk.

Above Playing at London's Camden Jazz Week in 1980, Eberhard Weber demonstrates his solid-bodied bass which combines features of both acoustic and electric instruments.

WORLD EVENTS

2 April Argentina invades the Falkland Islands

1 May British offensive to retake the Falklands begins

14 June Argentine troops surrender to British forces

20 December Death of Arthur Rubinstein

● Oscar-winners this year include Richard Attenborough's *Gandhi* (8 awards) and Steven Spielberg's blockbuster *E.T.* (3 awards)

Pat Metheny and the New Versatility

Guitarist Pat Metheny will undoubtedly be remembered as one of the most artistically resourceful and commercially successful artists of the 1980s and 1990s. His career has achieved a workable (and very rare) balance between a mass popular appeal – more typical of a rock musician than a jazz performer, and capable of filling a football stadium at a live gig – and a consistent devotion to musical innovation that has led him to collaborate with notable figures from the avant-garde. Predictably, this musical fence-straddling has elicited carping from both critical camps: his recent light-rock albums with his FUSION group have been criticized for their apparent complacency and easy-going tunefulness, while a seminal experimental album such as his collaboration with Ornette Coleman, *Song X* (● p. 205), has been viewed as a compromise merely because some of the session's most radical takes were not included in the release.

Born near Kansas City in Missouri (● p. 64), Metheny played with vibraphonist Gary Burton at

Left The Pat Metheny Group performs at Bracknell in 1980 (l. to r.): Lyle Mays (keyboards), Metheny (guitar), Mark Egan (electric bass) and Danny Gottlieb (drums).

the age of twenty, having already displayed his prodigious talents by teaching at Miami University and at Boston's Berklee College of Music while still a teenager. In 1976 he began working with pianist Lyle Mays, whose style was deeply rooted in the idiom of Bill Evans (● p. 156) and whose talents as co-composer injected considerable harmonic and structural sophistication into the work of the resulting Pat Metheny Group, which recorded its first album in 1978. Subsequent recordings for the German ECM label (● p. 177) showed Metheny to have absorbed the influence of American country music, which imparted melodic freshness to a style of guitar playing already reflecting the work of Wes Montgomery (● p. 99).

Like Joe Zawinul with Weather Report (● p. 174), Metheny found he could successfully package limited avant-garde experimentation in the context of popular fusion albums. His best-selling *Offramp* (released in 1982) sported an aggressive title track, in an ATONAL idiom of extreme textural and rhythmic unpredictability, alongside highly melodic compositions more akin to easy listening than self-conscious modernism. When his group switched to the Geffen label in 1985, its style grew notably lighter and began to betray the overt influence of Brazilian music by insistently including a (sometimes wordless) vocal line.

Lyle Mays went on to produce three albums as leader (● p. 211), the first in 1986, and continues to collaborate with Metheny after a fruitful association of more than two decades.

Guitar Synthesizer

Metheny's album *Offramp* featured striking effects created by a guitar synthesizer, used to control the powerful digital Synclavier operated by Lyle Mays' keyboard. Guitar synthesizers were launched by the Roland instrument company in 1977, and have been adopted by performers such as John McLaughlin, Al Di Meola, Bill Frisell and Lee Ritenour. Inspired by the unlimited range of sonorities possible on the keyboard synthesizers that entered jazz in the early 1970s (● p. 193), the guitar synthesizer adapted the technology to the playing technique of a stringed instrument. Three basic categories of sound are at the performer's disposal: electronic imitations of conventional instruments, pure electronic effects, and complex timbres created by the processing of material sampled from a live source.

April–May Electric guitarist John Scofield joins Miles Davis (● p. 216) on his European tour.

June Vibraphonist Lionel Hampton (● p. 70) plays in Tokyo.

15 June Alto saxophonist Art Pepper dies, Panorama, California.

23 July Charlie Parker's disciple, alto saxophonist Sonny Stitt, dies one month after recording his final sessions in New York.

● Trumpeter Shorty Rogers tours the UK with the National Youth Jazz Orchestra. ● Benny Goodman (● p. 84) reforms his original quartet with Teddy Wilson (piano) and Lionel Hampton (vibraphone). The deceased Gene Krupa is replaced by drummer Panama Francis. ● Chick Corea (● p. 178) records Mozart's Concerto for Two Pianos. ● Wynton Marsalis (● p. 196) leaves Art Blakey's Jazz Messengers (● p. 138). ● Bassist Jaco Pastorius leaves Weather Report (● p. 174) to start his own band.

1983-85
Prodigies

The dazzling talents of Wynton Marsalis and Tommy Smith suggest that jazz is being redefined by, and for, a much younger generation.

Right Veteran pianist Eubie Blake indulges in a little domestic music-making on a late visit to Norway.

WORLD EVENTS

1983

25 February Death of Tennessee Williams

8 March Death of William Walton

29 July Death of Luis Buñuel

October US troops invade Grenada

• First compact discs marketed.
• *Terms of Endearment* wins Oscar for Best Picture

1984

22 August First black franchise granted, South Africa

31 October Indira Gandhi assassinated

6 November Ronald Reagan elected to second term as US President

• Academy Award-winning films include *A Passage to India*, *The Killing Fields* and *Amadeus* (Best Picture)

1985

13 July Bob Geldof's charity concert "Live Aid" reaches a global audience

1 September Wreck of the *Titanic* located

2 December Death of poet and jazz critic Philip Larkin

7 December Death of Robert Graves

• Kurt Vonnegut's novel *Galapagos*
• *Out of Africa* wins Oscar for Best Picture

1983

January Pianist Keith Jarrett (● p. 185) makes his first recordings of STANDARDS with a trio featuring Gary Peacock (bass) and Jack DeJohnette (drums).

12 February STRIDE pianist Eubie Blake dies in New York, five days after his 100th birthday. Having eaten a fried breakfast every day of his adult life, as well as being a smoker and drinker, he said when interviewed shortly before his death, "If I'd known I was going to live this long, I'd have taken better care of myself."

9–10 March Anthony Braxton records his album *Four Compositions (Quartet) 1983* in Milan. Its title, like many of Braxton's creations, betrays the influence of avant-garde visual art.

22 April Pianist Earl Hines (● p. 124) dies, aged seventy-nine, Oakland, California.

May Miles Davis (● p. 216) tours Japan.

June Miles Davis releases his album *Star People*, featuring saxophonist Bill Evans, guitarist John Scofield and bassist Marcus Miller.

8–10 June Lee Konitz collaborates with German trombonist Albert Mangelsdorff (● p. 61) on the album *The Art of the Duo*, recorded at Villingen.

5 July Trumpeter Harry James dies, Las Vegas.

26–27 July British trumpeter Humphrey Lyttleton performs in Toronto. This year, he establishes his own record label under the name Calligraph.

August British saxophone prodigy, sixteen-year-old Tommy Smith, makes his recording debut, and goes on to join the Whizz Kids Band organized by Gary Burton at Berklee College.

October Bassist Dave Holland collaborates with Canadian trumpeter Kenny Wheeler on the ECM album *Jumpin' In.* ● The first of an annual series of "Floating Jazz Festivals" is held on the SS *Norway*, which departs from Miami on a musical cruise.

Left Herbie Hancock in 1986, showing how in live performances funk-orientated keyboard players liked to drape their instrument around the neck in the fashion of a guitar.

Below Hancock accepts his Grammy for "Best Rhythm and Blues Instrumental," won by his hit track "Rockit" in 1984.

Herbie Hancock, Megastar

Herbie Hancock's brand of electronic funk captivated listeners of pop music with such consummate ease in 1983 it scarcely seemed possible that two decades before he had been one of the most challenging musicians working in the jazz mainstream. An earlier indication of his commercial viability came ten years before with the phenomenal sales of his album *Headhunters,* and in his fluctuation between popular FUSION hits and less marketable ACOUSTIC jazz, Hancock's later career has been typical of many jazz musicians of his generation. He frankly admitted, however, that his increasing attraction to the popular marketplace arose from the realization that his jazz work could scarcely rival the awe-inspiring talents of geniuses such as Charlie Parker, John Coltrane or Miles Davis.

Like Wynton Marsalis (● p. 196), Hancock was a child prodigy who first revealed his skills to the world in the context of classical music. Trumpeter Donald Byrd (● p. 12) enticed him to move to New York from his home city of Chicago, and he recorded his first album, *Takin' Off,* in 1962. This disc, which includes the original version of his later hit "Watermelon Man," marked the beginning of a long and fruitful association with the Blue Note label (● p. 166), for which he went on to serve as house pianist. A year later he fell in with Miles Davis and, together with

bassist Ron Carter and drummer Tony Williams, formed the renowned RHYTHM SECTION for the trumpeter's second quintet. Meanwhile, his own career as leader blossomed with the appearance of his Blue Note albums *Empyrean Isles* (1964) and *Maiden Voyage* (1965). The former contains his popular composition "Cantaloupe Island," a SAMPLE from which formed the basis for the 1993 hit "Cantaloop," by the jazz-pop group US3.

On quitting Davis in 1968, Hancock began work with reed-player Bennie Maupin in the context of a sextet, and began to concentrate on electronic keyboards (a sign of the times: ● p. 193). In 1973, Hancock restructured the group as a quartet and issued *Headhunters,* with its hit opening track, "Chameleon," also released as a best-selling pop single. After his music became more pop-oriented in the later 1970s, he returned to orthodox jazz by reuniting his former Davis sidemen to create the group VSOP with trumpeter Freddie Hubbard, who had figured prominently on his earlier Blue Note albums. This group provided invaluable experience for Wynton Marsalis at the start of his career. Another former Blue Note associate, tenor saxophonist Dexter Gordon, made a moving acting appearance in the film *'Round Midnight* (● p. 208), for which Hancock composed (and performed on screen) an Oscar-winning soundtrack in 1987. Hancock's album *The New Standard* (1996) continued to reassess pop material by reworking songs by the rock group Nirvana, Peter Gabriel and the Beatles.

November Radio City Music Hall, New York, presents a tribute to Miles Davis ("An American Musical Legend"), hosted by comedian Bill Cosby (● p. 217). The trumpeter receives an honorary degree from Fisk University in Nashville, Tennessee.

December Pablo Records preserves Count Basie's last big-band performances on the live album *Fancy Pants*. ● SWING-era clarinetist and bandleader Artie Shaw emerges from retirement to play with Dick Johnson's band at the Glen Island Casino, once made famous by the music of Glenn Miller (● p. 107).

● Wynton Marsalis (● p. 196) makes musical history as the first artist to win simultaneous Grammy Awards for a jazz album (*Think of One*, recorded in collaboration with his saxophonist brother, Branford) and a classical recording (Haydn's Trumpet Concerto). ● Toshiko Akiyoshi and Lew Tabackin form their second big band. ● Ornette Coleman's *Skies of America* (● p. 179) is revived this year, and later performed in Verona (1987) and London (1988). ● Herbie Hancock's synthesized dance hit "Rockit," from the album *Future Shock*, reaches number 1 in the pop charts. ● Scott Joplin (● p. 21) appears on a US postage stamp.

1984

27 February Bandleader and keyboard player Sun Ra, aged seventy, visits Athens to perform at the Praxis 84 festival. This year he is also voted a member of *Down Beat*'s prestigious "Hall of Fame."

March The Soviet Union's Ganelin Trio (● p. 207) appear at London's Bloomsbury Theatre as part of their UK tour. Their collective artistry is demonstrated with an eccentric theatrical presentation recalling the avant-garde jazz of the 1960s.

New Jazz in Britain

Jazz had become such an international commodity by the 1980s that it might seem misleading to consider the work of musicians active in a single European country (as if nationalism ever had any meaning in jazz outside the nation in which it was born). But in Britain, the desolate years during which American musicians were banned from appearing in the country (● p. 85) had the regrettable consequence of ensuring that British jazz remained behind the times. Both traditional jazz and bop grew steadily in stature in the 1950s before a new, younger generation of musicians finally placed the UK firmly on the global jazz map in the midst of the growing stylistic indeterminacy of the post-FUSION 1980s.

The lead was taken by tenor saxophonists Courtney Pine and Andy Sheppard. Pine, who made his recording debut in 1986 (● p. 206) and whose playing revealed the influence of Sonny Rollins and John Coltrane (● p. 160), tirelessly sought to encourage black musicians in Britain to espouse the cause of jazz through his Abibi Jazz Arts organization. In the process, he admitted overtly West Indian musical characteristics into his style and successfully reached out to a large audience. After years of relative obscurity spent in Paris, Sheppard entered the record catalogues one year after Pine and progressed from a similar post-Coltrane background to achieve soundscapes more reminiscent of Jan Garbarek's distinctively European work with ECM (● p. 177). Both players were a potent inspiration to emerging young talents up and down the country.

In the sphere of jazz composition, the rise to prominence of keyboard player Django Bates and his group Loose Tubes set new and formidable standards at around the same time. Entering the recording studio in 1984 and causing a sensation at Ronnie Scott's in the following year (● p. 205), Loose Tubes offered a breathtaking fare of highly sophisticated arrangements, taking on board any stylistic material that caught their fancy. Such was the quality of their work that they were later promoted by producer Teo Macero, who had masterminded the recording of much of Miles Davis's music on the Columbia label. Bates also channeled his energies into work for the groups Human Chain, Earthworks and Delightful Precipice. The latter produced exciting music to accompany performances by the Snapdragon circus company in the early 1990s.

Right Saxophonist Courtney Pine: a tireless campaigner for the wider recognition of jazz in the UK.

Left A former sideman of Fletcher Henderson in the 1940s, Sonny Blount assumed the name Sun Ra and went on to dazzle audiences with his heady blend of music-theater, free jazz and popular styles.

Right The Dirty Dozen Brass Band appearing at the 14th JVC Grande Parade du Jazz at Nice in 1987.

Spring Saxophonist Lee Konitz is on tour in Scotland and the north of England.

April Guitarist John Abercrombie records *Night* for ECM with tenor saxophonist Mike Brecker and drummer Jack DeJohnette.

23 April Juan Tizol, composer of Ellington's hit "Caravan," dies in Inglewood, California.

26 April Count Basie dies in Hollywood, at seventy-nine. His autobiography, *Good Morning Blues,* is published posthumously.

May Wynton Marsalis records *Hot House Flowers*, with a lineup that includes brother Branford on saxophone and Ron Carter on bass.

July Steve Gadd, virtuoso of the modern drum kit (● p. 220), records his album *Gaddabout.*

August Gil Evans's band records live at the Sweet Basil club, Greenwich Village, where they have enjoyed a residency for the past year.

26 September Drummer Shelly Manne dies, Los Angeles.

December Miles Davis visits Denmark to receive a Sonning Foundation award (● p. 204). This year, he records *You're Under Arrest*, a pop-oriented album featuring singer Sting and guitarists John McLaughlin and John Scofield: the highlight of the disc is a re-interpretation of Michael Jackson's "Human Nature." This recording is his final release on the Columbia label after a twenty-nine-year association; he begins recording on the Warner label in 1986 (● p. 208). Warner pays him a seven-figure sum merely to sign up, but Davis declines to negotiate his publication rights and, as a result, his own compositions are not featured on his subsequent recordings.

● Trumpeters Malachi Thompson and Lester Bowie form the group Brass Fantasy.
● The early New Orleans style is reassessed from a modern perspective in the debut recording of the Dirty Dozen Brass Band, *My Feet Can't Fail Me Now.* ● Francis Ford Coppola's movie *The Cotton Club* reconstructs the atmosphere of the famous Harlem venue in 1928 (● p. 62).

1985

January Jack DeJohnette temporarily abandons his drum kit in favor of the keyboard to record *The Piano Album* for Landmark.

26 January Drummer Kenny Clarke dies at seventy-one, near Paris.

February Miles Davis (● p. 216) visits Denmark to record *Aura*, written in his honor by fellow trumpeter Palle Mikkelborg when Davis received his Sonning Award.

10 February Thad Jones returns to the US from Copenhagen to assume leadership of the Count Basie band.

22 February The re-launch of Blue Note (● p. 166) is celebrated by a concert at New York's Town Hall. Participants include Art Blakey (● p. 138), Ron Carter, Herbie Hancock (● p. 201), Freddie Hubbard, Cecil Taylor, Grover Washington, Jr., and Tony Williams.

25 February Art Blakey visits London to play at Ronnie Scott's.

Right The virtuoso British band Loose Tubes, which took London by storm in the mid-1980s.

Above Don Cherry: the archetypal "world musician," who mastered instruments from numerous ethnic traditions and promoted a brand of crossover jazz he liked to term "primal music."

Ethnic Crossovers

The barriers between jazz and classical music had been broken down as early as the 1920s (● p. 55), and by the 1980s the concept of THIRD STREAM music that synthesized the best of both worlds had become commonplace. New "crossover" ventures in the 1970s looked to more distant horizons by appropriating the musical traditions of exotic cultures, borrowing freely from ethnic music to create a musical potpourri entirely in keeping with the concept of the Global Village.

The most consistent champion of this approach has been trumpeter Don Cherry, who participated in the avant-garde jazz of the early 1960s (● p. 150) at a time when John Coltrane (● p.160) was demonstrating an interest in Indian ragas and Eric Dolphy's sights were also turning toward world music. In 1978, Cherry collaborated with Collin Walcott and Nana Vasconcelos in the first of a trilogy of recordings for ECM entitled *Codona*, in which Walcott played two Indian instruments – the sitar (a plucked stringed instrument) and the tablā (two small hand-beaten drums). Walcott's first important sitar recording was made in 1969 when he played for Tony Scott's album *Homage to Lord Krishna*, and the ethnic crossover movement proceeded to flourish alongside the phenomenal growth of jazz-rock FUSION. The tablā player Zakir Hussain was the linchpin of John McLaughlin's group Shakti (1973–77), in which the guitarist played a special instrument based on an Indian prototype.

Since 1980, the Danish bandleader Pierre Dørge and his New Jungle Orchestra have successfully combined features borrowed from East European, African and Japanese traditional music in a style rooted in the post-Ellington band tradition. Influences from the Indian subcontinent have remained prominent: saxophonist Jan Garbarek recorded his album *Ragas and Sagas* with Pakistani musicians as recently as 1990 (● p. 213).

Today, cross-cultural borrowings in all music (whether classical or jazz) are dangerously close to becoming *de rigeur*. In jazz circles, at any rate, they enjoy a continuing justification in the realization that pan-cultural artistic synthesis directly reflects the tension between African and European music that gave birth to jazz a century ago.

> "For jazz musicians to assume that they had any reason or any right to start playing with musicians of other cultures implied a new self-confidence on the part of the jazz community, and could probably only have happened thanks to the 1960s climate of the civil rights movement."
>
> Brian Priestley, 1995

May Loose Tubes appears at Ronnie Scott's London club. This twenty-one-piece British band, led by twenty-five-year-old keyboard player Django Bates, astonishes audiences with its heady mixture of vibrant musical idioms and irrepressible energy (● p. 202). ● Bassist Marc Johnson records *Bass Desires* for ECM, supported by guitarists Bill Frisell and John Scofield, and drummer Peter Erskine.

July Sonny Rollins records an album of live solo-saxophone improvisations at New York's Museum of Modern Art.

30 August Drummer Philly Joe Jones dies, Philadelphia. He is affectionately remembered for his "Philly lick," the distinctive use of a rim-shot on the final beat of a bar, best known from its appearance on Miles Davis's 1958 album *Milestones* (● p. 142).

15 September Trumpeter Cootie Williams dies, New York.

December Twenty-two-year-old new singing star Cassandra Wilson records *Point of View* with alto saxophonist Steve Coleman. ● Weather Report (● p. 174) records its final album, *This is This*.

12–14 December Guitarist Pat Metheny (● p. 198) explores avant-garde territory by collaborating with Ornette Coleman (● p. 150), Charlie Haden and Jack DeJohnette on the Geffen album *Song X* (to which Coleman contributes a characteristically idiosyncratic violin solo).

● Chick Corea (● p. 178) captivates a new youthful audience with his Elektric Band (● p. 215). Although denounced by purist critics, the group initiates a revival of interest in jazz-rock FUSION. After releasing an album featuring guitarist Scott Henderson, its membership stabilizes: Corea (keyboards), Eric Marienthal (saxophones), Frank Gambale (guitar), John Patitucci (bass) and Dave Weckl (drums). ● Saxophonist Branford Marsalis tours with pop singer Sting, who has recorded the jazzy album *The Dream of the Blue Turtles*. ● Benny Goodman (● p. 84), now seventy-six, fronts an orchestra founded by Loren Schoenberg to revive classics of the SWING-band repertoire. ● Drummer Mel Lewis celebrates twenty years of uninterrupted band performances at the Village Vanguard, Greenwich Village. ● Dave Grusin (keyboards) and Lee Ritenour (guitar) record their album *Harlequin* on Grusin's own GRP label (● p. 214).

1986-88

Envoi to the Last of the Great Leaders

An era closes with the passing of Benny Goodman, Teddy Wilson, Thad Jones, Woody Herman and Gil Evans.

1986

January Saxophonists Gerry Mulligan (● p. 134) and Scott Hamilton (● p. 189) record together in New York.

April The World Saxophone Quartet's *Plays Duke Ellington* shows that the Duke's masterpieces are as vibrant as ever twelve years after his death.

June Debut of Gary Giddins' American Jazz Orchestra at the Cooper Union, New York.

6 June Chet Baker (● p. 210) plays at Ronnie Scott's, London.

13 June Benny Goodman dies, aged seventy-seven, New York.

July Woody Herman's fiftieth-anniversary concert is staged at the Hollywood Bowl; another West Coast celebration is mounted in San Francisco.

31 July Pianist Teddy Wilson dies, New Britain, Connecticut.

July–August British saxophonist Courtney Pine (● p. 202) makes his recording debut with *Journey to the Urge Within*. His sextet features up-and-coming British talents Julian Joseph (piano) and Martin Taylor (guitar).

20 August Thad Jones dies, Copenhagen. His former position at the helm of the Count Basie band (● p. 204) is now held by saxophonist Frank Foster.

September Wynton Marsalis (● p. 196) cements his growing reputation as a performer of jazz STANDARDS with his album *Standard Time*.

November Alto saxophonist Benny Carter joins forces with Oscar Peterson (● p. 162) in Los Angeles.

WORLD EVENTS

1986

28 January Space shuttle *Challenger* explodes on launch

15 April US bombs Libya from British air base

26 April Nuclear disaster at Chernobyl, USSR

31 August Death of Henry Moore

● Oscar awarded to Oliver Stone's film *Platoon*, based on the war in Vietnam.

1987

22 February Death of Andy Warhol

17 August Hitler's deputy, Rudolf Hess, commits suicide in a Berlin prison

16 October UK devastated by freak hurricane

19 October Stock market crashes, New York

● Van Gogh's *Irises* sold for a record $45 million at auction

1988

26 January Climax of Australia's bicentennial celebrations

11 November George Bush elected US President

6 December Death of Roy Orbison

22 December Pan-Am jumbo jet explodes over Lockerbie, Scotland

Left An ageing Benny Goodman conveys his thanks after receiving a Grammy Award for "Lifetime Achievement" at a ceremony held in Los Angeles on 25 February 1986, less than four months before his death.

Above Soviet pianist Vyacheslav Ganelin, who formed the boldly innovative Ganelin Trio in 1971 with Vladimir Chekasin (reeds) and Vladimir Tarasov (drums).

Glasnost: the Jazz Resurgence in the USSR

The appearance of the first jazz recordings in 1917 inauspiciously coincided with the Russian Revolution, and for approximately a decade afterward the new music was welcomed in the Soviet Union under the watchful patronage of Lenin. Leopold Teplitsky was officially encouraged to travel abroad in search of American arrangements to bring back to the fledgling USSR (● p. 65). Classical composer Dmitri Shostakovich, who produced a witty orchestral arrangement of *Tea for Two* in 1928, went on to compose two suites for jazz band, but the conservative style of his later works demonstrates how the iron hand of Stalin had by the early 1930s tightened its grip on Soviet culture. American HOT jazz was now as much out of favor as it was in Nazi Germany (● p. 81), and was gradually replaced in official circles by innocuous dance music deemed more suitable for consumption by the masses. Genuine jazz was branded by *Pravda* as the music of the "fat bourgeoisie," and described by Stalinist author Maxim Gorky in savage terms that suggested it was still inextricably linked with the decadent and sexually depraved *demi-monde* that had allegedly created it. Posters soon began to appear declaring, "Today you play jazz: tomorrow you will betray your country."

Under Stalin's reign of terror, Teplitsky and other prominent Soviet musicians were sent into exile and the jazz scene remained barren until the leader's death in 1953. While cultural restrictions remained severe under the succeeding regime, the influence of BOP nevertheless belatedly began to assert itself behind the iron curtain. American musicians began to visit the USSR in 1962 (● p. 155), opening Soviet ears to

broader musical experiences. Notable American performers who toured there include Benny Goodman and Teddy Wilson in 1962, Earl Hines (● p. 165) in 1966, Charles Lloyd in 1967, Duke Ellington (● p. 177) in 1971, Oscar Peterson (● p. 182) in 1974 and Dave Brubeck (● p. 208) in 1987–88. Meanwhile, as in the sphere of classical music, a growing number of Soviet musicians defected to the West in search of wider artistic horizons.

The most remarkable aspect of Soviet jazz was undoubtedly the sudden flowering of the avant-garde during the 1970s. In terms of its political symbolism, this movement exactly paralleled the emergence of FREE JAZZ in the US in the early 1960s by representing the performers' need for civil as well as artistic liberation. The best known of the Soviet free-jazz groups was the influential piano trio led by Vyacheslav Ganelin, which began recording in the USSR in 1976 after an acclaimed tour to Poland (a vital center for the new Eastern bloc jazz since the foundation of the Sopot Festival in 1956). Ganelin's highly eclectic group synthesized elements borrowed from BOP, Chicago free jazz and the eccentric multi-instrumental effects developed by Roland Kirk (● p. 189), and presented its music in a vividly theatrical atmosphere. Recordings made by them in East Germany in 1977–82 were smuggled to the West. The more congenial climate prevailing in the Soviet Union in the 1980s allowed the trio to visit London in 1984 (● p. 202) and the USA in 1986, when they astonished audiences at the JVC Jazz Festival in New York. Ganelin thereupon decided to defect, and settled in Israel in 1987.

December Alto saxophonist Frank Morgan emerges from obscurity and re-establishes his reputation with a gig at the Village Vanguard, New York.

● Miles Davis (● p. 216) begins his Warner contract with the album *Tutu*, named after Desmond Tutu and inspired by the persisting racial tensions in South Africa. This year Davis takes a cameo role as a drug-dealing pimp in the television series "Miami Vice." ● Bertrand Tavernier's film *'Round Midnight*, with a score by Herbie Hancock (● p. 201), stars tenor saxophonist Dexter Gordon as a composite character amalgamated from incidents in the lives of Lester Young and Bud Powell. ● Keyboard player Bob James and saxophonist David Sanborn collaborate on the album *Double Vision* with Marcus Miller (bass) and Steve Gadd (drums). ● Keyboard player Lyle Mays (● p. 211) records his eponymous debut album for Geffen with a group including Bill Frisell (guitar), Alex Acuña (drums) and Nana Vasconcelos (percussion). ● Chick Corea (● p. 178) composes a Piano Concerto.

1987

February Eighty-year-old Benny Carter is honored with a major retrospective presented by the American Jazz Orchestra at the Great Hall of the Cooper Union.

22–24 February The Danish Radio Big Band tours Scotland and northern England.

March Dave Brubeck visits the Soviet Union.

March–April Pat Metheny's FUSION group achieves further commercial success when they record their album *Still Life (Talking)* for the Geffen label.

2 April Drummer Buddy Rich dies, Los Angeles.

May Doc Cheatham (● p. 195) visits Sweden to present a musical tribute to Billie Holiday (● p. 131).

10 July Record producer John Hammond dies, New York.

Ella Fitgerald receiving a Medal of Arts from President Ronald Reagan at the White House in June 1987 (*below*), and singing live a few days later (*above*).

John Hammond: Talent Spotter Extraordinaire

Progress in the arts is, very occasionally, shaped by the talents of entrepreneurs with a keen eye for both quality and commercial mileage. A prominent example from early in the twentieth century was the great impresario Serge Diaghilev, who nurtured the talents of composers such as Debussy, Ravel and Stravinsky by commissioning them to write works for his famous Ballets Russes. The strongest candidate for the appellation "the Diaghilev of jazz" is undoubtedly John Hammond, who died in 1987 after a lifetime devoted to the pursuit and promotion of the finest performing talent he could unearth.

Hammond's career as a record producer began in the early 1930s, when his samplings of Harlem musical life drew his attention to bandleaders such as Fletcher Henderson (● p. 71) and Teddy Wilson. Benny Goodman (● p. 84), Hammond's brother-in-law, was able to get his new band off to a flying start in 1934 thanks largely to Hammond's energetic assistance. The following year, Hammond organized Goodman's first appearance as a classical clarinetist, and he later initiated the fruitful partnership between Goodman and BOP guitarist Charlie Christian. In 1935 Hammond also made the major discovery of the phenomenal young singer Billie Holiday (● p. 131). It was Hammond's interest in Count Basie's band (● p. 86) that resulted in their relocation from Kansas City to New York and their subsequent rise to fame.

Hammond's association with the Brunswick record company was followed by a move to Columbia in 1939. Around that time he also organized influential jazz concerts at Carnegie Hall (● p. 91) that initiated, among other things, the revival of interest in BOOGIE-WOOGIE piano later exploited by Blue Note records. In later years, Hammond's outlook broadened to encompass the work of rock musicians, including Bruce Springsteen, and folk singers such as Bob Dylan.

> "Goodman watched Charlie approach the bandstand, looked around the room until he spotted me, and zapped me with the famous Goodman 'ray.' But before the opening night audience there was nothing he could do but go along [with Hammond's proposal that he try Christian out] . He chose 'Rose Room,' a standard familiar to Goodman audiences, though one he assumed Charlie would not know. This would be Benny's revenge for my interference.
>
> I am reasonably certain Christian had never heard 'Rose Room' before, because it was a West Coast song in the repertoire of most black bands. No matter. Charlie had ears like antennae ... Benny would play a chorus or two, Lionel [Hampton] would answer him, and their talent would inspire Charlie to greater improvisations of his own. Before long the crowd was screaming with amazement. 'Rose Room' continued for more than three-quarters of an hour and Goodman received an ovation unlike any even he had had before."

John Hammond describing how he introduced Charlie Christian to Benny Goodman at the Victor Hugo Restaurant, Beverly Hills, in 1939

Below The Diaghilev of Jazz: entrepreneur John Hammond in c. 1939.

17 July The twentieth anniversary of the death of John Coltrane (● p. 160) is commemorated by several albums, including *Blues for Coltrane* (Pharoah Sanders and McCoy Tyner) and *Homage to John Coltrane* (Dave Liebman).

21 July Saxophonist Andy Sheppard (● p. 202) makes his first album as leader in London, his style strongly influenced by John Coltrane.

August Loose Tubes (● p. 205) appear at the Royal Albert Hall, London, as part of the BBC Promenade Concerts.

14–15 September Charlie Haden (bass) records *Etudes* with trio partners Geri Allen (piano) and Paul Motian (drums).

21 September Bassist Jaco Pastorius dies, aged thirty-five, after he is beaten up in a nightclub brawl in Fort Lauderdale, Florida.

8 October Bob Wilber's big band presents their re-enactment of Benny Goodman's 1938 Carnegie Hall concert (● p. 91) at London's Royal Festival Hall.

29 October Woody Herman dies, aged seventy-four, in Los Angeles.

November Alto saxophonist Phil Woods, who this year signs his quintet up with the Concord label, tours Japan and records *Bop Stew* and *Bouquet* in Tokyo.

● Tenor saxophonist Mike Brecker records his eponymous first album as leader for the Impulse label. ● A big band is formed to celebrate Dizzy Gillespie's seventieth birthday and embarks on a world tour. ● Ornette Coleman is reunited with sidemen Don Cherry (trumpet), Charlie Haden (bass) and Billy Higgins (drums).

1988

1 January Miles Davis performs alongside pop star Prince in Minneapolis.

16 January Loren Schoenberg and Bob Wilber present a concert at Carnegie Hall celebrating the fiftieth anniversary of Benny Goodman's first appearance there, and reconstructing the original program.

The Rise and Fall of Chet Baker

Few faces can have displayed the ravaging effects of a lifetime's personal problems as graphically as that of Chet Baker, who died in 1988. The trumpeter's boyish good looks helped shoot him to prominence in the 1950s as the first popular idol of the COOL school (● p. 132); his laid-back image and adolescent sex appeal were immortalized in a series of photographs taken by William Claxton that set the tone for the decade and have remained influential in pop-music marketing strategies to this day. But when he died at the age of fifty-eight, Baker's craggy wrinkles told a very different story.

From the outset, Baker's trumpet and flugelhorn playing displayed the marked influence of Miles Davis's mature technique (notably in its studied lack of VIBRATO), and never really escaped from Davis's shadow. It was rather his crooning voice, coupled with a skillfully promoted commercial image, that did most to win him popular success. Chet Baker's work is best represented by recordings made with Gerry Mulligan (● p. 134) and Charlie Parker (● p. 128) in 1952–53, and in the work of his own quartet (1953–56), which adopted the piano-less format he had favored during his collaboration with Mulligan. Although Baker's recorded output was vast, few albums have proved themselves to be truly memorable. He will perhaps be most vividly remembered for his laconic treatment of "My Funny Valentine," which typified the understated approach of mainstream cool artists.

Baker's never-ending drug problems became public knowledge in the 1960s, thanks to a series of widely reported encounters with the law while traveling abroad (including a spell in an Italian jail) and occasional deportations. His affliction did not improve on returning to the USA, and in 1968 he was beaten up in a drug-related incident in San Francisco, in which he lost most of his teeth. This savage mugging effectively brought his American career to an end, although he managed to return to the European circuit in the mid-1970s and continued to play and record until his unexplained death.

February Singer Cassandra Wilson records *Blue Skies.*

16 February Charles Delaunay, pioneer of jazz discography (● p. 87), dies near Paris.

20 March Composer/arranger Gil Evans dies, Cuernavaca, Mexico. His orchestra undertakes a memorial tour of Italy in **July**.

13 May Former COOL idol, Chet Baker, is killed when he falls from his Amsterdam hotel window in mysterious circumstances. The trumpeter's life soon becomes the subject of a documentary, *Let's Get Lost,* filmed by fashion photographer Bruce Weber.

Below One of the finest electronic keyboard technicians in jazz, Lyle Mays's acoustic piano playing remains heavily indebted to the example of Bill Evans.

June At the age of seventy-one, Ella Fitzgerald (● p. 195) sings at Carnegie Hall.

18–19 August Alto saxophonist John Zorn records *Spy versus Spy: the Music of Ornette Coleman.*

17 October Pianist Keith Jarrett (● p. 185) gives a solo concert in Paris. He is nominated for a Grammy Award for his recording of the first book of J. S. Bach's *48 Preludes and Fugues* this year.

27 October Wynton Marsalis continues his systematic reassessment of the heritage of early jazz by recording the album *The Majesty of the Blues.*

● Lyle Mays issues his second album, *Street Dreams*. Musicians participating in this eclectic FUSION project include Bill Frisell (guitar) and drummers Peter Erskine and Steve Gadd (● p. 220). ● Verve issues a fusion album, *Echoes of Ellington*, featuring the talents of trumpeter Randy Brecker and saxophonists Tom Scott and Bill Evans. ● Avant-garde pianist Cecil Taylor tours with British drummer Tony Oxley. ● Dave Brubeck makes a return visit to the USSR. ● Joe Zawinul forms the Zawinul Syndicate with guitarist Scott Henderson. ● Brothers Dave and Don Grusin record their keyboard extravaganza, *Sticks and Stones* (GRP). ● Clint Eastwood directs the biopic *Bird*, dramatizing the final years of Charlie Parker's life and using Parker's original recordings as the basis for its soundtrack. ● *The New Grove Dictionary of Jazz* is published in two volumes by Macmillan under the editorship of Barry Kernfeld. Originally priced at £200 in the UK, a single-vol-ume reprint in 1994 is marketed for just £25 and (not surprisingly) achieves phenomenal sales.

1989-90

Messengers Retrospective

Art Blakey's Jazz Messengers, a group that nurtured several generations of exciting performers, are reunited just one year before the great drummer's death.

Above A vital link between swing and bop, trumpeter Roy "Little Jazz" Eldridge died in 1989.

Right Art Blakey, high priest of hard bop.

26 February Trumpeter Roy Eldridge dies, Valley Stream, New York.

March Ralph Sutton and Jay McShann celebrate the origins of jazz keyboard-playing in their album *Last of the Whorehouse Piano Players*.

9 May Already suffering from AIDS, trumpeter Woody Shaw, aged forty-five, dies from injuries sustained three months earlier when his left arm was severed by a subway train shortly after he left a gig at the Village Vanguard.

June Dizzy Gillespie (● p. 219) plays in a concert televised by the BBC from London's Royal Festival Hall. This year he undertakes a punishing schedule, performing over three hundred gigs in nearly thirty countries; home appearances are made in one hundred US cities across thirty-two states.

August A tribute to Jelly Roll Morton (● p. 45) is mounted at Alice Tully Hall, New York, by Wynton Marsalis and Dr. Michael White's New Orleans band.

October A seventieth-birthday celebration for drummer Art Blakey (● p. 138) is held in Leverkusen, West Germany, at which he is reunited with former Jazz Messengers stars Freddie Hubbard (trumpet) and Bennie Golson (tenor saxophone).

November Phil Woods's protégé, saxophonist Richie Cole, tours the Soviet Union.

December Drummer Max Roach appears with Cecil Taylor at New York's Town Hall. Roach also makes his first tour to the UK this year, fronting his own quartet.

● Nineteen-year-old trumpeter Roy Hargrove (● p. 223) records *Diamond in the Rough*. ● Alto saxophonist John Zorn records *Naked City* for Nonesuch. Prone to the use of eccentric sound effects (e.g., duck calls) that suggest the influence of Roland Kirk (● p. 189), Zorn makes his name as an important postmodernist capable of both popular appeal and musical freedom. ● Keith Jarrett's trio records STANDARDS live in Oslo for ECM. ● Charles Mingus's large-scale work *Epitaph*, completed and edited by Gunther Schuller, receives a posthumous first performance. The second volume of Schuller's definitive analytical history of jazz (● p. 169) is published this year under the title *The Swing Era*. ● Quincy Jones assembles a vast array of contemporary talent for his album *Back on the Block*, a heady mixture of BOP and popular styles, including rap.

WORLD EVENTS

1989

23 January Death of Salvador Dalí

February Salman Rushdie sentenced to death in Iran for his allegedly blasphemous novel *The Satanic Verses*

4 June Tiananmen Square massacre, Beijing, China

19 October Earthquake in San Francisco

10 November Berlin Wall opened

1990

11 February Nelson Mandela freed, South Africa

2 August Iraq invades Kuwait

15 October Mikhail Gorbachev awarded Nobel Peace Prize

● A. S. Byatt's novel *Possession*

Tributes to Art Blakey

Art Blakey (d. 1990)

"Blakey had developed a fiercely individual style that was simultaneously volcanic and severe. Blakey was amongst the least superfluously 'busy' drummers in jazz. His rhythmic sense was so sharp, and his foot and wrist control so precise, that he needed do little more than 'keep time' to create an atmosphere of tremendous power. His accompanying figures, sparsely used, came at the right moments to support the soloist with sudden bursts of energy. Likewise, Blakey's solos were usually structured around a few melodic motifs played against each other contrapuntally as he built to a climax. Musical coherence was never sacrificed to technical flash."

David H. Rosenthal, 1992

"Throughout the 1980s the roster of young talent that passed through Blakey's unique finishing school [the Jazz Messengers] continued unabated ... It is significant that many young musicians either came to the attention of the jazz world through Blakey's auspices or at least enhanced their reputation as a result of their tenure with him, most going on to shape the sound of mainstream bop on graduating from his ensemble – just as he intended."

Stuart Nicholson, 1990

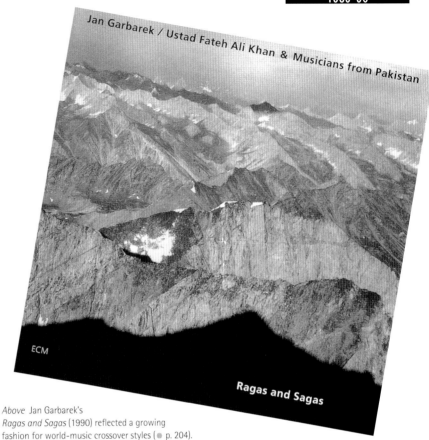

Above Jan Garbarek's *Ragas and Sagas* (1990) reflected a growing fashion for world-music crossover styles (p. 204).

1990

3 February Drummer Mel Lewis dies, New York.

18 March Pianist Ellis Marsalis, father of superstars Wynton (p. 196) and Branford, records a trio album with bassist Bob Hurst and drummer Jeff Watts.

3 April Vocalist Sarah Vaughan (p. 123) dies, Los Angeles.

25 April Saxophonist Dexter Gordon dies, Philadelphia.

May Jan Garbarek (p. 177) records *Ragas and Sagas* for ECM with Pakistani musicians, including singer Ustad Fateh Ali Khan.

4 May Thirty-three-year-old guitarist Emily Remler, former wife of Jamaican pianist Monty Alexander, dies of a heart attack during a tour of Australia.

July Saxophonist Pharoah Sanders tours London.

August Jan Garbarek records his album *I Take Up the Runes* in Oslo for ECM.

4 October Violinist Stephane Grappelli (p. 75), aged eighty-two, performs in Tokyo.

14 October Leonard Bernstein dies, New York.

16 October Art Blakey dies, New York.

● John McLaughlin records his *Mediterranean Concerto* with the London Symphony Orchestra under conductor Michael Tilson Thomas. ● Photographer Herman Léonard publishes his book *The Eye of Jazz*. Milt Hinton publishes his autobiography, *Bass Line*. Miles Davis (p. 216) brings out his best-selling and racy life story, *Miles: the Autobiography* (co-authored with Quincy Troupe). ● Spike Lee's movie *Mo' Better Blues*, with a musical score by his father, Bill Lee (double bass), features Denzel Washington as a jazz trumpeter.

Dave Grusin and GRP

Right Equally at home in popular fusion and hard-driving bop styles, pianist Dave Grusin has originated a stream of impressive Hollywood film scores.

In 1989, the motion picture *The Fabulous Baker Boys* made an unlikely singing star of actress Michelle Pfeiffer with a stunning jazz soundtrack composed and performed by Dave Grusin – and skillfully mimed on screen by the keyboard-playing Baker brothers, Jeff and Lloyd Bridges.

A highly experienced composer of major Hollywood scores (including *Tootsie* in 1982, *Havana* in 1983 and the Oscar-winning soundtrack to *The Milagro Beanfield War* in 1988), Grusin's international exposure in the cinema has long been in danger of overshadowing his talents as a performing artist and recording entrepreneur. Over sixty years after the demise of the silent-movie pianists, Grusin showed how simple music for a solo ACOUSTIC piano could provide an admirably flexible commentary to the on-screen action with his score for the Tom Cruise thriller *The Firm* (1993).

Grusin majored in piano at the University of Colorado, where he played with Art Pepper (alto saxophone), Johnny Smith (guitar) and Anita O'Day (vocal), before moving to New York in 1959 to study at the Manhattan School of Music. While serving as musical director for singer Andy Williams (until 1966), he recorded with the Benny Goodman Quintet and in a BOP piano trio and quintet (the latter featuring the talents of Thad Jones and Frank Foster). In the early 1970s he recorded with Sarah Vaughan, while acting as arranger to Quincy Jones and Carmen McRae.

In the early 1980s, his record company GRP (Grusin–Rosen Productions, which he co-founded with Larry Rosen) established itself as a stylish purveyor of an easygoing brand of jazz-rock FUSION which, although never greatly favored by the critics,

nevertheless restored melodic appeal to jazz when it most needed it. Grusin's own albums on this label include fine interpretations of standards by George Gershwin (1991), Duke Ellington (1993) and Henry Mancini (1997), and a virtuoso electronic duo session with brother and fellow keyboard-player Don Grusin (● p. 211).

Other artists who have augmented the growing GRP catalogue include Chick Corea's Elektric Band, guitarist Lee Ritenour, flautist Dave Valentin, singer Diane Schuur, the Duke Ellington Orchestra and pianist David Benoit. Of these, it is perhaps Corea's energetic young band that has been most successful in avoiding the pitfalls of overt commercialization by striving toward adventurous musical horizons.

Down Beat's Critics' Poll: Results Highlights

August 1990

Jazz Artist of the Year Benny Carter (alto saxophone)
Jazz Album of the Year Cecil Taylor, *In Berlin*
Composer Henry Threadgill
Arranger Toshiko Akiyoshi
Acoustic Group Phil Woods Quintet
Electric Group Ornette Coleman's Prime Time
Big Band Sun Ra's Arkestra
Acoustic Guitar Jim Hall
Electric Guitar Bill Frisell
Trumpet Lester Bowie
Acoustic Piano Cecil Taylor; Geri Allen
(Talent Deserving Wider Recognition)
Soprano Saxophone Steve Lacy
Alto Saxophone Phil Woods
Tenor Saxophone Sonny Rollins
Baritone Saxophone Hamiet Bluiett; John Surman
(Talent Deserving Wider Recognition)
Female Vocalist Betty Carter; Cassandra Wilson
(Talent Deserving Wider Recognition)

Above Chick Corea's Elektric Band helped revive the fortunes of fusion in the 1980s, and showcased the talents of drummer Dave Weckl (● p. 221).

Right Chick Corea at the piano in 1989.

1991

Farewell, Prince of Darkness

Miles Davis, arguably the most influential artist in the history of jazz, leaves the stage for the last time.

January Pat Metheny fights a copyright battle over the unauthorized use of his composition "Last Train Home" (from the album *Still Life (Talking)*: ● p. 208) in a television advertisement in Miami, Florida.

Spring The Koger Foundation donates $1 million to endow a series of courses in Great American Jazz at the University of North Florida.

April Pianist McCoy Tyner records *New York Reunion* with former quartet sidemen Joe Henderson (tenor saxophone), Ron Carter (bass) and Al Foster (drums).

June Lionel Hampton (● p. 70), aged eighty-two, records live with his Golden Men at the Blue Note club, New York, for Telarc. Lead trumpeter for the session is Clark Terry. ● Ornette Coleman (● p. 150) participates in the JVC Jazz Festival at Carnegie Hall. ● Foundation of the Smithsonian Institution's Jazz Masterworks Orchestra, directed by David Baker (University of Indiana) and Gunther Schuller. The band's activities are linked to a series of publications (the Jazz Masterworks Edition), and both ventures are supported by a grant in excess of $330,000 from Congressional funds.

6 June Saxophonist Stan Getz (● p. 153) dies, Malibu, California.

Miles Davis: Death of a Legend

On 8 July 1991, a visibly frail Miles Davis took the stage at the Montreux Jazz Festival, backed by a 50-piece orchestra under the direction of Quincy Jones, and played a tribute to his onetime collaborator, Gil Evans. Two days later, the sixty-five-year-old trumpeter was in Paris to receive the title Commander of Arts and Letters from the Ministry of Culture and play a reunion gig with former sidemen Wayne Shorter and Dave Holland. On 19 July he visited London for the last time and appeared at the Royal Festival Hall. A little over two months later, in California, the combination of pneumonia and a stroke took his life.

Davis probably accomplished more in his forty-seven-year career – an unusually long period of sustained activity for a jazz musician – than any other performer. As fellow trumpeter Ian Carr has recently put it, "his creativity and his influence as both player and conceptualist were sustained for more than four decades, an example which introduced the idea of permanent conceptual development into the jazz life. That is why he has been an inspirational figure for successive generations of musicians since the 1940s."

Born in East St. Louis, Davis moved to New York in 1944 to take up a place at the prestigious Juilliard School of Music. However, he quickly grew disillusioned with the school's stifling environment and preferred to gain practical jazz experience by seeking out Dizzy Gillespie and Charlie Parker on 52nd Street and in Harlem. Davis later explained, "We was all trying to get our master's degrees and Ph.D.s from Minton's University of

Bebop under the tutelage of Professors Bird and Diz."

By the close of 1945 he had begun recording with Parker and was serving a thorough apprenticeship in the BOP style. Somewhat limited in playing technique, Davis was unable to compete with Gillespie's pyrotechnics (for his remarks on this situation, ● p. 219), and in 1948 first asserted his stylistic individuality by forming with Gil Evans the celebrated nonet that initiated the COOL school (● p. 120). Although he continued to work with Evans in large-ensemble ventures, Davis spent much of the 1950s and 1960s developing a refined form of HARD BOP while experimenting with novel MODAL techniques (● p. 146).

His canny initiation of the jazz-rock FUSION movement in 1968–69 was sudden, unpredictable and hugely successful (● p. 170), and earned him an international status akin to that of a high-profile pop star. Not surprisingly, perhaps, he later collaborated with pop singers, such as Sting and Prince. But in the jazz sphere Davis's personal and health problems, coupled with an inability to sustain development of his own stylistic innovations, meant that his work in the 1970s and 1980s did not match up to the quality of performances by younger talents, many of whom had been nurtured in his own bands years before.

Davis's distinctive manner of trumpet playing was widely imitated, but not to everyone's taste. The poet and highly conservative jazz critic Philip Larkin, jazz reviewer for the *Daily Telegraph* in the 1960s, wrote of the trumpeter's "new inhumanity," and declared that Davis had "several manners: the dead muzzled slow stuff, the sour yelping fast stuff, and the sonorous theatrical arranged stuff, and I disliked them all."

Opposite Miles Davis at New York's JVC Jazz Festival in June 1987.

WORLD EVENTS

16 January Gulf War begins

25 February Warsaw Pact collapses

21 May Rajiv Gandhi assassinated

November Singer Freddie Mercury dies from AIDS

21 December Downfall of Soviet Union

July Miles Davis appears at the Montreux Jazz Festival with Quincy Jones and resurrects his early work with arranger Gil Evans (● p. 120). ● Keith Jarrett (● p. 185) gives one of his increasingly rare solo concerts at London's Royal Festival Hall.

Summer Chicago's Hot House launches an annual "Women of the New Jazz" festival, featuring pianist Geri Allen and singer Sheila Jordan.

September Bill Cosby receives a Lifetime Achievement Award from *Down Beat*. A drummer himself, the comedian is the popular host of the Playboy Jazz Festival, held at the Hollywood Bowl annually since 1979.

28 September Miles Davis dies at the age of sixty-five, Santa Monica, California.

October The first Akbank International Jazz Festival is held in Istanbul.

● Alto saxophonist David Sanborn, a popular FUSION artist, records *Another Hand* with a distinguished line-up including Bill Frisell, Charlie Haden, Marcus Miller and Jack DeJohnette. ● The eightieth birthday of Cuban trumpeter Mario Bauzá (● p. 144) inspires a resurgence of interest in "cubop" in New York.

1992-95

Henceforward...

Jazz moves into its tenth decade confronted with a richly varied but utterly unpredictable future.

1992

13 April   Widely respected jazz critic Martin Williams dies aged sixty-seven, Washington, D. C.

23 April   Pianist Lyle Mays (● p. 211) records an ACOUSTIC trio album, *Fictionary*, with Marc Johnson (bass) and Jack DeJohnette (drums).

August   Miles Davis's last studio album, the rap-based *Doo-Bop* (featuring Easy Mo Bee), and Wynton Marsalis's *Blue Interlude* both receive a grudging $4^1/_2$ out of 5 stars in *Down Beat* reviews.

November   The San Francisco Jazz Festival stages a pianists' tribute to the work of Jelly Roll Morton (● p. 45), featuring Wynton Marsalis's pianist Marcus Roberts. Morton's life is further celebrated this year in the Broadway musical *Jelly's Last Jam*.

December   Julius Hemphill's sextet recording *Fat Man and the Hard Blues* (July 1991) receives the maximum 5 stars in a *Down Beat* review.

● Keith Jarrett (● p. 185) records Dmitri Shostakovich's *Preludes and Fugues*. ● Bob Belden's recording of his jazz reinterpretation of themes from Puccini's *Turandot* (the opera having been popularized by its global exposure in television coverage of soccer's World Cup in 1990) is released only in Japan because of copyright restrictions imposed by Puccini's estate. ● In a sign of the increasing use of ethnic music in a jazz context, the Montreux Festival renames itself the Montreux Jazz and World Music Festival.

1993

30 May   Bandleader Sun Ra dies, aged seventy-nine, Birmingham, Alabama.

25 July   The Concord Jazz Festival celebrates its silver jubilee in California.

August   In *Down Beat*'s annual Critics' Poll, the Best Album is Joe Henderson's *So Near, So Far (Musings for Miles)* on the Verve label. Henderson goes on to win three awards in the same journal's Readers' Poll in **December**.

Above Tenor saxophonist Joe Henderson, who won major critical and popular acclaim in 1993.

Right A participant in Miles Davis's early fusion projects in 1969–71, formidable drummer Jack DeJohnette is also proficient as a pianist.

Dizzy Gillespie: Antics and Tributes

Dizzy Gillespie (died 6 January 1993)

"When Pee Wee Marquette finished announcing an attraction at Birdland, he usually walked off the bandstand leaving the microphone at the height he had adjusted it for himself, about three feet from the floor.

"One night, Pee Wee announced, 'And now, ladies and gentlemen, Birdland proudly presents, DIZZY GILLESPIE!' and walked away from the microphone. Out came Dizzy on his knees to accept the applause and announce the first tune. The microphone needed no adjustment."

Bill Crow, 1990

"I wanted to play high and fast like Dizzy just to prove to myself that I could do it. A lot of cats used to be putting me down back in the bebop days because their ears could only pick up what Dizzy was doing. That's what they thought playing the trumpet was all about. And when somebody like me came along, trying something different, he ran the risk of being put down."

Miles Davis, 1989

"Gillespie was one of the few of the early beboppers who did not destroy himself. He ran his career with intelligence, and even when later movements in music seemed to make bop obsolete, he continued to work, emerging, in the 1970s, as something as close to an elder statesman as the music has ever seen. Like [Coleman] Hawkins, he kept his standards and continued to play his own way despite shifts of taste."

James Lincoln Collier, 1978

One of Dizzy Gillespie's distinctive trumpets, on which the bells were bent sharply upwards, was sold by a London auction house in 1996. Gillespie himself described how the unusual modification came about on the night of 6 January 1953:

"The truth is that the shape of my horn was an accident . . . When I got back to the club [Snookie's, on 45th Street, New York], Stump 'n' Stumpy had been fooling around on the bandstand, and one had pushed the other, and he'd fallen back on to my horn. Instead of the horn just falling, the bell bent. When I got back, the bell was sticking up in the air. Illinois Jacquet had left. He said, 'I'm not going to be here when that man comes back and sees his horn sticking up at that angle.'

"When I came back, it was my wife's birthday and I didn't want to be a drag. I put the horn to my mouth and started playing it. Well, when the bell went back, it made a smaller hole because of the dent . . . The sound had been changed and it could be played softly, very softly, not blarey . . . I contacted the Martin Company, and I had Lorraine, who's also an artist, draw me a trumpet at a forty-five degree angle . . . They made me a trumpet and I've been playing one like that ever since."

Below Dizzy Gillespie shows off his two physical hallmarks: bulging cheeks containing enough air to produce a seemingly endless succession of brilliant notes, and his upward-thrusting trumpet bell.

WORLD EVENTS

1992

12 April EuroDisney opens, Paris

April–May Race riots in Los Angeles

3 November Bill Clinton elected US President

9 December Prince and Princess of Wales separate

• Civil war intensifies in former Yugoslavia

1993

15 October Nelson Mandela and F. W. de Klerk win Nobel Peace Prize

• Death of Frank Zappa • Steven Spielberg's holocaust movie *Schindler's List* receives Oscar for Best Picture, while his film *Jurassic Park* nets $500 million at the box office.

1994

26 April First multiracial election, South Africa

1 May Formula I driver Ayrton Senna killed in motor race

• Increasing NATO involvement in former Yugoslavia
• Edvard Munch's painting *The Scream* stolen from Oslo's National Gallery

1995

17 January Earthquake in Kobe, Japan

23 January Former football star O. J. Simpson's murder trial in Los Angeles receives global television coverage

February Civil unrest in Chechnya, former Soviet Union

December Milt Jackson (● p. 129) receives a special award from *Down Beat* for having won the vibraphone category of the journal's Critics' Poll for ten years in succession. ● Cassandra Wilson's first Blue Note album, *Blue Light 'Til Dawn*, receives five stars in the review pages of *Down Beat*.

● Dave Grusin records an album of Duke Ellington STANDARDS under the title *Homage to Duke* (GRP). ● Pianist Horace Silver records *It's Got to Be Funky* for Columbia. ● Canadian pianist Oscar Peterson (● p. 162) wins a $50,000 prize awarded in memory of his compatriot, classical pianist Glenn Gould. Twenty-nine-year-old pianist Benny Green receives $10,000 and the title "Glenn Gould Protégé in Music." ● Chick Corea's dynamic Elektric Band is refused permission to perform at Baden-Würtemberg, Germany, because of the pianist's membership in the controversial Church of Scientology (● p. 178). ● Jan Garbarek (● p. 177) scores both commercial success and critical acclaim with his unique album *Officium* (ECM), a CROSSOVER venture synthesizing jazz and medieval vocal music: Latin motets performed by the Hilliard Ensemble provide the backdrop for haunting saxophone improvisations.

Modern Drummers

1994

April The Verve record label celebrates its fiftieth birthday in New York.

23 May Guitarist Joe Pass dies, Brunswick, New Jersey.

27 May Trumpeter Red Rodney, formerly a close associate of Charlie Parker, dies in Boynton Beach, Florida.

6 June The *New York Times* says of Keith Jarrett's live recordings at the Blue Note, Greenwich Village, "Every new note sounds like a discovery." This year Jarrett records Baroque music by Handel.

July *Down Beat* publishes a special issue to commemorate its sixtieth anniversary.

28 July Singer Cleo Laine and saxophonist John Dankworth perform at the opening night of the first Hawaii International Jazz Festival.

August Pianist Maria Schneider receives 4¹/₂ stars from *Down Beat* for her album *Evanescence.*

Above Dave Weckl, who made his name while still in his twenties as the virtuosic timekeeper of Chick Corea's Elektric Band.

Left Steve Gadd at Nice in 1988.

One of the most significant developments affecting the course of jazz during the FUSION craze was the shift to a rock-influenced style of drumming. The SWUNG rhythms of earlier jazz were increasingly replaced in the late 1960s by "straight" rhythmic patterns that were often hard-driving and included emphatic BACKBEATS. At the same time, and in sharp contrast, avant-garde drummers concentrated on dissolving all sense of rhythmic pulse in an attempt to break away from conventional attitudes to METER.

As the first wave of experimentation abated and performers began to look back once again to earlier jazz styles for inspiration, jazz drumming readmitted traditional techniques alongside these new approaches. Since the 1980s, drummers have had at their disposal a phenomenal array of rhythmic resources, and the tension between "straight" rock patterns, "swung" jazz rhythms and metrical freedom has been maintained with generally impressive creative results. The succession of drummers who performed with Weather Report (● p. 174) – Alphonse Mouzon, Alex Acuña, Peter Erskine and Omar Hakim – exemplified varied but equally impressive syntheses of the available techniques. Versatile artists such as Barry Altschul and Steve Gadd have developed their own distinctive idioms. Gadd's "linear" style of playing employs a wide range of percussive timbres with unusual economy and clarity.

Weather Report was also typical of its time in featuring an additional performer playing exotic percussion instruments that were often heavily influenced by Brazilian music. The Brazilian virtuoso Nana Vasconcelos brought an extra dimension to the fusion sound with his colorful work with the Pat Metheny Group in the 1980s, and in his CROSSOVER ventures with Don Cherry and others (● p. 204).

Another product of the 1970s was the electronic drum pad, which produces synthesized drum sounds when struck. Models manufactured by Moog (● p. 193) and Simmons may either be used exclusively, or else rigged up alongside a conventional drum kit as an ancillary resource. Among the first exponents of the device were Tony Williams, who was Miles Davis's prodigious drummer, and Billy Cobham, who cemented his reputation with his exhilarating drumming for John McLaughlin's Mahavishnu Orchestra. Superb electronic drumming has more recently been demonstrated in Chick Corea's Elektric Band by Dave Weckl, who indulged in a drum battle with Steve Gadd on his 1990 album, *Master Plan.*

Once popular but now regarded with suspicion in jazz circles, the so-called drum-machine seemed in danger of supplanting live drummers altogether during the 1970s. Fully automated and capable of a rigorous metrical precision beyond even the best human performer, the drum-machine has remained an ideal tool in a disco environment but has proved to be too inflexible for the spontaneous creative context of the best jazz.

Above A set of six images of jazz and blues singers appeared as US postage stamps in 1994.

22 September Critic Leonard Feather dies, Encino, California.

● Pianist Geri Allen records her trio album *Twenty-One* for Blue Note with former Miles Davis and Herbie Hancock sidemen, Ron Carter and Tony Williams. ● A jazz-rap "summit" meeting is mounted in New York by Max Roach, Donald Byrd and rap artist Q-tip. ● Classical violinist Itzhak Perlman records a jazz album, *Side by Side*, for Telarc with Oscar Peterson.

1995

June Jan Garbarek records *Visible World* in Oslo for ECM.

September Maria Schneider is the featured composer at the thirty-eighth Monterey Jazz Festival.

October The Arts Council publishes a green-paper review of the state of jazz in England. It concludes that underfunding and underexposure of the work of native jazz musicians has resulted in "insufficient opportunity in this country for [their] important contribution to world music to be fully recognised."

December Trumpeter Roy Hargrove, aged 26, finally ousts Wynton Marsalis from first place in the *Down Beat* Readers' Poll (though Marsalis still tops the Critics' Poll).

● Ornette Coleman's group Prime Time makes a major comeback with their album *Tone Dialing*, issued by the saxophonist's own Harmolodic label (a subsidiary of Verve). Other albums recorded this year include John Scofield's *Groove Elation* (Blue Note) and Chick Corea's quartet disc *Time Warp*. ● Director Robert Altman films his movie *Kansas City*, which includes a reconstruction of a typical 1930s JAM SESSION. ● The Thelonious Monk Institute and Universal Studios, Florida, plan "Jazz-Fest USA," set for April 1996, to showcase the best young talent emerging from American colleges.

Right Free-jazz pioneer Ornette Coleman, seen here (second from right) with his quartet in a famous rehearsal picture from 1971, made a timely comeback in the mid-1990s.

Down Beat's Critics' Poll Results

August 1995

Hall of Fame Julius Hemphill (alto saxophone)
Jazz Artist of the Year Joe Lovano (saxophones)
Jazz Album of the Year Joe Lovano and Gunther Schuller, *Rush Hour* (Blue Note)
Reissue of the Year *The Complete Bud Powell* (Verve)
Composer Henry Threadgill
Arranger Toshiko Akiyoshi
Acoustic Group Charlie Haden's Quartet West
Electric Group John Scofield
Acoustic Guitar John McLaughlin
Electric Guitar John Scofield
Violin Stephane Grappelli
Acoustic Bass Charlie Haden
Trumpet Wynton Marsalis
Trombone J. J. Johnson
Keyboards Herbie Hancock
Soprano Saxophone Steve Lacy
Alto Saxophone Jackie McLean
Tenor Saxophone Sonny Rollins
Baritone Saxophone Gerry Mulligan
Drums Elvin Jones
Male Vocalist Joe Williams
Female Vocalist Betty Carter

The Readers' Poll results, published in December 1995, were strikingly similar. Notable exceptions were:

Hall of Fame J. J. Johnson
Trumpet Roy Hargrove
Alto Saxophone Phil Woods
Female Vocalist Cassandra Wilson

"Though a premature autopsy of jazz arrives every few years, either because of the deaths of giants or because the business of the music seems down for the count, jazz maintains a startling vitality in New York. This is made possible by the authority of the enduring masters, and by a growing body of young players ... When the elder statesmen of blues and swing are on the bandstand, one can hear nuances continuing to develop within their styles – the styles of musicians whose experience stretches back to the sixties, the fifties, the forties, the thirties, even (if you're talking about Doc Cheatham) to the twenties and the teens ... They convey the music's meaning through their gestures, their speech patterns, their anecdotes, their humor and camaraderie, their elegance, their grasp of romantic frailty ...

"Playing alongside them is the growing flock of younger musicians, who use the misdeeds of their predecessors as invaluable admonishments, and who cherish the timeless triumphs of the jazz idiom with an unprecedented depth of scholarship so tightly focused on the processes of art that it doesn't shrivel into the academic ... By ignoring the dictates of the mass media, they have become the truest rebels in American music, choosing an intricate and difficult discipline that demands courage, patience, and a willingness to cultivate one of the most fertile traditions this century has produced."

Stanley Crouch, "New York is Jazz"
The New Yorker, 26 August–2 September 1996

REFERENCE SECTION

Milt Gabler's busy Commodore Music Shop on 42nd Street, New York, in the 1940s, home to the record label he founded in 1938. Gabler watches on at extreme left, while a record is selected by his brother-in-law Jack Crystal (father of comedian Billy Crystal).

Biographical Index of Musicians

Muhal Richard Abrams
b. 19 September 1930, Chicago
Piano, composer.
Leading light of Chicago free jazz in the early 1960s and founder of the city's Association for the Advancement of Creative Music.

Julian "Cannonball" Adderley
b. 15 September 1928, Tampa, Florida
d. 8 August 1975, Gary, Indiana
Alto and soprano saxophones.
Brother of Nat Adderley.
Virtuoso bop performer schooled in the tradition of Charlie Parker.

Nat Adderley
b. 25 November 1931, Tampa, Florida
Trumpet.
Brother of Cannonball Adderley, with whom he served as a sideman for twenty years (1955–75).

Toshiko Akiyoshi
b. 12 December 1929, Dairen, Manchuria
Piano, composer, arranger.
Her sophisticated arrangements continue the tradition of big-band composition formulated by Duke Ellington and Gil Evans. She married fellow-arranger Lew Tabackin in 1970.

Monty Alexander
b. 6 June 1944, Kingston, Jamaica
Piano.
Versatile keyboard technician inspired by the style of Oscar Peterson. He was married to guitarist Emily Remler.

Geri Allen
b. 12 June 1957, Pontiac, Michigan
Piano.
One of the most prominent younger keyboard players, who made her first album as leader in 1983.

Barry Altschul
b. 6 January 1943, New York
Drums.

Eclectic performer equally proficient in bop and free-jazz idioms.

Albert Ammons
b. 23 September 1907, Chicago
d. 2 December 1949, Chicago
Piano.
Pre-eminent boogie-woogie pianist in Chicago during the 1930s and 1940s.

Arild Andersen
b. 27 October 1945, Oslo
Acoustic and electric bass, composer.
Sideman of Jan Garbarek in the late 1960s, and voted best European bass player in 1975.

Lilian Armstrong (née Hardin)
b. 3 February 1898, Memphis, Tennessee
d. 27 August 1971, Chicago
Piano.
Married to Louis Armstrong (1924–38), alongside whom she served in King Oliver's Creole Jazz Band.

Louis "Satchmo" Armstrong
b. 4 August 1901, New Orleans
d. 6 July 1971, New York
Cornet, trumpet, vocals.
The first virtuoso improviser in the history of jazz, Armstrong laid the foundations from which all mainstream jazz styles developed. He later reached a wide audience as a popular singer. Married to Lilian Hardin (1924–38).

Georgie Auld
b. 19 May 1919, Toronto
d. 8 January 1990, Palm Springs, California
Saxophones, clarinet.
Sideman of Artie Shaw and Benny Goodman who tutored Robert De Niro's mimed playing in the film *New York, New York*.

Albert Ayler
b. 13 July 1936, Cleveland, Ohio
d. (drowned) 25 November 1970, New York
Saxophones, composer.
Inimitable free-jazz performer,

inspired by the traditional popular music of pre-jazz New Orleans. Brother of Donald Ayler.

Donald Ayler
b. 5 October 1942, Cleveland
Trumpet.
Brother of Albert Ayler.

Mildred Bailey
b. 27 February 1907, Tekoa, Washington
d. (liver failure) 12 December 1951, Poughkeepsie, New York
Vocals.
Singer with Paul Whiteman's orchestra (1929–33), subsequently married to Red Norvo (1933–43).

Chet Baker
b. 23 December 1929, Yale, Oklahoma
d. (fell from hotel window) 13 May 1988, Amsterdam
Trumpet, flugelhorn, vocals.
Archetypal "cool" performer, whose boyish good looks shot him to prominence in the 1950s.

Chris Barber
b. 17 April 1930, Welwyn Garden City, UK
Trombone, composer.
Leading British bandleader with a solid reputation in continental Europe.

William "Count" Basie
b. 21 August 1904, Red Bank, New Jersey
d. 26 April 1984, Hollywood
Piano, organ, composer, bandleader.
Originator of a brand of Kansas City jazz that became the hottest big-band sound of the 1930s and 1940s.

Django Bates
b. 2 October 1960, Beckenham, UK
Keyboards, tenor horn, composer.
Wild compositional talent whose work with Loose Tubes in the 1980s exhibited dazzling eclecticism.

Mario Bauzá
b. 28 April 1911, Havana

d. 11 July 1993, New York
Trumpet, alto saxophone, composer, arranger.
Classically trained performer whose Afro-Cuban collaborators included Dizzy Gillespie.

Sidney Bechet
b. 14 May 1897, New Orleans
d. 14 May 1959, Paris
Clarinet, soprano saxophone.
Wayward talent of old New Orleans, popular in his adoptive France during the 1950s.

Leon "Bix" Beiderbecke
b. 10 March 1903, Davenport, Iowa
d. 6 August 1931, New York
Cornet, piano, composer.
The first white jazz performer widely admired by black musicians.

Bunny Berigan
b. 2 November 1908, Hilbert, Wisconsin
d. 2 June 1942, New York
Trumpet, vocals.
Sideman of the Dorsey brothers who absorbed the influences of Louis Armstrong and Bix Beiderbecke.

Leonard Bernstein
b. 25 August 1918, Lawrence, Massachusetts
d. 14 October 1990, New York
Composer, conductor.
Equally at home in classical and jazz idioms, he came to global prominence as the composer of *West Side Story* in 1957.

Barney Bigard
b. 3 March 1906, New Orleans
d. 27 June 1980, Culver City, California
Clarinet, tenor saxophone.
Sideman of Duke Ellington and Louis Armstrong.

Bernard "Acker" Bilk
b. 28 January 1929, Pensford, UK
Clarinet, bandleader.
Prominent exponent of British traditional jazz in the 1960s and 1970s.

Eubie Blake
b. 7 February 1883, Baltimore
d. 12 February 1983, New York
Piano.
His ragtime and stride playing spanned a century of jazz history.

Art Blakey
b. 11 October 1919, Pittsburgh
d. 16 October 1990, New York
Drums.
Hard-bop performer whose Jazz Messengers provided an apprenticeship for numerous young performers.

Carla Bley (née Borg)
b. 11 May 1938, Oakland, California
Keyboards, composer.
Original compositional talent who made her name with a distinctive brand of free jazz. Married Paul Bley in 1957.

Paul Bley
b. 10 November 1932, Montreal
Keyboards, composer.
A protégé of Charles Mingus, he later founded the record company Improvising Artists Inc. Married Carla Bley in 1957.

Hamiet Bluiett
b. 1940, Lovejoy, Illinois
Baritone saxophone.
Founder member of the World Saxophone Quartet in 1977.

Charles "Buddy" Bolden
b. 6 September 1877, New Orleans
d. 4 November 1931, Jackson, Louisiana
Cornet.
Legendary pioneer of New Orleans jazz, who never recorded.

George Botsford
b. 24 February 1874, Sioux Falls, South Dakota
d. 11 February 1949, New York
Ragtime composer.
His best-known composition is "Black and White Rag."

Lester Bowie
b. 11 October 1941, Frederick, Maryland

Trumpet, flugelhorn, composer.
Member of the Art Ensemble of Chicago, famous for his theatrical manner of performance.

Anthony Braxton
b. 4 June 1945, Chicago
Saxophones, clarinets, flute, composer.
Controversial free-jazz artist who has appealed more to avant-garde intellectuals than to a wide audience.

Michael Brecker
b. 29 March 1949, Philadelphia
Tenor and soprano saxophones, Electronic Wind Instrument.
Versatile fusion artist; brother of Randy Brecker.

Randy Brecker
b. 27 November 1945, Philadelphia
Trumpet.
Brother of Michael Brecker, with whom he formed The Brecker Brothers in 1974.

Willem Breuker
b. 4 November 1944, Amsterdam
Saxophones, composer, bandleader.
Dutch free-jazz guru, founder of the Instant Composers' Pool (1968) and Kollectief (1974).

Bob Brookmeyer
b. 19 December 1929, Kansas City
Trombone.
West Coast artist specializing in the neglected valve trombone.

Clifford Brown
b. 30 October 1930, Wilmington, Delaware
d. (automobile accident) 26 June 1956, Pennsylvania
Trumpet.
Bop performer and close associate of Max Roach.

Ray Brown
b. 13 October 1926, Pittsburgh
Double bass.
Mainstream artist, especially associated with Oscar Peterson. Married to Ella Fitzgerald (1948–52).

Dave Brubeck
b. 6 December 1920, Concord, California
Piano, composer.
West Coast performer, studied composition with Darius Milhaud. His rhythmically sophisticated music, achieved in collaboration with Paul Desmond, was enormously popular in the late 1950s and 1960s.

Gary Burton
b. 23 January 1943, Anderson, Indiana
Vibraphone, composer.
He revolutionized vibraphone technique in the late 1960s, and has since made a name as an influential music educator.

Don Byas
b. 21 October 1912, Muskogee, Oklahoma
d. 24 August 1972, Amsterdam
Tenor saxophone.
One of several bop performers who emigrated to Europe, settling in Paris in 1946.

Donald Byrd
b. 9 December 1932, Detroit
Trumpet, flugelhorn, composer.
Soul-jazz artist prominent in the Blue Note catalog.

George "Red" Callender
b. 6 March 1916, Haynesville, Virginia
d. 8 March 1992, Saugus, California
Double bass, tuba.
Popular on the West Coast in the 1940s, he was mentor to Charles Mingus.

Cabell "Cab" Calloway
b. 25 December 1907, New York
d. 18 November 1994
Vocals, bandleader.
Charismatic leader whose band succeeded Duke Ellington's at the Cotton Club in the early 1930s.

Harry Carney
b. 1 April 1910, Boston
d. 8 October 1974, New York
Baritone saxophone.

Stalwart sideman of Duke Ellington (1927–74).

Ian Carr
b. 21 April 1933, Dumfries, UK
Trumpet, flugelhorn, writer.
Founder of the fusion group Nucleus in 1969, and biographer of Miles Davis and Keith Jarrett.

Benny Carter
b. 8 August 1907, New York
Alto saxophone, trumpet.
Mainstream swing artist, prominent in Europe in the late 1930s and again in the 1970s.

Betty Carter
b. 16 May 1929, Flint, Michigan
Vocals.
Protégée of Lionel Hampton in the late 1940s, she continues to top popularity polls in the US.

Ron Carter
b. 4 May 1937, Ferndale, Michigan
Acoustic and electric bass.
Sideman to Miles Davis and Herbie Hancock in the 1960s, he has been a leader since 1976.

Al Casey
b. 15 September 1915, Louisville, Kentucky
Guitar.
Member of Fats Waller's Rhythm (1934–42).

"Big" Sid Catlett
b. 17 January 1910, Evansville, Indiana
d. (heart attack) 25 March 1951, Chicago
Drums.
Sideman to Benny Goodman, Louis Armstrong and early bop performers.

Paul Chambers
b. 22 April 1935, Pittsburgh
d. (tuberculosis) 4 January 1969, New York
Double bass.
Member of the Miles Davis Quintet (1955–63).

Adolphus "Doc" Cheatham
b. 13 June 1905, Nashville, Tennessee
Trumpet.
Traditionalist equally at home in New Orleans and Latin styles.

Don Cherry
b. 18 November 1936, Oklahoma City
d. 19 October 1995
Trumpet, piano, ethnic instruments.
Pioneer of "world music," he first made his name with Ornette Coleman in the late 1950s.

Charlie Christian
b. 29 July 1916, Dallas
d. (tuberculosis) 2 March 1942, New York
Electric guitar.
Innovative improviser who influenced the emerging bop style.

Kenny Clarke
b. 9 January 1914, Pittsburgh
d. 26 January 1985, Montreuil-sous-Bois, France
Drums.
After developing bop drumming techniques in the 1940s, he emigrated to France in 1956.

Stanley Clarke
b. 30 June 1951, Philadelphia
Acoustic and electric bass.
Founder member of Chick Corea's fusion band Return to Forever.

Tony Coe
b. 29 November 1934, Canterbury, UK
Saxophones.
Sideman to John Dankworth and Stan Tracey, he was the tenor soloist on Henry Mancini's popular "Pink Panther" theme.

Nat "King" Cole
b. 17 March 1917, Montgomery, Alabama
d. 15 February 1965, Santa Monica, California
Vocals, piano.
Originator of the piano-trio format and popular singing star on US television in the 1950s.

George Coleman
b. 8 March 1935, Memphis
Tenor and alto saxophones.
Member of the Miles Davis Quintet (1963–64).

Ornette Coleman
b. 19 March 1930, Fort Worth
Alto and tenor saxophones, trumpet, violin, composer.
Controversial pioneer of free jazz in the early 1960s.

John Coltrane
b. 23 September 1926, Hamlet, North Carolina
d. 17 July 1967, New York
Saxophones, composer.
Enormously influential on subsequent tenor saxophonists, he became a cultural icon in the 1960s through his spirituality and experiments with free jazz and oriental music.

Eddie Condon
b. 16 November 1905, Goodland, Indiana
d. 4 August 1973, New York
Guitar, bandleader.
Popular on US television after a ground-breaking broadcast from New York's Town Hall in 1942.

Will Marion Cook
b. 27 January 1869, Washington
d. 19 July 1944, New York
Composer, conductor.
His Southern Syncopated Orchestra took Sidney Bechet to Europe in 1919.

Aaron Copland
b. 14 November 1900, New York
d. 2 December 1990
Composer.
Foremost US classical composer of the twentieth century, who evolved a nationalistic symphonic-jazz idiom in the 1920s.

Chick Corea
b. 12 June 1941, Chelsea, Massachusetts
Keyboards, composer.
Sideman to Miles Davis in the early fusion era, his own fusion bands have included Return to Forever and the Elektric Band. Also a fine acoustic player in styles ranging from hard bop to free jazz.

Eddie Daniels
b. 19 October 1941, New York
Clarinet, tenor saxophone, flute.
Work with Thad Jones and Mel Lewis (1966–72) led to solo prominence on the GRP label in the 1980s.

John Dankworth
b. 20 September 1927, London
Alto saxophone, composer, bandleader.
Early promoter of bop in the UK in the late 1940s and early 1950s, he later headed a popular big band. Married to Cleo Laine since 1958; their son Alec (b. 1960) is a bass player.

Miles Davis
b. 26 May 1926, Alton, Illinois
d. 28 September 1991, Santa Monica, California
Trumpet, flugelhorn, composer.
Widely considered to be the most influential figure in jazz history, his early bop playing led to a number of seminal stylistic developments: "cool" jazz, orchestral jazz (with Gil Evans), modal jazz and jazz-rock fusion.

Claude Debussy
b. 22 August 1862, St Germain-en-Laye
d. 25 March 1918, Paris
Composer.
As an antidote to the French Impressionist style he had himself founded, he became the first European classical composer to flirt with ragtime.

Jack DeJohnette
b. 9 August 1942, Chicago
Drums, piano.
Member of the early Miles Davis fusion bands (1969–71), he has drummed for Keith Jarrett's trio since 1983.

Paul Desmond
b. 25 November 1924, San Francisco

d. 30 May 1977, New York
Alto saxophone, composer.
Member of the Dave Brubeck
Quartet (1951–67), who composed
"Take Five" in 1959.

Al Di Meola
b. 22 July 1954, Jersey City, New
Jersey
Acoustic and electric guitar.
Member of Chick Corea's Return
to Forever (1974–76),
subsequently leader of Al Di
Meola Project.

Warren "Baby" Dodds
b. 24 December 1898, New
Orleans
d. 14 February 1959, Chicago
Drums.
Brother of Johnny Dodds, with
whom he played in King Oliver's
Creole Jazz Band.

Johnny Dodds
b. 12 April 1892, Waverly,
Louisiana
d. (stroke) 8 August 1940,
Chicago
Clarinet, alto saxophone.
Leading clarinetist of early New
Orleans jazz, he worked with King
Oliver and Louis Armstrong.
Brother of Baby Dodds.

Eric Dolphy
b. 20 June 1928, Los Angeles
d. (heart attack) 29 June 1964,
Berlin
*Alto saxophone, flute, clarinet
and bass clarinet.*
Sideman to Charles Mingus and
John Coltrane in the early 1960s.

Arne Domnérus
b. 20 December 1924, Stockholm
Alto saxophone.
Pre-eminent Swedish performer
who made his name in the 1940s.

Pierre Dørge
b. 28 February 1946,
Copenhagen
Guitar, composer, bandleader.
Founder of the New Jungle
Orchestra in 1980, he has
absorbed elements borrowed from
a wide variety of styles and ethnic
traditions.

Kenny Dorham
b. 30 August 1924, Fairfield,
Texas
d. 5 December 1972, New York
Trumpet.
Bop performer who succeeded
Miles Davis as sideman to Charlie
Parker in 1948 and then created
the Jazz Messengers with Art
Blakey.

Jimmy Dorsey
b. 29 February 1904, Shenandoah,
Pennsylvania
d. 12 June 1957, New York
Clarinet, alto saxophone.
Brother of Tommy Dorsey, with
whom he co-led the Dorsey
Brothers Orchestra in 1934–35
and 1953–56.

Tommy Dorsey
b. 19 November 1905,
Shenandoah, Pennsylvania
d. 26 November 1956, Greenwich,
Connecticut
Trombone.
Brother of Jimmy Dorsey.

Honoré Dutrey
b. *c.* 1890, New Orleans
d. 21 July 1935, Chicago
Trombone.
Member of King Oliver's Creole
Jazz Band.

Billy Eckstine
b. 8 July 1914, Pittsburgh
d. 8 March 1993, Pittsburgh
Vocals, trumpet, bandleader.
His 1940s big band employed
emerging bop talents such as
Dizzy Gillespie, Charlie Parker
and Miles Davis.

Roy "Little Jazz" Eldridge
b. 30 January 1911, Pittsburgh
d. 26 February 1989, Valley
Stream, New York
Trumpet, flugelhorn.
Leading trumpeter of the late
1930s, whose style remained
conservative after the bop
revolution.

Edward Kennedy "Duke" Ellington
b. 29 April 1899, Washington
DC
d. 24 May 1974, New York
Piano, composer, bandleader.
Creator of numerous
masterpieces, many in
collaboration with Billy
Strayhorn, infusing jazz with the
intellectual appeal of classical
music. His orchestra found fame
at the Cotton Club (1927–31) and
in Europe, appeared annually at
Carnegie Hall (1943–48) and
later specialized in extended
works.

Peter Erskine
b. 5 June 1954, Somers Point,
New Jersey
Drums.
Member of Weather Report
(1978–82), now much in demand
as a session player.

James Reese Europe
b. 22 February 1881, Mobile,
Alabama
d. (murdered) 10 May 1919,
Boston
Bandleader.
Promoter of orchestrated ragtime,
which he took to Europe in
1918.

Bill Evans
b. 16 August 1929, Plainfield,
New Jersey
d. 15 September 1980,
New York
Piano, composer.
The most respected keyboard
player in modern jazz, whose
harmonic daring and rhythmic
subtlety influenced many
emerging talents in the 1960s.

Bill Evans
b. 9 February 1958, Clarendon
Hills, Illinois
Saxophones.
Sideman to Miles Davis (1980–84)
and a member of John
McLaughlin's Mahavishnu
Orchestra.

Gil Evans
b. 13 May 1912, Toronto
d. 20 March 1988, Cuernavaca,
Mexico
Composer, arranger.
His collaborations with Miles
Davis established the "cool" style

and later broke new ground in
the blending of pre-composed
orchestral music with jazz
improvisation.

Herschel Evans
b. 1909, Denton, Texas
d. 9 February 1939, New York
Tenor saxophone.
Member of Count Basie's band
(1936–39).

Leonard Feather
b. 13 September 1914, London
d. 22 September 1994, Sherman
Oaks, California
Piano, writer.
British critic and historian who
worked (as both composer and
producer) with numerous major
talents in the US.

Ella Fitzgerald
b. 25 April 1918, Newport News,
Virginia
d. 14 June 1996
Vocals.
Rising to prominence with the
Chick Webb Band in the late
1930s, she became renowned as
a superb scat singer and versatile
interpreter of a phenomenally
extensive repertoire of standards.
She was married to Ray Brown
(1948–52).

Frank Foster
b. 23 September 1938,
Cincinatti
Tenor saxophone.
Member of Count Basie's band in
the 1950s, and its leader from
1986.

Bill Frisell
b. 18 March 1951, Baltimore
Acoustic and electric guitar.
House guitarist for ECM in the
1980s, working with Jan
Garbarek, Eberhard Weber and
Charlie Haden.

Steve Gadd
b. 1945, Rochester, New York
Drums.
Leading jazz-rock drummer who,
since working with Chick Corea
in the 1970s, has been much in
demand as a session player.

Vyacheslav Ganelin
b. 17 December 1944, Kraskov,
Soviet Union
Piano.
Founder of the Ganelin Trio in
1971, and largely responsible for
bringing Soviet free jazz to an
international audience.

Jan Garbarek
b. 4 March 1947, Mysen,
Norway
Tenor and soprano saxophones.
One of the most distinctive
players in European jazz, he has
absorbed folk and rock influences
and boosted sales of the ECM
label.

Erroll Garner
b. 15 June 1921, Pittsburgh
d. 2 January 1977, Los Angeles
Piano.
Composer of "Misty," he became
a popular trio pianist after
deputizing for Art Tatum in the
mid-1940s.

Jimmy Garrison
b. 3 March 1934, Miami
d. 7 April 1976, New York
Double bass.
Sideman to John Coltrane in the
1960s.

George Gershwin
b. 26 September 1898,
New York
d. 11 July 1937, Hollywood
Composer, piano.
He laid the foundations for the
symphonic jazz of the 1920s with
Rhapsody in Blue, and in 1935
produced the "American folk
opera" *Porgy and Bess*. Songs
from the latter and from his
numerous Broadway musicals are
a staple part of the standards
repertoire.

Stan Getz
b. 2 February 1927, Philadelphia
d. 6 June 1991, Malibu,
California
Tenor saxophone.
Versatile performer who
spearheaded the bossa nova craze
in the 1960s, and straddled West
and East Coast styles.

Astrud Gilberto
b. 1940, Bahia, Brazil
Vocals.
Catapulted to stardom with "The
Girl from Ipanema" in 1963, she
collaborated with Stan Getz in
popularizing bossa nova. Was
married to João Gilberto.

João Gilberto
b. June 1931, Juaseiro, Brazil
Vocals, guitar.
Pioneer of the bossa nova style
in Brazil in the late 1950s
alongside Antonio Carlos
Jobim, he was married to
Astrud Gilberto.

John Birks "Dizzy" Gillespie
b. 21 October 1917, Cheraw,
South Carolina
d. 6 January 1993, Englewood,
New Jersey
Trumpet, composer.
Leading trumpeter of the
emerging bop style in the early
1940s, famed for his on-stage
antics, penetrating sound, and
unique instrument
(with its bell bent sharply
upwards). His later career took
him on worldwide concert tours
for the US Department of State.

Jean Goldkette
b. 18 March 1899, Valenciennes,
France
d. 24 March 1962, Santa Barbara
Piano, bandleader.
Popular dance-band director
of the 1920s and 1930s who
engaged Bix Beiderbecke
as soloist.

Paul Gonsalves
b. 12 July 1920, Boston
d. 14 May 1974, London
Tenor saxophone.
Sideman to Duke Ellington
(1950–74), best remembered
for his powerful solo during
Ellington's orchestra's appearance
at the Newport Festival in 1956.

Benny Goodman
b. 30 May 1909, Chicago
d. 13 June 1986, New York
Clarinet, bandleader.
The first jazz musician to be

equally at home in the world of
classical music, he became a
household name in 1935 and was
dubbed "The King of Swing."
In collaboration with Fletcher
Henderson, his work defined the
big-band sound of the swing era,
and his band became the first jazz
outfit to appear at Carnegie Hall
(1938).

Dexter Gordon
b. 27 February 1923,
Los Angeles
d. 25 April 1990, Philadelphia
Tenor saxophone.
Bop performer who moved to
Europe in 1962; best known
for his starring role in
the film *Round Midnight*
(1986).

Norman Granz
b. 6 August 1918, Los Angeles
Record producer.
Founder of the Jazz at the
Philharmonic tours, and the
Clef, Verve and Pablo record
labels.

Stephane Grappelli
b. 26 January 1908, Paris
Violin.
With Django Reinhardt, he
formed the backbone of the
Quintette du Hot Club de France
in the 1930s.

Sonny Greer
b. 13 December 1895, Long
Branch, New Jersey
d. 23 March 1982, New York
Drums.
Stalwart sideman of Duke
Ellington (1920–51) who added
many exotic percussion
instruments to the standard
drum-kit.

Dave Grusin
b. 26 June 1934, Denver,
Colorado
*Keyboards, composer, record
producer.*
With Larry Rosen, he directs the
GRP record label, and is active as
a versatile performer and
composer of numerous Hollywood
film scores.

Charlie Haden
b. 6 August 1937, Shenandoah,
Iowa
Double bass.
Sideman to Ornette Coleman
(1958–60) and founder in 1969
of the Liberation Music Orchestra,
which he re-formed in 1982.

Adelaide Hall
b. 20 October 1901, New York
d. 7 November 1992, London
Vocals.
She provided the haunting,
wordless vocal line in Duke
Ellington's "Creole Love Call"
(1927).

Scott Hamilton
b. 12 September 1954, Rhode
Island
Tenor saxophone.
Mainstream artist promoted by
the Concord label. He has served
as sideman for Benny Goodman
and Woody Herman.

John Hammond
b. 15 December 1910,
New York
d. 10 July 1987, New York
Record producer.
In the 1930s he promoted the
work of Benny Goodman, Count
Basie, Fletcher Henderson and
Billie Holiday, and mounted the
famous Carnegie Hall jazz
concerts of 1938 and 1939.

Lionel Hampton
b. 20 April 1908, Louisville,
Kentucky
Vibraphone, drums, bandleader.
Member of the Benny Goodman
Quartet in the 1930s, and later
responsible for heading the
longest surviving big band in
the history of jazz (1940–present
day).

Herbie Hancock
b. 12 April 1940, Chicago
Keyboards, composer.
Sideman of Miles Davis (1963–68)
and house pianist to Blue Note
records in the 1960s, he scored
major successes in the pop charts
with the electronic *Headhunters*
(1973) and "Rockit" (1983).

William Christopher Handy
b. 16 November 1873, Florence, Alabama
d. 28 March 1958, New York
Cornet, bandleader, composer.
Widely known as "The Father of the Blues," he published the first printed blues arrangement in 1912.

Roy Hargrove
b. 16 October 1969, Dallas
Trumpet, composer.
Since his début album in 1990, he has earned a reputation as a fine exponent of a modern brand of bop.

John Harle
b. 20 September 1956, Newcastle, UK
Soprano and alto saxophone, composer.
British artist equally at home in jazz and modern classical styles.

Ben Harney
b. 6 March 1871, Middletown, Kentucky
d. 11 March 1938, Philadelphia
Ragtime song composer.
His "You've Been a Good Old Wagon" (1895) was the first published ragtime song.

Coleman "Bean" Hawkins
b. 21 November 1904, St Joseph, Missouri
d. 16 May 1969, New York
Tenor saxophone.
After a decade in Fletcher Henderson's band (1924–34), his reputation as a soloist capable of lyrical improvisations was cemented with "Body and Soul" in 1939.

Roy Haynes
b. 13 March 1925, Roxbury, Massachusetts
Drums.
Bop drummer whose collaborators have included Charlie Parker, Sarah Vaughan, Miles Davis, Thelonious Monk, Lee Konitz, Stan Getz, John Coltrane, Chick Corea and Pat Metheny.

Percy Heath
b. 30 April 1923, Wilmington, North Carolina
Double bass.
Founder member of John Lewis's Modern Jazz Quartet.

Neal Hefti
b. 29 October 1922, Hastings, Nebraska
Composer, arranger.
Arranger for the Count Basie band in the 1950s, he composed the music for the movie *The Odd Couple* in 1968.

Julius Hemphill
b. 1940, Fort Worth
d. 2 April 1995
Alto saxophone.
Founder member of the World Saxophone Quartet, with whom he played from 1977 until 1990.

Fletcher Henderson
b. 18 December 1897, Cuthbert, Georgia
d. 28 December 1952, New York
Piano, arranger, bandleader.
Originator of the swing-band style of the late 1920s and 1930s. His arrangements were bought in 1934 by Benny Goodman's band, for which he served as staff arranger in 1939–41.

Joe Henderson
b. 24 April 1937, Lima, Ohio
Tenor saxophone, composer.
Sideman to Blue Note artists Horace Silver and Freddie Hubbard in the 1960s, he continues to top popularity polls in the US.

Woody Herman
b. 16 May 1913, Milwaukee, Wisconsin
d. 29 October 1987, Los Angeles
Clarinet, bandleader.
His various bands, called "Herman's Herds," created a polished swing music and inspired Igor Stravinsky to compose his *Ebony Concerto* in 1945.

Earl "Fatha" Hines
b. 28 December 1903, Duquesne, Pennsylvania
d. 22 April 1983, Oakland, California
Piano, bandleader.
The first keyboard player to break away from the stride idiom, Hines developed the more melodic and versatile "trumpet style" after working with Louis Armstrong in the 1920s. His big band later became a popular fixture at Chicago's Grand Terrace (1928–40).

Johnny "Rabbit" Hodges
b. 25 July 1907, Cambridge, Massachusetts
d. 11 May 1970, New York
Alto saxophone.
Endowed with a distinctively suave saxophone tone, his sensual playing is heard to best advantage in his work with Duke Ellington's orchestra (1928–51 and 1955–70).

Eleanor "Billie" Holiday
b. 7 April 1915, Baltimore
d. 17 July 1959, New York
Vocals.
Closely associated with Teddy Wilson and Lester Young, she made her name in the 1930s and is widely regarded as the finest jazz singer of all time: a self-taught artist who instinctively reshaped banal popular songs into memorable and highly expressive melodies.

Dave Holland
b. 1 October 1946, Wolverhampton, UK
Acoustic and electric bass.
Sideman to Miles Davis (1968–70) and member of Chick Corea's group Circle (1970–72); more recently he has worked with Kenny Wheeler and Pat Metheny.

Freddie Hubbard
b. 7 April 1938, Indianapolis
Trumpet, flugelhorn, composer.
After working with Ornette Coleman on *Free Jazz* (1960), he was a member of Art Blakey's Jazz Messengers until 1964 and

remained active on the Blue Note label with various groups.

Dick Hyman
b. 8 March 1927, New York
Piano.
A versatile artist embracing many styles in his early career, he has been well known since the 1970s as an advocate of the traditional jazz of New Orleans and the Harlem stride pianists.

Abdullah Ibrahim (Dollar Brand)
b. 9 October 1934, Cape Town
Piano, composer.
Unable to promote jazz freely in his native South Africa, he moved to Switzerland in 1962 where he was discovered by Duke Ellington.

Milt Jackson
b. 1 January 1923, Detroit
Vibraphone.
Leading bop vibraphonist and co-founder (with John Lewis) of the Modern Jazz Quartet in 1952.

Tony Jackson
b. 5 June 1876, New Orleans
d. (syphilis) 20 April 1921, Chicago
Ragtime pianist, composer.
Mentor of Jelly Roll Morton.

Illinois Jacquet
b. 31 October 1922, Broussard, Louisiana
Tenor saxophone.
Sideman of Lionel Hampton, Cab Calloway and Count Basie in the 1940s, he later toured with Jazz at the Philharmonic.

Ahmad Jamal
b. 2 July 1930, Pittsburgh
Piano.
His piano-trio work influenced Miles Davis during the 1950s.

Bob James
b. 25 December 1939, Marshall, Michigan
Keyboards, composer.
Fusion artist and composer of the signature tune to the US television comedy series *Taxi.*

Harry James
b. 15 March 1916, Albany,
Georgia
d. 5 July 1983, Las Vegas
Trumpet, bandleader.
Principal trumpeter with Benny
Goodman's band (1937–39), and
later a popular big-band leader
in his own right.

Keith Jarrett
b. 8 May 1945, Allentown,
Pennsylvania
Piano, composer.
Sideman to Miles Davis
(1970–71), he soon abandoned
electronic keyboards and became
famous for his large-scale solo
improvisations at European
venues. He has recorded a
sizeable quantity of classical
music, and regularly interprets
standards with his trio partners
Gary Peacock and Jack
DeJohnette.

Antonio Carlos "Tom" Jobim
b. 25 January 1927, Rio de
Janeiro
d. 8 December 1994, New York
Guitar, piano, composer.
Co-founder (with João Gilberto)
of the bossa nova style in the late
1950s, he appeared at Carnegie
Hall with Dizzy Gillespie in 1962.

Bunk Johnson
b. 27 December 1889,
New Orleans
d. 7 July 1949, New Iberia,
Louisiana
Trumpet.
Sideman to the legendary Buddy
Bolden, he came to prominence
in the revival of New Orleans jazz
in the 1940s.

J. J. Johnson
b. 22 January 1924, Indianapolis
Trombone.
Leading bop trombonist and
sometime sideman to Miles Davis
and Sonny Stitt. He founded a
quintet with fellow trombonist
Kai Winding in the 1950s.

James P. Johnson
b. 1 February 1894, New
Brunswick

d. 17 November 1955, New York
Piano, composer.
Pre-eminent stride artist and
teacher of Fats Waller. He
composed the hit song
"Charleston" in 1923.

Pete Johnson
b. 24 March 1904, Kansas City
d. 23 March 1967, Buffalo
Piano.
Boogie-woogie performer,
sometime duet partner of Albert
Ammons.

Elvin Jones
b. 9 September 1927, Pontiac,
Michigan
Drums.
Brother of bandleader Thad
Jones. He worked with John
Coltrane during the 1960s,
playing in a bop style heavily
influenced by Max Roach and
Kenny Clarke.

Philly Joe Jones
b. 15 July 1923, Philadelphia
d. 30 August 1985, Philadelphia
Drums.
Sideman to Miles Davis
throughout the 1950s.

Quincy Jones
b. 14 March 1933, Chicago
Composer, arranger.
After early work with Lionel
Hampton (1951–53), he arranged
for Count Basie and then became
active as a record producer. He
founded his own label, Qwest, in
1980 and has worked with high-
profile popular artists such as
Frank Sinatra, Michael Jackson
and Aretha Franklin.

Thad Jones
b. 28 March 1923, Pontiac,
Michigan
d. 21 August 1986, Copenhagen
Trumpet, flugelhorn, bandleader.
Brother of Elvin Jones. With Mel
Lewis, he co-led a virtuoso big
band at New York's Village
Vanguard (1965–78) before
emigrating to Copenhagen. He
returned to the US briefly in the
mid-1980s to lead Count Basie's
band.

Scott Joplin
b. 24 November 1868, Texarkana,
Texas
d. 1 April 1917, New York
Ragtime composer and pianist.
The most successful ragtime
composer, who attempted to
transform the popular genre into
an art form. His achievements
only came to be fully recognized
during a 1970s revival of his
work.

Julian Joseph
b. 11 May 1966, London
Piano, composer.
After work with Branford
Marsalis in 1986, he made his
début album as leader in 1991.

Wynton Kelly
b. 2 December 1931, Jamaica
d. 12 April 1971, Toronto
Piano.
Sideman to Miles Davis
(1959–63), he left to set up his
own trio with Paul Chambers
and Billy Cobb.

Stan Kenton
b. 19 February 1912, Wichita,
Kansas
d. 25 August 1979,
Los Angeles
Composer, piano, bandleader.
Originator of a style of West
Coast "progressive jazz" in the
late 1940s, borrowing elements
from Latin American music and
modern classical techniques.

Freddie Keppard
b. 27 February 1890,
New Orleans
d. (tuberculosis) 15 July 1933,
Chicago
Cornet.
A first-generation jazz musician
whose playing represented the
transition from Buddy Bolden to
the style of Louis Armstrong.

Barney Kessel
b. 17 October 1923, Muskogee,
Oklahoma
Guitar.
Session performer who worked
with Oscar Peterson's original
piano trio in the early 1950s.

Rahsaan Roland Kirk
b. 7 August 1936, Columbus,
Ohio
d. (stroke) 5 December 1977,
Bloomington, Indiana
Saxophones, flute, whistles.
Eccentric talent who developed a
manner of playing three wind
instruments simultaneously, but
transcended this ostensible
gimmickry to produce music
reflecting the values of
conventional jazz.

Lee Konitz
b. 13 October 1927, Chicago
Saxophones.
Leading performer of the West
Coast "cool" school, closely
associated with the work of Stan
Kenton and Lennie Tristano in
the 1950s.

Gene Krupa
b. 15 January 1909, Chicago
d. 16 October 1973, Yonkers,
New York
Drums, bandleader.
Charismatic sideman to Benny
Goodman (1934–38), later a
leader in his own right.

Steve Lacy
b. 23 July 1934, New York
Soprano saxophone, composer.
Eclectic artist who worked with
Cecil Taylor, Gil Evans and
Thelonious Monk between 1955
and 1964, taking free jazz to Italy
and France in the late 1960s.

Scott LaFaro
b. 3 April 1936, Newark,
New Jersey
d. (automobile accident) 6 July
1961, Geneva, New York
Double bass.
Enormously influential player
whose tragically short career
peaked in the Bill Evans Trio
(1959–61).

Cleo Laine
b. 27 October 1927, Southall,
UK
Vocals.
Married to John Dankworth since
1958, she has embraced all styles
from classical to pop.

Joseph Lamb
b. 6 December 1877, Montclair, New Jersey
d. 3 September 1960, New York
Ragtime composer.
With Scott Joplin and James Scott, he was one of the team of leading ragtime composers published by John Stark.

Brian Lemon
b. 11 February 1937, Nottingham, UK
Piano.
Having made his name during the 1960s and 1970s by accompanying visiting US stars such as Ben Webster, Milt Jackson and Benny Goodman, he went on to lead his own trio.

John Lewis
b. 3 May 1920, La Grange, Illinois
Piano, composer.
Active as a bop pianist in the 1940s, he participated in Miles Davis's *Birth of the Cool* sessions in 1949. With the establishment of the Modern Jazz Quartet in the early 1950s, he gained a global reputation as a composer of refined musical structures reflecting strong classical influences.

Meade "Lux" Lewis
b. 4 September 1905, Chicago
d. (automobile accident) 7 June 1964, Minneapolis
Piano.
Popular boogie-woogie artist who composed "Honky Tonk Train Blues."

Mel Lewis
b. 10 May 1929, Buffalo, New York
d. 2 February 1990, New York
Drums, bandleader.
Co-leader, with Thad Jones, of the successful big band based at New York's Village Vanguard from 1965 until 1978, when he assumed sole leadership.

Charles Lloyd
b. 15 March 1938, Memphis
Saxophones, flute.

After working with Cannonball Adderley and Keith Jarrett in the 1960s, he became one of the more popular free-jazz artists.

Joe Lovano
b. 29 December 1952, Cleveland
Saxophones.
Sideman to Woody Herman in the late 1970s, and a prominent leader on the Blue Note label in the 1990s.

Jimmie Lunceford
b. 6 June 1902, Fulton, Mississippi
d. (collapsed on stage) 12 July 1947, Seaside, Oregon
Bandleader.
His band made its reputation at New York's Cotton Club in the mid-1930s.

Humphrey Lyttleton
b. 23 May 1921, Eton, UK
Trumpet, writer.
A popular broadcaster on British radio, he took part in the Dixieland revival of the late 1940s and became a champion of traditional jazz.

Howard McGhee
b. 6 February 1918, Tulsa, Oklahoma
d. 17 July 1987, New York
Trumpet.
After participating in early bop performances, he joined Jazz at the Philharmonic in 1947 and was voted Best Trumpeter by *Down Beat* in 1949.

John McLaughlin
b. 4 January 1942, Kirk Sandall, UK
Acoustic and electric guitar, composer.
Sideman to Miles Davis in 1969, then leader of his own fusion group, The Mahavishnu Orchestra (1970–75, re-formed in 1984). In this outfit and his smaller group Shakti (1975–77), he showed himself to be strongly influenced by Indian music.

Teo Macero
b. 30 October 1925, Glens Falls,

New York
Composer, record producer.
He masterminded most of Miles Davis's recordings from 1957 onwards, but is also respected as a saxophonist and composer in his own right.

"Machito" (Raúl Grillo)
b. 16 February 1912, Tampa, Florida
d. 15 April 1984
Bandleader.
Brother-in-law of Mario Bauzá, he participated in the Latin jazz boom of the 1940s.

Albert Mangelsdorff
b. 5 September 1928, Frankfurt
Trombone, composer.
Eclectic performer who developed the radical technique of playing chords (multiphonics) on his instrument.

Shelly Manne
b. 11 June 1920, New York
d. 26 September 1984, Los Angeles
Drums.
Sideman to Stan Kenton and Woody Herman in the late 1940s, he founded Shelly's Manne Hole in Los Angeles in 1951.

Fate Marable
b. 2 December 1890, Paducah, Kentucky
d. (pneumonia) 16 January 1947, St. Louis
Piano, bandleader.
Director of a jazz band on the Streckfus Line steamboats plying the Mississippi River.

Branford Marsalis
b. 26 August 1960, Breaux Bridge, Louisiana
Soprano and tenor saxophone.
Son of Ellis Marsalis. Sideman to Art Blakey, Miles Davis, Herbie Hancock and his brother Wynton Marsalis in the 1980s.

Ellis Marsalis
b. 14 November 1934, New Orleans
Piano, composer.

Father of Branford and Wynton Marsalis.

Wynton Marsalis
b. 18 October 1961, New Orleans
Trumpet.
Brother of Branford Marsalis and son of Ellis Marsalis. Wynton worked with Art Blakey and Herbie Hancock before becoming a prominent champion of traditional jazz values through a series of high-profile Columbia recordings in the 1980s. He is also a virtuoso on classical trumpet, and a noted music educator.

Warne Marsh
b. 26 October 1927, Los Angeles
d. 18 December 1987, North Hollywood
Tenor saxophone.
Sideman to Lee Konitz and Lennie Tristano in the 1950s.

Lyle Mays
b. 27 November 1953, Wausaukee, Wisconsin
Keyboards, composer.
Fusion artist closely associated with Pat Metheny since 1976.

Pat Metheny
b. 12 August 1954, Lee's Summit, Missouri
Electric guitar, guitar synthesizer, composer.
Leader of the popular fusion band Pat Metheny Group since 1977, this versatile artist works in styles ranging from country and rock to avant-garde free jazz.

Palle Mikkelborg
b. 6 March 1941, Copenhagen
Trumpet, composer.
Danish player who came to international prominence when he composed *O* for Miles Davis in 1984.

Bubber Miley
b. 3 April 1903, Aiken, South Carolina
d. (tuberculosis) 20 May 1932, New York
Trumpet.
Sideman to Duke Ellington

(1923–29) who developed the "growl" style of trumpet playing.

Darius Milhaud
b. 4 September 1892, Aix-en-Provence
d. 22 June 1974, Geneva
Composer.
French composer whose ballet *Le Boeuf sur le toit* (1923) contained jazz elements. He taught extensively in the US, where he numbered Dave Brubeck amongst his composition pupils.

Glenn Miller
b. 1 March 1904, Clarinda, Iowa
d. (aircraft crash) 15 December 1944, English Channel
Trombone, bandleader.
Composer of "In the Mood" and "Moonlight Serenade." His hugely popular band reached its peak in 1939–42, before he formed a new band for the US Army Air Force and entertained Allied troops in Europe.

Charles Mingus
b. 22 April 1922, Nogales, Arizona
d. 5 January 1979, Cuernavaca, Mexico
Double bass, composer.
Experimental composer who blended elements from bop and free jazz. His sophisticated bass playing was heard to best advantage in duets with Eric Dolphy in the early 1960s.

Thelonious Sphere Monk
b. 11 October 1917, Rocky Mount, North Carolina
d. 17 February 1982, Weehawken, New Jersey
Piano, composer.
Central figure of the early bop movement whose eccentric keyboard style remains inimitable. His compositions became a core part of the standards repertory, and are characterized by harmonic and rhythmic unpredictability.

Wes Montgomery
b. 6 March 1925, Indianapolis

d. (heart attack) 15 June 1968, Indianapolis
Guitar.
His sophisticated melodic improvisations were enormously influential on post-war guitarists.

Lee Morgan
b. 10 July 1938, Philadelphia
d. (shot by mistress) 19 February 1972, New York
Trumpet, composer.
Hard-bop performer who played with Art Blakey's Jazz Messengers (1958–61), then became a leader on the Blue Note label, where his successes included *The Sidewinder* (1964).

Ferdinand "Jelly Roll" Morton
b. 20 October 1890, New Orleans
d. 10 July 1941, Los Angeles
Piano, vocals, composer.
The first jazz composer and intellectual, his group The Red Hot Peppers recorded polished music in the New Orleans style in 1926–27. In 1938 he emerged from obscurity to make a series of retrospective recordings for the Library of Congress.

Bennie Moten
b. 13 November 1894, Kansas City
d. 2 April 1935, Kansas City
Piano, bandleader.
Pioneer of Kansas City big-band jazz and mentor of the young Count Basie.

Paul Motian
b. 25 March 1931, Rhode Island
Drums.
Sideman to Bill Evans (1959–64) and Keith Jarrett (1966–77).

Gerry Mulligan
b. 6 April 1927, New York
d. 20 January 1996
Baritone saxophone, composer.
After participating in Miles Davis's *Birth of the Cool* sessions (1949), he became a leading figure in the West Coast "cool" school when he formed a quartet with Chet Baker in 1952.

David Murray
b. 19 February 1955, Berkeley, California
Saxophone, composer.
Founder member of World Saxophone Quartet in 1977.

Ray Nance
b. 10 December 1913, Chicago
d. 28 January 1976, New York
Trumpet, violin.
Sideman to Duke Ellington (1940–63).

Joe "Tricky Sam" Nanton
b. 1 February 1904, New York
d. 20 July 1946, San Francisco
Trombone.
Sideman to Duke Ellington (1926–46) who adapted the "growl" style of trumpet playing for use on the trombone.

Fats Navarro
b. 24 September 1923, Key West, Florida
d. (tuberculosis) 7 July 1950, New York
Trumpet.
Sideman to leading bop musicians whose early death prevented him from reaching his full potential.

Jimmie Noone
b. 23 April 1895, New Orleans
d. (heart attack) 19 April 1944, Los Angeles
Clarinet, alto saxophone.
He took the New Orleans style to Chicago in the 1920s and influenced the playing of Barney Bigard and Benny Goodman.

Kenneth "Red" Norvo
b. 31 March 1908, Beardstown, Illinois
Vibraphone, xylophone.
Featured soloist with Woody Herman, Charles Mingus, and Benny Goodman. Married to Mildred Bailey (1933–43).

Joe "King" Oliver
b. 11 May 1885, Louisiana
d. 10 April 1938, Savannah, Georgia
Cornet, bandleader.

Leader of King Oliver's Creole Jazz Band, his work in Chicago in the early 1920s laid the foundations for later jazz and provided an apprenticeship for the young Louis Armstrong.

Niels-Henning Ørsted Pederson
b. 27 May 1946, Ørsted, Denmark
Double bass.
Virtuoso sideman to Oscar Peterson in the 1970s and 1980s.

Edward "Kid" Ory
b. 25 December 1886, La Place, Louisiana
d. 23 January 1973, Hawaii
Trombone, vocals.
Exponent of the "tailgate" style of New Orleans trombone playing.

Tony Oxley
b. 15 June 1938, Sheffield, UK
Drums.
Leading British drummer, well known since his appearance on John McLaughlin's album *Extrapolation* in 1969.

Walter Page
b. 9 February 1900, Gallatin, Missouri
d. 20 December 1957, New York
Double bass.
Bassist in Bennie Moten's and Count Basie's Kansas City bands.

Charlie "Yardbird" Parker
b. 29 August 1920, Kansas City
d. 12 March 1955, New York
Alto saxophone.
The most revered and enigmatic character of the bop movement, a phenomenal improviser who influenced all subsequent reed players. He became as famous for his drug habit and its harrowing consequences as for his innovative playing.

Joe Pass
b. 13 January 1929, New Brunswick
d. 23 May 1994
Guitar.
His technical fluency made him an ideal partner for Oscar

Peterson and other mainstream artists managed by Norman Granz in the 1970s.

Jaco Pastorius
b. 1 December 1951, Norristown, Pennsylvania
d. (killed in brawl) 22 September 1987, Fort Lauderdale, Florida
Electric bass.
Member of Weather Report in the mid-1970s and early sideman to Pat Metheny, he led his own groups in the 1980s.

Gary Peacock
b. 12 May 1935, Barley, Idaho
Double bass.
Sideman to Bill Evans (1962–63), Albert Ayler and Paul Bley, and a member of Keith Jarrett's standards trio.

Art Pepper
b. 1 September 1925, Gardena, California
d. 1 June 1982, Panorama, California
Saxophones.
Member of Stan Kenton's band (1946–51), who subsequently developed a bop-oriented brand of West Coast jazz.

Oscar Peterson
b. 15 August 1925, Montreal
Piano.
A performer of staggering technical ability with a prodigious recorded output, he made his name in trio work during the 1950s and has been closely associated with Norman Granz since 1949.

Oscar Pettiford
b. 30 September 1922, Okmulgee, Oklahoma
d. 8 September 1960, Copenhagen
Double bass.
Sideman to Roy Eldridge and Dizzy Gillespie in the early 1940s, he moved to Europe in 1958.

Courtney Pine
b. 18 March 1964, London
Tenor and soprano saxophones.

Leading figure in the British jazz resurgence of the 1980s.

Jean-Luc Ponty
b. 29 September 1942, Avranches, Normandy
Violin and electric violin.
After working in John McLaughlin's Mahavishnu Orchestra (1974), he has played in all styles from swing to fusion and free jazz.

Bud Powell
b. 27 September 1924, New York
d. 31 July 1966, New York
Piano.
Leading bop pianist and protégé of Thelonious Monk, he spent the period 1959–64 in Paris with Kenny Clarke.

Chano Pozo
b. 7 January 1915, Havana
d. (murdered) 2 December 1948, New York
Vocals, percussion.
Latin drummer who collaborated with Dizzy Gillespie in 1947–48.

André Previn
b. 6 April 1929, Berlin
Pianist, composer, conductor.
West Coast pianist and Hollywood film composer who gained international fame as conductor of the London Symphony Orchestra in the 1970s.

Brian Priestley
b. 10 July 1940, Manchester, UK
Piano, writer.
He transcribed Ellington's music in the 1970s and is popular in the UK as a broadcaster and author.

Flora Purim
b. 6 March 1942, Rio de Janeiro
Vocals, guitar, percussion.
Brazilian singer who worked with Chick Corea's Return to Forever in the early 1970s.

Ike Quebec
b. 17 August 1918, Newark, New Jersey

d. 16 January 1963, New York
Tenor saxophone.
Bop performer who worked as artists and repertory agent for Blue Note records, of which he became assistant musical director in 1959.

Gertrude "Ma" Rainey
b. 26 April 1886, Columbus, Georgia
d. 22 December 1939, Rome, Georgia
Vocals.
Popular blues singer of the 1920s.

Dewey Redman
b. 17 May 1931, Fort Worth
Saxophones.
Sideman to Ornette Coleman (1967–74) and Charlie Haden (1969 and 1982).

Don Redman
b. 29 July 1900, Piedmont, West Virginia
d. 30 November 1964, New York
Saxophones, arranger.
His collaboration with Fletcher Henderson in the 1920s laid the foundations for the big-band style of the swing era.

Django Reinhardt
b. 23 January 1910, Charleroi, Belgium
d. 16 May 1953, Fontainebleau, France
Guitar.
Flamboyant gypsy performer who starred alongside Stephane Grappelli in the Quintette du Hot Club de France during the 1930s.

Emily Remler
b. 18 September 1957, New York
d. (heart attack) 4 May 1990, Sydney, Australia
Guitar.
Influenced by Wes Montgomery, she worked with Astrud Gilberto (1978–81) and was married to Monty Alexander.

Buddy Rich
b. 30 June 1917, New York
d. 2 April 1987, Los Angeles
Drums, bandleader.

Sideman to Tommy Dorsey (1939–42, 1944–45 and 1954–55), he moved smoothly from the swing to bop styles.

Lee Ritenour
b. 1 November 1952, Los Angeles
Guitar.
Fusion artist closely associated with Dave Grusin and the GRP label.

Sam Rivers
b. 25 September 1930, El Reno, Oklahoma
Saxophones, composer.
Sideman to Miles Davis (1964) and Cecil Taylor (1968–73).

Max Roach
b. 10 January 1924, New Land, North Carolina
Drums.
Alongside Kenny Clarke, the most influential of early bop drummers. His work in the 1960s was associated with the black civil rights movement in the US.

Luckey Roberts
b. 7 August 1887, Philadelphia
d. 5 February 1968, New York
Piano.
Stride performer based in Harlem in the 1940s.

Marcus Roberts
b. 7 August 1963, Jacksonville, Florida
Piano.
Sideman to Wynton Marsalis (1985–91).

Robert "Red" Rodney
b. 27 September 1927, Philadelphia
d. 27 May 1994
Trumpet.
Sideman to Charlie Parker (1949–51).

Sonny Rollins
b. 7 September 1930, New York
Tenor and soprano saxophones.
Early bop work in the 1950s led to a brief collaboration with

Miles Davis before he made his name as a leader. His playing formed a link between the styles of Charlie Parker and John Coltrane.

George Russell
b. 23 June 1923, Cincinnati
Composer.
Theorist who formulated the procedures of modal jazz in the 1950s.

Johnny St. Cyr
b. 17 April 1890, New Orleans
d. 17 June 1966, Los Angeles
Banjo, guitar.
Member of King Oliver's and Louis Armstrong's Chicago bands in the 1920s.

David Sanborn
b. 30 July 1945, Tampa, Florida
Alto saxophone.
Fusion artist with a distinctively intense tone, whose album *Voyeur* won a Grammy in 1981.

Pharoah Sanders
b. 13 October 1940, Little Rock, Arkansas
Tenor and soprano saxophone, composer.
A disciple of John Coltrane, with whom he played in the mid-1960s, he has remained notorious for his strident tone colors.

Maria Schneider
b. 27 November 1960, Windom, Minnesota
Piano, arranger.
Her work was featured prominently at several US jazz festivals in the mid-1990s.

Gunther Schuller
b. 11 November 1925, Jackson Heights, New York
Composer, conductor, writer, French horn.
His horn playing (which included work alongside Miles Davis in 1949) has been overshadowed by his conducting and writing careers. He is the author of the most thorough musical analyses of mainstream jazz yet to have appeared in print.

John Scofield
b. 26 December 1951, Dayton, Ohio
Guitar, composer.
Sideman to Miles Davis (1982–85), his playing continues to top US popularity polls in the 1990s.

James Scott
b. 12 February 1885, Neosho, Missouri
d. 30 August 1938, Kansas City
Ragtime composer.
With Scott Joplin and Joseph Lamb, he was one of the team of leading ragtime composers published by John Stark.

Ronnie Scott
b. 28 January 1927, London
d. 23 December 1996, London
Tenor saxophone, club owner.
A participant in the British bop movement of the 1950s, his clubs in London and Birmingham remain the foremost UK venues for live jazz.

Artie Shaw
b. 23 May 1910, New York
Clarinet, bandleader.
His band recorded its hit "Begin the Beguine" in 1938.

Woody Shaw
b. 24 December 1944, Laurinburg, North Carolina
d. (train accident) 10 May 1989, New York
Trumpet, flugelhorn.
A member of Art Blakey's Jazz Messengers in the early 1970s, he also collaborated with Eric Dolphy, Horace Silver and Chick Corea.

George Shearing
b. 13 August 1919, London
Piano.
Blind performer of "cool" jazz featuring a "locked-hands" style of block-chord playing.

Archie Shepp
b. 24 May 1937, Fort Lauderdale
Saxophones, composer.
Free-jazz performer influenced by

John Coltrane in the early 1960s.

Andy Sheppard
b. 20 January 1957, Warminster, UK
Tenor and soprano saxophones, composer.
Sideman to Gil Evans and George Russell in the late 1980s, he has worked in the 1990s with Carla Bley and his own big band and trio.

Wayne Shorter
b. 25 August 1933, Newark, New Jersey
Tenor and soprano saxophones, composer.
Sideman to Miles Davis (1964–70) and member of Weather Report (1970–85).

Horace Silver
b. 2 September 1928, Norwalk, Connecticut
Piano, composer.
Leading hard-bop pianist long associated with the Blue Note label (1952–80).

Bessie Smith
b. 15 April 1895, Chattanooga, Tennessee
d. (automobile accident) 26 September 1937, Clarksdale, Mississippi
Vocals.
Her magnificently earthy singing earned her the sobriquet "Empress of the Blues" in the 1920s.

Clarence "Pine Top" Smith
b. 11 June 1904, Troy, Alabama
d. (shot in brawl) 15 March 1929, Chicago
Piano.
Boogie-woogie performer popular in Chicago in the late 1920s.

Mamie Smith
b. 26 May 1883, Cincinnati
d. 30 October 1946, New York
Vocals.
Her 1920 blues recordings were the first to be cut by a black jazz singer.

Willie "The Lion" Smith
b. 25 November 1897, Goshen, New York
d. 18 April 1973, New York
Piano, composer.
Stride artist and early mentor of Duke Ellington.

Elmer Snowden
b. 9 October 1900, Baltimore
d. 14 May 1973, Philadelphia
Bandleader.
His band, The Washingtonians, became Duke Ellington's first orchestra when Snowden was deposed as leader in 1924.

Rex Stewart
b. 22 February 1907, Philadelphia
d. 7 September 1967, Los Angeles
Trumpet.
Sideman to Duke Ellington (1934–45).

Sonny Stitt
b. 2 February 1924, Boston
d. 22 July 1982, Washington
Saxophones.
His fluent and expressive bop style was an impressive development of Charlie Parker's improvisatory techniques.

Igor Stravinsky
b. 17 June 1882, Lomonosov, Russia
d. 6 April 1971, New York
Composer.
He created modernistic distortions of the ragtime style in 1918–19 and composed *Ebony Concerto* for Woody Herman's Herd in 1945.

Billy "Sweetpea" Strayhorn
b. 29 November 1915, Dayton, Ohio
d. 31 May 1967, New York
Piano, composer, arranger.
Composer of "Take the 'A' Train" and "Satin Doll," he created many of Duke Ellington's finest scores in the period 1939–67.

Sun Ra
b. 22 May 1914, Birmingham, Alabama

d. 30 May 1993, Birmingham, Alabama
Keyboards, composer, bandleader.
Colorful fusion artist whose Myth-Science Arkestra was a potent force in the free jazz emerging in Chicago during the 1950s.

John Surman
b. 30 August 1944, Tavistock, UK
Baritone and soprano saxophones.
Influenced by John Coltrane, his expertise first came to attention on John McLaughlin's album *Extrapolation* in 1969.

Ralph Sutton
b. 4 November 1922, Hamburg, Missouri
Piano.
Modern exponent of the Harlem stride style.

Lew Tabackin
b. 26 May 1940, Philadelphia
Tenor saxophone.
With his wife Toshiko Akiyoshi, whom he married in 1970, he led a successful big band from 1973.

Art Tatum
b. 13 October 1909, Toledo, Ohio
d. 5 November 1956, Los Angeles
Piano.
Near-blind performer who revitalized jazz piano playing in the 1940s with a heady blend of virtuosity and harmonic daring.

Cecil Taylor
b. 25 March 1929, New York
Piano, composer.
He worked sporadically in a free-jazz idiom throughout the 1960s, and gained greater exposure in the late 1970s.

Martin Taylor
b. 20 October 1956, Harlow, UK
Guitar.
Sideman to Stephane Grappelli in the 1980s, he became a popular solo artist in the UK during the 1990s.

Jack Teagarden
b. 29 August 1905, Vernon, Texas
d. 15 January 1964, New Orleans
Trombone, vocals.
After working in Paul Whiteman's orchestra in the 1930s, he formed his own big band and joined Louis Armstrong's All Stars in 1947.

Clark Terry
b. 14 December 1920, St Louis
Trumpet, flugelhorn, vocals.
Early work with Count Basie (1948–51) led to a stint with Duke Ellington (1951–59) and a close involvement with leading bop musicians.

Juan Tizol
b. 22 January 1900, San Juan, Puerto Rico
d. 23 April 1984, Inglewood, California
Trombone, composer.
Specializing in the valve trombone, he worked with Duke Ellington (1929–44, 1951–53 and 1960–61) and composed "Caravan" in 1937.

Stan Tracey
b. 30 December 1926, London
Piano, composer.
Pianist at Ronnie Scott's London club during the 1960s, he played for Sonny Rollins's *Alfie* film score in 1966. His son Clark (b. 1961) is a drummer.

Lennie Tristano
b. 19 March 1919, Chicago
d. 18 November 1978, New York
Piano, composer.
Blind performer who branched out from a bop background into an experimental brand of "cool" jazz in the 1950s.

McCoy Tyner
b. 11 December 1938, Philadelphia
Piano, composer.
Member of the John Coltrane Quartet (1960–65), and a leader since the 1970s.

Nana Vasconcelos
b. 2 August 1944, Recife, Brazil
Percussion, vocals.
Member of Collin Walcott's and Don Cherry's world-music trio Codona (founded in 1978), and Pat Metheny's fusion group (1980–83).

Sarah "Sassy" Vaughan
b. 27 March 1924, Newark, New Jersey
d. 3 April 1990, Los Angeles
Vocals.
Early exposure with Billy Eckstine's band in the mid-1940s launched her on a solo career ranging from invigorating bop standards to lush arrangements of popular songs.

Joe Venuti
b. 16 September 1903, Philadelphia
d. 14 August 1978, Seattle
Violin.
Duet partner of guitarist Eddie Lang in the late 1920s, he influenced Stephane Grappelli.

Collin Walcott
b. 24 April 1945, New York
d. 8 November 1984, Magdeburgh, Germany
Sitar, tabla, percussion.
Advocate of world music who specialized in traditional Indian instruments and formed the trio Codona with Don Cherry and Nana Vasconcelos in 1978.

Thomas "Fats" Waller
b. 21 May 1904, New York
d. 15 December 1943, Kansas City
Piano, organ, vocals, composer.
Popular comic songwriter and virtuoso stride pianist of the 1930s.

Dinah Washington
b. 29 August 1924, Tuscaloosa, Alabama
d. (overdose) 14 December 1963, Detroit
Vocals.
Membership of Lionel Hampton's band (1943–46) led to a wide-ranging solo career embracing blues and pop in addition to jazz.

Grover Washington Jnr.
b. 12 December 1943, Buffalo, New York
Saxophones.
His polished performances of soul jazz have brought him numerous chart successes since the mid-1970s.

Sadao Watanabe
b. 1 February 1933, Tochigi, Japan
Alto saxophone.
Leading Japanese bop and fusion artist.

Chick Webb
b. 10 February 1909, Baltimore
d. 16 June 1939, Baltimore
Drums, bandleader.
Hunchback bandleader who hired the teenage Ella Fitzgerald in 1934.

Eberhard Weber
b. 22 January 1940, Stuttgart
Double bass, composer.
His group Colours met with critical acclaim in the mid-1970s when he became a key artist on the ECM label.

Ben Webster
b. 27 March 1909, Kansas City
d. 20 September 1973, Amsterdam
Tenor saxophone.
Sideman to Duke Ellington (1935–36, 1940–43 and 1948–49), he emigrated to Denmark in 1964.

Dave Weckl
b. 8 January 1960, St. Louis
Drums.
Dynamic member of Chick Corea's Elektric Band since 1986, proficient on both acoustic and electronic drums.

Kenny Wheeler
b. 14 January 1930, Toronto
Trumpet, flugelhorn.
Based in the UK since 1952, he became an established ECM artist in the mid-1970s and has collaborated with Keith Jarrett and Jan Garbarek.

237

Paul Whiteman
b. 28 March 1890, Denver, Colorado
d. 29 December 1967, Doylestown, Pennsylvania
Bandleader.
Dubbed "The King of Jazz," he promoted symphonic jazz by commissioning *Rhapsody in Blue* from George Gershwin in 1924. His bands produced polished dance music typical of the 1920s.

Charles "Cootie" Williams
b. 24 July 1910, Mobile, Alabama
d. 15 September 1985, New York
Trumpet.
Sideman to Duke Ellington (1929–40 and 1962–74) and Benny Goodman (1941), and a leader in his own right during the 1940s.

Clarence Williams
b. 8 October 1898, Plaquemine Delta, Louisiana
d. 6 November 1965, New York
Piano, vocals.
He collaborated with Sidney Bechet, Louis Armstrong and Bubber Miley in the 1920s.

Mary Lou Williams
b. 8 May 1910, Atlanta, Georgia
d. 28 May 1981, Durham, North Carolina
Piano, composer.
Her *Zodiac Suite* was performed by the New York Philharmonic Orchestra in 1946. She wrote scores for Benny Goodman and Duke Ellington, and was the first front-rank female instrumentalist in jazz.

Tony Williams
b. 12 December 1945, Chicago
d. 23 February 1997, Daly City, California
Drums.
A child prodigy, he joined Miles Davis at the age of seventeen and remained his sideman until 1969, also playing for Herbie Hancock. He formed the energetic fusion group Lifetime with John McLaughlin on his departure from Davis.

Cassandra Wilson
b. December 1963, Jackson, Mississippi
Vocals.
Strongly influenced by the blues, she made her highly acclaimed first album for Blue Note in 1993.

Teddy Wilson
b. 24 November 1912, Austin, Texas
d. 31 July 1986, New Britain, Connecticut
Piano, bandleader.
Leading pianist of the swing era, famous for his work with Billie Holiday and Benny Goodman's chamber groups in the 1930s.

Kai Winding
b. 18 May 1922, Aarhus, Denmark
d. 7 May 1983, Yonkers, New York
Trombone.
Along with J. J. Johnson, the foremost trombonist working in the bop style during the 1950s.

Phil Woods
b. 2 November 1931, Springfield, Massachusetts
Alto saxophone.
Early work with Buddy Rich, Dizzy Gillespie and Benny Goodman revealed his strong debt to Charlie Parker. He continued to top *Down Beat*'s popularity polls in the mid-1990s.

Lester "Pres" Young
b. 27 August 1909, Woodville, Mississippi
d. 15 March 1959, New York
Tenor saxophone.
Soulmate and frequent accompanist to Billie Holiday, he played in Count Basie's band (1936–41 and 1943–44) and was renowned for his light, clear tone.

Joe Zawinul
b. 7 July 1932, Vienna
Keyboards, composer.
His expertise with synthesizers in the jazz-rock group Weather Report (1970–85), which he co-led with Wayne Shorter, enriched the soundscapes of the early fusion period.

John Zorn
b. 2 September 1953, New York
Alto saxophone, bird imitations.
Experimental free-jazz artist who began stamping his personal imprint on compositions by Ornette Coleman and others during the 1980s.

Glossary of Musical Terms

Acoustic Live sound that has not been electronically enhanced. Used to distinguish an instrument from its electric version.

Acoustic recording A recording made before the advent of the electrical process in 1926.

Antiphony The spatial contrast between groups of instruments located in different positions, or differentiated by timbre (e.g. brass versus reeds). In jazz, musical ideas are often passed from one instrumental group to another (see CALL-AND-RESPONSE).

Atonality The avoidance of a sense of key, generally through a consistent use of DISSONANCE. The idea was imported into jazz from classical music, which began to dissolve conventional TONALITY in the early years of the twentieth century.

Backbeat Placing a heavy emphasis on the beats of the measure traditionally regarded as the weakest (beats two and four in a four-beat measure).

Ballad Any slow jazz piece characterized by melodic lyricism.

Banjo An instrument developed by slave musicians in the nineteenth century from African prototypes, and common in jazz bands until supplanted by the guitar in the 1930s. The most popular model has five strings stretched over a circular body supporting a skin resonator; the strings are plucked with the aid of plectra. Six-string banjos were common in early jazz.

Be-bop A style of jazz developed in the early 1940s by small ensembles, characterized by virtuosic solo IMPROVISATIONS based on complex harmonic progressions and often promoting melodic angularity and metrical disruption.

Block chords The parallel motion of chords, in which all underlying parts move in the same RHYTHM as the melody; a defining characteristic of the SWING-band style of the 1930s and 1940s.

Blue note A microtonal flattening of the third, fifth or seventh note of the major scale for expressive effect, thought to be derived from African music. Blue notes sound noticeably harsher on keyboard instruments, which have no pitch-bending capability.

Blues An improvised genre for solo voice, generally accompanied by a single instrument (e.g. guitar) in CALL-AND-RESPONSE patterns, which exerted a major influence on the development of jazz.

Blues progression See TWELVE-BAR BLUES.

Boogie-woogie A keyboard version of the BLUES in which the harmonies are articulated by the player's left hand in repeated rhythmic figurations.

Bop See BE-BOP.

Bossa nova ("new wave") A jazz style popular in the 1960s, reflecting strong Brazilian influences in its restrained and lyrical use of SYNCOPATION.

Break A short improvised passage, usually performed by a solo instrument, inserted between adjacent sections of a piece by way of punctuation.

Cakewalk A dance popular at the turn of the century and similar to RAGTIME in style, originally evolved by black communities to parody the pretentious behaviour of white folk. The name derives from the tradition of awarding a cake to the best performer of the dance.

Call-and-response A musical pattern of "question-and-answer" in which a short theme is passed rapidly from one performer (or group of performers) to another in ANTIPHONY. The technique probably derived from the antiphonal singing common in slave working parties.

Changes The repeating pattern of CHORDS on which a conventional jazz IMPROVISATION is based.

Chord The simultaneous playing of different notes to create a single HARMONY.

Chorus In jazz, a single statement of the CHANGES on which a piece is based. Solo improvisations are normally of more than one chorus in duration. The term can also describe the refrain of a popular song, preceded by a "verse."

Chromatic The "chromatic scale" employs all 12 semitones available in a single octave. Thus "chromatic HARMONY" utilizes CHORDS with their root notes a semitone apart; the expression generally implies harmonic complexity and instability.

Combo Jazz slang for a small instrumental group (cf. "combination").

Cool The opposite of HOT, usually applied to any style of jazz marked by emotional restraint.

Counterpoint The simultaneous combination of more than one melodic line, sometimes referred to as polyphony.

Crossover Any musical venture that transcends perceived stylistic or commercial barriers, e.g. idioms that synthesize jazz and rock (see FUSION), jazz and classical music, jazz and ethnic music, etc.

Cross-rhythm The combination of rhythmic patterns to create displaced accents (see SYNCOPATION) that conflict with the main pulses of the METER.

Cutting contest An informal competition between instrumentalists who try to out-play each other in a JAM SESSION.

Dissonance A combination of notes that sounds "wrong" (more correctly, "discordant"). In classical music before the twentieth century, dissonances required resolution to "consonances"; in jazz, many milder dissonances have become standard elements of the harmonic vocabulary.

Dixieland Early New Orleans ensemble jazz, as performed by white groups. The term "Dixie" refers to the southern states of the USA.

Electric piano An electric keyboard instrument that imitates the sound of an ACOUSTIC piano. The metallic timbre of the Fender-Rhodes electric piano was popular with FUSION groups in the 1970s, but now sounds dated.

239

Field holler A work song (or shout) originated by slaves on US plantations.

Free jazz Generic term for several styles of jazz, pioneered by the 1960s avant-garde, which abandon conventional harmonic, melodic and rhythmic procedures in pursuit of greater musical freedom. At times, this dissolution of traditional musical grammar has consciously symbolized the black community's need for political and social freedom.

Funk A term used in the 1950s to describe down-to-earth jazz styles (i.e. those characterized by powerful rhythms and prominent BLUE NOTES), especially in contrast to COOL jazz. The term "funk" is synonymous with SOUL jazz and should not be confused with its more modern pop-music derivative.

Fusion A stylistic amalgamation of features from jazz and rock music, first introduced by Miles Davis in the late 1960s. See also CROSSOVER.

Gig Jazz parlance for a professional engagement.

Glissando (plural **glissandi**) Sliding from one note to a higher or lower one by sounding the intermediate pitches. On a piano, all individual pitches between the two notes are clearly audible; on other instruments and in vocal technique a blurred effect is produced.

Gospel Successor to the SPIRITUAL as the principal vocal genre in popular black religious music.

Growl A manner of playing wind instruments intended to portray the rough sound of the human voice, or a manner of "dirty" vocal production common in the work of female BLUES singers.

Hard bop A loose term usually indicating a development of BE-BOP in the 1950s in which the hard-driving rhythmic characteristics and BLUES mannerisms were intensified. Sometimes synonymous with FUNK and SOUL jazz, or used to indicate the importation of GOSPEL features.

Harmony The use of CHORDS as a basis for musical textures, generally organized into a pre-determined "chord progression" (see CHANGES). Static harmony, which tends to avoid chord progressions, is a characteristic of some MODAL jazz.

Head The statement of a theme at the opening and/or conclusion of a piece, before and/or after the improvised solo CHORUSES.

Hot A term popular in early jazz, referring to the elements of a performance which sound "jazzy" (e.g. SWUNG RHYTHM, SYNCOPATION, BLUE NOTES, and expressive tone).

Improvisation The spontaneous production of musical ideas by a performer, involving no conscious element of PRE-COMPOSITION.

Jam session An informal group IMPROVISATION.

Licks The characteristic (and sometimes idiosyncratic) melodic or rhythmic formulae habitually used by an individual player, sometimes referred to as "signatures."

March A genre derived from military music, popular in America during the nineteenth century. Its multi-sectional structures and simple harmonic schemes provided the foundation for RAGTIME.

Meter The organization of rhythmic pulses into regular stress patterns.

Minstrel show A comic musical entertainment, highly popular in America from the 1840s onwards, in which white performers blackened their faces and caricatured the behaviour of colored people. Later in the nineteenth century, black musicians participated in such shows; many early jazz musicians began their careers in this way.

Modal jazz A style of jazz, pioneered by Miles Davis and others towards the end of the 1950s, in which IMPROVISATIONS are based on MODES rather than conventional CHANGES. See also HARMONY.

Mode Musical SCALE. In the twentieth century, both classical and jazz musicians grew frustrated with the major and minor scales that had dominated Western music for several centuries, and began experimenting with less familiar modes. Some of these scales were inspired by pre-classical music of the Renaissance, while others were borrowed from non-Western musical traditions.

Multiphonics A technique used by avant-garde wind players to produce more than one note simultaneously.

Mute A device inserted into the bell of a brass instrument to alter its natural timbre, generally resulting in a more subdued tone. Manufactured from a variety of substances, mutes are available in numerous designs, each with a different sonorous character.

Novelty A popularized style of RAGTIME successful in the 1910s and 1920s, favoring pieces with fanciful titles and sometimes containing musical gimmicks.

Ostinato (Italian "obstinate") A short musical motif subjected to more than one immediate repetition. See also RIFF.

Piano roll A roll of paper which records a keyboard performance as a sequence of perforations. When passed through the mechanism of a player piano (pianola), an approximation of the original performance is produced.

Plugger Employee of a music publisher responsible for promoting the company's latest issues.

Polyphony See COUNTERPOINT.

Polyrhythm The superimposition of two or more conflicting rhythmic patterns.

Polytonality The superimposition of two or more conflicting keys.

Pre-composition Planning the structure and details of a musical work in advance of its performance, usually preserving them in the form of a notated score. The historical development of jazz has frequently involved a fruitful creative tension between varying degrees of pre-composition and spontaneous IMPROVISATION.

Professor Informal title awarded to early jazz pianists who were capable of reading music.

Progressive jazz A predominantly PRE-COMPOSED big-band style promoted in the 1940s and 1950s by Stan Kenton as an amalgamation of jazz and modern classical music.

Race records Recordings specifically aimed at the escalating black consumer market in the 1920s and 1930s.

Rag Any piece in the RAGTIME style.

Ragtime Early precursor of jazz in which highly SYNCOPATED melodies were supported by solid musical structures borrowed from the MARCH. Ragtime was PRE-COMPOSED, and circulated in the form of songs, piano pieces and orchestral dance music. See also CAKEWALK.

Reeds Generic term for wind instruments that use a reed to generate their sounds, principally clarinets and saxophones (single reeds), and oboes and bassoons (double reeds).

Rhythm The temporal organization of music as patterns of weak, strong, long and short beats. Rhythms are usually governed by the constraints of a prevailing METER.

Rhythm section Members of a jazz COMBO or big band responsible for maintaining the rhythmic and harmonic foundation of the music, and accompanying solo performers. A standard rhythm section comprises a harmony instrument (guitar, banjo or keyboard), bass instrument and drums.

Riff Any short, catchy OSTINATO figure. Riffs were a common device in big-band music of the SWING era, where they sometimes appeared as accompanying figures, or as the main melody. The device was retained as a prominent feature of the BOP style.

Rip An exhilarating upwards GLISSANDO on a brass instrument.

Scale The arrangement of any group of musical pitches in ascending or descending order. See also MODE.

Sampling A technique in electronic music by which a segment of natural sound is extracted ("sampled") from a source, and then converted into digital information to provide the raw material for computerized transformations.

Scat singing Singing an improvised melodic line to nonsense syllables, often in imitation of instrumental music.

Sequencing The computerized repetition or juxtaposition of digitally SAMPLED sounds.

Side Before the introduction of long-playing records, a single recorded piece was often referred to as a "side" since it normally occupied one complete side of a 78rpm disc.

Sideman Any player in a group other than the leader.

Soul A brand of HARD BOP

incorporating elements borrowed from black church music.

Spiritual Vocal music of the black American church, developed under the influence of European hymns in the late nineteenth century.

Standard Any song melody forming part of the "standard" repertoire of themes used by jazz musicians as raw material on which to base their IMPROVISATIONS.

Storyville Red-light district of old New Orleans, traditionally considered to have been the cradle of jazz in the early twentieth century.

Stride piano The first important style of jazz piano playing, at its height in the 1930s. It evolved directly from RAGTIME and took its name from the "striding" motion of the player's leaping left hand.

Swing Type of (largely PRE-COMPOSED) big-band dance music internationally popular in the 1930s and 1940s, which gave its name to the "Swing Era."

Swung rhythm The tendency of jazz performers to anticipate the main beats of a METER through SYNCOPATION or to alternate notes of long and short rhythmic values. Both techniques propel the music forwards with a strong rhythmic drive.

Symphonic jazz Hybrid style combining elements of jazz and classical music, popularized by Gershwin and others in the 1920s and 1930s.

Syncopation The accentuation of a weak beat to disrupt the expected stress patterns of a regular METER. See also CROSS-RHYTHM.

Synthesizer Electronic instrument capable of producing a theoretically infinite range of sound colours.

Tonality The conventional system of major and minor keys prevailing in all Western music until the twentieth century. See also ATONALITY.

Trumpet style Melodic style of piano playing developed by Earl Hines in the late 1920s.

Twelve-bar blues The most common harmonic progression in all jazz. It comprises twelve measures based on tonic (I), dominant (V) and subdominant (IV) harmonies, organized in the simple pattern I-I-I-I-IV-IV-I-I-V-V-I-I. Much variety has been injected into this configuration through the use of additional and substitute chords.

Vaudeville A staged variety show popular in America at the turn of the century, broadly comparable to the music-hall tradition in Britain. Like the MINSTREL SHOW, its musical content was important to the early development of jazz.

Vibrato The creation of a rich tone color by the rapid oscillation between two notes of very slightly differing pitch. Various methods are used by string, brass and wind players and vocalists, but the technique is not possible on ACOUSTIC keyboard instruments.

West Coast A style of COOL jazz originating in California during the 1950s.

Guide to International Jazz Festivals and Venues

Major Jazz Festivals

Dates in parentheses indicate year of foundation. All festivals are held annually unless otherwise stated.

NORTH AMERICA

Canada
Montreal International Jazz Festival (1980): June–July
Jazz City International Jazz Festival (1980): June–July, Edmonton

United States of America
Atlanta Free Jazz Festival (1978): August–September, Georgia
Berkeley Jazz Festival (1967): August–September, University of California at Berkeley
Bix Beiderbecke Memorial Festival (1972): July, Davenport, Iowa (specialist Dixieland festival)
Chicago Jazz Festival (1979): August–September, Illinois
Concord Jazz Festival (1969): August, California
Dixieland Jubilee (1974): May, Sacramento, California
Floating Jazz Festival (1983): autumn jazz cruises operated out of Miami by Norwegian Caribbean Lines
Globe Jazz and Heritage Festival (1966): March, Boston
Greenwich Village Jazz Festival (1982): August–September, New York
Jacksonville Jazz Festival (1983): October, Florida
Jazz and Heritage Festival (1968): April–May, New Orleans
Jazz Picnic (1976): June, Waterloo Village, New Jersey
JVC Jazz Festival Newport (1984): August, Rhode Island
JVC Jazz Festival New York (1972): June
Kool Jazz Festival (1980): August–September, Detroit (in association with the Montreux Festival, Switzerland)
Mellon Jazz Festival (1984): June, Pittsburgh
Monterey Jazz Festival (1958): September, California
Playboy Jazz Festival (1979): June, Hollywood Bowl, Los Angeles

EUROPE

Austria
International Jazz Festival Salzburg (1982): March–April
Blue Danube Jazz Summit (1987): July, Vienna

Belgium
Free Music Antwerp (1974): August (specialist festival for free jazz)
Middelheim Jazz Festival (1969): August (biennial)

Denmark
Copenhagen Jazz Festival (1979): July

Republic of Eire
Guinness Jazz Festival (1978): October, Cork

Finland
Pori Jazz (1966): July, Pori

France
Antibes/Juan-les-Pins International Jazz Festival (1960): July
Jazz Pulsations (1973): October, Nancy
JVC Grande Parade du Jazz (1974): July, Nice
Paris Jazz Festival (1980): October–November

Germany
Berlin Jazz Festival (1964): October–November
Frankfurt Jazz Festival (1953): February–March
International New Jazz Festival (1972): May–June, Moers
Jazz Ost-West (1966): May–June (biennial), Nuremberg

Greece
Praxis (1978): November, Athens (specialist festival for free jazz)

Italy
Pescara International Jazz Festival (1969): July
Ravenna Jazz Festival (1974): July
Umbria Jazz Festival and Clinic (1982): July
Verona International Jazz Festival (1986): July–August

The Netherlands
NOS Jazz Festival (1980): August–September, Amsterdam
North Sea Jazz Festival (1976): July, The Hague
Oude Stijl Jazz Festival (1971): May, Breda

Norway
Night Jazz (1973): May–June, Bergen
Molde International Jazz Festival (1961): July–August
Oslo Jazz Festival (1986): August

Poland
International Jazz Jamboree Festival (1959): October, Warsaw

Spain
Madrid Jazz Festival (1981): November
San Sebastián Jazz Festival (1966): July

Sweden
Åhus Jazz Festival (1987): July
Jazz and Blues All Star Festival (1980): June–July, Stockholm

Switzerland
Festa New Orleans Music (1974): June–July, Ascona
Lugano Jazz Festival (1979): July
Montreux International Jazz Festival (1967): July
Zurich International Jazz Festival (1978): October–November

United Kingdom
Birmingham International Jazz Festival (1985): July
Brighton Jazz Festival (1983): May
Chichester Jazz Festival (1978): October
Edinburgh International Jazz Festival (1979): August
JVC/Capital Radio Jazz Parade (1979): July, London
London International Jazz Festival: November
Soho Jazz Festival (1986): October, London

REST OF WORLD

Australian Jazz Convention (1946): December, different city each year
Budweiser Newport Jazz Festival at Madarao (1982): August, Tokyo, Japan
Israel Jazz Festival (1981): July–August, varying locations
Jazzyatra (1978): February–March (biennial), Bombay, India
Autumn Rhythms (1986): November, St. Petersburg, Russia
Moscow Jazz Festival (1978): May (biennial)

Major Jazz Venues

NORTH AMERICA

Canada

L'Air du Temps, Rue St Paul,
Montreal
George's Spaghetti House, 290
Dundas Street East, Toronto
(1956)
Massey Hall, Shuter Street,
Toronto
Yardbird Suite, 1023 86 Street,
Edmonton (1984)

United States of America

Atlanta
Café au Lait, Snellville
La Carousel, Paschel's Motel, MLK
Boulevard

Boston
The Gallery, 956 Massachusetts
Avenue
Sculler's, 400 Soldiers Field Road

Cambridge, Massachusetts
Nightstage, 838 Main Street
(1985)
1369 Club, 1369 Cambridge Street
(1980)
Regattabar, Charles Hotel, Harvard
Square (1985)

Chicago
Andy's, 11 East Hubbard Street
(1977)
Bop Shop, 1897 West Division
Bull's, 1916 North Lincoln Park
West
Fairbank's, 300 East Ohio Street
George's, 230 West Kenzie Street
(1980s)
Jazz Showcase, Blackstone Hotel,
Balboa
New Regal Theater, 79th Street
(1987)

Los Angeles
Catalina's Bar and Grill, 1640
North Cahuenga Boulevard
Hollywood Bowl
Indigo Jazz Club, 111 East Artesia
La Ve Lee, 12514 Ventura
Boulevard, Studio City (Latin
jazz)
World Stage, 4344 Degnan
Boulevard

New Orleans
Blue Room, Fairmount Hotel,
University Place
Municipal Auditorium, Saratoga
Street

Fairgrounds Race Track, near
City Park
Preservation Hall, 726 St Peter
Street (1961)
Snug Harbor, 626 Frenchman
Street

New York
Angry Squire, 216 Seventh
Avenue (1981)
Arthur's Tavern, 57 Grove Street
(1950s)
Birdland, 2745 Broadway
Blue Note, 131 West Third Street
(1981)
Bottom Line, 15 West Fourth
Street (1974)
Bradley's, University Street
Café Carlyle and Bemelmans Bar,
Hotel Carlyle, Madison Avenue
(1970s)
Carnegie Hall, West 57th Street
Fat Tuesday, 190 Third Avenue
(1979)
Greene Street, 101 Greene Street
(1986)
Indigo Blues, 221 West 46th
Street
Knickerbocker Saloon, 33
University Place (1978)
Sweet Basil, 88 Seventh Avenue
South (1975)
Village Gate, 160 Blecker Street
(1958)
Village Vanguard, 178 Seventh
Avenue (1935)
West End, 2911 Broadway (1973)
Zinno's, 126 West 13th Street
(1982)

Philadelphia
Blue Note, Washington Lane
Natalie's Lounge, 4003 Market
Street (1960s)
Ortlieb's Jazz House, 847 North
Third Street
Prince Total Experience Lounge,
1410 Hunting Park Avenue
(1980s)

Pittsburgh
The Balcony, 5520 Walnut Street
Cardillo's, South 12th Street

San Francisco
Great American Music Hall, 859
O'Farrill Street (1970s)
Kimball's, 5800 Shellmound,
Farmer's Market, Emeryville
Milestones, 376 Fifth Street
(1980s)

Washington, D.C.
Blues Alley, 1073 Rear Wisconsin
Avenue, Georgetown (1965)
Constitution Hall, 18th Street
One Step Down, 2517
Pennsylvania Avenue

EUROPE

Austria
Wiener Metropol, Hernalser
Hauptstrasse 55, Vienna (1981)

Belgium
Lazy River Jazz Club,
Stadhuissteeg 5, Ghent (1966)
Palais des Beaux Arts, Brussels
Sounds, 28 Rue de la Tulipe,
Brussels

Denmark
Montmartre Jazzhus, Nørregade
41, Copenhagen (1976)

Estonia
Kiko, 12 Vaike-Karja Street,
Tallinn (1981)

Finland
Columbia City Jazz Club, Café Jazz
and Verve Jazz Club, Jazz Street,
Helsinki

France
Alliance, 7–11 Rue St.-Benoît, Paris
Caveau de la Huchette, 5 Rue de la
Huchette, Paris
Jazz Club Lionel Hampton, Hôtel
Meridien, 81 Boulevard
Gouvion-St.-Cyr, Paris
Le Petit Journal, 71 Boulevard St.-
Michel, Paris
Le Petit Journal, 13 Rue du
Commandant Mouchotte, Paris
Salle Pleyel, 252 Rue du Faubourg-
St.-Honoré, Paris

Germany
Haus der Jungen Talente,
Klosterstrasse 68, Berlin
Jazzclub Tonne, Tzschirnerplatz 3,
Dresden (1981)
Jazzclub Unterfahrt, Kirchenstrasse
96, Munich (1978)
Der Jazzkeller, Kleine
Bockenheimerstrasse 18a,
Frankfurt (1952)
Jazz Studio, Paniersplatz 27,
Nuremberg (1954)

Italy
Alpheus, Via del Commercio 36,
Rome
Fonclea, Via Crescenzio 82a, Rome
(1978)
Jive, Via Libetta 7, Rome
Mississippi Jazz Club, Borgo
Angelico 16, Rome (1979)
Music Empire Jazz Club, 15 Via S.
Maria Fulcorina, Milan
La Scimmia, Navigli, Milan

The Netherlands
BIM-huis, Oude Schans 73,
Amsterdam (1973)

Norway
Bergen Jazz Forum, Sardinen,
Kulturhuset
Oslo Jazzhus,
Sjokoladefabrikken
Storyville Jazz Club, Molde

Poland
Akwarium, Ulica Emilii Plater 49,
Warsaw (1977)

Portugal
Hot Club of Portugal, Praça da
Alegria 39 (1950)

Russia
Café of the Cultural Palace of
Seamen, 2 Vinolavskaya Street,
Petersburg (1986)
Kvadrat, 47 Professor Popov
Street, St. Petersburg (1965)
Sinyaya Ptitsa, 23 Chekhov Street,
Moscow (1986)

Sweden
Fasching, Kungsgatan 63,
Stockholm (1975)

Switzerland
Casa Bar, 30 Münster-Gasse,
Zurich

United Kingdom
Barbican Centre, London
Bull's Head, Lonsdale Road,
London (1960)
Jazz Café, Camden Parkway,
London
100 Club, 100 Oxford Street,
London (1958)
606 Club, 90 Lots Road, London
Pizza Express, 10 Dean Street
(1970s)
The Rhythmic, The Angel, London
(1995)
Ronnie Scott's, 47 Frith Street,
London (1959)
Ronnie Scott's, Broad Street,
Birmingham
South Bank Centre, London:
Purcell Room, Queen Elizabeth
Hall, Royal Festival Hall
Town Hall, Victoria Square,
Birmingham

REST OF WORLD

Australia
The Basement, 29 Reiby Place,
Circular Quay, Sydney (1973)
Jazz Club of Western Australia,
Hyde Park Hotel, Fitzgerald
Street, Perth
Soup Plus Restaurant, 383 George
Street, Sydney (1974)

Select Discography

The following discography is organized chronologically by musical style in order to facilitate the selection of a personal anthology reflecting the historical development of jazz. Musicians within each section are listed in alphabetical order. Items are restricted to titles available on compact disc at the time of writing, although attention should be drawn to the flourishing (and increasingly expensive) trade in second-hand albums on vinyl. Many early jazz recordings, and certain live performances from the 1950s and 1960s, are widely available on CD in the form of low- and mid-price compilations that provide an inexpensive starting point for a listener wishing to build up a comprehensive collection. Remarkably full catalogs of such discs have been marketed in the low-price Italian "Giants of Jazz" series, and the French "Hot'n'Sweet" and "Jazz Archives" series (EPM/Auvidis Distribution). Both ranges helpfully provide accurate information on personnel and recording dates in their liner notes, in contrast to many other cheap reissues.

Ragtime and Harlem Stride Piano

Eubie Blake: *Memories of You* (Biograph BCD112).

James P. Johnson: *James P. Johnson – Harlem Stride Piano, 1921–9* (Hot'n'Sweet AD065); *Snowy Morning Blues* (MCA/GRP 16042).

Scott Joplin: The composer's own recordings of his compositions on piano rolls are available on *King of Ragtime* (Giants of Jazz 53004), *The Entertainer* (Jazz Archives 15, 157262) and numerous other inexpensive reissues.

Joshua Rifkin: *Digital Ragtime* (Angel CDC747199-2).

Willie "The Lion" Smith: *Willie "The Lion" Smith, 1925–37* (Classics 662), *1937–8* (667) and *1938–40* (692).

Ralph Sutton: *At Café des Copains* (Sackville SKCD2-2019).

Fats Waller: *Piano Masterworks*, volumes 1 and 2 (Hot'n'Sweet 151062/151132); *The Joint is Jumpin'* (RCA Bluebird ND86288); *The Last Years, 1940–43* (RCA Bluebird ND 90411, 3 CDs).

Blues and Boogie-Woogie Piano

Albert Ammons, Meade Lux Lewis, Pete Johnson, James P. Johnson and others: *Blue Boogie – Boogie-Woogie, Stride and the Piano Blues* (Blue Note CDP 7990992).

Louis Armstrong and the Blues Singers, 1924–30 (Affinity AFS1018-6, 6 CDs), including Ma Rainey, Bessie Smith and more than 20 other vocalists.

Ma Rainey: *Ma Rainey's Black Bottom* (Yazoo YAZCD1071); *Ma Rainey* (Milestone MCD47021-2).

Bessie Smith: *Bessie Smith, Empress of the Blues 1923–33* (Giants of Jazz 53090); *Sings the Jazz 1923–33* (Jazz Archives 61, 157902); *Complete Recordings* (Columbia; 4 double-CD sets).

New Orleans

Louis Armstrong: *Hot Five and Hot Seven*, volumes 1 and 2 (Columbia 460821-2/463052-2, 4 CDs); *Hot Five and Hot Seven Masterpieces, 1925–28* (Giants of Jazz 53001); *Louis Armstrong Masterpieces* (Jazz Archives 158132); *Plays W. C. Handy* (Columbia 450981); see also under "Small Groups of the Swing Era" and "Mainstream Soloists" below.

Sidney Bechet: *The Chronological Sidney Bechet, 1923–26* (Classics 583); *Bluebird Sessions, 1932–43* (RCA Bluebird ND90317, 5 CDs); *The Young Bechet* (Jazz Archives 22, 157392).

Bunk Johnson: *Bunk Johnson and His Superior Jazz Band* (Good Time Jazz 12048).

Jelly Roll Morton: *The Complete Jelly Roll Morton* (RCA Bluebird ND82361, 5 CDs); *Jelly Roll Morton*, vols. 1 to 5 (JSP CD321-5); *The Best of Jelly Roll Morton* (Jazz Archives 16, 158012).

King Oliver and his Creole Jazz Band: *King Oliver, Volume 1: 1923–29* (CDS RPCD607) and *Volume 2: 1927–30* (CDS RPCD608); *King Oliver's Jazz Band 1923* (Jazz Archives 13, 157462).

Original Dixieland Jazz Band: *Sensation* (ASV AJA5023R); *75th Anniversary* (RCA Bluebird ND90650).

Kid Ory: *New Orleans Creole Jazz* (Jazz Archives 9, 157162).

Symphonic Jazz

Aaron Copland: *Early Orchestral Works, 1922–35* (Sony SM2K 47232, 2 CDs) includes the Piano Concerto and *Music for the Theater*.

George Gershwin: Recordings of *Rhapsody in Blue*, *An American in Paris* and the Piano Concerto in F are too numerous to list, but the composer's own 1927 recording of *Rhapsody in Blue* with Paul Whiteman is available on Halcyon DHDL101; complete recordings of the opera *Porgy and Bess* are available on the EMI, RCA and Decca labels, alongside a multitude of albums comprising varied selections of extracts from the opera.

The Simon Rattle Jazz Album (EMI CDC 7479912) includes Darius Milhaud's *La Création du Monde*, Igor Stravinsky's *Ebony Concerto*, Leonard Bernstein's *Prelude, Fugue and Riffs*, the original version of Gershwin's *Rhapsody in Blue* and several vocal numbers in their Paul Whiteman arrangements.

Dance Bands

Jean Goldkette: *Bix Beiderbecke Volume 2: At the Jazz Band Ball* (Columbia 460825-2).

Paul Whiteman: *Bix'n'Bing*, featuring Bix Beiderbecke and Bing Crosby (ASV AJA5005); *Jazz Portraits: Paul Whiteman* (Jazz Portraits 14521); see also under "Symphonic Jazz" above.

Big Bands of the Swing Era

Count Basie: Early work in the period 1936–41 is well represented on *The Essential Count Basie*, volumes 1 to 3 (Columbia 460061-2, 460828-2 and 461098-2). A selection of tracks from the 1950s and 1960s is available on *Jazz Masters: Count Basie* (Verve 519819-2). Many live recordings from Basie's last years have been issued by Pablo.

Benny Goodman: *Live at Carnegie Hall* (Columbia 450983-2, 2CDs). This famous 1938 concert is also available in the "Giants of Jazz" series (53101 and 53102), the second disc of which includes part of the second Carnegie Hall concert in 1939. A comprehensive collection of earlier Goodman is available on RCA Bluebird as *The Birth of Swing, 1935–36* (ND90601, 3 CDs).

Lionel Hampton: *Compact Jazz: Lionel Hampton* (Verve 833287-2).

244

Recordings from the period 1937–41 have been issued on four Classics discs.

Fletcher Henderson: *Jazz Classics in Digital Stereo: Fletcher Henderson 1929–37* (BBC CD682). Most of Henderson's work from 1923 to 1938 has been reissued on the Classics label as a 15-CD series, each disc available separately.

Woody Herman: *The Thundering Herds, 1945–47* (Columbia 460825-2).

Earl Hines: *Earl "Fatha" Hines: Piano Man, 1928–55* (Giants of Jazz, 53118).

Jack Hylton: *The Cream of Jack Hylton* (Flapper PASTCD 9775).

Harry James: *The Best of Harry James: the Capitol Years* (Capitol CDP798952-2).

Glenn Miller: *The Popular Recordings, 1938–42* (RCA Bluebird ND90412); *The Army Air Force Band, 1943–44* (RCA Bluebird ND86360).

Bennie Moten: *Basie Beginnings, 1929–32* (RCA Bluebird ND90403). Earlier recordings have been issued on four separate CDs by Classics.

Royal Air Force Squadronaires: *Big Band Spectacular* (Bandleader BNA5007).

Artie Shaw: *Begin the Beguine* (RCA Bluebird ND82432).

Chick Webb: *Spinnin' the Webb* (MCA GRP 16352) covers the period 1929–39.

Compilations: *Best of the Big Bands*, featuring Goodman, Basie, Ellington, James, Krupa, Hampton, Herman and others (Verve 833281-2); *An Anthology of Big-Band Swing, 1930–55*, featuring Duke Ellington, the Dorsey Brothers, Count Basie, Chick Webb and others (GRP 26292).

Excellent examples of the up-dated big-band sound of the late 1960s and 1970s are provided by *Thad Jones/Mel Lewis* (LRC CDC9004) and *The Toshiko Akiyoshi/Lew Tabackin Big Band* (Novus ND83106).

See also under "Duke Ellington" below.

Small Groups of the Swing Era

Europe: *Swing from Paris*, featuring Stephane Grappelli, Django Reinhardt and the Quintette du Hot Club de France (ASV CD AJA5070); a comparable collection is available on *Swingin' with*

Django (Pro Arte CDD549), and on numerous low-price imports from France and Italy.

USA: *After You've Gone*, featuring the Benny Goodman Quartet (RCA Bluebird ND85631); *Charlie Christian: Genius of Electric Guitar*, featuring the Benny Goodman Sextet (Giants of Jazz 53049); *Small Combos: Lionel Hampton, 1937–40* (Giants of Jazz 53050); *The Duke's Men: Small Groups*, volumes 1 and 2, featuring Duke Ellington's small-group work in the period 1934–39 (Columbia 468618-2 and 472994-2, two double-CD sets); *Esquire Jazz Concert [Metropolitan Opera House, 1944]*, featuring Armstrong, Tatum, Hawkins, Hampton, Holiday and many others (Giants of Jazz 53035).

Duke Ellington

Early work: *Duke Ellington: Masterpieces 2* (Jazz Archives 158142) covers the most famous recordings from 1927–42, which are also available as a series of discs on the Classics label. A good selection of sides from 1927–34 is to be found on *Early Ellington* (RCA Bluebird 86852).

Middle period: *Duke Ellington and his Orchestra, 1941–51* (Giants of Jazz 53057). The Carnegie Hall appearances from 1943 to 1948 have been issued on four Prestige double-CD sets, including *Black, Brown and Beige* (Prestige 34004). The five CDs of Columbia's *The Complete Duke Ellington* cover the period 1947–52. The famous 1956 Newport Festival concert is to be found on the album *At Newport* (Columbia 450986-2).

Later work: 1960s output includes *The Far East Suite* (RCA Bluebird ND87640) and the *Second Sacred Concert* (Prestige P24045).

Mainstream Soloists

Louis Armstrong: *Louis Armstrong and Duke Ellington: The Complete Sessions* (Roulette CDP 793844-2); *Louis Armstrong Meets Oscar Peterson* (Verve 825713-2); see also under "New Orleans" and "Small Groups of the Swing Era" above.

Ella Fitzgerald: Early work with Chick Webb is featured on *Ella Fitzgerald* (ASV AJD055, 2 CDs). Verve has reissued the entire 'Songbook' series on 18 CDs, alongside the useful single-disc

sampler *Best of the Songbooks* (Verve 519804-2).

Coleman Hawkins: *Coleman Hawkins, 1926–40* (Jazz Archives 41, 157202); *April in Paris* (RCA Bluebird ND90636).

Billie Holiday: A series of nine discs entitled *The Quintessential Billie Holiday* has been issued by Columbia, covering the period 1933–42. *Jazz Masters: Billie Holiday* (Verve 519825-2) presents a selection of recordings from her final years (1952–56). A good mid-price compilation is to be found on the French import *Billie Holiday: Her Best Recordings, 1935–42* (Best of Jazz 4003), featuring her work with Teddy Wilson and Paul Whiteman.

Sarah Vaughan: *16 Most Requested Songs* (Columbia 474399-2); *Jazz Masters: Sarah Vaughan* (Verve 518199-2).

Ben Webster: *King of the Tenors* (Verve 519806-2); *Art Tatum and Ben Webster* (Pablo 2310-737).

Lester Young: *Classics in Swing: Lester Young* (Commodore 72725).

Bop

Kenny Clarke: *Special Kenny Clarke, 1938–59* (Jazz Time 799702).

Miles Davis: see *The Charlie Parker Story* (below). Davis's early bop recordings from 1947 are also to be found on *Charlie Parker Memorial*, volume 1 (Savoy SV 0101).

Dizzy Gillespie: *Groovin' High* (Savoy SV0152); *Pleyel 48*, preserving his historic performances in Paris in 1948 (Vogue 74321); *Night in Tunisia: Small Groups, 1945–50* (Giants of Jazz 53122); *Gillespiana/Carnegie Hall Concert [1961]* (Verve 519809-2).

Thelonious Monk: *Genius of Modern Music*, volumes 1 and 2 (Blue Note 781510 and 781511); *Thelonious Monk: 'Round Midnight* (Giants of Jazz 53008); *At Town Hall* (Original Jazz Classics 206); *Art Blakey's Jazz Messengers with Thelonious Monk* (Atlantic 7567-81332-2).

Charlie Parker: *The Charlie Parker Story*, featuring Miles Davis, Dizzy Gillespie, Bud Powell and Max Roach (Savoy SV 0105); *Bird in Boston: Live at the Hi-Hat, 1953–54* (Fresh Sound

FSCD 1006); *Compact Jazz: Charlie Parker* (Verve 833288-2); *The Complete Dial Sessions, 1946–47* (Spotlite SPJ4101, 4 CDs); *Bird: the Complete Charlie Parker on Verve* (Verve 837141, 10 CDs).

Bud Powell: *The Genius of Bud Powell* (Verve 827901); *The Amazing Bud Powell*, volumes 1 and 2 (Blue Note B21Y-81503/4).

Max Roach: *Jazz in 3/4 Time* (Mercury 826456); *Deeds Not Words* (Original Jazz Classics 304).

Hard Bop

Cannonball Adderley: *Somethin' Else*, featuring Miles Davis and Art Blakey (Blue Note CDP 746338-2).

Art Blakey and his Jazz Messengers: *Moanin'* (Blue Note B21Y-46516-2); *Free For All* (B12Y-84170); *The Best of Art Blakey and the Jazz Messengers* (Blue Note CDP 793205-2); see also under "Bop" (Thelonious Monk) above.

Miles Davis: *Walkin'* (Original Jazz Classics 213); *Cookin'* (Original Jazz Classics OJC 128); *Relaxin'* (Original Jazz Classics OJC 190); *Workin'* (Original Jazz Classics 296); *Steamin'* (Original Jazz Classics 391).

Dexter Gordon: *Doin' Alright* (Blue Note B21Y-84077-2).

Lee Morgan: *The Sidewinder* (Blue Note 784157).

Sonny Rollins: *Saxophone Colossus* (Original Jazz Classics 291).

Wayne Shorter: *Speak No Evil* (Blue Note B21Y-46509).

Horace Silver: *Song for My Father* (Blue Note CDP 784185-2).

Sonny Stitt: *Sonny Stitt/Bud Powell/J. J. Johnson* (Original Jazz Classics 009).

Compilation: *The Best of Blue Note*, including the title tracks of Morgan's "The Sidewinder", Silver's "Song for My Father", Blakey's "Moanin'", and Coltrane's "Blue Train" (Blue Note CDP 796110-2).

Piano Trios

Monty Alexander: *Full Steam Ahead* (Concord CCD4287); *Fridaynight* (Limetree MCD0022).

Nat King Cole: *The Best of the Nat King Cole Trio* (Capitol CDP 7982882).

Bill Evans: *Trio '64* (Verve 815057-2); *Waltz for Debby* (Original Jazz Classics 210);

Conversations with Myself (Verve 8219884-2); see also under "Modal Jazz" below.

Erroll Garner: *The Original Misty* (Mercury 834910-2).

Keith Jarrett: *Standards*, volumes 1 and 2 (ECM 1255 and 1289); *Bye Bye Blackbird* (ECM 1467); see also under "ECM" below.

Lyle Mays: *Fictionary* (Geffen 24521); see also under "Jazz-Rock Fusion" below.

Oscar Peterson: *Night Train* (Verve 821724); *Very Tall*, featuring Milt Jackson (Verve 827821-2); *Satch and Josh*, featuring Count Basie (Pablo J33J20013); see also under "Mainstream Soloists" above (Louis Armstrong).

Art Tatum: *The Art Tatum Solo Masterpieces*, volumes 1 to 7 (Pablo 2405-432/3/4/5/6/7/8); *Art Tatum: the Genius of Keyboard* (Giants of Jazz 53019); see also under "Mainstream Soloists" above (Ben Webster).

Cool Jazz and West Coast

Chet Baker: *My Funny Valentine* (Pacific Jazz 828262); *Chet Baker: Inspired by the Motion Picture "Let's Get Lost"* (Giants of Jazz 53100).

Dave Brubeck Quartet, featuring Paul Desmond: *Jazz at Oberlin* (Original Jazz Classics 046); *Time Out* (Columbia 460611-2 62068).

Miles Davis: *Birth of the Cool* (Capitol CDP 792862).

Stan Getz: *At The Shrine*, featuring Bob Brookmeyer (Verve 513753-2); *Getz Meets Mulligan in Hi-Fi* (Verve 849392-2); see also under "Afro-Cuban, Latin and Bossa Nova" below.

Stan Kenton: *The Best of Stan Kenton [1943-61]* (Capitol CDP72438 31504-2 7).

Lee Konitz: *Konitz Meets Mulligan* (Pacific Jazz B21Y-46847); *From Newport to Nice [1955-80]* (Philology W65).

Modern Jazz Quartet: *No Sun in Venice* (Atlantic 1284-2); *MJQ 40* (Atlantic 782330-2, 4 CDs).

Gerry Mulligan: *The Best of the Gerry Mulligan Quartet with Chet Baker* (Pacific Jazz CDP 795481-2); *Birth of the Cool, Volume 2* (Capitol 798935).

George Shearing: *Midnight on Cloud 69*, featuring Charles Mingus (Savoy SV0208).

Lennie Tristano: *Lennie Tristano/The New Tristano*, featuring Lee Konitz (Rhino/Atlantic R271595).

Afro-Cuban, Latin and Bossa Nova

Mario Bauzá: *My Time is Now* (Messidor 158252).

Djavan: *Puzzle of Hearts* (Epic 4669632).

Stan Getz: *Jazz Samba* (Verve 810061-2); *Big Band Bossa Nova* (Verve 825771-2); *Getz/Gilberto* (Verve 810048-2); *The Girl from Ipanema* (Verve 823611-2, 4 CDs).

Astrud Gilberto: *The Girl from Ipanema* (Prestige/BBC CDPC5009).

João Gilberto: *The Legendary João Gilberto* (World Pacific CDP 793891-2).

Dizzy Gillespie and Machito: *Afro-Cuban Jazz Moods* (Original Jazz Classics 447).

Irakere: *Live at Ronnie Scott's* (EMI CDP7805982).

Antonio Carlos Jobim: *Brazilian Tropical Orchestra and Singers* (Compact Club CCV8905); *Compact Jazz: Antonio Carlos Jobim* (Polydor 843273-2).

Flora Purim: *Butterfly Dreams* (Original Jazz Classics 315-2).

Compilations: *Compact Jazz: Best of Bossa Nova* (Verve 833289-2); *Latin Jazz Volume 2* (BGP 1027).

Modal Jazz

Bill Evans: *Everybody Digs Bill Evans* (Original Jazz Classics 068).

Miles Davis: *Milestones* (Columbia 460827); *Kind of Blue* (Columbia 460603-2), both featuring John Coltrane and Cannonball Adderley.

Herbie Hancock: *Maiden Voyage* (Blue Note BST-84195); *The Best of Herbie Hancock: The Blue Note Years* (Blue Note CDP791142-2).

John Coltrane

Blue Train (Blue Note CDP 7460952); *Giant Steps* (Atlantic 781337-2); *My Favorite Things* (Atlantic 782346-2); *Olé Coltrane* (Atlantic 1273-2); *A Love Supreme* (MCA MCLD19029).

See also under "Hard Bop", "Modal Jazz" and "Free Jazz".

Miles Davis

L'Ascenseur pour l'échafaud (Fontana 836305); *Porgy and Bess* (Columbia 450985); *Sketches of Spain* (Columbia 460604); *The Complete Concert 1964: My Funny Valentine and Four & More* (Columbia 471246); *E.S.P.* (Columbia 467899); *Miles Smiles* (Columbia 471004); *Aura*

(Columbia 463351).

For other recordings from the 1940s and 1950s, see "Bop", "Hard Bop" and "Modal Jazz" above; for jazz-rock recordings, see under "Jazz-Rock Fusion" below.

Charles Mingus

Pithecanthropus Erectus (Atlantic 81456); *New Tijuana Moods* (Bluebird ND85644); *Mingus at Antibes* (Atlantic 90532, 2 CDs); *The Black Saint and the Sinner Lady* (MCA MCAD39119).

Free Jazz

Anthony Braxton: *Three Compositions of New Jazz* (Delmark DS423); *Seven Compositions (Trio) 1989* (Hat Art CD6025).

Art Ensemble of Chicago: *Art Ensemble 1967–68* (Nessa NCD25005).

Albert Ayler: *Witches and Devils* (Freedom 74101); *Spiritual Unity* (ESP Disk 1002).

Ornette Coleman: *The Shape of Jazz to Come* (Atlantic 781339-2); *Free Jazz* (Atlantic 781364-2); *At the Golden Circle, Stockholm*, volumes 1 and 2 (Blue Note B21Y-84224/5); see also under Pat Metheny below.

John Coltrane: *The Major Works of John Coltrane*, including both versions of "Ascension" (Impulse GRD21132, 2 CDs); *The Avant-Garde*, featuring Don Cherry (Atlantic 90041-2).

Chick Corea: *The Song of Singing* (Blue Note B21Y-84353).

Pat Metheny: *Song X*, featuring Ornette Coleman (Geffen 924096).

Sun Ra: *The Magic City* (Evidence ECD22069).

Cecil Taylor: *Unit Structures* (Blue Note B21Y-84237).

Jazz-Rock Fusion

Chick Corea: *Where Have I Known You Before* (Polydor 825206-2); *No Mystery* (Polydor 827149-2); *Elektric Band* (GRP 95352); *Inside Out* (GRP 96012); see also under "Free Jazz" above and "ECM" below.

Miles Davis: *In a Silent Way* (Columbia 450982); *Bitches Brew* (Columbia 460602, 2 CDs); *Jack Johnson* (Columbia 471003).

Dave Grusin: *Harlequin*, featuring Lee Ritenour (GRP D-9522); *Sticks and Stones*, featuring Don Grusin (GRP D-9562).

Herbie Hancock: *Head Hunters* (Columbia 471239); *Future Shock* (Columbia 25540); see also under "Modal Jazz" above.

Bob James: *One* (Columbia CK36835); *The Best of Bob James*, including the theme from the American TV comedy *Taxi* (Renaissance CCSCD807).

John McLaughlin: *Extrapolation* (Polydor 841598); *The Inner Mounting Flame*, featuring the Mahavishnu Orchestra (Columbia 31067).

Bob James and David Sanborn: *Double Vision* (WEA 925393-2).

Lyle Mays: *Lyle Mays* (Geffen GFLD19193); *Street Dreams* (Geffen GFLD19194); see also under "Piano Trios" above.

Pat Metheny: *As Falls Wichita, So Falls Wichita Falls*, featuring Lyle Mays (ECM 1190); *Offramp* (ECM 1216); *First Circle* (ECM 1278); *Still Life (Talking)* (Geffen GED24468); see also under "Free Jazz" above and "ECM" below.

Lee Ritenour: *Color Rit* (GRP 95944); see also under Dave Grusin above.

David Sanborn: *Voyeur* (Warner Brothers 256900).

Grover Washington Jr: *Winelight* (Elektra 60338).

Weather Report: *Heavy Weather* (Columbia 468209); *Black Market* (Columbia 468210); *This is This* (Columbia 57052).

ECM

Gary Burton: *Works*, featuring Chick Corea and Pat Metheny (ECM 823267).

Chick Corea: *Children's Songs* (ECM 8156802).

Jan Garbarek: *I Took Up The Runes* (ECM 1419); *Ragas and Sagas*, featuring Pakistani musicians (ECM 1442); *Twelve Moons* (ECM 1500); *Visible World* (ECM 1585).

Keith Jarrett: *The Köln Concert* (ECM 8100672); *Belonging*, featuring Jan Garbarek (ECM 1050); see also under "Piano Trios" above.

Pat Metheny: *Bright Size Life* (ECM 1073); *Watercolors* (ECM 1097); *80/81*, featuring Dewey Redman and Michael Brecker (ECM 843169-2).

Collin Walcott, Don Cherry and Nana Vasconcelos: *Codona*, 1, 2 and 3 (ECM 1132, 1177 and 1243).

Eberhard Weber: *Yellow Fields* (ECM 1066).

Talents of the 1980s

Geri Allen: *Home Grown* (Minor Music 8004).

Michael Brecker: *Michael Brecker* (Impulse MCA5980).

Human Chain: *Cashin' In* (Editions EG 57).

Roy Hargrove: *With the Tenors of Our Time*, featuring Branford Marsalis and Joe Henderson (Verve 523019-2).

Loose Tubes: *Open Letter* (Editions EG 55).

Wynton Marsalis: *Wynton Marsalis* (Columbia 468708); *Marsalis Standard Time, Volume 1* (Columbia 468713-2); *The Majesty of the Blues* (Columbia 465129-2).

Courtney Pine: *Journey to the Urge Within* (Island 842687-2).

Cassandra Wilson: *Blue Light 'Til Dawn* (Blue Note CDP 7781357-2).

World Saxophone Quartet: *W.S.Q.* (Black Saint BSR0046); *Plays Duke Ellington* (Elektra Musician 979137).

Suggested Further Reading

Reference

Gérald Arnaud and Jacques Chesnel, *Masters of Jazz* (Paris, 1988 and Edinburgh, 1991)

Ian Carr, Digby Fairweather and Brian Priestley, *Jazz: the Rough Guide* (London, 1995)

Richard Cook and Brian Morton, *The Penguin Guide to Jazz on CD, LP and Cassette* (Harmondsworth, 1992; third edition 1996)

Barry Kernfeld (ed.), *The New Grove Dictionary of Jazz*, 2 volumes (New York and London, 1988; single-volume reprint, 1994)

David Meeker, *Jazz in the Movies* (London, second edition 1981)

Autobiographies and Memoirs

Louis Armstrong, *Satchmo: My Life in New Orleans* (New York, 1954)

Count Basie and Albert Murray, *Good Morning Blues: the Autobiography of Count Basie* (New York, 1985)

Sidney Bechet, *Treat it Gentle: an Autobiography* (New York and London, 1960)

Bill Crow, *Jazz Anecdotes* (New York and Oxford, 1990)

Miles Davis and Quincy Troupe, *Miles: the Autobiography* (London, 1990)

Duke Ellington, *Music is My Mistress* (Garden City and London, 1973)

Dizzy Gillespie, *To Be, or not ... to Bop: Memoirs* (Garden City, 1979)

Benny Goodman and Irving Kolodin, *The Kingdom of Swing* (New York, 1939)

Billie Holiday and William Dufty, *Lady Sings the Blues* (Garden City, 1956)

Charles Mingus, *Beneath the Underdog* (New York and London, 1971)

General Histories

Joachim Berendt, *The Jazz Book: from Ragtime to Fusion and Beyond* (St Albans, 1976; revised edition, 1992)

Samuel Charters and Leonard Kunstadt, *Jazz: a History of the New York Scene* (New York, second edition 1981)

Donald Clarke, *The Rise and Fall of Popular Music* (New York and London, 1995)

James Lincoln Collier, *The Making of Jazz: a Comprehensive History* (London, 1978)

Mervyn Cooke, *Jazz: A Concise History* (Thames & Hudson 'World of Art' series; London, 1998)

Juliet Coryell, *Jazz-rock Fusion: the People, the Music* (London, 1978)

Jim Godbolt, *A History of Jazz in Britain, 1919–50* (London, 1984)

Jim Godbolt, *A History of Jazz in Britain, 1950–70* (London, 1989)

John Edward Hasse, *Ragtime: its History, Composers, and Music* (New York and London, 1985)

André Hodeir, *Jazz: its Evolution and Essence* (New York, 1956)

Ekkerhard Jost, *Free Jazz* (Graz, 1974)

Stuart Nicholson, *Jazz: the 1980s Resurgence* (New York, 1995)

Paul Oliver, *The Story of the Blues* (London, 1969)

Thomas Owens, *Bebop: the Music and its Players* (New York and Oxford, 1995)

Hugues Panassié, *Hot Jazz* (Paris, 1934; English translation, London and New York, 1936)

Hugues Panassié, *The Real Jazz* (New York and Toronto, 1942)

David H. Rosenthal, *Hard Bop* (Oxford, 1992)

Keith Shadwick, *Jazz: An Illustrated History* (London, 1991)

George Simon, *The Big Bands* (New York, 1967; fourth edition, 1981)

Eileen Southern, *The Music of Black Americans: a History* (New York and London, second edition 1983)

Marshall Stearns, *The Story of Jazz* (New York and Oxford, 1956)

Barry Ulanov, *A History of Jazz in America* (New York, 1952)

Criticism

Krin Gabbard, *Jammin' at the Margins: Jazz and the American Cinema* (Chicago, 1996)

Constant Lambert, *Music Ho!: a Study of Music in Decline* (London, 1934)

Philip Larkin, *All What Jazz: A Record Diary, 1961–71*

(revised edition, London and New York, 1985; original edition 1970)

Martin Williams (ed.), *The Art of Jazz: Essays on the Nature and Development of Jazz* (New York, 1959)

Martin Williams, *Jazz in its Time* (New York and Oxford, 1989)

Musical Techniques and Analysis

Michael J. Budds, *Jazz in the Sixties: the Expansion of Musical Resources and Techniques* (Iowa City, 1978; expanded edition, 1990)

Mark Gridley, *Jazz Styles* (Englewood Cliffs, New Jersey, 1978–85)

Barry Kernfeld, *What to Listen for in Jazz* (New Haven, 1995)

Lewis Porter, Michael Ullman and Ed Hazell, *Jazz: From Its Origins to the Present* (Englewood Cliffs, New Jersey, 1993)

Gunther Schuller, *Early Jazz* (New York and Oxford, 1969)

Gunther Schuller, *The Swing Era: the Development of Jazz, 1930–45* (New York and Oxford, 1989)

Studies of Individual Musicians

Ian Carr, *Miles Davis: a Critical Biography* (London, 1988)

Ian Carr, *Keith Jarrett: the Man and his Music* (London, 1991)

Donald Clarke, *Wishing on the Moon: the Life and Times of Billie Holiday* (Harmondsworth, 1994)

Gary Giddins, *Celebrating Bird: the Triumph of Charlie Parker* (New York, 1987)

James Lester, *Too Marvelous for Words: the Life and Genius of Art Tatum* (New York and Oxford, 1994)

Alan Lomax, *Mister Jelly Roll* (New York, 1950)

Brian Priestley, *Mingus: a Critical Biography* (London, Melbourne and New York, 1982)

Ken Rattenbury, *Duke Ellington: Jazz Composer* (New Haven, 1990)

Mark Tucker (ed.), *The Duke Ellington Reader* (New York and London, 1993)

Richard Williams, *The Man in the Green Shirt: Miles Davis* (London, 1993)

List of Illustrations

Index

James, Bob 191, 208
James, Harry 84, 91, 106, 119, 137, **142**, 200
Janis, Harriet 116, 125
Jarrett, Keith 139, 156, 175, 176, 177, 181, 184, **184**, 185, **185**, 186, 192, 200, 211, 212, 217, 218, 221
Jazz At The Philharmonic 106, 112, 122, 128, **129**, 130, 139, 162, **187**, 195
Jazz Composers' Workshop 190
Jazz Messengers 117, 137, 138-9, 140, 142, 143, 152, 194, 196, 199, 212
jazz-rock fusion, see fusion
Jobim, Antonio Carlos 143, 153
Johnson, Alphonso 127
Johnson, Bill **5**, 48
Johnson, Bunk 22, 25, 100, 108, **109**, 116, **116**, 122
Johnson, Dick 202
Johnson, J. J. 61, 120, 135, 223
Johnson, James P. 27, 31, 32, 43, 44, **46**, 47, 53, 59, 63, 65, 66, 67, **78**, 91, 97, 104, 105, 137, 166
Johnson, Marc 205, 218
Johnson, Pete 91, 98, 166
Johnson, Robert 27
Jolson, Al 63
Jones, Elvin 160, 223
Jones, Hank 186
Jones, Irving 18
Jones, Philly Joe 137, 205
Jones, Quincy 141, 212, 214, 216
Jones, Spike **101**
Jones, Thad 33, 163, 165, **165**, 168, 169, 181, 189, 193, 204, 206, 214
Jones, Wallace 91
Joplin, Scott 16, 18, 19, 20-1, **21**, 22, 25, 26, 31, 32, 39, 46, 175, 179, 180, **180**, 181, 184, 189, 202
Jordan, Duke 186
Jordan, Joe 31
Jordan, Sheila 217
Joseph, Julian 206
Jost, Ekkehard 182
Joyce, William ("Lord Haw-Haw") 81, 96
Jungle Club (Washington D.C.) **90**
jungle style 49, 63, 118

Kaminsky, Max **122**
Kansas City 11, 18, 49, 51, 64, 65, 66, 71, 76, 86, 87, 104, 136, 198, 209, 222
Kay, Connie 128
Kazan, Elia 126
Kelly, Wynton 176
Kennedy, John F. 156, 158
Kenton, Stan 99, 114, 122, 134, 139, 142, 153, 192, **192**
Kentucky Club (New York) 51, 60
Keppard, Freddie 22, 25, 27, 28, 39, **51**, 52, 76
Kern, Jerome 29, 55, 138

Kernfeld, Barry 211
Kessel, Barney 99
Keynote (New York) 191
Kirk, Andy 66
Kirk, Roland **13**, 131, 161, 189, **189**, 207, 212
Koenigswarter, Baroness Pannonica de 136, 179
Konitz, Lee 120, **120**, 126, 134, 189, 200, 203
Kool Festival 195
Koussevitzky, Serge 63, 120
Krell, William H. 16
Krenek, Ernst 65
Krupa, Gene 82, 84, **84**, 90, **91**, 98, 104, 118, 135, 137, 141, 147, 180, 199

Lacy, Steve 181, 189, 215, 223
Ladnier, Tommy 43
LaFaro, Scott 152, 153, 156
Laine, Cleo 161, 221
Lake, Oliver 189
Lamb, Joseph 21, 22, 31
Lang, Eddie 98
Lang, Ronny 184
Lange, J. Bodewalt 20
Larkin, Philip 11, 150. 153, 155, 175, 200, 216
LaRocca, Nick 32, 37, **37**, 40, 152
La Scala (Milan) 143
Latin jazz 96, 114, 115, 140, 143, 178, 190, 191
Lawrence, Jacob **144**
Ledbetter, Huddie "Ledbelly" **116**
Lee, Bill 213
Leeds Festival 143
Leigh, Vivien 126
Leipzig 65, 81
Léger, Fernand **53**
Lemon, Brian 176
Lenin 207
Leningrad 65, 194
Lévy, Charles **10**
Lewis, John 113, 115, 120, 126, 128-9, 135, 140, 141, 142, 147, 188
Lewis, Meade Lux 86, 91, 117, **158**, 166
Lewis, Mel 163, 165, 181, 189, 193, 205, 213
Lewis, Ted 72
Library of Congress (Washington D.C.) 45, 90
Liberty (record label) 163, 167
licks 57, 136
Liebman, Dave 209
Lifetime 170
Lincoln, Abraham 17, 55
Lindsay, Johnny **34**
Lion, Alfred 94, 166
Little Rock **150**
Ljubljana 168
Lloyd, Charles 166, 207
Lomax, Alan 8, 45, 90, 116, 125, **125**
London 18, 19, 28, 31, 36, 42, 44, 48, 53, 57, 60, 72, 74, 76, 77, 81,

87, 90, 91, 92, 112, 119, 130, 143, 147, 148, 151, 154, 157, 159, 163, 166, 167, **169**, 174, 175, 176, 177, 180, 181, 182, 185, 189, 191, **193**, 198, 202, 206
London Palladium, see Palladium
Longshaw, Fred 67
Loose Tubes 202, 205, **205**, 209
Los Angeles 12, 48, 76, 83, 84, 88, 98, 100, 106, 108, 112, 113, 119, 122, 124, 128, 130, 132-4, 136, 138, 139, 151, 159, 162, 163, 167, 181, 192, 203, 206, 208
Louisiana Five 40
Lovano, Joe 223
Luftwaffe 81, 104
Lunceford, Jimmie 63, 80
Lyttleton, Humphrey 139, **139**, 200

Macero, Teo 157, 202
Machito 114, **114**
Mahavishnu Orchestra 177, 179, 180, 182, 184, 186, 221
Mainieri, Mike 195
Malle, Louis 140
Mancini, Henry 141, 176
Mandela, Nelson 198
Mangelsdorff, Albert 61, 200
Manhattan Transfer 174, 193
Mann, Herbie 130
Manne, Shelly 120, 133, 134, 151, 203
Manone, Wingy **52**
Marable, Fate 40, **40**, 115
marching bands, see brass bands
Marienthal, Eric 205
Marquette, Pee Wee 219
Marsalis, Branford 160, 196, 202, 203, 205, 213
Marsalis, Ellis 213
Marsalis, Wynton **13**, 97, 139, 184, 194, 196, **197**, 199, 201, 202, 203, 206, 211, 212, 213, 218, 222, 223
Marsh, Warne 126
Marx Brothers 87
Mason, Harvey 181
Massey Hall (Toronto) 130
Maupin, Bennie 181, 201
Matthews, Artie 28, 44
Mayer, John 169
Mays, Lyle 141, 156, 189, 193, 194, 198, 199, **199**, 208, 211, **211**, 218
McGhee, Howard **97**
McLaughlin, John 170, 171, 177, **178**, 179, 180, 182, 184, 186, 199, 203, 204, 213, 221, 223
McLean, Jackie 223
McRae, Carmen 214
McShann, Jay 98, 212
Melrose Brothers 45
Mercer, Johnny 138
Mercury (record label) 129
Metheny, Pat 64, 99, 127, 141, 153, 177, 184, 189, 193, 194,

198-9, **199**, 205, 208, 216, 221
Metronome 106, 126
Metropolitan Opera House (New York) 106, **106**, 109, **109**, 126, 165
Metropol Jazzhus (Oslo) 148, **149**, 154, 156, 169
Miami 199, 200, 216
Micheal, Don 152
Michelot, Pierre 140
Mikkelborg, Palle 204
Miles, Reid 167
Miley, Bubber 49, 51, 60, 63, 66, 74
Milhaud, Darius 53, 59, 134, 188
Miller, Glenn 60, 92, 93, 102, **102**, 104, 106, 107, **107**, 135, **135**, 141, 202
Miller, Marcus 196, 200, 208, 217
Mineo, Sal 141
Mingus, Charles 99, 128, 129, 130, 131, 135, 136, 137, 138, 140, 141, 142, 147, 148, 151, 152, 154, 156, 157, 159, 161, 163, 175, 177, 179, 186, 187, 189, 190, **190**, 192, 212
Mingus Dynasty 190, 192
Mingus, Susan Graham Ungaro 192
Minimoog 193
minstrel shows 17, 66, 101
Minton, Henry 97
Minton's Playhouse (New York) 97, **97**, 98, 136, 154
Mitchell, George **34**
Mitchell, Louis 27, 31, 36
Mobley, Hank 137, 139
modal jazz 12, 24, 141, 142, 143, 146-7, 150, 156, 177, 188, 190, 216
Modern Jazz Quartet 70, 113, 120, 128-9, 135, 140, 141, 142, 147, 148, 182, 196
Moffett, Charnett 152
Molde 165
Mondrian, Piet **107**
Monk, Thelonious 11, 96, 97, **97**, 105, 106, 113, 115, **115**, 116, 124, 132, 136, 137, 140, 146, 152, 154-5, **155**, 156, 163, 165, 166, 167, 175, 177, 179, 186, 198
Monroe's Uptown House (New York) 97
Monterey Jazz Festival 143, 151, 161, 163, 189, 191, 193, 196, 222
Montgomery, Monk 127
Montgomery, Wes 99, 168, 199
Montmartre Jazzhus (Copenhagen) 169, 189
Montreal 130, 163
Montreux Festival 107, 167, 174, 184, 189, **189**, 191, 194, 216, 218
Montrose, Jack **132**
Moody, James 96
Moog 193, 221